Intertextuality
and Contemporary American Fiction

INTERTEXTUALITY

AND
CONTEMPORARY
AMERICAN
FICTION

Edited by Patrick O'Donnell
and Robert Con Davis

═══

THE JOHNS HOPKINS UNIVERSITY PRESS

Baltimore and London

© 1989 The Johns Hopkins University Press
All rights reserved
Printed in the United States of America

The Johns Hopkins University Press, 701 West 40th Street,
Baltimore, Maryland 21211
The Johns Hopkins Press Ltd., London

The paper used in this publication meets the minimum
requirements of American National Standard for Information
Sciences—Permanence of Paper for Printed Library
Materials, ANSI Z39.48–1984.

Library of Congress Cataloging-in-Publication Data

Intertextuality and contemporary American fiction /
Patrick O'Donnell and Robert Con Davis, editors.
p. cm.
Bibliography: p.
ISBN 0-8018-3773-1 (alk. paper)
1. American fiction—20th century—History and criticism.
2. Intertextuality.   I. O'Donnell, Patrick, 1948–   .
II. Davis, Robert Con, 1948–   .
PS374.I56I58   1989
813'.5'09—dc19   88-46066

Contents

===

CONTENTS

INTERTEXTUAL AFTERWORDS

Acknowledgments

Bringing together a book such as this is always a little more trouble than one at first imagines. For the editors of this book, two great pleasures kept the project attractive and satisfying. The first was the opportunity this book gave us to explore contemporary American fiction from the variety of new perspectives designated by "intertextuality." In the very best sense that collaborative critical projects make possible, we have learned about American fiction from each other and have gained insights and recognitions that were not there before. The second was the occasion to collaborate with the critics who have also been thinking about American fiction in the new ways that interest us. We were fortunate to be working with the scholars in this collection—most of them friends, we are happy to say—who take joy in the kind of work we do. We are deeply appreciative of their contributions to this volume.

We also have some other specific debts that are a pleasure to acknowledge. We want to thank the University of Arizona and the University of Oklahoma for the many kinds of support they gave to this project. Particularly, the University of Oklahoma Office of Research Administration provided research support at a critical moment. Professor Richard Macksey of the Johns Hopkins University helped us to shape this project and gave valuable encouragement when it meant the most. We appreciate his generosity. Eric Halpern of the Johns Hopkins University Press gave patient and good advice as we conceived and worked through this book; his support of the project from its inception has been essential to its completion. Donna Larger of the English Department at Arizona typed and retyped the manuscript for us with amazing care and cheerfulness.

We would also like to thank Diane, Sean, and Sara O'Donnell for their love and support of the editor at Tucson, and Ronald Schleifer, Alan Velie, David Gross, and James Comas—the Oklahoma Criticism Group—for their continual support of the editor in Norman.

Patrick O'Donnell
Robert Con Davis

Introduction

Intertext and Contemporary
American Fiction

====

Since the late 1960s and the work of Julia Kristeva, Gérard Genette, Jacques Derrida, and Michael Riffaterre, among others, much
has been written about the concept of intertextuality in relation to
practical criticism. On the model of the "word" or the "signifier,"
semioticians have tended to see texts (like all language) as radically
"differential," that is, as a system of signs made up "only [of] differences *without positive terms*" (Saussure 120). These signs can then
be treated as distinctive features and "bundled" together as texts.
The formed texts, in turn, must be read in practical criticism as
virtual rather than substantial objects, that is, constituted by language and not regarded as self-evident, or transparent, "views of
reality." But as Thaïs Morgan (in this collection) and others show,
the development of the concept of intertextuality arises within the
larger history of modern literature and literary criticism and encompasses many textual models. In modern criticism, from the late
1930s through the 1950s, the New Critics defined textuality as a set
of images organized by two tropes reflecting the structure of the
human imagination, paradox and irony. For them, all texts were
subject to analysis as intertexts insofar as individual texts manifested these tropes. In somewhat related fashion, the myth critics
who followed imagined texts to be the reflection, or fragmented
presentation, of archetypes—ideal and fundamental forms of human experience. They saw a "text" as the shadow of virtual (archetypal) objects, an assemblage of imperfect textual fragments par-
ticipating in a larger textual (mythic) order. The structuralists,
subsequently, redefined "texts" semiotically, as situated in systems
of signs and codes that in turn are organized and transformed by
underlying rules formulable in a kind of grammar. This development led fairly directly to the formulation of intertextuality as we
are applying the term in this book.

In some ways drawing on all of these models, this book's general
view of intertextuality is fundamentally an attempt to conceive—or
redefine—the concept of the "text" dynamically, as an ongoing operation (what Derrida calls "structuration") involving the continual

play of referentiality between and within texts. This means that intertextuality, most directly informed by semiotics and derived from the work of structuralism, defines a text as always in process, continually changing its shape. In this view, a text is a fabric simultaneously being woven and unwoven, made up not of a uniform "material" (like the New Critical "paradox" manifested in images) but by the traces of other texts. At an extreme, this definition projects all texts as further divisible into other texts, and these into yet other texts (or signifiers), ad infinitum.

The format of this book is a model of this concept of intertextual weaving. This collection is constructed to look like, and to a degree function as, a continuous discussion organized by the pattern of its topic. In short, it is a book "on" intertextuality and contemporary American fiction. Also, however, this collection exists as a separate and disparate series of approaches *to* contemporary American fiction. Each essay posits a somewhat different sense of intertextuality, under various cultural and ideological constraints, and then reads its expectations against particular authors and works. In one sense, this diversity of readings resembles an extended intertextual approach, a double reading of American fiction. But as Henry Louis Gates, Jr., shows in his discussion of Afro-American texts, and as Gabriele Schwab and John Carlos Rowe suggest in their discussions of television, texts, and the "bodies" of mass culture, the certainty about American fiction as a definite body of texts—a fixed and decidable set of books—has all but vanished. American fiction, indeed the canon of American literature, is now widely conceived to be an intertext in several senses, an a-literate, surfictional cyborg, as Schwab says, of multimedia events and influences—a monstrosity of partial and potential significations. Thus, like intertextuality itself, this collection "coheres" only through the co-presence of constituent differences.

Accordingly, we have deliberately chosen essays for this collection that—individually and as a whole—emphasize the variety, dynamism, sense of play, and comic sensibility of intertextuality. At the same time, these essays tend to resist (or postpone) the calcification of narrow literary categories and subgenres. These choices suggest, as we wish to show further, our own sense of intertextuality as offering a particularly important opening for the (re)interpretation of contemporary American fiction.

For example, in the parodic flurry of quotations, conversations, and plagiarized texts that make up William Gaddis's recently "rediscovered" *The Recognitions*, the following passage stands as one among many that reveals a comic version of "intertextuality" as the historicization of cultural reading and writing. Max, a pop artist, Stanley, a misplaced religious aesthete, and Otto, an ersatz dramatist, are discussing, as they walk along the streets of Manhattan, the relation between improvisation and invention in art:

> —But it isn't making it up, inventing music [said Otto], it's like . . . remembering, and like, well van Gogh says about painting, when he would take a drawing of Delacroix as a subject and improvise with colors, not as himself, he says, but searching for memories of their pictures, the "vague consonance of colors," the memory that was himself, his own interpretation.
> They stopped together at another curb. A store loudspeaker poured out upon them a vacuous tenor straining,—I'm dreaming of a white Christmas . . . with insipid mourning hope [. . .]
> —Well it isn't . . . they have no right to . . . Stanley tried to speak, out of breath [. . .]
> —What do you want on Sixth Avenue, *The Messiah*?
> —They have no right to . . . cheapen . . .
> —Ask them to play *Yes We Have No Bananas*, Max said, smiling.
> —That's from *The Messiah*, and it's more their line.
> —What do you mean? [. . .]
> —I mean *Yes We Have No Bananas* was lifted right out of Handel's *Messiah*. Come on, Max said taking his arm, and looking around for Otto.—What's the matter with both of you today?
> —You don't have to . . . tell me things like that, Stanley said, pulling away. [. . .]
> —You might say that the man who wrote *Yes We Have No Bananas* was searching from memories? a vague consonance of sounds? . . . Max began good-humoredly. Then looking at Otto he said, —What's the matter, you look all disjointed. (461–62; editors' ellipses in brackets)

The world of *The Recognitions* is one in which cheap imitations of all art forms—themselves humbled "originals" to superior antecedents—abound, where the myth of originality is exposed for its sentimentalization of individuality and "genius," and where the real artists are the counterfeiters, the authors of faked, newly discovered "originals," the Pierre Menards. The conversation recorded above suggests that, for modernism, invention is an act of improvisation where the past is neither transformed nor transcended but re-membered. In the anesthetizing noise and mass consumerism of the modern city, of what use is "originality" where every "invention" or variation can be immediately copied, counterfeited, and disseminated? If a part of Handel's *Messiah* can be quoted, unrecognized, in a popular song with nonsensical lyrics, then what substance can be attached to Handel's name or "genius"

xi

in a culture where those who could recognize Handel's originality are vastly outnumbered by those who know the refrain to *Yes We Have No Bananas*?

In an age of "felt ultimacies," as John Barth refers to the post-modern era in the infamous "Literature of Exhaustion," questions regarding the origins and ends of discourse loom large (67). Much of that enterprise to which we presently give the name literary theory has devoted itself to speculating upon the origins of language, or discourse, or culture, or their intertwined histories, or the priority of one over the others—at each turn, with the growing sense that originality and priority are romantic diversions, and that our true subject is relation without beginning or end. Perhaps we would hesitate to put it as formalistically as Gramsci does, but his comment in *The Prison Notebooks* that *the* subject is "the synthesis not only of existing relations, but the history of these relations" (353) provides us with a working definition of text (as a series of existing relations) and intertextuality (as the profaned or "fallen" history of these relations) at the present time.

Clearly, as Gaddis's novel suggests, the recognition and definition of these relations (to what remembered past? within what predetermined or inferred contexts?) may lead to a depressing sense of the touted scarcities and artificiality of American culture. They may also lead, however, to a reconceptualization of such entities as text, author, discourse, history, and origin, to the extent that their integrity is broken down while their interdependencies are seen as critical, for better or worse, to their continuance. In the case of Handel, what is worse: that he be recognized and heard by a select few, or that he (at least a piece of him) be retained by the cultural memory in the musical phrases of a popular lyric? The seeming levity of such questions as this posed within the historical framework of a belated, palimpsestic, consumerist postmodern culture hints at the more complicated issues that arise within this collection. We wish, by way of introduction, to state these issues and, thus, to provide a context for the work undertaken here by critics who concern themselves with intertextuality as a constitutive element of contemporary literature.

II

Thaïs Morgan shows in her survey of intertextuality's complex history and practice that the phenomenon of intertextuality has accrued to itself an array of definitions, each with its own set of formal, aesthetic, and ideological assumptions. One could immediately ask that most ironic question for the study of intertextuality: where does it begin? The question is put in spatial (where) rather than temporal terms (when) because it is generally assumed that even the most literal-minded scrutiny of quotations and revisions in any text reveals a lineage of predecessors—fathering or mothering models, echoes of the past—as well as the semblance of an originary ur-text. The fact, nonetheless, that the term *intertextuality* has emerged within the past two decades in the general critical lexicon only tells us that we may have found a different, *historically* framed means to discuss perennial matters of allusion, reference, parody, and imitation. That difference is crucial for the essays in this collection, each of which redefines intertextuality as a way of writing and reading contemporary texts. The difference, nevertheless, is hardly original. A theory of intertextuality cannot claim for itself a unique historical presence, any more than the quantum theory of light could claim that its paradoxical material qualities came into being only with its own formulation. Just as light is alternatively wave and particle depending on a chosen viewpoint, so the historical and literary contexts of intertextuality change and are changed by our cognizance of reading, writing, and memory as components constituting a perspective of interpretation.

Intertextuality, then, is not new. It is the oldest troping we know, the most ancient textual (con)figuration, though its presence as a specific form of attention may be located within the loose amalgamation of poststructuralist critical theories. As John Hollander remarks, textual echo, that oblique and partial repetition, is the metaphor for "language answering language" (21). Intertextuality—"language answering language"—is a constant linguistic "fact," a representation of language's ever-unfolding filiation with itself, its posited objects, its network of references. And yet, the problems of originality, reference, or reflexivity are not solved by recognizing and naming intertextuality as a dimension of writing. Intertextuality, rather, signals an *anxiety* and an *indeterminacy* regarding authorial, readerly, or textual identity, the relation of present culture to past, or the function of writing within certain historical and political frameworks. The latter point suggests, too, that intertextuality, as a "fact" of writing, can only be located within its own particular manifestations, and that these are always specified within a series of histories—cultural, literary, authorial, and int*ra*textual.

It could be said that contemporary American literature has no history proper, especially in that many of its authors purportedly reject "history" in favor of (according to one recent estimate) escapism, hedonism, or the supposed delights and reliefs offered by metafiction and fabulation (see Graff). Further, there is little of a canon for postmodern literature, much of which avidly seeks to avoid inclusion in a "canon" in the first place. We thus see that the present literary situation complicates the discussion of intertextuality. Yet it is precisely within the particularly volatile range of recent letters that a discussion of intertextuality can prove most useful, for in the unfolding literary event labeled (with a desirable flexibility) "contemporary" we can find the ongoing redefinition of several kinds of history, so to speak, in the making. One definition suggests that intertextuality is the simultaneous repression and remembering of the past. The desire for originality (repression of the past) involves a necessary recognition of how much any writing is "language answering language" (remembrance of the past). The special poignancy that this formulation has for much recent writing, or, for that matter, any writing that foregrounds its own "contemporaneity," is that the *amount* of the indebtedness to the literary, historical, or cultural past increases with any attempt to cancel that debt. Within this economy, then, the discussion of intertextuality becomes crucial, for through it we discover the terms of the indebtedness that literary "borrowing" imposes. Narrative offers a particularly fruitful area for this discussion because its generic and discursive largesse allows for a rich mixing of texts, histories, stories, and voices where the work of intertextuality is often at its most fervent.

III

In this volume the reader will find a collection of essays unified by their attempt to construct an approach toward intertextuality in an examination of contemporary American fiction. The essays herein precisely question the boundaries of "contemporary American fiction": periodic, national, generic. Dynamic in nature, intertextuality "at work" inevitably takes the form of boundary-crossing; it creates crises, aporiae, ideology wherever it goes—for, as is inherent in the nature of signs, the intertextual relation generates the deferral and rewriting of "parent" texts, themselves bastardized deformations of the texts that came before them. Intertextuality challenges those systems of signification which allow us to mark off the formal terrains of "literary period," "genre," "author," "subject," "nation," "text." While it may be argued that (as some of the essays here suggest) this challenge often results in a reflexive textual "self-awareness" that conserves rather than dispossesses us of the literary past—its ideological baggage intact—it may equally be said that the work of intertextuality is at the bottom of the process which Michael Holquist and Caryl Emerson characterize for Bakhtin as "novelization":

> "Novel" is the name Bakhtin gives to whatever force is at work within a given literary system to reveal the limits, the artificial constraints of that system. Literary systems are comprised of canons, and "novelization" is fundamentally anticanonical. It will not permit generic monologue. Always it will insist on the dialogue between what a given system will admit as literature and those texts that are otherwise excluded from such a definition of literature. What is more conventionally thought of as the novel is simply the most complex and distilled expression of this impulse. (*Dialogic Imagination xxxi*)

This "force," or "impulse," we would argue, is that of intertextuality, which might be defined as the noisy communicative device within the "system" that—through parody, quotation, imitation, deformation—permits the recognition of systematic limits and encourages the intertextual dialogue that will dissolve and reconfigure those limits. Yet we are still within a communicative "system" and, therefore, we must still worry about what lies outside: can the discussion of intertextuality successfully address problems of extra-literary reference, or is its explosive force merely "interlinear," contained within an ever-renewed system or structure whose changing boundaries reflect the conservative nature of intertextuality? How sound, ideologically, is the investment in the attention to and appraisal of the intertextual process? Where does that process (the question refuses to go away) "come from," and what is the agenda of the sources of its inducements?

These are questions for the reader of this collection, but they are not questions which the contributors to it shy away from, nor is there any common agreement among them about the nature of or answers to questions of intertextuality. What does exist as a commonality is the sense that the study of intertextuality makes problematic our received notions concerning the nature of literature and the various schemes we have created to understand it as a means of communication. Some of those schemes involve generic and period distinctions which an intertextual approach, brought to bear upon specific texts, is at odds to critique—thus, once again, the inherent irony in a title that proclaims as its subject "contemporary American fiction." The reader will find that several of the essays take liberties with this subject precisely because issues of contemporaneity, fictionality, and the cultural assumption of "Americanness" are at stake when a theory of intertextuality is foregrounded. Yet there is an insistence in these essays that the questions about forms, limits, and temporality that the discussion of intertextuality raises do not *collapse* generic distinctions so much as *historicize* them within those literary and cultural contexts pointed out by the study of intertextuality. The essays in this collection are firmly situated within historical, cultural, ideological contexts provided by "contemporary," "American," and "fiction," even as these terms are questioned and redefined. Indeed, the broadest view of the essays gathered here would suggest that, in various ways, they all address the projects and limits of "discourse" within the multidiscursivity of contemporary American culture.

We have arranged the essays so that the reader, proceeding through them one by one, will encounter a series of issues related to intertextuality: sexuality and textuality; parody; the relation between contemporary texts and their modern predecessors; postmodern texts and culture; ideology; and the history, presence, and definition of intertextuality in contemporary American fiction. Within these groups there is often debate, and the categories tend to merge in ways that trace out a cluster of diverse, interrelated themes and topics focused around intertextuality and contemporary American fiction. To begin, in a prelude to the discussion of specific texts, Linda Hutcheon studies the varieties and forms intertextuality takes in a broad range of contemporary texts. She sees parody as the contemporary "sign" of intertextuality at work, most often present in texts which complicate the relation between fiction and history as they generate their own history by forming a parodic relation to prior texts. Hutcheon views parody as essentially regenerative in that it marks the continual reconstitution of intra- and intertextual relations—a mutability she deems essential to maintaining open-ended connections between literary discourse and the other discourses of history.

Hutcheon's essay provides a fitting background and context for the collection's first group of essays, headed "Intertextuality and Parody." Here John T. Matthews, Heide Ziegler, and Alan Singer are variously concerned with parody as the primary mode where intertextuality is evident and where its intentions can be located. As Michael McKeon has recently argued, parody contextualizes and historicizes texts: "The generic capacity of a work is defined by its intertextual affiliations with some works and by its intertextual detachment from others. Indeed, the notion of 'parody' is as fruitful as it is to Bakhtin because it conflates these two movements into a single dialectical gesture of recapitulation and repudiation, imitation and disillusion, continuity and rupture" (12–13). The double movement of affiliation and detachment that parody conveys interests Matthews, Ziegler, and Singer as "the intertextual effect," the semantics of which varies with each critic. Matthews views parody as a literary device that generates intertextual relations but has the capacity to repress the ideological content of the text. He develops a theory of intertextuality as revealing the "political unconscious" of the author—in this case, John Barth—and argues that the relation between the author and the state which Barth portrays in the prefaces to the nonfiction pieces of *The Friday Book* is re-represented and fictionalized in his novels, particularly *Chimera* and *Sabbatical*. For Matthews, this relation is parodic and parasitical, and he tests its ideological implications in light of Barth's well-known statement about the exhaustion and renewal of literary traditions in postmodernism.

In reading *Beowulf* against *Grendel*, *The Good Soldier* against *The Blood Oranges*, Ziegler locates the activity of parody as either regressive or progressive. She argues that the movement of filiation and distancing which McKeon defines reflects an "erotics" of parody that both manifests and problematizes authorial identity within the shifting frameworks of classic, modern, and postmodern literature. Ziegler's view of intertextuality as, essentially, an erotic/parodic relation interestingly contrasts with Matthews' portrayal of Barth's intertextuality as sustained by a parasitic relation between author and state.

Singer regards intertextual parody as a matter of temporality. As the echoing or ventriloquizing of past texts in present ones, parody acts to provide a historical context for the latter because it temporalizes as it creates repetitions between "then" and "now." By developing a theory of historical contradiction out of Althusser, Singer offers a reading of William Gaddis's *Carpenter's Gothic* in order to show how a decisively postmodern text rejects traditional notions of historicity and chronicity while generating its own horizon of temporality through the management of intertextual relations. This entails, for Singer, not merely a redefinition of the relation between history and fiction, but also a redefinition of the subject who lives in one and reads the other.

Questions about temporality and periodicity are implicitly evoked by the next group of essays, under the title "Revisionary Intertextuality." Considering the "modern/contemporary" or "modern/postmodern" continuum—or discontinuity—Charles Caramello, Ronald Schleifer, and Henry Louis Gates, Jr., address what might be called a "near relation," for we are still debating whether or not postmodernism, viewed as an epoch, offers an apocalyptic break from modernist mastery, improves upon it, or merely repeats it in an inflated, fallen form (for the terms of this debate, see Newman, Wilde, Klinkowitz, Hassan, and Lyotard). Caramello discusses "portrait narration" in James and Stein, who are usually represented as roughly contingent in the evolution of the modernist movement. In Caramello's view, however, Stein is James's contemporary, or rather, she is to James what contemporaneity is to modernism. Because she is so concerned with the matter of contemporaneity, Caramello suggests that she remains our contemporary and that her writing—which makes "improvements" upon James as one would anchor an abstraction within the specificities of the present context—figures a relation to a literary ancestor which questions periodicity. As Caramello portrays her, Stein is both near and far from James, and this distancing has as much to do with specific syntactical relations as it does with time and influence.

Ronald Schleifer sees Theodore Dreiser through Norman Mailer, and Mailer through Dreiser. In so doing Schleifer traces a history of violence in American literature—a lineage of ruptures and displacements—which is also a history of the unspeakable, and the confrontation between writing and that which cannot be written. In *The Executioner's Song* Mailer rewrites *An American Tragedy*, but the intertextual relation he forms to the "fathering" text is one in which the authored relation itself is displaced in an attempt to deauthorize the text so that the unnameable can be recorded, so that there is no authorial or subjective mediation between the inscription and the violent, chaotic reality it inscribes. What stood for Stein as an improvement of James becomes in Mailer's hands, according to Schleifer, not so much a disfiguration as a rubbing out of the authorial function—this in a novel whose subject is crime and punishment in contemporary America.

For Henry Louis Gates, Jr., the perceived relation between Zora Neale Hurston's *Their Eyes Were Watching God* and Alice Walker's *The Color Purple* is quite different from that between Dreiser and Mailer: already doubly marginalized by virtue of their being black and female, in different ways Hurston and Walker overturn authority and conventional authorial relations. Confronted with the difficulty of finding and inscribing a voice in a cultural situation where only submission to divine or human (male) masters allows them access to official, authorized channels of communication, Hurston and Walker—Gates argues—represent a tradition within a tradition, that nurturing, repressed declension of orality transformed into writing. To use Gates's phrase, Walker "signifies upon" Hurston by converting Hurston's "self as spoken" (though this self, paradoxically, is represented in the writing down of oral discourse) into the "self as written." Gates sees Walker's success in this endeavor as a sign of renewal and continuance. Intertextuality, in this instance, is the process which marks the emergence of the black, female writing subject.

In the next group of essays, "Intertextuality and the Postmodern Subject," the constitution of subjectivity in postmodern culture is of interest to Kathleen Hulley, Gabriele Schwab, and John Carlos Rowe, who see intertextuality as the culture-bound transcription of relations between text, economy, and desire. Hulley provides a path-breaking analysis of Kathy Acker's work, particularly her *Algeria*, which crosses the boundaries of narrative and drama, literature and performance art. Hulley's feminist critique exposes in Acker—whose work is often described as "nonliterary," anarchistic, pornographic—the sexual politics of intertextuality within a capitalist economy and a representational, engendered language which accompanies it. For Hulley, Acker stands as a kind of "limit-case" whose work refigures the female subject while it defines the acquisition, familiarization, and endorsements of the economized body by the hegemonic state.

Schwab scrutinizes a variety of contemporary artifacts and fictions in order to assess the "cyberneticization" of postmodern culture. Citing such evidence as the science fiction of Stanislav Lem, medical transplants, and the childhood cultural underground represented in the comic strips of "The Garbage-Pail Kids," Schwab is concerned to show how the postmodern representation of the body, as a form of intertextuality (relations between body parts, between separate bodies, and between bodies and machines), rests upon a "belief" in metonymy and a desire for omnipotence through replaceability. For Schwab, cyberneticization is the result of fears generated in a culture bent on its self-destruction and, simultaneously, fantasizing its own perpetuation while, literally, incorporating that destructive power in the body. Conversely, she sees cybernetics and the systems theories which found it as offering the possibility of a new holism where the boundary between interior and exterior (or "nature" and "culture") is erased. In its place, there is an epistemology where the body/culture intertext is allowed its fullest, most unrepressed representation. Schwab does not fail to observe the duality that cyberneticization poses, or the sinister futurist implications of its technological optimism.

John Carlos Rowe discusses an old literary problem in light of the new texts offered by American television from the 1950s to the 1980s—the relation between the audience and the text, and the text's reflection upon its own form and content. For Rowe, who sees situation comedies as complicated enactments of the present cultural situation, the audience–text connection is affected by the technology and economy of contemporary video productions, which are multiauthored and which comment upon their own lack of cultural authority in a peculiar manner. These "texts" reflect material desires through the immateriality of significatory processes in postmodern times. In his reading of the serial video fictions of (among other) *The Honeymooners* and *I Love Lucy*, Rowe argues that television situations incorporate popular desires for autonomy, meaningful work, sexual equality, relief from economic duress, etc., while at the same time countering these through the portrayal of the workplace and of other competing, more glamorized desires for sexual dominance and control over the modes of production. The success of such shows depends precisely upon their ability to generate a set of referential relations so that the audience can see itself in these typical comic situations or vignettes of modern life. Schwab and Rowe thus assess the role of what might be called "technological fictions" in an intensely layered, postmodern culture bent on the complex representation of itself.

In the final group of the collection, "Intertextual Afterwords," we have included an essay on the history of intertextuality by Thaïs Morgan, an interview with Julia Kristeva conducted by Margaret Waller, and a selected bibliography of work on intertextuality and contemporary American fiction by Jennifer Jenkins. Morgan's essay is broad and informative: she narrates the critical history of intertextuality in recent thought and in the work of such crucial individual theorists as Kristeva, Bakhtin, Genette, and Riffaterre. Morgan analyzes the assumptions underlying the intertextual "project," its prevalence in poststructuralist theory, and its effect upon literary study. This scrutiny reveals, for Morgan, that intertextuality is, essentially, a "conservative" function of literature, a way of maintaining the past in the present, though not unproblematically or through any prescribed modes of representation. It is fitting that an interview with Julia Kristeva follows Morgan's recounting of the scene and history of intertextuality, in that Kristeva's own involvement with intertextuality forms a crucial part of that history. Kristeva is sometimes, ironically, credited with being the inventor of the term *intertextuality*, and though her present interests in psychoanalysis and the poetics of abjection may seem distant from her early studies, there is a bridge between the potential "revolution in poetic language" associated with intertextuality and the revolution in the constitution of the subject implied by Kristeva's revelations regarding abjection and melancholy. In this new interview, Kristeva talks candidly of intertextuality, of past and present interests, of how, in her view, the speaking subject is always "intertextual." Readers of *Powers of Horror* know that this intertextual subject is complex in its definition and constitution. "Pieced together" from the repressed fragments of the abjected symbolic being, the intertextual subject signifies both the limitations of subjectivity and the horrors of its evolution. Still, this subjectivity, as "marked" by language—as textualized—remains a source of fascination and interest for Kristeva, and its potential for rupture or change resides in the poetic or emotive moment which may never be purely represented. What might be called the romanticism of intertextuality is paired with its own strong demythologizings of the romantic subject and its representability. Kristeva's thought, in general, negotiates this paradox. The collection concludes with Jennifer Jenkins' selective, yet extensive bibliography of theoretical works on intertextuality and specific critiques of intertextuality in contemporary American fiction.

When we began thinking about this collection, the book we imagined was focused on much that is traditionally literary, and matters of literary influence, tradition, and troping are often discussed in these pages. But these essays are concerned, too, and rather pointedly, with establishing "intertextual" relations to "extraliterary" discourses, or texts not usually conceived of as texts—voice, culture, violence, portraiture, body, sex. Intertextuality, of course, simply does not recognize the boundaries of discipline and is at work in the whole of the world text. Intertextuality leads, by circuitous routes, to an understanding of centrifugal relations between texts, rather than merely to a concentration on centripetal "literary relations." The study of intertextuality—broadly conceived—provides a context for contemporary literary productions as they reinscribe and transform the representations of the cultural past. This study, then, can assist us in defining and coming to terms with the emergent sensibility we have labeled postmodern. That this sensibility, as is the case with all contemporary sensibilities, arises in the midst of things expresses both a hope for continuance and a sense of indebtedness to a past that (as both Eliot *and* Derrida insist) must constantly be resituated and shown up for its fictive assumptions.

Works Cited

Bakhtin, Mikhail. *The Dialogic Imagination: Four Essays*. Edited by Michael Holquist. Translated by Caryl Emerson and Michael Holquist. Austin: University of Texas Press, 1981.

Barth, John. "The Literature of Exhaustion." In *The Friday Book: Essays and Other Nonfiction*. New York: Putnam, 1984.

Gaddis, William. *The Recognitions*. 1955. Reprint. New York: Penguin, 1983.

Graff, Gerald. "Under Our Belt and Off Our Backs: Barth's LETTERS and Postmodern Fiction." *TriQuarterly* 52 (1981): 150–64.

Gramsci, Antonio. *Selections from the Prison Notebooks*. Edited and translated by Quentin Hoare and Geoffrey Norwell Smith. New York: International Publishers, 1983.

Hassan, Ihab. *Paracriticisms: Seven Speculations of the Times*. Urbana: University of Illinois Press, 1975.

Hollander, John. *The Figure of Echo: A Mode of Allusion in Milton and After*. Berkeley and Los Angeles: University of California Press, 1981.

Klinkowitz, Jerome. *Literary Disruptions: The Making of a Post-Contemporary American Fiction*. 2d ed. Urbana: University of Illinois Press, 1980.

Lyotard, Jean-François. *The Postmodern Condition: A Report on Knowledge*. Translated by Geoff Bennington and Brian H. Massumi. Theory and History of Literature, vol. 10. Minneapolis: University of Minnesota Press, 1984.

McKeon, Michael. *The Origins of the English Novel, 1600–1740*. Baltimore: Johns Hopkins University Press, 1987.

Newman, Charles. *The Post-Modern Aura: The Act of Fiction in an Age of Inflation*. Evanston, Ill.: Northwestern University Press, 1985.

Saussure, Ferdinand de. *Course in General Linguistics*. Translated by Wade Baskin. 1959. Reprint. New York: McGraw-Hill, 1966.

Wilde, Alan. *Horizons of Assent: Modernism, Postmodernism, and the Ironic Imagination*. Baltimore: Johns Hopkins University Press, 1981.

PRELUDE

Historiographic Metafiction

Parody and the Intertextuality
of History

===

LINDA HUTCHEON

Il y a plus affaire à interpréter les interprétations qu'à interpréter les choses, et plus de livres sur les livres que sur autre
sujet: nous ne faisons que nous entregloser.
—Montaigne

The frontiers of a book are never clear-cut: beyond the title,
the first lines, and the last full-stop, beyond its internal configuration and its autonomous form, it is caught up in a system of references to other books, other texts, other sentences: it is a node within a network.
—Foucault

What we tend to call postmodernism in literature today is usually
characterized by intense self-reflexivity and overtly parodic intertextuality. In fiction this means that it is usually metafiction that is
equated with the postmodern. Given the scarcity of precise definitions of this problematic period designation, such an equation is
often accepted without question. What I would like to argue is that,
in the interests of precision and consistency, we must add something else to this definition: an equally self-conscious dimension of
history. My model here is postmodern architecture, that resolutely
parodic recalling of the history of architectural forms and functions. The theme of the 1980 Venice Biennale, which introduced
postmodernism to the architectural world, was "The Presence of
the Past." The term *postmodernism*, when used in fiction, should, by
analogy, best be reserved to describe fiction that is at once metafictional *and* historical in its echoes of the texts and contexts of the
past. In order to distinguish this paradoxical beast from traditional
historical fiction, I would like to label it "historiographic metafiction." The category of novel I am thinking of includes *One Hun-
dred Years of Solitude, Ragtime, The French Lieutenant's Woman*, and
The Name of the Rose. All of these are popular and familiar novels
whose metafictional self-reflexivity (and intertextuality) renders
their implicit claims to historical veracity somewhat problematic, to
say the least.

3

In the wake of recent assaults by literary and philosophical theory on modernist formalist closure, postmodern American fiction, in particular, has sought to open itself up to history, to what Edward Said (*The World*) calls the "world." But it seems to have found that it can no longer do so in any innocent way: the certainty of direct reference of the historical novel or even the nonfictional novel is gone. So is the certainty of self-reference implied in the Borgesian claim that both literature and the world are equally fictive realities. The postmodern relationship between fiction and history is an even more complex one of interaction and mutual implication. Historiographic metafiction works to situate itself within historical discourse without surrendering its autonomy as fiction. And it is a kind of seriously ironic parody that effects both aims: the intertexts of history and fiction take on parallel (though not equal) status in the parodic reworking of the textual past of both the "world" and literature. The textual incorporation of these intertextual past(s) as a constitutive structural element of postmodernist fiction functions as a formal marking of historicity—both literary and "worldly." At first glance it would appear that it is only its constant ironic signaling of difference at the very heart of similarity that distinguishes postmodern parody from medieval and Renaissance imitation (see Greene 17). For Dante, as for E. L. Doctorow, the texts of literature and those of history are equally fair game.

Nevertheless, a distinction should be made: "Traditionally, stories were stolen, as Chaucer stole his; or they were felt to be the common property of a culture or community . . . These notable happenings, imagined or real, lay outside language the way history itself is supposed to, in a condition of pure occurrence" (Gass 147). Today, there is a return to the idea of a common discursive "property" in the embedding of both literary and historical texts in fiction, but it is a return made problematic by overtly metafictional assertions of both history and literature as human constructs, indeed, as human illusions—necessary, but none the less illusory for all that. The intertextual parody of historiographic metafiction enacts, in a way, the views of certain contemporary historiographers (see Canary and Kozicki): it offers a sense of the presence of the past, but this is a past that can only be known from its texts, its traces—be they literary or historical.

Clearly, then, what I want to call postmodernism is a paradoxical cultural phenomenon, and it is also one that operates across many traditional disciplines. In contemporary theoretical discourse, for instance, we find puzzling contradictions: those masterful denials of mastery, totalizing negations of totalization, continuous attestings of discontinuity. In the postmodern novel the conventions of both fiction and historiography are simultaneously used and abused, installed and subverted, asserted and denied. And the double (literary/historical) nature of this intertextual parody is one of the major means by which this paradoxical (and defining) nature of postmodernism is textually inscribed. Perhaps one of the reasons why there has been such heated debate on the definition of postmodernism recently is that the implications of the doubleness of this parodic process have not been fully examined. Novels like *The Book of Daniel* or *The Public Burning*—whatever their complex intertextual layering—can certainly not be said to eschew history, any more than they can be said to ignore either their moorings in social reality (see Graff 209) or a clear political intent (see Eagleton 61). Historiographic metafiction manages to satisfy such a desire for "worldly" grounding while at the same time querying the very basis of the authority of that grounding. As David Lodge has put it, postmodernism short-circuits the gap between text and world (239–40).

Discussions of postmodernism seem more prone than most to confusing self-contradictions, again perhaps because of the paradoxical nature of the subject itself. Charles Newman, for instance, in his provocative book *The Post-Modern Aura*, begins by defining postmodern art as a "commentary on the aesthetic history of whatever genre it adopts" (44). This would, then, be art which sees history only in aesthetic terms (57). However, when postulating an American version of postmodernism, he abandons this metafictional intertextual definition to call American literature a "literature *without* primary influences," "a literature which lacks a known parenthood," suffering from the "anxiety of *non*-influence" (87). As we shall see, an examination of the novels of Toni Morrison, E. L. Doctorow, John Barth, Ishmael Reed, Thomas Pynchon, and others casts a reasonable doubt on such pronouncements. On the one hand, Newman wants to argue that postmodernism at large is resolutely parodic; on the other, he asserts that the American postmodern deliberately puts "distance between itself and its literary antecedents, an obligatory if occasionally conscience-stricken break with the past" (172). Newman is not alone in his viewing of postmodern parody as a form of ironic rupture with the past (see Thiher 214), but, as in postmodernist architecture, there is always a paradox at the heart of that "post": irony does indeed mark the difference from the past, but the intertextual echoing simultaneously works to affirm—textually and hermeneutically—the connection with the past.

When that past is the literary period we now seem to label as

5

modernism, then what is both instated and then subverted is the notion of the work of art as a closed, self-sufficient, autonomous object deriving its unity from the formal interrelations of its parts. In its characteristic attempt to retain aesthetic autonomy while still returning the text to the "world," postmodernism both asserts and then undercuts this formalistic view. But this does not necessitate a return to the world of "ordinary reality," as some have argued (Kern 216); the "world" in which the text situates itself is the "world" of discourse, the "world" of texts and intertexts. This "world" has direct links to the world of empirical reality, but it is not itself that empirical reality. It is a contemporary critical truism that realism is really a set of conventions, that the representation of the real is not the same as the real itself. What historiographic metafiction challenges is both any naive realist concept of representation and any equally naive textualist or formalist assertions of the total separation of art from the world. The postmodern is selfconsciously art "within the archive" (Foucault 92), and that archive is both historical and literary.

In the light of the work of writers such as Carlos Fuentes, Salman Rushdie, D. M. Thomas, John Fowles, Umberto Eco, as well as Robert Coover, E. L. Doctorow, John Barth, Joseph Heller, Ishmael Reed, and other American novelists, it is hard to see why critics such as Allen Thiher, for instance, "can think of no such intertextual foundations today" as those of Dante in Virgil (189). Are we really in the midst of a crisis of faith in the "possibility of historical culture" (189)? Have we ever *not* been in such a crisis? To parody is not to destroy the past; in fact, to parody is both to enshrine the past and to question it. And this is the postmodern paradox.

The theoretical exploration of the "vast dialogue" (Calinescu 169) between and among literatures and histories that configure postmodernism has, in part, been made possible by Julia Kristeva's early reworking of the Bakhtinian notions of polyphony, dialogism, and heteroglossia—the multiple voicings of a text. Out of these ideas she developed a more strictly formalist theory of the irreducible plurality of texts within and behind any given text, thereby deflecting the critical focus away from the notion of the subject (here, the author) to the idea of textual productivity. Kristeva and her colleagues at *Tel Quel* in the late sixties and early seventies mounted a collective attack on the founding subject (alias: the "romantic" cliché of the author) as the original and originating source of fixed and fetishized meaning in the text. And, of course, this also put into question the entire notion of the "text" as an autonomous entity, with immanent meaning.

In America a similar formalist impulse had provoked a similar attack much earlier in the form of the New Critical rejection of the "intentional fallacy" (Wimsatt). Nevertheless, it would seem that even though we can no longer talk comfortably of authors (and sources and influences), we still need a critical language in which to discuss those ironic allusions, those re-contextualized quotations, those double-edged parodies both of genre and of specific works that proliferate in modernist and postmodernist texts. This, of course, is where the concept of intertextuality has proved so useful. As later defined by Roland Barthes (*Image* 160) and Michael Riffaterre (142–43), intertextuality replaces the challenged author–text relationship with one between reader and text, one that situates the locus of textual meaning within the history of discourse itself. A literary work can actually no longer be considered original; if it were, it could have no meaning for its reader. It is only as part of prior discourses that any text derives meaning and significance.

Not surprisingly, this theoretical redefining of aesthetic value has coincided with a change in the kind of art being produced. Postmodernly parodic composer George Rochberg, in the liner notes to the Nonesuch recording of his String Quartet no. 3 articulates this change in these terms: "I have had to abandon the notion of 'originality,' in which the personal style of the artist and his ego are the supreme values; the pursuit of the one-idea, uni-dimensional work and gesture which seems to have dominated the esthetics of art in the 20th century; and the received idea that it is necessary to divorce oneself from the past." In the visual arts too, the works of Shusaku Arakawa, Larry Rivers, Tom Wesselman, and others have brought about, through parodic intertextuality (both aesthetic and historical), a real skewing of any "romantic" notions of subjectivity and creativity.

As in historiographic metafiction, these other art forms parodically cite the intertexts of both the "world" and art and, in so doing, contest the boundaries that many would unquestioningly use to separate the two. In its most extreme formulation, the result of such contesting would be a "break with every given context, engendering an infinity of new contexts in a manner which is absolutely illimitable" (Derrida 185). While postmodernism, as I am defining it here, is perhaps somewhat less promiscuously extensive, the notion of parody as opening the text up, rather than closing it down, is an important one: among the many things that postmodern intertextuality challenges are both closure and single, centralized meaning. Its willed and willful provisionality rests largely upon its acceptance of the inevitable textual infiltration of prior discursive

7

practices. Typically contradictory, intertextuality in postmodern art both provides and undermines context. In Vincent B. Leitch's terms, it "posits both an uncentered historical enclosure and an abysmal decentered foundation for language and textuality; in so doing, it exposes all contextualizations as limited and limiting, arbitrary and confining, self-serving and authoritarian, theological and political. However paradoxically formulated, intertextuality offers a liberating determinism" (162).

It is perhaps clearer now why it has been claimed that to use the term *intertextuality* in criticism is not just to avail oneself of a useful conceptual tool: it also signals a "prise de position, un champ de référence" (Angenot 122). But its usefulness as a theoretical framework that is both hermeneutic and formalist is obvious in dealing with historiographic metafiction that demands of the reader not only the recognition of textualized traces of the literary and historical past but also the awareness of what has been done—through irony—to those traces. The reader is forced to acknowledge not only the inevitable textuality of our knowledge of the past, but also both the value and the limitation of that inescapably discursive form of knowledge, situated as it is "between presence and absence" (Barilli). Italo Calvino's Marco Polo in *Invisible Cities* both is and is not the historical Marco Polo. How can we, today, "know" the Italian explorer? We can only do so by way of texts—including his own (*Il Milione*), from which Calvino parodically takes his frame tale, his travel plot, and his characterization (Musarra 141).

Roland Barthes once defined the intertext as "the impossibility of living outside the infinite text" (*Pleasure* 36), thereby making intertextuality the very condition of textuality. Umberto Eco, writing of his novel *The Name of the Rose*, claims: "I discovered what writers have always known (and have told us again and again): books always speak of other books, and every story tells a story that has already been told" (20). The stories that *The Name of the Rose* retells are both those of literature (by Arthur Conan Doyle, Jorge Luis Borges, James Joyce, Thomas Mann, T. S. Eliot, among others) and those of history (medieval chronicles, religious testimonies). This is the parodically doubled discourse of postmodernist intertextuality. However, this is not just a doubly introverted form of aestheticism: the theoretical implications of this kind of historiographic metafiction coincide with recent historiographic theory about the nature of history writing as narrativization (rather than representation) of the past and about the nature of the archive as the textualized remains of history (see White, "The Question").

In other words, yes, postmodernism manifests a certain introversion, a self-conscious turning toward the form of the act of writing itself; but it is also much more than that. It does not go so far as to "establish an explicit literal relation with that real world beyond itself," as some have claimed (Kiremidjian 238). Its relationship to the "worldly" is still on the level of discourse, but to claim that is to claim quite a lot. After all, we can only "know" (as opposed to "experience") the world through our narratives (past and present) of it, or so postmodernism argues. The present, as well as the past, is always already irremediably textualized for us (Belsey 46), and the overt intertextuality of historiographic metafiction serves as one of the textual signals of this postmodern realization.

Readers of a novel like Kurt Vonnegut's *Slaughterhouse-Five* do not have to proceed very far before picking up these signals. The author is identified on the title page as "a fourth-generation German-American now living in easy circumstances on Cape Cod (and smoking too much), who, as an American infantry scout *hors de combat*, as a prisoner of war, witnessed the fire-bombing of Dresden, Germany, 'The Florence of the Elbe,' a long time ago, and survived to tell the tale. This is a novel somewhat in the telegraphic schizophrenic manner of tales of the planet Tralfamadore, where the flying saucers come from. Peace." The character, Kurt Vonnegut, appears in the novel, trying to erase his memories of the war and of Dresden, the destruction of which he saw from "Slaughterhouse-Five," where he worked as a POW. The novel itself opens with: "All this happened, more or less. The war parts, anyway, are pretty much true" (7). Counterpointed to this historical context, however, is the (metafictionally marked) Billy Pilgrim, the optometrist who helps correct defective vision—including his own, though it takes the planet Tralfamadore to give him his new perspective. Billy's fantasy life acts as an allegory of the author's own displacements and postponements (i.e., his other novels) that prevented him from writing about Dresden before this, and it is the *intra*texts of the novel that signal this allegory: Tralfamadore itself is from Vonnegut's *The Sirens of Titan*, Billy's home in Illium is from *Player Piano*, characters appear from *Mother Night* and *God Bless You, Mr. Rosewater*. The *inter*texts, however, function in similar ways, and their provenience is again double: there are actual historical intertexts (documentaries on Dresden, etc.), mixed with those of historical fiction (Stephen Crane, Céline). But there are also structurally and thematically connected allusions: to Hermann Hesse's *Journey to the East* and to various works of science fiction. Popular and high-art intertexts mingle: *Valley of the Dolls* meets the poems of William Blake and Theodore Roethke. All are fair game and all get re-contextualized in order to challenge the imperialistic (cultural and political) mentalities that bring about the Dresdens of history. Thomas Pynchon's *V.* uses double intertexts in a similarly "loaded" fashion to formally enact the author's related theme of the entropic destructiveness of humanity. Stencil's dossier, its fragments of the texts of history, is an amalgam of literary intertexts, as if to remind us that "there is no one writable 'truth' about history and experience, only a series of versions: it always comes to us 'stencillized' " (Tanner 172). And it is always multiple, like V's identity.

Patricia Waugh notes that metafiction such as *Slaughterhouse-Five* or *The Public Burning* "suggests not only that writing history is a fictional act, ranging events conceptually through language to form a world-model, but that history itself is invested, like fiction, with interrelating plots which appear to interact independently of human design" (48–49). Historiographic metafiction is particularly doubled, like this, in its inscribing of both historical and literary intertexts. Its specific and general recollections of the forms and contents of history writing work to familiarize the unfamiliar through (very familiar) narrative structures (as Hayden White has argued ["The Historical Text," 49–50]), but its metafictional self-reflexivity works to render problematic any such familiarization. And the reason for the sameness is that both real and imagined worlds come to us through their accounts of them, that is, through their traces, their texts. The ontological line between historical past and literature is not effaced (see Thiher 190), but underlined. The past really did exist, but we can only "know" that past today through its texts, and therein lies its connection to the literary. If the discipline of history has lost its privileged status as the purveyor of truth, then so much the better, according to this kind of modern historiographic theory: the loss of the illusion of transparency in historical writing is a step toward intellectual self-awareness that is matched by metafiction's challenges to the presumed transparency of the language of realist texts.

When its critics attack postmodernism for being what they see as ahistorical (as do Eagleton, Jameson, and Newman), what is being referred to as "postmodern" suddenly becomes unclear, for surely historiographic metafiction, like postmodernist architecture and painting, is overtly and resolutely historical—though, admittedly, in an ironic and problematic way that acknowledges that history is not the transparent record of any sure "truth." Instead, such fiction corroborates the views of philosophers of history such as Dominick LaCapra who argue that "the past arrives in the form of texts and textualized remainders—memories, reports, published writings, archives, monuments, and so forth" (128) and that these texts interact with one another in complex ways. This does not in any way deny the value of history-writing; it merely redefines the conditions of value in somewhat less imperialistic terms. Lately, the tradition of narrative history with its concern "for the short time span, for the individual and the event" (Braudel 27), has been called into question by the Annales School in France. But this particular model of narrative history was, of course, also that of the realist novel. Historiographic metafiction, therefore, represents a challenging of the (related) conventional forms of fiction and history through its acknowledgment of their inescapable textuality. As Barthes once remarked, Bouvard and Pécuchet become the ideal precursors of the postmodernist writer who "can only imitate a gesture that is always anterior, never original. His only power is to mix writings, to counter the ones with the others, in such a way as never to rest on any of them" (*Image* 146).

The formal linking of history and fiction through the common denominators of intertextuality and narrativity is usually offered not as a reduction, as a shrinking of the scope and value of fiction, but rather as an expansion of these. Or, if it is seen as a limitation—restricted to the always already narrated—this tends to be made into the primary value, as it is in Lyotard's "pagan vision," wherein no one ever manages to be the first to narrate anything, to be the origin of even her or his own narrative (78). Lyotard deliberately sets up this "limitation" as the opposite of what he calls the capitalist position of the writer as original creator, proprietor, and entrepreneur of her or his story. Much postmodern writing shares this implied ideological critique of the assumptions underlying "romantic" concepts of author and text, and it is parodic intertextuality that is the major vehicle of that critique.

Perhaps because parody itself has potentially contradictory ideological implications (as "authorized transgression," it can be seen as both conservative and revolutionary [Hutcheon 69–83]), it is a perfect mode of criticism for postmodernism, itself paradoxical in its conservative installing and then radical contesting of conventions. Historiographic metafictions, like Gabriel García Márquez's *One Hundred Years of Solitude*, Günter Grass's *The Tin Drum*, or Salman Rushdie's *Midnight's Children* (which uses both of the former as intertexts), employ parody not only to restore history and memory in the face of the distortions of the "history of forgetting" (Thiher

202), but also, at the same time, to put into question the authority of any act of writing by locating the discourses of both history and fiction within an ever-expanding intertextual network that mocks any notion of either single origin or simple causality.

When linked with satire, as in the work of Vonnegut, V. Vampilov, Christa Wolf, or Coover, parody can certainly take on more precisely ideological dimensions. Here, too, however, there is no direct intervention in the world: this is writing working through other writing, other textualizations of experience (Said *Beginnings* 237). In many cases *intertextuality* may well be too limited a term to describe this process; *interdiscursivity* would perhaps be a more accurate term for the collective modes of discourse from which the postmodern parodically draws: literature, visual arts, history, biography, theory, philosophy, psychoanalysis, sociology, and the list could go on. One of the effects of this discursive pluralizing is that the (perhaps illusory but once firm and single) center of both historical and fictive narrative is dispersed. Margins and edges gain new value. The "ex-centric"—as both off-center and de-centered—gets attention. That which is "different" is valorized in opposition both to elitist, alienated "otherness" and also to the uniformizing impulse of mass culture. And in American postmodernism, the "different" comes to be defined in particularizing terms such as those of nationality, ethnicity, gender, race, and sexual orientation. Intertextual parody of canonical classics is one mode of reappropriating and reformulating—with significant changes—the dominant white, male, middle-class, European culture. It does not reject it, for it cannot. It signals its dependence by its *use* of the canon, but asserts its rebellion through ironic *abuse* of it. As Edward Said has been arguing recently ("Culture"), there is a relationship of mutual interdependence between the histories of the dominators and the dominated.

American fiction since the sixties has been, as described by Malcolm Bradbury (186), particularly obsessed with its own past—literary, social, and historical. Perhaps this preoccupation is (or was) tied in part to a need to find a particularly American voice within a culturally dominant Eurocentric tradition (D'haen 216). The United States (like the rest of North and South America) is a land of immigration. In E. L. Doctorow's words, "We derive enormously, of course, from Europe, and that's part of what *Ragtime* is about: the means by which we began literally, physically to lift European art and architecture and bring it over here" (in Trenner 58). This is also part of what American historiographic metafiction in general is "about." Critics have discussed at length the parodic intertexts of the work of Thomas Pynchon, including Conrad's *Heart of Darkness* (McHale 88) and Proust's first-person confessional form (Patteson 37–38) in *V.* In particular, *The Crying of Lot 49* has been seen as directly linking the literary parody of Jacobean drama with the selectivity and subjectivity of what we deem historical "fact" (Bennett). Here the postmodern parody operates in much the same way as it did in the literature of the seventeenth century, and in both Pynchon's novel and the plays he parodies (John Ford's *'Tis Pity She's a Whore*, John Webster's *The White Devil* and *The Duchess of Malfi*, and Cyril Tourneur's *The Revenger's Tragedy*, among others), the intertextual "received discourse" is firmly embedded in a social commentary about the loss of relevance of traditional values in contemporary life (Bennett).

Just as powerful and even more outrageous, perhaps, is the parody of Charles Dickens' *A Christmas Carol* in Ishmael Reed's *The Terrible Twos*, where political satire and parody meet to attack white Euro-centered ideologies of domination. Its structure of "A Past Christmas" and "A Future Christmas" prepares us for its initial Dickensian invocations—first through metaphor ("Money is as tight as Scrooge" [4]) and then directly: "Ebenezer Scrooge towers above the Washington skyline, rubbing his hands and greedily peering over his spectacles" (4). Scrooge is not a character, but a guiding spirit of 1980 America, one that attends the inauguration of the president that year. The novel proceeds to update Dickens' tale. However, the rich are still cozy and comfortable ("Regardless of how high inflation remains, the wealthy will have any kind of Christmas they desire, a spokesman for Neiman-Marcus announces" [5]); the poor are not. This is the 1980 replay of "Scrooge's winter, 'as mean as a junkyard dog'" (32).

The "Future Christmas" takes place after monopoly capitalism has literally captured Christmas following a court decision which has granted exclusive rights to Santa Claus to one person and one company. One strand of the complex plot continues the Dickensian intertext: the American president—a vacuous, alcoholic, ex-(male) model—is reformed by a visit from St. Nicholas, who takes him on a trip through hell, playing Virgil to his Dante. There he meets past presidents and other politicians, whose punishments (as in the *Inferno*) conform to their crimes. Made a new man from this experience, the president spends Christmas Day with his black butler, John, and John's crippled grandson. Though unnamed, this Tiny Tim ironically outsentimentalizes Dickens': he has a leg amputated; he is black; his parents died in a car accident.

In an attempt to save the nation, the president goes on television to announce: "The problems of American society will not go away . . . by invoking Scroogelike attitudes against the poor or saying humbug to the old and to the underprivileged" (158). But the final echoes of the Dickens intertext are ultimately ironic: the president is declared unfit to serve (because of his televised message) and is hospitalized by the business interests which really run the government. None of Dickens' optimism remains in this bleak satiric vision of the future. Similarly, in *Yellow Back Radio Broke-Down*, Reed parodically inverts Dostoevsky's "Grand Inquisitor" in order to subvert the authority of social, moral, and literary order. No work of the Western humanist tradition seems safe from postmodern intertextual citation and contestation today: in Heller's *God Knows* even the sacred texts of the Bible are subject to both validation and demystification.

It is significant that the intertexts of John Barth's LETTERS include not only the British eighteenth-century epistolary novel, *Don Quixote*, and other European works by H. G. Wells, Mann, and Joyce, but also texts by Henry David Thoreau, Nathaniel Hawthorne, Edgar Allan Poe, Walt Whitman, and James Fenimore Cooper. The specifically American past is as much a part of defining "difference" for contemporary American postmodernism as is the European past. The same parodic mix of authority and transgression, use and abuse characterizes intra-American intertextuality. For instance, Pynchon's *V.* and Morrison's *Song of Solomon*, in different ways, parody both the structures and theme of the recoverability of history in William Faulkner's *Absalom, Absalom!*. Similarly, Doctorow's *Lives of the Poets* (1984) both installs and subverts Philip Roth's *My Life as a Man* and Saul Bellow's *Herzog* (Levine 80).

The parodic references to the earlier, nineteenth-century or classic American literature are perhaps even more complex, however, since there is a long (and related) tradition of the interaction of fiction and history in, for example, Hawthorne's use of the conventions of romance to connect the historical past and the writing present. And indeed Hawthorne's fiction is a familiar postmodern intertext: *The Blithedale Romance* and Barth's *The Floating Opera* share the same moral preoccupation with the consequences of writers taking aesthetic distance from life, but it is the difference in their structural forms (Barth's novel is more self-consciously metafictional [Christensen 12]) that points the reader to the real irony of the conjunction of the ethical issue.

The canonical texts of the American tradition are both undermined and yet drawn upon, for parody is the paradoxical postmodern way of coming to terms with the past. Given this, it is not surprising that contemporary American literature should abound in parodic echoes of Herman Melville's *Moby-Dick*, the great novel of naming and knowing—concerns that postmodernism obviously shares: Roth's "Call me Smitty" (*The Great American Novel*), Vonnegut's "Call me Jonah" (*Cat's Cradle*), or Barth's less direct, but more postmodernly provisional, "In a sense, I am Jacob Horner" (*The End of the Road*). Novels that deal with historical and technological fact and/or that recount the pursuit of seemingly unconquerable Nature are also bound to recall Melville's text. For instance, in Norman Mailer's *Of a Fire on the Moon* the moon/whale sought after by Aquarius/Ishmael comes alive in a familiar (but here, ironic) language that mixes technical concreteness with transcendent mystery (Sisk).

Somewhat by way of parenthesis, it is worth noting here that, like historiographic metafiction, the nonfictional novel—whatever its claims to factual veracity of historical reporting—overtly structures its report on fictive intertexts: Tom Wolfe's *The Electric Kool-Aid Acid Test* parodies Jack Kerouac's *On the Road*, Poe's "A Descent into the Maelstrom," and works by Thoreau, Ralph Waldo Emerson, and Arthur C. Clarke (see Hellmann 110–13); Hunter S. Thompson's *Fear and Loathing in Las Vegas* recalls *Moby-Dick*, American romances, and the picaresque genre (Hellmann 82–87); another of the intertexts of Mailer's *Of a Fire on the Moon* is *The Education of Henry Adams* (Taylor); John Hersey's *The Algiers Motel Incident* and Mailer's *The Armies of the Night* both parody John Dos Passos's *USA*. Of course a good case might be made for Dos Passos's trilogy itself being an earlier form of historiographic metafiction in its use and abuse of the conventions of history, fiction, biography, autobiography, and journalism (Malmgren 132–42). The fragmented form and the constant play with reader expectations do indeed begin to subvert the authority of those conventions, but perhaps in the end there is more resolution of formal and hermeneutic tensions than would characterize the more open and contradictory fiction of postmodernism.

Historiographic metafiction, like the nonfictional novel, however, does turn to the intertexts of history as well as literature. Barth's *The Sot-Weed Factor* manages both to debunk and to create the history of Maryland for its reader through not only the real Ebenezer Cooke's 1708 poem (of the same name as the novel) but also the raw historical record of the Archives of Maryland. From these intertexts, Barth rewrites history, taking considerable liberty— sometimes inventing characters and events, sometimes parodically inverting the tone and mode of his intertexts, sometimes offering connections where gaps occur in the historical record (see Holder 598–99). Thomas Berger's *Little Big Man* recounts all the major historical events on the American plains at the end of the nineteenth century (from the killing of the buffalo and the building of the railway to Custer's last stand), but the recounting is done by a fictive, 111-year-old character who both inflates and deflates the historical heroes of the West and the literary clichés of the Western genre alike—since history and literature share a tendency to exaggerate in narrating the past.

Berger makes no attempt to hide his intertexts, be they fictional or historical. The mythic stature of Old Lodge Skins is meant to recall that of Natty Bumppo—and to parody it (Wylder); the account of his death is taken almost word for word from John G. Neilhardt's report of Black Elk's, and Custer's final mad talk is lifted directly from his *My Life on the Plains* (Schulz 74–75). Even the fictional Jack Crabb is defined by his intertexts: the historical Jack Cleybourne and the fictive John Clayton from Will Henry's *No Survivors*, both of them temporally and geographically coextensive with Crabb.

It is not just literature and history, however, that form the discourses of postmodernism. Everything from comic books and fairy tales to almanacs and newspapers provide historiographic metafiction with culturally significant intertexts. In Coover's *The Public Burning* the history of the Rosenbergs' execution is mediated by many different textualized forms. One major form is that of the various media, through which the concept of the disparity between "news" and "reality" or "truth" is foregrounded. The *New York Times* is shown to constitute the sacred texts of America, the texts that offer "orderly and reasonable" versions of experience, but whose apparent objectivity conceals a Hegelian "idealism which mistakes its own language for reality" (Mazurek 34). And one of the central intertexts for the portrayal of Richard Nixon in the novel is his famous televised Checkers speech, the tone, metaphors, and ideology of which provide Coover with the rhetoric and character of his fictionalized Nixon.

Historiographic metafiction appears willing to draw upon any signifying practices it can find operative in a society. It wants to challenge those discourses and yet to milk them for all they are worth. In Pynchon's fiction, for instance, this kind of contradictory subversive inscribing is often carried to an extreme: "Documentation, obsessional systems, the languages of popular culture, of advertising: hundreds of systems compete with each other, resisting assimilation to any one received paradigm" (Waugh 39). Perhaps.

But Pynchon's intertextually overdetermined, discursively over-loaded fictions both parody and enact the tendency of all dis-courses to create systems and structures. The plots of such narra-tives become other kinds of plots, that is, conspiracies that invoke terror in those subject (as we all are) to the power of pattern. Many have commented upon this paranoia in the works of contemporary American writers, but few have noted the paradoxical nature of this particularly postmodern fear and loathing: the terror of total-izing plotting is inscribed within texts characterized by nothing if not by overplotting and overdetermined intertextual self-reference. The text itself becomes the ultimately closed, self-referring system.

Perhaps this contradictory attraction/repulsion to structure and pattern explains the predominance of the parodic use of certain familiar and overtly conventionally plotted forms in American fic-tion, for instance, that of the Western: *Little Big Man*, *Yellow Back Radio Broke-Down*, *The Sot-Weed Factor*, *Welcome to Hard Times*, *Even Cowgirls Get the Blues*. It has also been suggested that "the one thing the Western is always about is America rewriting and reinterpret-ing her own past" (French 24). The ironic intertextual use of the Western is not, as some have claimed, a form of "Temporal Escape" (Steinberg 127), but rather a coming to terms with the existing tra-ditions of earlier historical and literary articulations of American-ness. As such, obviously, parody can be used to satiric ends. Doc-torow's *Welcome to Hard Times* recalls Stephen Crane's "The Blue Hotel" in its portrayal of the power of money, greed, and force on the frontier: through intertextuality it is suggested that some noble myths have capitalistic exploitation at their core (Gross 133). In parodically inverting the conventions of the Western, Doctorow here presents a nature that is not a redemptive wilderness and pio-neers who are less hardworking survivors than petty entrepre-neurs. He forces us to rethink and perhaps reinterpret history, and he does so mainly through his narrator, Blue, who is caught in the dilemma of whether we make history or history makes us. To un-derline the intertextual intertwining of discourses, he writes his story in the ledger book where the town records are also kept (see Levine 27–30).

Ishmael Reed's parody of the Western in *Yellow Back Radio Broke-Down* is even more ideologically "loaded." Loop Garoo Kid is both the ironically black cowboy hero and a parody of the Haitian Congo spirit Bacca Loupgerow (Byerman 222). The genre's tradi-tional assumptions of the long (good) hero fighting lawless evil and corruption are here inverted as the demonic, anarchic cowboy must combat the repression and corruption of the very forces of law and order. Reed uses other generic parodies to similar critical effect. In *The Free-Lance Pallbearers* he transcodes the American success-story (Horatio Alger) plot into scatological terms to underline his theme of human waste. In *Mumbo Jumbo*, Papa LaBas parodies the American detective in his climactic unveiling of the history of the motives behind the crime—but here the crime is aboriginal and the motives go back to prehistory and myth. The detective tale's plotting, with its reliance on rationality, becomes another plot, another oppressive, ordering pattern.

Reed's fiction clearly asserts not just a critical American "difference" but also a racial one. His parodic mixing of levels and kinds of discourse challenges any notion of the "different" as either coherent and monolithic or original. It draws on both the black and white literary and historical narrative traditions, rewriting Zora Neale Hurston, Richard Wright, and Ralph Ellison as easily as Plato or T. S. Eliot (see McConnell 145; Gates 314), while also drawing on the multiple possibilities opened up by the folk tradition. Implicitly opposing community and heterogeneous voicings to single, fixed, homogenizing identity, these folk materials are "historical, changing, disreputable, and performative" (Byerman 4)—a perfect postmodernist vehicle for a challenge to the universal, eternal, ahistorical "natural."

Reed's *Flight to Canada* "signifies upon" or parodies the historical and literary versions of the slave narrative—as written by both blacks and whites (i.e., *Uncle Tom's Cabin*). As Henry Louis Gates, Jr., has shown at great length, *Mumbo Jumbo* is an extended and multiple parodic polemic, and one of its major intertexts comes from a poem by Reed, itself a parodic response to the epilogue to Ellison's *Invisible Man*, which asserts that men [*sic*] are different, that "all life is divided," and that such division is healthy. Reed replies in "Dualism: in ralph ellison's invisible man" (*Conjure* 50):

> i am outside of
> history. i wish
> i had some peanuts, it
> looks hungry there in
> its cage.
>
> i am inside of
> history. its
> hungrier than i
> thot.

Here Reed is obviously serious, as he always is, beneath his parodic play. It is this seriousness that critics have frequently been blind to when they accuse postmodernism of being ironic—and therefore trivial. The assumption seems to be that authenticity of experience and expression are somehow incompatible with double-voicing and/or humor. This view seems to be shared, not only by Marxist critics (Jameson; Eagleton), but by some feminist critics: Elaine Showalter seems to see Virginia Woolf's parody in *A Room of One's Own* as "teasing, sly, elusive" (284). And yet it is feminist writers, along with blacks, who have used ironic intertextuality to such powerful ends—both ideologically and aesthetically (if the two could, in fact, be so easily separated). Parody for them is more than just a key strategy through which "feminine duplicity" is revealed (Gilbert and Gubar 80), though it is one of the major ways in which women both use and abuse, set up and then challenge male traditions in art. The link between gender and genre is clear in *Orlando's* parodic play with biographical conventions, and Monique Wittig has re-en-gendered the male epic (*Les Guérillères*) and the patriarchal/filiative *Bildungsroman* (in *L'Opoponax*).

In fact, the *Bildungsroman* has been a most obvious and popular parodic model. Marge Piercy's *Small Changes* inverts the male narrative pattern of education and adventure to offer a radical feminist escape from (rather than integration into) the patriarchal state (see Hansen 215–16). Toni Morrison's *Song of Solomon* uses a traditional male protagonist but parodically inverts the usual focus on the individual in the world to make us consider the community and the family in a new light (Wagner 200–1). In a similar way, Alice Walker calls upon ironic versions of familiar fairy tales in *The Color Purple*: Snow White, the Ugly Duckling, and Sleeping Beauty. But the significance of the parodies is not clear until the reader notices the gender and race reversal effected by her irony: the world in which she lives happily ever after is a female and black one (see Byerman 161).

The ex-centric in America is not just a matter of gender or race or nationality, but also one of class, for the fifty United States do not really constitute an economic and social monolith. Even within black feminist novels, for instance, the issue of class enters. With intertextual echoes of Ike McCaslin in Faulkner's "The Bear," Milkman in *Song of Solomon* must be stripped of the physical symbols of the dominant white culture and submit to a trial by endurance in order to be accepted. The reason? The blacks in Shalimar perceive the class issue beneath the racial one. They know that "he had the heart of the white men who came to pick them up in the trucks when they needed anonymous, faceless laborers" (269). And in the same novel, the petit bourgeois Ruth, the doctor's daughter, scorns her nouveau-riche husband. In Doctorow's *Ragtime* the issues of ethnicity (Tateh) and race (Coalhouse) both merge with that of class. In *Loon Lake* art itself is brought into the equation. Joe feels that it is his social background that prevents his full appreciation of Warren Penfield's poetry: "How could I have been listening with the attention such beautiful words demanded, people from my world didn't talk with such embellishment such scrollwork" (85). Readers may be tempted to equate grammar with class until they notice that Penfield's poetry often lacks punctuation.

Doctorow's fiction, like Reed's, reveals the kind of powerful impact, on both a formal and an ideological level, that parodic intertextuality can have. Under enemy fire in 1918, *Loon Lake's* Warren Penfield, a signaler in the signal corps, sends—not the message desired by his commander, but—the first few lines of Wordsworth's "Ode: Intimations of Immortality from Recollections of Early Childhood." The ironic appropriateness of its themes of past glory and present reality makes Doctorow's point about war better than any didactic statement could have. This novel presents us with all the kinds of intertextual parody that we have seen in American fiction in general: of genre, of the European tradition, of American canonical works (classic and modern), of the texts of popular culture and of history. On the level of genre, Joe is and is not the picaresque hero, both in his adventures on the road and in his narration of them: he usually narrates in the third person when recounting his past life, but often the first-person voice interferes.

Specifically British intertexts abound in the novel, from the Wordsworthian signal message to a parody of D. H. Lawrence's *Sons and Lovers*: like Paul Morel, Warren Penfield grows up in a coal-mining community with a mother who feels he is special, "a rare soul, a finer being" (38). Doctorow demystifies and ironizes Lawrence's serious idealization by making his poet a clumsy, awkward man. And, as with Morel, at the end of the novel it is not clear whether he is, in fact, a real artist or not. The opening of Joyce's *A Portrait of the Artist as a Young Man* is recalled in *Loon Lake's* early passages about the infant's relations both to his body and to language. But the parodic element enters when we acknowledge differences: unlike Stephen Dedalus, this child recalls no names and is alone. He cannot place himself in his family, much less his universe. Yet both boys will end up as poets. Or will they? No intertext used by Doctorow is without its cutting edge. His loon may indeed recall Keats's nightingale, but the cliché of "crazy as a loon" is never far in the background.

One of the protagonists, Joseph Korzeniowski, gives up his name to become the nominal son of F. W. Bennett. The use of Joseph Conrad's original name here is, of course, hardly accidental in a novel about identity and writing. But Joe hails from Paterson, New Jersey, a place that has other literary associations for Americans. Places, in fact, resound with intertextual echoes in *Loon Lake*. In American literature lakes tend to be symbols of the purity of nature: Cooper's Lake Glimmerglass, Thoreau's Walden (Levine 66), but here they stand for corruption and, above all, economic commodity. Fittingly, this interpretation is prompted by another intertext: the Bennett estate unavoidably suggests Gatsby's, just as the young, indigent Joe with his dream of a woman follows the trail of the same self-made, self-named American literary hero.

But it is not only the literary canon that is drawn upon in this novel. In fact, the entire portrait of 1930s America is developed from the popular culture of the period: Frank Capra comedies, gangster films, strike novels, James M. Cain's melodramas (see Levine 67). The significance of this is both literary and historical: the novel actually enacts the realization that what we "know" of the past derives from the discourses of that past. This is not documentary realism (if that were even possible); it is a novel about our understanding or our picture of the past, our discourse *about* the thirties. I think this is what Doctorow meant when he said, in an interview, about *Ragtime*, that he could not "accept the distinction between reality and books" (in Trenner 42). For him there is no neat dividing line between the texts of history and literature, and so he feels free to draw on both. The question of originality obviously has a different meaning within this postmodern theory of writing.

The focus of that novel, *Ragtime*, is America in 1902: Teddy Roosevelt's presidency, Winslow Homer's painting, Houdini's fame, J. P. Morgan's money, news of cubism in Paris. But the intertexts of history double up with those of literature, especially Heinrich von Kleist's "Michael Kohlhaas" and Dos Passos's *USA*. Doctorow himself has pointed critics to the Kleist text (in Trenner 39) and much work has been done already linking the two (Levine 56; Foley 166, 176–77n; Ditsky). Briefly, the story of Coalhouse Walker has many parallels with that of Michael Kohlhaas (beginning with the naming of the protagonist). In Kleist's tale, Kohlhaas is a medieval horse dealer who refuses to pay an unjust fine to Wenzel von Tronka's servant and so loses his beautiful horses. Doctorow's Coalhouse faces similar injustices at the hands of Willie Conklin, but the horses have been replaced by his new model T. Failing to obtain legal redress from the Elector of Saxony, Kohlhaas's wife—like Coalhouse's—attempts to intervene and is killed in a manner which Doctorow again updates but basically retains. The strongly implied similarities between the corrupt feudal society and the equally corrupt and unstable modern one are not lost on the reader. In the German novella the hero leads a rebel army and, though his horses are returned, he is executed. Doctorow's novel ironically transcodes this plot into American turn-of-the-century terms, complementing it with echoes of the climax of another intertext, George Milburn's *Catalogue*. In all, we are dealing with people who cannot find justice in a society that pretends to be just. In both "Michael Kohlhaas" and *Ragtime* historical characters mix with fictional ones: the hero meets Martin Luther in the one and Booker T. Washington in the other. But in neither, I would argue, does this imply any overvaluing of the fictional (see Foley 166). It is the narrativity and the textuality of our knowledge of the past that are being stressed; it is not a question of privileging the fictive or the historical.

Again, many critics have teased out the connections between *Ragtime* and Dos Passos's *USA* (Foley; Seelye; Levine). The echoes are thematic (the Lawrence textile strike, the San Diego free speech fight, portraits of events and personages such as the Mexican Revolution and Red Emma), formal (fiction mixing with history; Boy/Camera Eye naively recording events), and ideological (a critique of American capitalism of the same period). But the same critics have been careful to acknowledge serious differences, ones that, I would argue, the very intertextual echoes themselves force us to consider. Doctorow does not share his predecessor's trust in the objective presentation of history, and it is his ironic intermingling of the factual and the fictive and his deliberate anachronisms that underline this mistrust. As Barbara Foley notes, *USA* implies that historical reality is "knowable, coherent, significant, and inherently moving" (171). Doctorow, however, appears to feel, on the one hand, that fiction is as well, and, on the other, that *both* need questioning in regard to these assumptions. Narrativized history, like fiction, reshapes any material (in this case, the past) in the light of present issues, and this interpretive process is precisely what this kind of historiographic metafiction calls to our attention: "Walker's meeting with Booker T. Washington, for instance, echoes the contemporary debate between integrationists and black separatists. Similarly, Henry Ford is described as the father of mass society and Evelyn Nesbit is depicted as the first goddess of mass culture" (Levine 55).

The ideological as well as epistemological implications of inter-textuality are even clearer in Doctorow's earlier novel, *The Book of Daniel*. Here, too, we find the same range of kinds of parodic inter-texts. The title cannot avoid pointing us to its biblical namesake: the alienation of modern Jews recapitulates their ancestor's fate (see Stark). The first epigraph is from Daniel 3:4 and concerns the king's call for all to worship the "golden image" or be cast in the "burning and fiery furnace." This sets up the fate of those who challenge the new golden image of modern capitalism, and the Jews in this tale will *not* survive in the cold war climate of anti-Semitic and anticommunist suspicion. The king who sentenced the biblical Daniel's brothers to that furnace has become here the more impersonal state, which sentences this Daniel's parents to the elec-tric chair. The Babylonian furnace image is also picked up in the Isaacsons' apartment building's furnace and its outcast black at-tendant. (The Nazi ovens—which do not have to be mentioned directly—are clearly part of the historical intertext.)

But the intertextual uses of the biblical Book of Daniel are not without their ironies, too. Doctorow's Daniel calls his namesake "a Beacon of Faith in a Time of Persecution" (15). The irony is two-fold: the present-day Daniel both persecutes his own wife and child and seeks for faith—desperately. The biblical Daniel is also a mar-ginalized personage, a "minor if not totally apocryphal figure" (21), a Jew in difficult times. He is not an actor in history so much as an interpreter (with God's help) of the dreams of others who remains confused about his own. Such is the model of the writer for Doc-torow's Daniel, who also tries to list "mysteries" and then examine them (26ff.) and who, as a survivor, is haunted by nightmares he cannot interpret. The result of the two Daniels' writing is also ironi-cally similar. The modern writer calls the biblical text one "full of enigmas," a mixture of familiar stories and "weird dreams and vi-sions" (15), a disordered text with none of the closure of revelation or truth. So, too, is Doctorow's *Book of Daniel*, in its generic mixing of journal form, history, thesis, and fiction. Both are works *about* the act of interpreting—and then judging. The narrative voices in both move from impersonally omniscient third person to person-ally provisional first person, but the customary authority of the bib-lical omniscience is ironized into the modern Daniel's futile at-tempts at distance and self-mastery.

When their parents were first arrested the Isaacson children were informed of their fate by Williams, that demonic black tender of the furnace in the basement. The text then cites a Paul Robeson song: "Didn't my Lord deliver Daniel?" (143). But the rhetorical question of the song is rendered ironic by its immediate context and our knowledge of the ultimate destiny of the parents. Robeson's rally, of course, had offered the young Daniel an important insight into his own father's (Paul's) beliefs and principles. The multiple and complex echoing points to the different possible functions of intertextuality in historiographic metafiction, for it can both thematically and formally reinforce the text's message, *or* it can ironically undercut any pretensions to borrowed authority, certainty, or legitimacy. "Daniel's Book" (318) actually ends as it began, self-conscious about being "*written in the book*" (319). Its final words are of closure *sous rature* in a way, because they are not its own, but those of its biblical namesake: "*for the words are closed up and sealed till the time of the end*" (319). The two songs of lamentation and prophecy (Levine 49) come to an end, as their words are opened up by our act of reading.

In a similar sense, the Isaacsons' fate "opens up" the Rosenbergs' case once again. Here the intertexts, for the reader, are the many books written (before and after the novel) on that incident of recent American history, including the one by the Rosenberg children. Time has not resolved the doubts and questions that surround this case even today. Analysts of all ideological persuasions line up to "prove" every possible interpretation. These range from the view that the Rosenbergs were innocent victims of a specific (or general) anti-Semitic (or even Jewish) plot to the view that Julius Rosenberg can only be done proper justice by history if we do accept his identity as a conscientious Soviet spy, with his wife's devotion and support. What many seem to see in the trial and its outcome are the social and ideological determinations of so-called universal, objective justice. It is this that Doctorow enacts in his Daniel's tortured investigation of his "family truth." In Althusserian terms, both the Repressive and the Ideological State Apparatuses conspire to condemn the Isaacsons, and, by implication, perhaps, the Rosenbergs. The intertextual voices of official historical texts and Karl Marx's writings play off against each other in this novel with ironic and doubly undercutting force.

Doctorow himself compared the Isaacson/Rosenberg paralleling to that of Crusoe/Selkirk in Defoe (in Trenner 46), and critics have also noted the intertextual parallels between this novel and *Hamlet* (and through it to Freud): the analytic intellectual trying to deal with emotional and political realities connected to the murder of a parent; the pressure of the past upon the present; the textual self-reflexivity (Knapp). Significantly, Doctorow's version is a postmodern, parodic one because the villain is not one known individual but the U.S. government and judiciary, perhaps even all of American society. And it is the presence of a major cultural intertext that underlines this difference within the novel: Disneyland becomes the incarnation of a debased intertextuality, one that denies the historicity of the past. Disneyland is offered as a manipulative, consumerist transgression of the boundaries of art and life, of past and present. But, in itself, it is not a critical and parodic transgression that might provoke thought; it is intended for instant consumption as a spectacle void of historical and aesthetic significance. It tames the past into the present. And it is the past of both literature and history that is being trivialized and recuperated: "The life and lifestyle of slave-trading America on the Mississippi River in the 19th century is compressed into a technologically faithful steamboat ride of five or ten minutes on an HO-scale river. The intermediary between us and this actual historical experience, the writer Mark Twain, author of *Life on the Mississippi*, is now no more than the name of the boat" (304). Disneyland's ideological reduction comes at the expense of the complexity and diversity of American society: Daniel notices that there are no hippies, no Hispanics, and certainly no blacks in this fantasy America.

Doctorow, of course, is by no means the only American writer to use intertextuality so powerfully. In *The Sot-Weed Factor* Barth both uses and subverts the conventions and implications of the eighteenth-century novel, with its ordered, coherent world vision, and in so doing sets up a parodic inversion of other intertexts—the cultural cliché, for instance, of the virginal wilderness, which instead becomes a place of vice, treachery, and the pox. Here innocence begins to look more like ignorance as Jefferson's America reveals its hidden connections with Eisenhower's. Such a critique goes beyond an urge to "mythopoetize" experience in the face of the loss of traditional values (see Schulz 88–89). Far from being just another form of aesthetic introversion, parodic intertextuality works to force us to look again at the connections between art and the "world." Any simple mimesis is replaced by a problematized and complex set of interrelations at the level of discourse—that is, at the level of the way we talk about experience, literary or historical, present or past. The fact is that, in practice, intertexts unavoidably call up contexts: social and political, among others. The "double contextualizability" (Schmidt) of intertexts forces us not only to double our vision, but to look beyond the centers to the margins, the edges, the ex-centric.

This gaze reveals intertextual parody crossing genre boundaries without reserve: Milan Kundera's play *Jacques and His Master* is subtitled *An Homage to Diderot in Three Acts* and represents what the author calls "an encounter of two writers but also of two centuries. And of the novel and the theater" (10). American writer Susan Daitch's recent novel *L.C.* offers an even more complex generic interaction that is directly tied to its dense intertextuality. The core of the novel's narrative is the journal of a (fictive) woman, Lucienne Crozier, witness to the (real) 1848 revolution in Paris. The first of two modern frames for this journal is by Willa Rehnfield, its first translator. Her "Introduction" reminds us of the contradiction of the year 1848 in terms of two symbolic intertexts: *Wuthering Heights* and the *Communist Manifesto*, both published that year. And these are indeed the contradictions of the journal (at least as translated by Rehnfield): Lucienne has strong socialist politics but is rendered ineffective by her marginalization (by the Left) and her melodramatic dying of tuberculosis, all but abandoned by her lover in Algiers. Rehnfield sees Lucienne as formed by "Marxism and fluff" (2)—that is, the feuilletons of the day. But, in fact, the journal reveals her critique of that popular literary form as being unfaithful to the social and economic realities of real life, despite its surface realism of language (136–37). Is this a radicalized Emma Bovary?

In fact, this question is raised by the text itself: "Madame Lucienne Crozier was doomed from the day she married" (207). So, of course, was Madame Bovary, as the title of the novel constantly reminds us. But Lucienne is a parodic inversion of Emma. Though they share a hatred for the provinces, their extramarital affairs and their reading, mutually motivated in both cases, lead them in opposite directions: Emma into fantasy and rejection of responsibility, and Lucienne into political action. In the text there is also an editorial attempt—by means of one word of slang—to link *Madame Bovary* to Marx, through his daughter Eleanor's translation of the novel (124). The clearest political connection, however, is to the journal's second editor and translator, who has taken the pseudonym Jane Amme. This surname is obviously Emma backwards, but this is where the intertextual echoes begin to proliferate: Emma Bovary is joined by Emma Goldman and Jane Austen's Emma. *Jane Eyre* is also not far in the background when a footnote refers (with deliberate modern critical echoes, too) to "the mad woman in the attic, real or theoretical" (198n). This frame figure defines herself as "the sort Jane Austen's characters would have called 'a most agreeable and obliging young lady'" (246), at least until her feminist radicalization at the hands of both the sexist male New Left at Berkeley in 1968 and the rapist who attacks her. Rejecting (as Lucienne does as well—at least in Amme's translation) the "mute role of an automatic participant" (246), she bombs the home of the capitalist "global rapist" who was also her sexual attacker. She writes her story, rejecting muteness for herself and for the other women writers whose intertexts are woven into the fabric of her text. Lucienne's own journal uses visual art in much the same way. Daumier's satiric works against women enrage her, as does the stand of Delacroix, her lover, against the political reality outside his window: he prefers to paint flowers and compliant women—with his back to that window.

Contemporary Latin American fiction has also turned to art forms other than literature or history and has thereby forced us to broaden what we must consider as intertexts. The various "films" described by Molina in Manuel Puig's *Kiss of the Spider Woman* are, on one level, only more verbal narratives; on another level, they are parodic plays with cinematic genres (horror movie, war propaganda, romantic melodrama) that politicize the apolitical (or repoliticize the propagandistic) in terms of gender, sexual preference, and ideology. The English (only) title of Alejo Carpentier's novel *Explosion in a Cathedral* refers to a real painting within the novel— and in reality (by Monsu Desiderio). As Gabriel Saad has shown, the descriptions of Madrid at the end of the novel are, in fact, quite literally descriptions of specific works by Goya, the ones of the second and third of May 1808 and the "Disasters of War" series. Carpentier uses a double intertext here, and the historical one is activated through the aesthetic one: those works represent the Madrid uprising which went on to spark the Spanish and Latin American wars of independence. In other words, there is an external historical dimension as well as an internal novelistic one to the intertextual reference.

But we do not have to go this far from home to be confronted with intertextual echoing. Many rock videos have tried to recall a filmic or television tradition in their form (Queen's "Radio Gaga" cites Fritz Lang's *Metropolis*) and settings (Manhattan Transfer uses the *I Love Lucy* living-room set in their videos), but the parodic edge that might provoke some critical perspective seems generally to be missing here. In art galleries, though, we can find works such as Michelangelo Pistoletto's *Venus of Rags* and *Orchestra of Rags*, which do suggest ironic critique. Pistoletto uses real rags, the end product of consumption: art represents the detritus of culture within the consumer ethic. His mica reproduction of a classical Venus may parodically represent the static, "universal" principle of aesthetic beauty, but here it faces (and is blocked by) a large pile of those rags. While many have argued that all paintings are intertextually

27

connected to other paintings (see Steiner), postmodern ones seem more tendentiously ironic in their interrelations. Even music, considered by most to be the least representational of the arts, is being interpreted these days in terms of the intertextual linking of the past to the present, as an analogue of the necessary linking of artistic form and human memory (Morgan 51).

Postmodernism is less a period than a poetics or an ideology. It clearly attempts to combat what has come to be seen as modernism's hermetic, elitist isolationism that separated art from the "world," literature from history. But it often does so by using the very techniques of modernist aestheticism against themselves. The autonomy of art is maintained; metafictional self-reflexivity even underlines it. But within this seemingly introverted intertextuality another dimension is added through the ironic inversions of parody: art's critical relation to the "world" of discourse—and beyond that to society and politics. History and literature provide the intertexts in the novels examined here, but there is no question of a hierarchy, implied or otherwise. They are both part of the signifying systems of our culture. They both make and make sense of our world. This is one of the lessons of that most didactic of postmodern forms: historiographic metafiction.

Works Cited

Angenot, Marc. "L'Intertextualité: enquête sur l'émergence et la diffusion d'un champ notionnel." *Revue des sciences humaines* 189, no.1 (1983): 121–35.
Barilli, Renato. *Tra presenza e assenza*. Milan: Bompiani, 1974.
Barth, John. *The Sot-Weed Factor*. New York: Doubleday, 1960.
———. LETTERS. New York: Putnam, 1979.
Barthes, Roland. *The Pleasure of the Text*. Translated by Richard Miller. New York: Hill & Wang, 1975.
———. *Image, Music, Text*. Translated by Stephen Heath. New York: Hill & Wang, 1977.
Belsey, Catherine. *Critical Practice*. London: Methuen, 1980.
Bennett, Susan. "Horrid Laughter." Paper presented at the annual meeting of the Canadian Comparative Literature Association, Montreal, 2 June 1985.
Berger, Thomas. *Little Big Man*. New York: Dial, 1964.
Bradbury, Malcolm. *The Modern American Novel*. Oxford: Oxford University Press, 1983.
Braudel, Fernand. *On History*. Translated by Sarah Matthews. Chicago: University of Chicago Press, 1980.
Byerman, Keith E. *Fingering the Jagged Grain: Tradition and Form in Recent Black Fiction*. Athens: University of Georgia Press, 1985.

Calinescu, Matei. "Ways of Looking at Fiction." In Garvin 155–70.

Canary, Robert H., and Henry Kozicki, eds. *The Writing of History: Literary Form and Historical Understanding.* Madison: University of Wisconsin Press, 1978.

Christensen, Inger. *The Meaning of Metafiction: A Critical Study of Selected Novels by Sterne, Nabokov, Barth, and Beckett.* Bergen and Oslo: Universitetsforlaget, 1981.

Coover, Robert. *The Public Burning.* New York: Viking, 1977.

Daitch, Susan. *L.C.* London: Virago, 1986.

Derrida, Jacques. "Signature Event Context." In *Glyph 1: Johns Hopkins Textual Studies,* 172–97. Baltimore: Johns Hopkins University Press, 1977.

D'haen, Theo. "Postmodernism in American Fiction and Art." In Fokkema and Bertens 211–31.

Ditsky, John. "The German Source of *Ragtime*: A Note." In Trenner 179–81.

Doctorow, E. L. *Welcome to Hard Times.* New York: Simon & Schuster, 1960.

———. *The Book of Daniel.* New York: Bantam, 1971.

———. *Ragtime.* New York: Random House, 1975.

———. *Loon Lake.* New York: Random House, 1979.

Eagleton, Terry. "Capitalism, Modernism, and Postmodernism." *New Left Review* 152 (1985):60–73.

Eco, Umberto. *Postscript to* The Name of the Rose. Translated by William Weaver. New York: Harcourt Brace Jovanovich, 1983.

Fokkema, Douwe W., and Hans Bertens, eds. *Approaching Post-modernism.* Amsterdam: Benjamins, 1986.

Foley, Barbara. "From *USA* to *Ragtime*: Notes on the Forms of Historical Consciousness in Modern Fiction." In Trenner 158–78.

Foucault, Michel. *Language, Counter-Memory, Practice.* Translated by D. F. Bouchard and S. Simon. Ithaca, N.Y.: Cornell University Press, 1977.

French, Philip. *Westerns.* London: Secker & Warburg, 1973.

Garvin, Harry R., and James Heath, eds. *Romanticism, Modernism, Postmodernism.* Lewisburg, Pa.: Bucknell University Press, 1980.

Gass, William H. *Habitations of the Word: Essays.* New York: Simon & Schuster, 1985.

Gates, Henry Louis, Jr. "The Blackness of Blackness: A Critique of the Sign and the Signifying Monkey." In Gates 284–321.

———, ed. *Black Literature and Literary Theory.* London: Methuen, 1984.

Gilbert, Sandra, and Susan Gubar. *The Madwoman in the Attic: The Woman Writer and the Nineteenth-Century Literary Imagination.* New Haven: Yale University Press, 1979.

Graff, Gerald. *Literature Against Itself: Literary Ideas in Modern Society.* Chicago: University of Chicago Press, 1979.

Greene, Thomas M. *The Light in Troy: Imitation and Discovery in Renaissance Poetry.* New Haven: Yale University Press, 1982.

Gross, David S. "Tales of Obscene Power: Money and Culture, Modernism and History in the Fiction of E. L. Doctorow." In Trenner 120–50.

Hansen, Elaine Tuttle. "Marge Piercy: The Double Narrative Structure of *Small Changes*." In Rainwater and Scheick 208–28.

Hellmann, John. *Fables of Fact: The New Journalism as New Fiction*. Urbana: University of Illinois Press, 1981.

Holder, Alan. "'What Marvelous Plot . . . Was Afoot?' History in Barth's *The Sot-Weed Factor*." *American Quarterly* 20 (1968):596–604.

Hutcheon, Linda. *A Theory of Parody: The Teachings of Twentieth-Century Art Forms*. London and New York: Methuen, 1985.

Jameson, Fredric. "Postmodernism, or the Cultural Logic of Late Capitalism." *New Left Review* 146 (1984):53–92.

Kern, Robert. "Composition as Recognition: Robert Creeley and Postmodern Poetics." *Boundary* 2 26–27 (1978):211–30.

Kiremidjian, G. K. "The Aesthetics of Parody." *Journal of Aesthetics and Art Criticism* 28 (1969):231–42.

Knapp, Peggy A. "Hamlet and Daniel (and Freud and Marx)." *Massachusetts Review* 21 (1980):487–501.

Kristeva, Julia. *Séméiotiké: Recherches pour une sémanalyse*. Paris: Seuil, 1969.

Kundera, Milan. *Jacques and His Master: An Homage to Diderot in Three Acts*. Translated by Michael Henry Heim. New York: Harper & Row, 1985.

La Capra, Dominick. *History and Criticism*. Ithaca, N.Y.: Cornell University Press, 1985.

Lee, A. Robert, ed. *Black Fiction: New Studies in the Afro-American Novel Since 1945*. London: Vision Press, 1980.

Leitch, Vincent B. *Deconstructive Criticism: An Advanced Introduction*. New York: Columbia University Press, 1983.

Levine, Paul. *E.L. Doctorow*. London: Methuen, 1985.

Lodge, David. *The Modes of Modern Writing: Metaphor, Metonymy, and the Typology of Modern Literature*. London: Edward Arnold, 1977.

Lyotard, Jean-François. *Instructions paiennes*. Paris: Galilée, 1977.

McConnell, Frank. "Ishmael Reed's Fiction: Da Hoodoo Is Put on America." In Lee 136–48.

McHale, Brian. "Modernist Reading: Post-Modern Text: The Case of *Gravity's Rainbow*." *Poetics Today* 1, nos. 1–2 (1979):85–110.

Malmgren, Carl Darryl. *Fictional Space in the Modernist and Postmodernist American Novel*. Lewisburg, Pa.: Bucknell University Press, 1985.

Mazurek, Raymond A. "Metafiction, the Historical Novel, and Coover's *The Public Burning*." *Critique* 23, no. 3 (1982):29–42.

Morgan, Robert P. "On the Analysis of Recent Music," *Critical Inquiry* 4, no. 1 (1977):33–53.

Morrison, Toni. *Song of Solomon*. New York: Signet, 1977.

Musarra, Ulla. "Duplication and Multiplication: Post-modernist Devices in the Novels of Italo Calvino." In Fokkema and Bertens 135–55.

Newman, Charles. *The Post-Modern Aura: The Act of Fiction in an Age of Inflation*. Evanston, Ill.: Northwestern University Press, 1985.

Patteson, Richard. "What Stencil Knew: Structure and Certitude in Pynchon's *V*." *Critique* 16, no. 1 (1974):30–44.

Pynchon, Thomas. *The Crying of Lot 49*. New York: Bantam, 1966.

Rainwater, Catherine, and William J. Scheick, eds. *Contemporary American Woman Writers: Narrative Strategies*. Lexington: University Press of Kentucky, 1985.

Reed, Ishmael, *Yellow Back Radio Broke-Down*. Garden City, N.Y.: Doubleday, 1969.

———. *Conjure: Selected Poems 1963–1970*. Amherst: University of Massachusetts Press, 1972.

———. *Mumbo Jumbo*. Garden City, N.Y.: Doubleday, 1972.

———. *The Terrible Twos*. New York: St. Martin's/Marek, 1982.

Riffaterre, Michael. "Intertextual Representation: On Mimesis as Interpretive Discourse." *Critical Inquiry* 11, no. 1 (1984): 141–62.

Rochberg, George. Jacket notes for *String Quartet no. 3*. Nonesuch H–71283.

Saad, Gabriel. "L'Histoire et la révolution dans *Le Siècle des lumières*." In *Quinze Etudes autour de El Siglo de las luces de Alejo Carpentier*, 113–22. Paris: L'Harmattan, 1983.

Said, Edward. *Beginnings: Intention and Method*. New York: Basic Books, 1975.

———. *The World, the Text, and the Critic*. Cambridge: Harvard University Press, 1983.

———. "Culture and Imperialism" course at University of Toronto, Fall 1986.

Schmidt, S. J. "The Fiction Is That Reality Exists: A Constructivist Model of Reality, Fiction, and Literature." *Poetics Today* 5, no. 2 (1984): 253–74.

Schulz, Max F. *Black Fiction of the Sixties: A Pluralistic Definition of Man and His World*. Athens: Ohio University Press, 1973.

Seelye, John. "Doctorow's Dissertation." *New Republic* 174, no. 15 (1976): 21–3.

Showalter, Elaine. *A Literature of Their Own: British Woman Novelists from Brontë to Lessing*. Princeton: Princeton University Press, 1977.

Sisk, John. "Aquarius Rising." *Commentary* (May 1971): 83–84.

Stark, John. "Alienation and Analysis in Doctorow's *The Book of Daniel*." *Critique* 16, no. 3 (1975): 101–10.

Steinberg, Cobbett. "History and the Novel: Doctorow's *Ragtime*." *Denver Quarterly* 10, no. 4 (1976): 125–30.

Steiner, Wendy. "Intertextuality in Painting." *American Journal of Semiotics* 3, no. 4 (1985): 57–67.

Tanner, Tony. *City of Words: American Fiction 1950–1970*. New York: Harper & Row, 1971.

Taylor, Gordon O. "Of Adams and Aquarius." *American Literature* 46 (1974): 68–82.

Thiher, Allen. *Words in Reflection: Modern Language Theory and Postmodern Fiction*. Chicago: University of Chicago Press, 1984.

Trenner, Richard, ed. *E. L. Doctorow: Essays and Conversations*. Princeton: Ontario Review Press, 1983.

Vonnegut, Kurt, Jr. *Slaughterhouse-Five or the Children's Crusade: A Duty-Dance with Death*. New York: Delacorte Press, 1969.

31

Wagner, Linda W. "Toni Morrison: Mastery of Narrative." In Rainwater and Scheick 190–207.

Waugh, Patricia, *Metafiction: The Theory and Practice of Self-Conscious Fiction.* London: Methuen, 1984.

White, Hayden. "The Historical Text as Literary Artifact." In Canary and Kozicki 41–62.

———. "The Question of Narrative in Contemporary Historical Theory." *History and Theory* 23 (1984): 1–33.

Wimsatt, W. K., Jr. *The Verbal Icon.* 1954. Reprint. Lexington: University Press of Kentucky, 1967.

Wylder, Delbert E. "Thomas Berger's *Little Big Man* as Literature." *Western American Literature* 3 (1969): 273–84.

INTERTEXTUALITY AND PARODY

Intertextual Frameworks

The Ideology of Parody in John Barth

JOHN T. MATTHEWS

Metafiction, Parody, and Intertextuality

I will shortly cite my epigraph from John Barth's brief essay on epigraphs in his collection of miscellaneous nonfiction pieces, *The Friday Book*. As is Barth's wont, he turns the essay into a parody, nothing but a very long epigraph itself, attributed to a work entitled "Epigraphs," from a collection identified as *The Friday Book*. Having evoked this typically Barthian *mise en abîme*, let me quote Barth on the epigraph, that customary gesture of liminal intertextuality: "Epigraphs," he begins, "should be avoided" (xii).

For all Barth's marvelous structural dexterity, for all the largesse of invention in his fiction, this epigraphic table-turning—a playful temporizing until something turns into nothing—will represent for many readers the limitations of Barth's artistry. Barth's steadfast practice of metafiction strikes many as a strategic retreat from the social interests of representational art or the moral intentions of polemical art. The self-quotation and self-reference that abound in Barth's work constitute a deeply recessed intertextuality, what might be called in*tra*textuality.[1] LETTERS is only the sublimest example in Barth's work of autopropagation, a process that makes the writer's former words the objects of intertextual appropriation. Such massive textual self-involvement appears to drive the scene of writing far from the "outside," from facticity or cultural discourse.

Many defenses of this postmodernist aesthetic point at least to the broader metaphysical subversiveness of metafiction, its potential for upsetting the stable division of reality from representation.[2] Yet Barth himself, who sometimes professes this line of justification, also refuses to disavow the sheer luxury of self-regarding narratives. Barth never tires of reminding us that the lucubrations of storytelling, like those of lovemaking, please him through their devotion to sheer technique. Barth may affirm that the "proper subject of literature" is "human life, its happiness and its misery" (*Friday Book* 218), but he does so with the understanding that life, like literature, is itself fundamentally an effect of language. Drawing his authority from Wittgenstein and Schopenhauer, Barth con-

35

cludes that the world we know is the product of our representation of it, and so, "Reality—to a greater or lesser extent, but strictly speaking—is our shared fantasy" (*Friday Book* 221).

Barth has marked off a zone for his fiction whose perimeters are the self representing the world to itself. Although the characters whose imaginations are most fertile, like Scheherazade, the Burlingames, Ambrose Mensch, or Perseus, may accrue worldly influence, heroic stature, or magical power, their sphere of accomplishment radiates from the palace of art. My argument will ultimately propose that Barth's fiction, as it rules out social or political involvement with the real, fixes its own ideological position. His fiction betrays, as all art must, its relation to the historical context that grounds the figure of the text. Barth may seek to locate the origin of experience in the "shared fantasy" produced by the autonomous imaginations of consenting adults. But his texts display the inevitable stresses and fissures of the political, economic, social—in a word, historical—basis of all experience. I shall argue that Barth's preferred mode—metafictive parody—constitutes a strategy by which the author can both rule out contemporaneous history from his fiction and at the same time permit it a marginalized appearance. Barthian parody serves to contain the political dimension of his material.

In 1965, Barth pleads, "Muse, spare me (at the desk, I mean) from social-historical responsibility, and in the last analysis from every other kind as well, except artistic" (*Friday Book* 55). Barth adds that fiction may be "responsive" to its age, but should never feel responsible to it. Between the author's crafting of tales and the citizen's engaging in politics runs a well-maintained barrier. "For reasons of temperament more than of philosophy," Barth remarks, "during the period of our war in Vietnam I remained apart from, though sympathetic to, the great antiwar demonstrations in our cities" (*Friday Book* 91). As a writer of fiction, Barth takes his role to be quite different from such activism. The remarkably Barth-like genie in *Chimera*, who is himself a composer of novellas in late 1960s Maryland, tells Scheherazade that he hopes in his life to add at least some "artful trinket or two, however small, to the general treasury of civilized delights . . . : he meant the treasure of art, which if it could not redeem the barbarities of history or spare us the horrors of living and dying, at least sustained, refreshed, expanded, ennobled, and enriched our spirits along the painful way" (17). Barth's creative temperament carries him away from the material of his historical context and toward a timeless treasure of art that "enriches" the inner lives of author and reader.

We may recognize here the premises of the kind of high-order metafiction Barth turns to after his earliest works of realism: "The eschewing of contemporaneous, 'original' material is a basic literary notion" (*Friday Book* 58). How can the textual space be protected from the encroachments of contemporaneous matter? Barth answers with literary parody. By making his own art repeat and transform works of the past (including his own), Barth hopes to restrict literature to a dialogue with itself about itself. "The use of . . . legendary material, especially in a farcical, even a comic, spirit, has a number of virtues, among which are esthetic distance and the opportunity for counterrealism" (*Friday Book* 59). Barth's fiction reflects not the matter of its age—the use of which "is but an occasional anomaly and fad of the last couple centuries" (*Friday Book* 58)—but the transhistorical constants of narrative—of yarns exchanged for love and life, of heroes' storied exploits, of tales of tales of tales.

Barth's originality arises from his virtuoso revoicings of older narrative scores. Before we were reading Bakhtin, Barth reminded us that the novel as a genre is constituted by parody. All literature "has been done long since" (*Friday Book* 73), and the novel perpetuates itself by permuting itself, remaking itself out of its leavings, parodying its forebears into novelty. "If this sort of thing sounds unpleasantly decadent," Barth allows, "nevertheless it's about where the genre began" (*Friday Book* 72); "with *Don Quixote*, the novel may be said to *begin* in self-transcendent parody and has often returned to that mode for its refreshment" (*Friday Book* 205).

Genuinely original parody is much more than the simple recitation of earlier texts. For Barth, parody demands a thorough rearrangement of the source material. The present-day writer seeks to appropriate his antecedent texts so fully that they appear as his own products. The exemplary case is the genie of Barth's novella, "Dunyazadiad," who is summoned by Scheherazade from his future writing desk to tell her the tales she will eventually compose and he will eventually read. One might, with Harold Bloom, choose a psychoanalytic model to account for Barth's authorial behavior, but in fact Barth's precursors are mainly anonymous framed tale cycles. Barth does not so much incorporate other authors as other stories, other tellers as other texts. One understands why he disfavors that weaker form of intertextuality—simple epigraphic quotation. Unlike the fuller reappropriations of parody, the epigraph puts the writer, he says, in "a posture of awe before some palimpsestic Other Text; a kind of rhetorical attitudinizing" (*Friday Book* xix).

If intertextuality may be distinguished as the presence in a text of those "elements exhibiting a structure created previous to the text, above the level of the lexeme, of course, but independently of the level of that structure" (Jenny 40), then we might consider parody as a strong form of intertextuality. Laurent Jenny puts the relation concisely: "While parody is always intertextual, intertextuality is not reducible to parody" (38). Linda Hutcheon attempts to specify the distinguishing characteristics of parody by arguing that it requires the reader's *detection* of the author's parodic *intention* in order to be activated. Parody is a more intense intertextuality because it relies on the constraint of pragmatic semiotic recognition (in addition to the fundamental formal constraint of verbal repetition): "Although my theory of parody is intertextual in its inclusion of both the decoder and the text, its enunciative context is even broader: both the encoding and the sharing of codes between producer and receiver are central" (37).

Defined as a form of intertextuality, parody appears to direct a work's attention toward other works rather than toward "the world." "Parody is one of the major forms of modern self-reflexivity; it is a form of inter-art discourse" (2). Hutcheon emphatically restricts parody to "intramural" relations—"inter-art discourse," reserving for the term *satire* any ironic representation of extramural social and moral realms (43). Such a view of the intertextual purity of parody coincides with Barth's understanding of his major fictive practice. For Bakhtin and Julia Kristeva, literary parody's status as a *textual* phenomenon signals its distance from the original subversiveness of parody as a social and moral practice during carnival. The truly liberating possibilities of carnivalesque parody involve its totally unrestrained, heterodox, and irreverent energies. The cries of the people, for example, fall "outside the norms of official speech" (Bakhtin 191). Literary parody, on the other hand, marks an absorption of the carnivalesque back into official speech, into the authorized recitation of canonical utterance:

> The word "carnivalesque" lends itself to an ambiguity one must avoid. In contemporary society, it generally connotes parody, hence a strengthening of the law. There is a tendency to blot out the carnival's *dramatic* (murderous, cynical, and revolutionary in the sense of *dialectical transformation*) aspects, which Bakhtin emphasized. (Kristeva 80)

Modernist parody tends toward a reinscription of prevailing modes of literary production. Hutcheon would recuperate the subversiveness of literary parody by arguing for its paradoxical nature:

Parody can also be seen, however, to be a threatening, even an-archic force, one that puts into question the legitimacy of other texts . . . Nevertheless, parody's transgressions ultimately remain authorized—authorized by the very norm it seeks to subvert. Even in mocking, parody reinforces . . . It is in this sense that parody is the custodian of the artistic legacy, defining not only where art is, but where it has come from. (Hutcheon 75)

Moreover, by restricting parody to an intramural phenomenon, Hutcheon must argue that its subversiveness works allegorically at most: "[Literary] norms are like social ones in the sense that they are human constructs which are authoritative only to those who have constructed or at least accepted them as *a priori*" (77). Hutcheon maintains the inseparability of aesthetic and "ideological" judgments (77), but if parody subverts and reauthorizes literary norms intramurally, then there needs to be some account of the dynamic by which the intramural distinguishes itself from the ex-tramural in the first place. Second, if parody is an authorized trans-gression, the effect of its so working out is a *management* of the subversive energies brought into play by the impulse to parody. We will need recourse to a model of textuality that emphasizes the dy-namic process of this working out, as opposed to Hutcheon's more static conceptualization of the "paradox of parody" (69).

Framing and Reframing

If Barth prefers parody as the *mode* that seeks to keep literature emphatically literary, framing is the literary *device* that undergirds the mode. Barth's passion for frame narratives in his fiction ap-pears insatiable. It may interest us that Barth the university profes-sor once conducted a systematic study of the varieties of frame sto-ries. This was, he confesses, during the "palmy mid-1960s" (*Friday Book* 224), when he had a graduate assistant at the University of Buffalo and no very good idea how to occupy him or her. To keep themselves busy, Barth and his assistant sifted through two hun-dred frame narratives, categorizing them by the degree of plot in-volvement between frame and enframed, and by the levels of nar-rative recess. Aside from indulging Barth's appetite for technique, this project also led him to the conviction that "not only is all fiction fiction about fiction, but all fiction about fiction is in fact fiction about life" (*Friday Book* 236).

Framing, then, helps execute the program of literary parody. Barth's efforts to outdo the contrivances of earlier frame works depend on reworking them and ornamenting them with his own frames. Barth loves to manipulate narrative structures, as if his most exquisite pleasure arises from the friction of fitting and counterfitting narrative parts. Framing and parody cooperate in providing the technical openings through which prior texts make their appearances in transmogrified form. By establishing the channels through which Barth's texts reactivate past texts, framing also protects literature from the merely contemporaneous. Like a kind of wrapping, narrative frames enclose and insulate the space of invention. This quarantining from the outer world is frequently their internal function in individual works, too: one thinks of the retreat of the members of the *Decameron* party from the sanctuary of the church to their country houses. It is as if the purpose of the *Decameron*'s frame is to establish that communication with the world of Florence is contamination, that storytelling requires a sanitized zone. This idea of the frame harbors a longing for literature that is free from the infection of representation altogether. Its purest embodiment for Barth may be the eloquent blank space at the dead center of his story "Menelaid," a space articulated by seven bracketing sets of quotation marks.

Whether they are prefatory essays, introductions, epigraphs, or embedded diegetic narratives, frames seek to control contextual matters. They attempt to determine boundaries between the work and all that is not the work, between what it is and is not about, between licit and illicit interpretations, between authorial motive and textual drift. In Barth, even more strenuously, they serve as the sites for parody and other forms of controlled, deliberate intertextuality. Yet these frame functions turn out to be double-edged. By establishing a border with the text's con-texts, frames open an articulated relation between figure and ground. Parody in Barth profits from this relation; frames formally bind the several instances of a story. As the term's etymology suggests, these conjoined texts, laid side by side, constitute the parodic relation. From Barth's viewpoint, the frame would need to be a selectively permeable membrane, then, keeping out the contemporaneous matter of the work's present historical context, but passing along the parodied matter of the literary historical context.

The frame observes a dynamic of recognition and refusal. I will argue that this dynamic radically endangers the freedom from the contemporaneous Barth seeks. Because the frame serves as a bar of differentiation between opposing entities, it is always liable to reversal and penetration. Moreover, just as the device of the frame may fail to police the work's borders, so parody inadvertently makes historical context fundamental rather than secondary to its operation. In order for a text by Barth, say, to parody the *Arabian Nights*, the reader must perceive a process of recontextualization. Hutcheon has referred to this process as "trans-contextualization" (12) in order to point up the way parody lifts an earlier work out of its original context and transports it into a new one made for it by the later work. But I want to maintain the term *recontextualization* in order to emphasize the process by which parody—which purports to establish strictly intramural relations between works and so make them independent of their historical contexts—actually exposes the inseparability of text and context. The identity of the text cannot be determined at all aside from the background of its historical setting. In the case of Barth's metafictive parodies, the material realities of mid-century America impinge on his work as the traces of their own suppression or repression. I will demonstrate how these two processes of refusal work in the example of *Chimera*.

In "The Literature of Exhaustion" Barth recounts the plot of Borges's "Pierre Menard, Author of the Quixote," a story about an author who "by an astounding effort of imagination, produces— not *copies* or *imitates*, but *composes*—several chapters of Cervantes's novel" (*Friday Book* 68). The story comments significantly on parody, for Menard's composition stands as the minimum case of recontextualization: "It would have been sufficient for Menard to attribute the novel to himself in order to have a new work of art" (*Friday Book* 69). The only difference between Cervantes's and Menard's *Quixote*s would be, that is, their contexts. The documents would be identical, but they would be different texts because the second resituates the first. The context determines the text.

The Denial of Context

We may see parody as a more luminescent form of the relation of text to context; parody may pretend to exclusive concentration on the intramural matter of its host texts, but the act of recontextualization that parody involves traces the outline of the original contexts in the ragged edges of the lifted text. The contemporaneous appears as what is missing. We are not so far here from Fredric Jameson's view of the status of history in literary texts. If history is precisely what is incapable of representation because, for Jameson, it cannot be perfectly subjected to the control of representational forms, then history appears in texts as what is repressed, as the unconscious. Jameson proposes "that history is *not* a text, not a narrative, master or otherwise, but that, as an absent cause, it is inac-

41

cessible to us except in textual form, and that our approach to it and to the Real itself necessarily passes through its prior textualization, its narrativization in the political unconscious" (35). As a mode of literary production, parody attempts overtly to repress historical context; Jameson's analysis of the effects of such textual dynamics puts us in a position to appreciate the ideology of parody in Barth's work:

> ideology is not something which informs or invests symbolic production; rather the aesthetic act is itself ideological, and the production of aesthetic or narrative form is to be seen as an ideological act in its own right, with the function of inventing imaginary or formal "solutions" to unresolvable social contradictions. (79)

I think we can pinpoint the way in which parodic fiction proposes a formal solution to the social contradictions that configure Barth's writing. By virtue of his position as a white, male, middle-aged, successful writer and university teacher in mid-twentieth century America, Barth flourishes under the very social and economic conditions his fiction exposes as fundamentally unjust. By examining the ways in which Barth's fiction attempts to keep this kind of recognition at bay, I hope to show the intimate relation between the historical context of Barth's writing and its parodic intertextuality. Barth's fiction seeks to exclude the contemporaneous because it would indict the very privilege that makes his authorship possible. The parodic mode allows Barth to manage this contradictory position formally. As Barth practices it, literary parody converts the author's social dependence and parasitism into the acceptable form of *narrative* dependence and parasitism.[3]

I hope to examine two ways in which Barth's metafiction reckons with the force of the real. My first objective will be to determine the fate of the contemporaneous in one of Barth's most emphatically counterrealistic books, *Chimera*. This triad of novellas, particularly the first as published, "Dunyazadiad," presents our problem compactly. The work is generated as a self-conscious parody of the *Arabian Nights'* scene of storytelling, the scene that Barth calls the most compelling he knows. One can hardly imagine a more avowedly metafictive work, moreover; the protagonist's problem is writer's block, and he discovers in the course of his adventures with Scheherazade's storytelling that to write about his block is to cure it: the key to the treasure is the treasure. At the same time, like its two companion pieces, "Dunyazadiad" explicitly considers the question of women's oppression by what is called the "patriarchy." The two lords in the *Arabian Nights* who despoil and slay one virgin per day in their despair over female perfidy represent a patriarchy responsible for the "gynocide" ravaging their kingdoms. For all that, Barth insists—oddly—that "the book *Chimera* . . . has nothing to do with politics at all" (*Friday Book* 97). According to my theoretical model of the double movement of parody, this apparent contradiction is what we might expect. The concentrated parody of the *Arabian Nights*, kept under tight control by the shifting frames of narration, inadvertently opens the text to contamination by the contemporary historical ground.[4]

Why does Barth want to maintain that *Chimera* has nothing to do with politics even as he admits that "the idea of revolution floats through my recent novellas" and that "one of the notions I've been most preoccupied with as a private citizen is the women's lib movement" (*First Person* 131)? Barth allows that "a simple-minded critic could say my trio of novellas is about women's lib. It *is* one of the themes that holds them together, although that's not at all what it's about for me" (*First Person* 131). Barth's animadversion to committed art can be made compatible with the presentation of social issues like feminism in his work. Barth's strategy allows him to suppress the *political* component of feminism while he magnifies its *personal* import. For Barth, these two realms stand tragically at odds. Shah Zaman's first lover, the equivalent of his brother's Scheherazade, takes the "Tragic View of Sex and Temperament":

> to wit, that while perfect equality between men and women was the only defensible value in that line, she was not at all certain it was attainable; even to pursue it ardently, against the grain of things as they were, was in all likelihood to spoil one's chances for happiness in love; *not* to pursue it, on the other hand, once one had seen it clearly to be the ideal, no doubt had the same effect. (45)

Though these words express only one character's views, they chime with similar positions taken by other characters, and with Barth's in his nonfiction. Nor are they gainsaid in the novel. The narrator points out that "even without regard to the interesting 'public' state of affairs" it is the King's "epical despair" that ravages the kingdom in the *Arabian Nights* (*Friday Book* 58). "For though the death of one person is not the death of a people, even mankind's demise will have to consist of each of our dyings. In this respect, all apocalypses are ultimately personal" (*Friday Book* 58). Or as Shah Zaman insists to the submissive Dunyazad: "Besides, between any two people, you know—what I mean, it's not the patriarchy that makes you take the passive role with your sister, for example" (42).

Once the story has personalized gender questions, it is in position further to muffle their political overtones. Barth's metafictive interests defuse some of the conflict between the sexes by turning their struggle into a metaphor for the engagement of storyteller and listener. The genie proclaims to the appreciative Sherry that the "very relation between teller and told was by nature erotic. The teller's role, he felt, regardless of his actual gender, was essentially masculine, the listener's or reader's feminine, and the tale was the medium of their intercourse" (25–26). Even as a metaphor of narrative engendering, of course, this conceit excludes less phallocentric models. But its very status *as* metaphor loosens the grip of the contemporaneous frame on the subject of gender roles. The metafictive fascination both obscures and confirms Scheherazade's insistence that fiction accomplishes very little in the face of actual gynocide. Stories only temporarily spell the horror: "For the present, it's our masters' pleasure to soften their policy; the patriarchy isn't changed: I believe it will persist even to our Genie's time and place" (37).

I characterize the placement of feminism in *Chimera*, then, as marking the suppression of politics, a self-conscious act that restricts the frame of reference. Feminism becomes the "theme" of *Chimera* because it is "more fascinating in many ways than the other liberation movements. For one thing, it's more complicated—morally, psychologically, and aesthetically" (*First Person* 131). But disregarding the political frame—the ideological or structural situation—of the issue produces only the passive regard of "fascination." It reminds us that Scheherazade's violent plot to overthrow the patriarchy and exact her revenge finally falls before a power that controls the ultimate frame of authority. The story repeatedly pulls back to reveal that the female narrator who seems to be in charge is actually subject to the delegation of authority from a higher source. The final take on Scheherazade comes from Shah Zaman, who himself narrates from a position of political authority, and who details his brother's triumph over revolution: "'A man couldn't stay king very long if he didn't even know what was going on in the harem!'" (54).

In recontextualizing the original mythic material, *Chimera* must recognize the contemporary pertinence of the myth's consideration of patriarchal power. The narrative works to contain "the women's liberationists" (231) through the balance of *Chimera*. The long last novella, "Bellerophoniad," presents its tarnished mythical hero, Bellerophon, as a reformed sexist: "I've had my consciousness raised" (222). "For all my transgressions against womankind—not least my apparent inability to treasure one of their number above all else in life, as did many so-called sexist pigs—I was contrite, and did not expect absolution" (285). Yet Bellerophon's acknowledgment of guilt and his understanding of social inequality cannot annul the ingrained dominance of the patriarchy. Melanippe the elder may represent the Amazon project of establishing a "militant gynocracy to oppose the forcible suppression of their sex" (218),[5] but her daughter instantly betrays their political program for the chance to love a hero and escape "the misanthropy" (287) of her feminist cohorts. Every political objective turns into the opportunity for personal advantage. Consider, for example, Philonoe's attainment of a groom (the younger Bellerophon) and a "matrilineal-but-patriarchal home rule for the Xanthians, a compromise grudgingly accepted by the shaken marecultists" (232)— all in the single stroke of extracting a dowry from her father. Or consider the vengeful Anteia's strident reverse sexism, a position that even manages to expose classical mythology as the "propaganda of the winners" in the gender context; yet the force of her critique collapses into a pathetic effort to seduce Bellerophon one last time. The force of *Chimera* as a whole drives the issue of women's liberation toward the manageably personal and psychological.[6]

Barth deprives feminism of its political status by personalizing ideological relations and metaphorizing social conflict. Such effects follow from the text's meticulous concentration on its literary models rather than its historical content. The new American feminism, however, is not the only contemporaneous matter to lose its political frame. Barth may prefer women's liberation as a theme because it is the most fascinating of the revolutionary movements he could observe in the late sixties, but it was certainly not all readers might have seen in Barth's fable of gynocide. The period of *Chimera*'s composition Barth characterizes as the "High Sixties": 1965–1973. The novellas come toward the end (1972), the notorious "Literature of Exhaustion" toward the beginning (1967). Rereading the latter, Barth says "I sniff traces of tear gas in its margins; I hear an echo of disruption between its lines" (*Friday Book* 64). In the margins of this chapter of Barth's writing career stands the Vietnam war—a genocide that hides behind a gynocide.

Chimera pictures a morose, disillusioned despot consigning the virgin youth of his land to certain ravishment and death. The plot and language of "Dunyazadiad" suggest a subliminal version of America's experience of the war in Vietnam. One imagines Lyndon Johnson, like Shahryar, bound to a futile program of gradual extermination—both of his adversaries and his own populace. How sadly accurate is Scheherazade's observation that "Shahryar would really like to quit what he's doing before the country falls apart, but needs an excuse to break his vow without losing face" (13). Like any good Buffalo undergraduate of the late sixties, Scheherazade studies political science and then psychology in an unavailing effort to learn how to stop Shahryar from "wrecking the country" (6). Sherry concludes that there is "no popular base for guerrilla war" since the victims are "upper-caste," but she grows daily more desperate as the body-count of "deflowered and decapitated" rises (6). (A later monarch in the novel, Bellerophon, points to the security of his reign: "My children were filially pious, my wife adored me, the silent majority of Lycians supported my administration" [142]). When Shah Zaman's lover first proposes an alternative to the two brothers' policies, a key feature is the establishment of a separate country to which the endangered virgins might flee after their night of defloration. Says the appreciative King, "[N]one, she imagined, would choose death over emigration, and any who found their new way of life not to their liking could return to Samarkand if and when I changed my policy, or migrate elsewhere in the meanwhile" (49).

Though the resemblances are not so precise or plentiful as to demand allegorization, Barth clearly gives us the Vietnam crisis in the margins of these novellas so otherwise taken up with women's liberation. In his *Friday Book* headnote to "The Literature of Exhaustion," Barth refers to the American High Sixties as a time when "the Vietnam War was in overdrive" and the "U.S. economy was fat and bloody" (62). Another essay details the achievements of a former student who traveled to Vietnam several times during the war; some of his missions were dedicated to airlifting burned children back to the United States for treatment, but the last trip was to record traditional Vietnamese oral poetry endangered—like everything else in the country—by the hostilities. Barth admits that the student's "poetical rescue work absolves us of nothing, any more than the rescue of those burned children does—but thank heaven he did it" (*Friday Book* 96). The mention of absolution suggests a sensitivity to moral responsibility and guilt, but Barth remains steadfast in his refusal to see how fiction itself can work on these problems. The guilt, I suggest, arises as much from Barth's convictions about the luxuries of art in a "fat and bloody" time as from the determination of national policy. What must it cost to write in *Chimera* that Samarkand's troubles strike the Genie as very similar to his own country's—"crises as desperate and problematical, he avowed, as ours, and as inimical to the single-mindedness needed to compose great works of art or the serenity to apprehend them" (10)?

Chimera domesticates the women's liberation movement by absorbing its subversiveness into metaphor, psychology, theme, and metanarrative. These strategies succeed in suppressing the politics of feminism, just as they screen the mechanism of repression that keeps the Vietnam war "out" of the novellas. It is only through the strength of denial that Barth can claim that *Chimera* has "nothing to do with politics at all." I have argued that parody in Barth protests its innocence of all that is not literary and yet betrays context as its very constitution. In this it limns out the situation of all textuality. Further, to the extent we recognize history as the contingent material factors that condition any work of art, history turns out to be context denied as content. Parody controls the contemporaneous in Barth's fiction; surely *Chimera*'s references to women's liberation and the Vietnam War are conscious and intended, and yet they are forced to the perimeter by Barth's concentration on the formal exercises of metafiction. My point will be misunderstood, I must add, if history is taken as the proportion of simple references to current or past events. It is not the nature or number of topical allusions that constitute history in a text; rather, history is precisely what the author's ideological position makes unavailable—or felt as absent—in a text. In the case of Barth, this position involves the author's retainment as a guest of the state, as a kind of tenured entertainer who amuses in exchange for comfort and security.

Parody/Parasitism

Though Scheherazade's plight moves the Genie/narrator of "Dunyazadiad," it is Dunyazad with whom he identifies; the Genie explains to her that she is the title character of his story because her "circumstances, on my 'wedding-night-to-come,' he found as arresting for taletellers of his particular place and time as was my sister's for the estate of narrative artists in general" (32). Dunyazad's belatedness makes her more the modern author. She has seen all the tricks of love, all the techniques of narrative; yet she must please her own king, tell her own story when the time comes. *Chimera* abounds with the notion that the post-mythic hero must reenact earlier feats, and that the storyteller must repeat familiar tales. Dunyazad functions as a superfluous third party to the intimate relations between lovers and taletellers, living and loving vicariously on the bounty of her retainer. Dunyazad's *structural* relation with her host makes her situation an emblem of the traditional association of parody with parasitism. The Genie recognizes that like Dunyazad, he feeds at a table set by others long before his arrival.

I am not activating this view of parody in order to reduce it to a literary practice by which one text drains life from another in order to sustain its own. The dialogic relations between the parodied and the parodying cannot, it is true, be accounted for either by simple predatory or simple symbiotic parasitism. We can, however, expand the idea of parasitism to describe a set of relations that govern the indebtedness of the derived work to its source. In doing so, we may locate the point of contact between Barth's most prevalent literary mode and its ideological ramifications.

In a work called *The Parasite*, Michel Serres has capitalized on a double meaning in his original French: the word "parasite" refers to a biological parasite (and so figuratively to a social parasite), and alternatively to the interference or static in a channel of communication. Serres meditates on how these senses inform each other. His principal notion is that the parasitic relation (literally an "eating next to") is foundational for all intersubjective relations: from the child at the mother's breast, the figure of parasitism characterizes biological and social ratios of dependence. According to Serres, this relation also suggests a single main vector of sustenance, from host to guest. These relations may be interlocked in long chains whose links may play guest to one host and host to the next guest. Yet the "arrow" of parasitism points inevitably toward death; parasitism follows the law of entropy. Serres applies this dynamic to communicative relations as well, noting that the medium of communication always provides noise or interference produced by the operation of the system itself. Without such static, however, communication would disappear because it would be unnecessary; it is interference itself that both constitutes the channel of communication and offers the resistance necessary to draw out the communicative impulse. ("Maybe I understood the message only because of the noise" [70].)

Although Serres's dense speculation can hardly be abstracted successfully, I think I can make clear the ways in which his enlarged view of parasitic relation bears on Barth's practice of parody and on its reflection of the author's place in a capitalist, mass consumer society. The problem that precipitates "Dunyazadiad," we recall, is the writer's block afflicting the Genie. The production of writing, in other words, suffers an obstruction. In psychological terms the misery may be clear enough, but in cultural terms the crisis may involve the obstacles placed before the production of "pure" art by the necessities of social reform, by the guilt of living off the labor of others, by the anxiety of being spared by others' blood. Barth's fictions repeatedly fend off the horror that his amusements depend on real human inequity, that having the key to the treasure is strictly to have the treasure itself.

My first observation about the parodist as parasitist involves the currency passed between the host and guest. Serres points out that the "parasite is invited to the *table d'hôte*; in return, he must regale the other diner with his stories and his mirth. To be exact, he exchanges good talk for good food; he buys his dinner, paying for it in words" (34). Looked at from the host's standpoint, we might say too that the host pays for amusement with his food. The exchange may put both participants in the roles of guest and host, as the French word "*hôte*" implies by denoting both.

Besides the many invocations of the epic custom of exchanging a story for bed and board, Barth's writing displays anxieties in other ways about the demands of hospitality on his art. Many of the explanatory headnotes attached to the nonfictional pieces in *The Friday Book* recount the circumstances under which the essays were written. Almost invariably these prefatory frames become occasions for considering who paid what for Barth's prose. A portrait emerges of a successful author trading his insubstantial words for material pleasures. This condition is no more marvelous for Barth than for any other writer who has actually made coppers ring on the other side of the keyboard, but Barth's meticulous accounting of his payments does beg for some explanation.

The most stunning example of this concern comes at the end of an essay entitled "Tales Within Tales Within Tales." Barth wants to illustrate the idea that the technique of narrative embeddedness establishes an isomorphy between syntactic and narrative structures, and writes a dazzlingly recessed sentence whose subject is itself an illustration of the tale-within-a-tale pattern. The sentence is about a series of chores that Barth and his wife have to perform each spring to ready their sailboat for the season. Wanting to set sail, they need first to fit out the boat, which involves painting the bottom, which involves going to town to buy new paint, etc. This task-within-a-task illustration is raised many powers, but its main relevance to my argument derives from Barth's yoking of writing to the pleasures of consumerism. He begins his story of the *mise en abîme* errand by remarking that he has "fortunately managed to secure a wife whom I enjoy living with, a house on the water that I enjoy living in, and a sailboat to sail on that water from that house with that wife for our innocent recreation when our more serious work is done" (*Friday Book* 237). In the course of his trip, moreover, Barth stops for gasoline, and pauses to "tisk my tongue about the price of fuel and shake my head at the narrative connection, so to speak, between the gasoline in my tank and the American hostages in Teheran" (*Friday Book* 238). The "narrative connection" is trivialized in a tisk, of course; the real connection has to do with the goods that Barth's "serious work" has "managed to secure" for him.

Though I cannot develop all the corroborating episodes in *The Friday Book* in this detail, I will mention a number of others that point to a model of artistic production essentially at peace with the ideology of a consumerist capitalism of commodification. During the most violent period of antiwar demonstrations at Buffalo, the "hawkish" Ralph Ellison was invited to lecture. Fearing student agitation, the university cancelled the lecture. As a result, Barth notes, "four or five of us . . . at great expense to the State of New York, spent a quiet evening with our visitor" (*Friday Book* 92). This kind of connection between political quietism and state patronage appears elsewhere. Barth contrasts the mood of "The Literature of Replenishment" to its "Exhaustion" predecessor by pointing out that the later piece appeared in "a calmer place and time—Johns Hopkins, Jimmy Carter" (*Friday Book* 193). It has a "more tenured, middle-aged air about it," he comments, while acknowledging that to readers in Romania or mainland China such pieces might seem "unintelligible or hopelessly luxurious" (*Friday Book* 193).

I want to make it clear that I am not attacking Barth's politics here, even if one could infer them from his miscellaneous remarks about his writing, or, even more treacherously, if one would extrapolate them from his fiction. Rather, I am interested in the practice of ideology in Barth's parodic fiction. The figure of the parasite for parody shows us how to understand the authorial impulse to "intoxicate, engorge oneself with *story*." These words come from Barth's famous account of discovering frame narratives in the Oriental stacks at the Johns Hopkins library, where he realizes that if anything will make a writer of him it will "be the digestion of that enormous, slightly surreptitious feast of narrative" (*Friday Book* 57).

Barth's parody functions to underscore the parasitic relation between authority and authorship. As a guest at the table of the mass economy, Barth enjoys what his prose can buy. As a guest at the table of the state, Barth cherishes its guarantee of the serenity needed to compose works of art. As a guest at the "feast of narrative," Barth parodically replenishes fiction from the "treasury of art." *Parody is the very mode of literary production that most nearly enacts*

Barth's place in contemporary social and economic modes of production. It both opens and forecloses an articulated relation with historical context. It proposes the parasitism of literary intertextuality as a formal solution to the predicament of social parasitism. The social and economic position of the author as revealed in Barth's writing may be characterized as dependent—derivative of benefit at others' expense. Of course, this situation is not unique to Barth as a contemporary author in a developed Western capitalist democracy; I wish to demonstrate how Barth's work manages this general problem, not to claim especially that Barth fails to align his writing with any politically "correct" position. Moreover, the reader must face his or her own implication in the consumption of the word in a mass economy and its reinforcement of a status quo. If these aspects of parasitism deepen the threat to the author of the contemporaneous, a process we saw begin with the very nature of literary parody, the second sense of *parasite* helps to explain the force of denial we have identified in Barth's attitude toward history.

When Barth sniffs tear gas in the margins of his sixties work and hears disruption between the lines, I contend he is picking up the noise of repression in his text. Serres comments on this textual phenomenon:

> To chase: push out, drive out, uproot, dismiss, purge, repress. We repress what bothers us. What is repressed, but remains anyway, still parasites communication. (77)

As in the fable of the country mouse and the city mouse, Serres reminds us, it is the noise of interruption (by the cat) that recalls the lines of parasitism and privilege governing the relation. Disturbance raises the parasitic function to the surface—as meaningful but indecipherable. In a literal way, Dunyazad performs this function in *Chimera*; the first novella begins with the sound of Dunyazad's planned interruption of her sister. As the unnecessary third, Dunyazad acts as the resistance that constitutes the exchange between Scheherazade and the King. Her interruption establishes the pretext under which a suspended narrative may be exchanged for a suspended death sentence.

The Ideology of Parody: Managing History

Chimera itself was an interruption. "The Author" of LETTERS recalls putting aside his work in progress "in pursuit of a new chimera called *Chimera*" in the period 1969–1971 (LETTERS 49). This interruption pertains to my reading of Barth's formal solutions to the impingement of history because he considers the resumption of his bicentennial novel a return "to history, to 'realism' " (LETTERS 49). In one sense, much of Barth's fiction seems to ground itself in history; he points to the historical, realistic roots of *The Sot-Weed Factor* and *Giles Goat-Boy*. LETTERS not only swims in seas of historical detail but identifies social revolution as its aim. Its earlier versions— NOTES and NUMBERS—aspire to "*the New, the Second Revolution, an utterly novel revolution*" according to Polyeidus's letter (*Chimera* 244). The ambiguity of a "novel revolution," however, precisely measures the protective confusion of intramural and extramural effect: "The document seemed to set forth its author's plan for completing a project that sometimes appeared to be a written work of some heroically unorthodox sort, at other times a political revolution" (*Chimera* 247). The unorthodoxy of such a novel, in fact, involves transcending "the limitations of particularity; . . . it will represent nothing beyond itself, have no content except its own form, no subject but its own processes" (*Chimera* 256).

This is a typically Barthian contradiction: a return to history in a novel that represents only itself. Precisely as it turns history into narrative, LETTERS seeks to manage the Real; the dazzling manipulations of historical events and personalities solve formally or deflect—in the way all fictional texts must—the threats of social and formal contradictions to the writing project. "History," A. B. Cook approvingly quotes his father, "is your grandest fiction" (319), and LETTERS presents history subject to the authority of narrative. In the first place, history appears as inevitably *scripted*. It is always a form of narrative. One of the novel's numerous aesthetic innovators, André Castine (one of Lady Amherst's lovers), proposes to practice "'action historiography': the *making* of history as if it were an avant-garde species of narrative" (72–73). One effect of such a sense of history is to personalize it; history invariably functions as the record of individual intrigues and the unfolding of genealogy in LETTERS. Notice how the syntax of the following sentence confines what history might mean: André Castine "disagreed point for point with [his parents'] interpretations of history, in particular the history of their own family's dark pursuits" (73). History remains indistinguishable from the processes by which the past is narrativized and the self created.[7]

LETTERS defends against the contingency of history by interiorizing it intertextually. For the compositional situation, Barth may suggest the image of contamination by outlying material, but the process turns out to be a kind of auto-infection. For example, the

Backwater Ballads "tales are told from the viewpoint of celestial Aedes Sollicitans, a freshmarsh native with total recall of all her earlier hatches" who "infects" the author "with her narrative accumulation" (28–29). The chronicle-like fictions and incessant catalogues of contemporaneous events (which reach an apotheosis in the author's last letter to the reader [771–72]) create an effect of massive historicity. Yet this effect actually arises in concert with the novel's powerful efforts to resist everything but regard for its own narrative processes; wholly narrativized history protects the fictive space from interference by those historical forces that cannot be reconciled. The text's position resembles Ambrose Mensch's resolve "to put by not only history, philosophy, politics, psychology, self-confession, sociology, and other such traditional contaminants of fiction, but also, insofar as possible, characterization, description, dialogue, plot—even language, where I could dispense with it" (151). This may be the empowering ideal of the Barthian text as well. His version of parody allows the restriction of the question of context to inter- and intratextual relations.

I have been arguing that the "return" to history, realism, and the work of a novel revolution in LETTERS only apparently redirects Barth's counterrealistic aesthetic. I take *Sabbatical* to confirm this reading of Barth's fiction since it displays—sometimes ferociously— the mechanisms of suppression and repression encountered earlier. *Chimera's* unease about the injustices of sexual and political oppression has boiled into anguish over the violence inflicted on the powerless. The narrators of *Sabbatical*, Fenwick Turner, a CIA agent turned novelist, and Susan Seckler, a professor of American literature, struggle to maintain a sanctuary for their private intellectual and carnal pleasures in the face of a vicious world. Repeatedly they fret over the seeming irrelevance of literature to social and political realities: Susan wonders how she can go on "correcting . . . comma faults, pretending that art and moral values and subject-verb agreement matter, while my husband and my stepfather-brother-in-law and their buddies kill Patrice Lumumba and overthrow Mohammed Mossadegh and Salvador Allende" (118). The awful contradiction that their consciences and sensibilities are the very products of a leisure bled from the downtrodden informs countless passages of guilt in *Sabbatical*:

> Susan's got her *New York Review of Books*, picked up improbably at Solomons; Fenn, Shakespeare's *Tempest* for the hundredth time. We are reasonably healthy, reasonably successful, reasonably well

off, well fed, well fucked, unpersecuted, unoppressed, and still in love after seven years of marriage: the favored of the earth. What is that light on for, at the end of that dock?

Good night, good night. (201)

Put this way, of course, the problem already dictates its answer. And Barth does not flinch. The way to go on writing novels is to look away. When gypsies surround the house in Spain rented by Fenn and his first wife, imploring them for food and holding their starving infants up to the windows, the would-be novelist finally decides to draw the curtains and "say no to presumably hungry people" (34). Or, to compose a later portion of their story, Susan and Fenn agree to "turning our eyes . . . from the sustained ordeal and most of Earth's human population, who still in 1980 go to bed hungry when they have bed to go to, and, if they woke, woke hungrier, weaker, damaged five days further in body and mind" (127).

To fend off the untenable contradictions of the novelist's situation in American culture, the writers in *Sabbatical* finally just accept their privilege. Fenn has all along been calmer about enjoying his mere good fortune; we are led to believe that Susan is more doubtful (338). Yet by the novel's conclusion we find the lovers happily ensconced in their vessel's cabin, again doting on each other; "as his familiar hand calmly takes her breast, she feels like a confident Scheherazade" (363). Here the master's touch rekindles the age-old forms of property and propriety, of privilege and authority, of indulgence and indolence. That these perquisites should appear as the necessary conditions of those who produce literature confirms the incapacity of the Barthian text to articulate a more productive stance toward its historical conditions.

Barth's parodic metafiction, so richly laminated with the technique of framing, attempts to clear a space for a literature about literature, for a fiction that is about life by being only about language. Yet the efforts of parody to exclude the merely contemporaneous, like the efforts of framing to rule out the merely contextual, turn out to cross up their own ends. Parody intensifies the dynamics of all textuality by practicing forms of suppression and repression. These methods of control include as felt absences what they seek to exclude. In the case of Barth's writing, parody smuggles context into play in the very process of banishing it. The contemporaneous matter of history contaminates the text through the channels meant to contain it. Parody's parasitism opens Barth's writing to relations of dependence and derived sustenance that have ideological as well as narrative implications.

Notes

I gratefully acknowledge a Fellowship for Independent Research in 1984–1985 from the National Endowment for the Humanities, which supported my work on framing in literature. I also wish to thank my colleague Michael McKeon for his helpful comments on the draft of this article.

1. Morgan uses the term "intratextuality" to isolate an intertextual relation between works by a single author; she cites the phenomenon as an example of intertextual relations that escape the model of literary influence (see chapter 11).

2. Following Bakhtin's explanation of the power of parody in the carnival, Hutcheon remarks: "Contemporary metafiction ... exists—as does the carnival—on that boundary between literature and life ... Both its form and content can operate to subvert formalistic, logical, authoritarian structures" (73).

3. This method of analysis may avoid the absorption of History (in Jameson's sense) by literary history alone. Such an absorption takes place in Hutcheon's unsuccessful attempt to address the ideological implications of literary parody. She argues that parody teaches us about "broader historical and ideological contexts implied by that act [of parodying]" (109). Yet Hutcheon allows her intramural model to commandeer history and turn it into the conscious representation of other aesthetic objects: "Parody historicizes by placing art within the history of art" (109). This inconsistency remains a problem for Hutcheon throughout her often suggestive consideration of parody; although her semiotic model of parody calls for an examination of broader contexts, her actual analyses concentrate entirely on the individual work's relation to other works of art.

4. Even Barth's host text displays such contamination. In the foreword to his authoritative translation of *The Book of the Thousand Nights and a Night*, Richard Burton, writing fifteen years before *Lord Jim*, recommends his work as an instrument of cultural domination. In this prefatory frame, which introduces the political even as it marginalizes it, the language of political conflict and control reflects the anxiety of a British empire hoping to maintain itself:

> [The reader] will not think lightly of my work when I repeat to him that with the aid of my annotations supplementing Lane's, the student will readily and pleasantly learn more of the Moslem's manner and customs, laws and religion than is known to the average Orientalist; and, if my labours induce him to attack the text of The Nights he will become master of much more Arabic than the ordinary Arab owns. This book is indeed a legacy which I bequeath to my fellow-countrymen in their hour of need ... Apparently England is ever forgetting that she is at present the greatest Mohammedan empire in the world ... We may, perhaps, find it hard to restore to England those pristine virtues, that tone and temper, which made her what she is; but at any rate we (myself and a host of others) can offer her the

means of dispelling her ignorance concerning the Eastern races with whom she is continually in contact. (xx–xxi)

5. Barth recycles the myths of prehistorical matriarchies like those embodied in the stories of the Amazons and Bellerophon. As Bamberger has argued, however, such myths of matriarchies (which exist only in patriarchal societies since there seem to be no documented matriarchies extant) inevitably recount the loss of power by women as a result of their immorality or incompetence. Such myths ought to be interpreted as rationalizations of their own power by patriarchal societies, a function more of the dynamic of domination than historical record. From this standpoint, then, the very form that the liberationist impulse is given in *Chimera* acts as a strategy of containment. I am grateful to my colleague at Boston University, Carolyn Williams, for calling Bamberger's work to my attention.

6. The novel's form functions like a closed loop, a moebius-strip that continuously folds the politics of feminism to face away from the text. Originally, Barth had imagined "Dunyazadiad" coming last, a sequence that would have shown the gradual burial of the feminist question in the shrouds of metafictive parody, and would have ended with the revelation that the male king still ruled after all. The suggestion that Barth start with the shorter, simpler novella was made by his editor, a woman whose name is, remarkably, Anne Freedgood (Morrell 162).

7. O'Donnell makes this point in his study of the textuality of history and self in LETTERS: "The significance that is born of such a textual, historical world comes about through the relations *between* its events and letters . . . Each writer becomes a sign in a system that is the narration of a being in history, which is, precisely the collection of documents and narratives that record the genealogy of the self" (65). This formulation perfectly characterizes the novel's own grasp of what it is doing. What I wish to pursue is what eludes that grasp—the history that appears only between the lines.

Works Cited

Bakhtin, Mikhail. *Rabelais and His World*. Translated by Helene Iswolsky. Bloomington: Indiana University Press, 1984.

Bamberger, Joan. "The Myth of Matriarchy: Why Men Rule in Primitive Society." In *Woman, Culture, and Society*, edited by Michelle Zimbalist Rosaldo and Louise Lamphere. Stanford: Stanford University Press, 1974.

Barth, John. "Interview. November 19, 1971." In *First Person: Conversations on Writers and Writing*, edited by Frank Gado. Schenectady, N.Y.: Union College Press, 1973.

———. *Chimera*. New York: Random House, 1972.

———. LETTERS. New York: Putnam, 1979.

———. *Sabbatical: A Romance*. New York: Putnam, 1982.

————. *The Friday Book: Essays and Other Nonfiction.* New York: Putnam, 1984.

Burton, Richard F., trans. *The Book of the Thousand Nights and a Night.* Vol. 1. Privately printed by the Burton Club. N.P., n.d.

Hutcheon, Linda. *A Theory of Parody: The Teachings of Twentieth-Century Art Forms.* London: Methuen, 1985.

Jameson, Fredric. *The Political Unconscious: Narrative as a Socially Symbolic Act.* Ithaca, N.Y.: Cornell University Press, 1981.

Jenny, Laurent. "The Strategy of Form." In *French Literary Theory Today,* edited by Tzvetan Todorov, translated by R. Carter. London: Cambridge University Press, 1982.

Kristeva, Julia. *Desire in Language: A Semiotic Approach to Literature and Art.* Edited by Leon S. Roudiez. Translated by Thomas Gora, Alice Jardine, and Leon S. Roudiez. New York: Columbia University Press, 1980.

Morgan, Thaïs. "The Space of Intertextuality," in this volume.

Morrell, David. *John Barth: An Introduction.* University Park: Pennsylvania State University Press, 1976.

O'Donnell, Patrick. *Passionate Doubts: Designs of Interpretation in Contemporary American Fiction.* Iowa City: University of Iowa Press, 1986.

Serres, Michel. *The Parasite.* Translated Lawrence R. Schehr. Baltimore: Johns Hopkins University Press, 1982.

Love's Labours Won

The Erotics of Contemporary Parody

=

HEIDE ZIEGLER

"Intertextuality" denotes not a state of affairs between texts, but the result of semiotic and deconstructive approaches to texts. It is, therefore, a historically founded literary phenomenon which—like all new approaches to texts—nevertheless contends, at least implicitly, that past perspectives on the interrelationship among texts are wrong. Such a contention is valid as long as the practitioner of intertextuality remains conscious of its epistemological limitations. One must keep an ironic distance from one's own fascination with intertextuality, always regarding it as a new method and not as a new "weltanschauung"—even if intertextuality calls the state of reality into question in the name of fiction. The very term *intertextuality* as such is in need of deconstruction insofar as it seems to presuppose the existence of discrete texts among which multiple influences can be noted. But actually the term is meant to convey the idea of overlapping textual systems which defy classification and allow for chains of signifiers to freely constitute themselves as so many fictional worlds. These fictional worlds seem to be all there is to those who agree with Raymond Federman that "there cannot be any truth nor any reality exterior to fiction" (12).

At first glance it seems as though the question of parody that is necessarily raised when one surveys contemporary American fiction cannot be approached intertextually. For parody presupposes first, that on the level of the text both the literary model and its parody should be discrete and that this particular quality should be marked as such; second, that on the authorial level the intention of the later author to parody the earlier text is a given and will become obvious to the reader; and, finally, that on the level of reception the reader will recognize citations from and allusions to the prior text in the later one. These parodic features require the author and the reader to be (to a greater or lesser extent) connoisseurs of a certain literary tradition; yet this tradition has to be regarded in strictly diachronic fashion and cannot be represented as a number of overlapping textual systems. Otherwise, the opportunity to establish hierarchies of texts would be lost, and without such hierarchies no evaluative attitude—for instance, the traditional mocking or denigrating attitude of the parodist—would be possible. Thus, the need for the author's parodic intention to become obvious in the text also seems to defy the concept of intertextuality, since the parodist appropriates the privileged position of historical heir, even when he considers himself aesthetically inferior to his model. And since intertextuality attempts to dissolve any distinct borderlines between texts, the claim for discreteness between at least two texts, which is necessary to define a parodic relationship, once more seems to indicate the necessity of a diachronic textual approach.

This essay nevertheless seeks to show that, as contemporary American literature has definitely absorbed intertextual tendencies and strategies to the point where they redefine the aesthetic value of texts as such, the traditional concept of parody has had to give way to a broader concept whose distinguishing feature can be seen as the attempt to recast, in seemingly synchronic fashion, the diachronic tradition of parody. Due to the particular history of the idea of parody in America, this process of recasting not only took place here (rather than in Europe, especially in France, where semiotic and deconstructive approaches to literature did, after all, come into being), but spread almost like wildfire, so that one may venture to say that—after the eighteenth century—a new parodic age is upon us. I would like to suggest that contemporary American parody should not be perceived as presenting a polemical approach to the literary model (or models) it is concerned with, but rather as entering into a seemingly erotic relationship with the prior text. The basic condition for the emergence of such an erotic relationship is a shift in the parodist's concern, from the style of a prior text (a literary concern that spawned much of Russian formalism) to the whole body of that text. The single features of the prior text become less important than the challenge to its existence as such. This recent change in the parodist's attitude coincides with the interest in margins demonstrated by those practitioners of intertextuality who locate significance, either more traditionally, in the interstices between distanced texts, or more radically, somewhere "outside" or "beneath" the tissue of literary interconnections altogether. This change may be the result of unconscious influence (the zeitgeist), or of the conscious struggle to meet the challenges implicit in a theory of intertextuality.

Two specific examples—a comparison of *Beowulf* (eighth century) and John Gardner's *Grendel* (1971), as well as a comparison of Ford Madox Ford's *The Good Soldier* (1915) and John Hawkes's *The*

Blood Oranges (1971)—shall serve to demonstrate that a description of parody in erotic terms can supplant a diachronically based definition of the term with one of supposed synchrony, and that this supposed synchrony is indeed the artistic outcome of the historical interdependence between contemporary American writing and the conscious formation of intertextual strategies. However, the two comparisons will also point to a difference within this new conception of parody which may ultimately serve to illustrate both its dangers and its possibilities. Without attempting to evaluate the following two terms along traditional lines, I would like to call Gardner's form of parody *regressive*, and that of Hawkes *progressive*. The reason why an evaluation of these terms should be initially suspended must be seen precisely in the synchronic aspect provided by intertextuality to the parodies of these authors. The dissolution of parody's diachronic features forbids any immediate use of synonyms such as "anachronistic" or "epigonal" for regressive parody, and "utopian" or "innovative" for progressive parody. Instead, the outcome of the subsequent analysis deserves adumbration at this point. *Regressive* and *progressive* will reveal themselves as opposing, yet not complementary, terms. They function on different levels of awareness. Whereas the term *regressive* relates to the moral and, by extension, traditional aspects of a text, *progressive* texts strive to be independent as texts, treating the prior text as the unaccountable Other. They suggest an encounter on equal terms; they engage literary tradition in order to overcome its forbidding impact. The erotics of progressive parody signify the attempt to do away with the hierarchical, patriarchal aspects of texts; the erotics of regressive parody signify a succumbing to that hierarchy and paternalism. Therefore, regressive parody tends to turn to canonized texts (*Beowulf*), while progressive parody prefers more canonically problematic, "comparable" texts (*The Good Soldier*).

What is meant by "the erotics of parody" is an evaluating extension of, say, Linda Hutcheon's definition of modern parody. In *A Theory of Parody* she states that "unlike what is more traditionally regarded as parody, the modern form does not always permit one of the texts to fare any better or worse than the other. It is the fact that they *differ* that this parody emphasizes and, indeed, dramatizes" (31). I refer to this difference as erotic because it implies in the emotional stance of the later writer towards the earlier text (and its author) a mixture of devotion (or homage) and aggression (or mockery)—the emotional attitude bringing the earlier text up to date, as it were. However, this definition seems to be geographically, rather than historically, delimited: what Hutcheon calls

"modern parody" may indeed be a specifically American phenomenon—one, moreover, that has begun to influence recent European
literature as well. The reasons for the development of this particular kind of contemporary parody lie in the American writer's
attitude towards tradition as such, especially towards European
tradition. Many contemporary American writers are steeped in
European literary lore; in fact their knowledge very often is almost
encyclopedic. However, they relate to the *whole* literary tradition,
not, say, to Homer as opposed to Dante, or to Shakespeare as opposed to Milton. This attitude of general homage at the same time
requires constant rebellion: it creates a love–hate relationship.
Therefore, American writers have always more or less attempted
to treat the parodied text as if it were another body, as if its author
could be "met." American contemporary writers whose distinguishing feature is self-reflexivity have let this love–hate relationship
determine the narrative structure of their texts, inscribing the
parodied together with the parody into the text and thus redefining the genre of parody from an internal, yet generalizing, point
of view.

In *Grendel*, John Gardner retells the Beowulf legend from the
monster's point of view. This shift of perspective is made possible
by the historical development of philosophy, psychology, and the
natural sciences that has taken place in the eleven centuries that
have elapsed between the composition of the Old English epic and
the twentieth-century novel. In seemingly postmodernist fashion,
Gardner transforms the effects of this historical development into
the causes for the fictional development of his "medieval" novel.
The monster Grendel can be regarded with sympathy—a result
helped along by the first-person narrative point of view—because
he has to cope with theories historically beyond the possible scope
of his understanding. On the one hand, Gardner implicitly de-
nounces the Middle Ages as "the dark ages," when people believed
in monsters as representatives of the devil and endowed them with
terrifying supernatural features, although in fact these features
were nothing but the projections of their own fear of the future.
On the other hand, the empathy established between the main
character and the author constitutes an emotional basis from which
Gardner then attempts to criticize present life and art. Gardner lets
the cultural assets of his own age parody an earlier time as represented in an early text while hardly parodying that text *as* a text.
He can then use *Beowulf* as the moral framework within which he
implicitly criticizes present-day life as inhuman, unheroic, and
ugly. In other words, he attempts to make the parody work both

ways. If, according to Gardner, the Scyldings of Heorot hall should not have boasted of their humanity as compared to the outcast spirit whom they themselves had alienated, then neither should the people of today pride themselves upon their advancements in the realm of human learning, which serve, at best, to illuminate their past mistakes. Gardner's double-edged parody contaminates past and present, fiction and reality, and, without superficially calling into question the discreteness of the two texts that have seemingly entered into a parodic relationship, actually creates an erotic fusion between them. "Eros," in this sense, suggests an undifferentiated intermingling rather than a mutual attraction of texts.

All of the heroes of the Beowulf legend appear in Gardner's novel as either brutal, unthinking men of action, like the legendary hero himself, or as thoughtful yet melancholy weaklings, like King Hrothgar. Interesting exceptions are the men of words, like the king's spokesman, Unferth, and the minstrel. Unferth, who in the legend "sits at the feet" of the king and combines the duties of entertainer, orator, satirist, and general counselor, might be called the representative historian, and the minstrel the exemplary artist. In Gardner's novel, Unferth, a privileged yet treacherous man and an unpunished fratricide to boot, becomes the image of self-reflexive modern man. He is the only one, before Beowulf, who dares to attack the monster, even searching him out in his subterranean cave. Grendel, however, despises Unferth for his ceaseless talking and, to the would-be hero's chagrin, spares him time and again. Grendel despises words, yet he falls prey to the minstrel's songs. For the minstrel's songs probe the possible, whereas Grendel, who knows that his whole existence depends on nothing so much as the author's words, has to accept the words he is given as an unshakable reality. By talking—orality at least having the advantage of appearing spontaneous as opposed to the written word—he continually attempts to create a distance between himself and the world: "Talking, talking. Spinning a web of words, pale walls of dreams, between myself and all I see" (4).

Since Gardner's present-day monster, unlike the medieval Grendel, can no longer be believed to exist, he must be constituted through the text. The first-person narrative thus gains an existential function: for Grendel, it is literally life-giving. So, in other ways, are the songs of the minstrel or Shaper, as he is called in Gardner's novel:

His fingers picked infallibly, as if moved by something beyond his power, and the words stitched together out of ancient songs, the scenes interwoven out of dreary tales, made a vision without seams, an image of himself yet not-himself, beyond the need of any shaggy old gold-friend's pay: the projected possible. (42)

To create, through his fiction, an image of himself yet not-himself seems a fair paraphrase of Gardner's artistic credo. The "projected possible," having the potential of becoming real in *Grendel*, seems to make Gardner, like the Shaper, part of his own projected fictional world. Through parody, the author himself wants to partake of an intertextual realm. He not only wants the Old English epic and his own novel to become one; his vision, as the projector of the possible, is to create the text in his own image and, thus, to participate in its fate. When the Shaper in Gardner's novel quotes the first lines of *Beowulf*, moving Grendel to believe in his own future destruction as a possibility, he is identical with the later author who repeats that same song.

This encompassing use of parody poses two questions. First, even in the Old English epic, the deeds of Beowulf become part of the minstrel's song immediately after they are completed—that is, they are cited within the frame of the epic itself:

> hwilum cyninges thegn,
> guma gilp-hlaeden, gidda gemyndig,
> se the eal-fela eald-gesegena
> worn gemunde, word other fand
> sothe gebunden. Secg eft ongan
> sith Beowulfes snyttrum styrian
> ond on sped wrecan spel gerade,
> wordum wrixlan. (11.867−74)[1]

However, while the process of assimilating life into art in *Beowulf* appears on the surface to be similar to Gardner's procedure, the distinction between deed and word remains unquestionable: indeed, Beowulf could not listen to the song celebrating his heroic deeds were he fulfilling those deeds at the time. Therefore, he is not like Gardner's Grendel, who lives by and through his words because he cannot exist otherwise. Second, in the parodic recension of the ancestral text, the realm of the possible does not pertain to the past in the same way as it does to the present and the future, not even as far as fiction is concerned. For whereas other possible versions of the Beowulf legend could have come into existence at the time of its composition that would have contained a similar outlook on life and art, it is impossible to assume that such a version could still be written today. (This is the problem that Jorge Luis

Borges most conspicuously calls attention to in his story "Pierre Menard, Author of Don Quixote.") Yet regressive parody, such as *Grendel*, always treats the earlier text as the unchangeable Other. It attempts to project itself into the time of the other text at the risk of losing its own identity and becoming totally dependent on the past text. The identity of a progressive parody, on the other hand, consists precisely in its insistence on the present point of view, while treating the past text as if it were contemporary. It is because of this at times painful insistence on its own identity that the progressive parody can point to future narrative possibilities.

When John Hawkes wrote his parody of Ford Madox Ford's *The Good Soldier* over five decades after that novel appeared, he chose a quotation from the end of the 1915 novel as the motto for his own:

> Is there then any terrestrial paradise where, amidst the whispering of the olive-leaves, people can be with whom they like and have what they like and take their ease in shadows and in coolness? (213)

Hawkes's novel attempts to answer this question by placing two couples with a certain resemblance to those portrayed by Ford into just such an environment. Hawkes's characters live in an imaginary southern land called Illyria, a country without seasons, where amidst whispering olive trees they can be with whom they like and have what they like, and take their ease in Dionysian fashion, having sex, drinking wine and playing the grape-tasting game in shadows and in coolness. The novel takes up Ford's longing for a terrestrial paradise, yet only in order to show how the apparently ideal, timeless landscape causes the moral deterioration of its inhabitants.

Ford's novel is set in America and Europe and is itself a parody of one of the main topics of the novels of Henry James, the so-called international theme. Ford's partial parody serves to offset Hawkes's more comprehensive endeavor. Ford's narrator and his wife are from Philadelphia and New England respectively. The other couple, called the Ashburnhams, own an estate in southern England, and the two couples meet in Nauheim, a German spa. Ford reverses the Jamesian pattern, in which American heroes tend to be ignorant of European culture but possessed of laudable moral convictions, while European heroes are sophisticated yet opportunistic. The American narrator of *The Good Soldier* is notoriously unreliable as a character. Florence, his wife, seems to have earned her telling name through her inclination to function as a sort of walking Guide Bleu and Baedecker rolled into one. The Ashburnhams, on the other hand, lack not culture, but sophistication. In fact, on first meeting Edward Ashburnham, the narrator, in an outburst of jealousy, describes the latter's eyes as "perfectly honest, perfectly straightforward, perfectly, perfectly stupid" (33). While this parodic version of James's international theme reflects a kind of moral reversal, the international setting remains the same— complete with the presence of a third meeting place on the Continent as a stage for the dramatization of differences between England and America. The similar setting serves to bring out the reversal of the values that Ford attaches to Americans and Europeans, whereas in Hawkes's novel the translocation of the plot into an imaginary Illyria ultimately calls into question the attribution of values as such. The parodic series of locations from James through Ford to Hawkes, while it seems to form a progression from wilderness to civilization to' terrestrial paradise—at least as far as the American characters are concerned—in fact ends by positing moral chaos as the condition of the new Eden. Hawkes implicitly voices the criticism that American literature still suffers from having replaced a European teleological concept of history with the myth of the virgin land, since for him the tension between the two concepts prevents the constitution of any unified set of values. At the same time, Hawkes's landscape of the imagination attempts to solve this American problem by treating it, ironically, as metaphor rather than "history."

In order to understand what this means, one should not see Ford's *The Good Soldier* simply as a link between James and Hawkes. The novel's unreliable narrator is not simply a continuation of a device developed by James, but also serves as a parody of that device, thus preparing the way for Hawkes's moral chaos to appear as a narrative problem. Ford dissolves the convention of the closed literary model as a necessary precondition for any parody by introducing the parody of a character as unreliable narrator. Normally parody can function only on the basis of two separate yet reliable narrative stances. However, Ford treats the international theme as if it were dependent on narrative instead of cultural values; that is, he opposes and questions two sets of values as if they were constituted through narrative representation. Thus Ford prepares for Hawkes's doubly unreliable narrator, whose unreliability can no longer be understood except when considered from the point of view of his ironic alter ego in the text itself. If Ford's narrator is unreliable because he cannot be trusted to exist exclusively as a "character" within his "tale of passion" (thus the subtitle of the novel), Hawkes's narrator is doubly unreliable because he assumes the role of narrator and author of the imagined world of Illyria. He not only manipulates the other characters' lives, but also distorts whatever traditional narrative topics he employs to explain himself—whether it be the topic of the pastoral idyl or of the tragic hero or of the Christian saint.

Cyril, Hawkes's narrator, whose last name (like those of the other characters) is never given, attempts to create an erotic idyl by establishing a sexual bond between himself and his wife, Fiona, and the married couple, Hugh and Catherine. Cyril would like their sexual quartet to be timeless, containing cyclical patterns of repetition and change. The two men and the two women can take turns making love to one another while remaining true to each other. The crucial question for Cyril is not one of morality, but of how this quartet can be set up without any loose ends and, even more importantly, how it can be secured and defended against loss of continuity. However, Hugh resents Cyril's machinations; he clings to traditional morals and, in the end, commits more or less accidental suicide. Even after this cataclysm, Cyril is still not ready to give up his plan for perfection. By telling the story of how he attempted to create this timeless erotic idyl to Catherine, who after Hugh's death has had a nervous breakdown and (conveniently for the narrator) refuses to speak, Cyril replaces the experiential idyl with a narrative idyl that is supposed to have similar qualities. This attempt at recasting "life" into narrative must fail, because it is belated, because it is a parody of life; this is not easy for Cyril to understand, since the similar interdependence between repetition and change created in the process of reading or listening to a text does indeed seem to justify his renewed impulse to achieve timelessness.

Cyril's desire is the same as that of his author: he wants to create synchrony within the narrative order. His story seeks to recreate the earlier idyl and, at the same time, to improve it in order to prevent a second failure. Improvement in this case means that Cyril breaks up the chronological sequence of events into short narrative vignettes or chapters and reorders them according to his own principle of emotional coherence. To give an example: when the two couples hold hands, they can never form the circle Cyril craves because Hugh has only one arm. They can only form a line. Since Cyril's plan requires Fiona to be connected with Hugh, the foursome must always hold hands in the following order: Catherine, Cyril, Fiona, Hugh. Now, when Cyril retells the story, he describes a visit he and Fiona had made to an old village church before the reader ever laid eyes on Hugh, so to speak. During this visit, Cyril at one point notices a life-sized wooden arm protruding over the edge of the pulpit. He points out to Fiona "the comic miracle of the arm in space, the wooden hand that no one would ever hold" (22). When Fiona fails to respond to this comic miracle, he argues to himself that the aesthetic pleasures of the wooden arm might be too subtle, even for the sensitive Fiona. If Fiona misses the comedy, the reader certainly should not, since the narrator implies that this is proof of an inability to perceive aesthetic pleasures. The reader at this point is also ignorant of the wooden arm's importance, and is only asked to note that it is, in some way, significant. Later, Hugh is presented to the reader as having the face of Saint Peter carved into the granite arch of the entrance to the church, and the reader can hardly help but conclude that Cyril is fitting the wooden arm, to which he had earlier drawn attention, into its proper place. By distorting the time sequence, the narrator creates the conditions necessary for the formation of a circle by four persons holding hands before the reader even knows that there is a need for such a circle. Thus Cyril constantly translates his cyclical time concept from life into story, relating it to the synchrony sought by the story's author.

The narrator in Ford's *The Good Soldier* is forced to distinguish between life and story (that is, he becomes a narrator in the first place) only because he never participates in the life story of the other characters. His very narrative presupposes his deficiency as a character. The life of Ford's narrator is completely eventless erotically: to all the women he meets, including his wife, he becomes, as he terms it, a male nurse. In contrast, the life of Edward Ashburnham, the narrator's antagonist and, as he would have it, alter ego, is punctuated by his various love affairs; their chronological sequence provides the only appearance of plot for the narrator's tale, which would otherwise seem to be completely confused. The story thus necessarily ends with Edward Ashburnham's final love, his all-consuming passion for his and his wife's ward, called "the girl." Remembering this episode, which ended with Edward's suicide and the girl's madness, the narrator ruminates about the nature of passion, asking himself why a man would fall in love with one woman after another, each time believing that this time he has found the one woman for him:

> It is impossible to believe in the permanence of any early passion. As I see it, at least, with regard to man, a love affair, a love for any definite woman—is something in the nature of a widening of the experience. With each new woman that a man is attracted to there appears to come a broadening of the outlook, or, if you like, an

acquiring of new territory. A turn of the eyebrow, a tone of the voice, a queer characteristic gesture—all these things, and it is these things that cause to arise the passion of love—all these things are like so many objects on the horizon of the landscape that tempt a man to walk beyond the horizon, to explore . . . And yet I do believe that for every man there comes at last a woman—or no, that is the wrong way of formulating it. For every man there comes at last a time of life when the woman who then sets her seal upon his imagination has set her seal for good. He will travel over no more horizons; he will never again set the knapsack over his shoulders; he will retire from those scenes. (108–9)

Ford's novel is constructed in accordance with this argument, or if the listener/reader prefers, in accordance with this belief of the narrator. The novel explores, in widening circles and going back and forth in time, the new features added to Edward's realm of experience by each new passion. The novel thereby manages to do what time denies the narrator's alter ego: it changes the sequence of love affairs into a continuum, or, in other words, it paradoxically manages to make Edward remain faithful to each of his loves. Up to the end Ford's novel thematizes what Cyril, in *The Blood Oranges*, becoming his author's alter ego, seeks to make into the structural principle of "his" characters' lives: the timeless continuum of repetition and change. The final failure of Cyril's design is foreshadowed by the observation of Ford's narrator, borne out by the structure of *The Good Soldier*, that a man's imagination will eventually be sealed to further experience by one final passion; Edward's suicide and the girl's madness are, in a sense, as much a failure of the narrator's imagination to otherwise end his novel as they are an existential failure of the characters themselves.

Hawkes's novel takes up these two tragic events in parodic fashion—with Catherine's nervous breakdown, which is not quite madness, and Hugh's questionable suicide. Hawkes is fascinated by the existential impact of these events and, at the same time, repelled by the narrative treatment they receive. His own novel therefore gives an answer to Ford's in the form of an erotic challenge. He denies the closure that Ford was ultimately willing to accept in the idea of one final passion, and by retelling the whole story in a different fashion—just as his narrator Cyril retells *his* story in a different fashion—he broadens the premises of his pre-text. "A turn of the eyebrow, a tone of the voice, a queer characteristic gesture," the things that, according to Ford, arouse the passion of love, can also be seen as metaphors of authorial strategies. Hawkes the author responds to Ford as in an erotic relationship, bestowing on that author's novel a fresh meaning by placing it within the enlarged context of Cyril's artistic reconstruction (subject to further interpretations/reconstructions) of his "life." At the same time, however, his own novel attempts to be like that last woman, setting its seal on Ford's novel for good. By having his own narrator revert to his past life story (a story like the one that the narrator of *The Good Soldier* tells, but in which he cannot participate), that is, by having him imitate yet transcend the role of Ford's narrator, Hawkes wants to preclude any further possible rewriting of Ford's novel.

The erotic relationship between texts, which I have portrayed as a love–hate relation, contains the respective authors' will to power as well as "mutual" respect. The will to power is exhibited when the later author makes use of his chronologically privileged position, which permits him to take up, transform, or even mock former literary themes or narrative strategies. However, just as for each individual woman within the string of Edward Ashburnham's mistresses, this privileged position is never secure: there may be yet another, more successful rewriting or parody of the same story, a rewriting that reduces its immediate predecessor's value. The evaluating process may also be reversed when the earlier text gains strength with each rewriting; this might be called an instance of the earlier author's will to power. It may instigate a later parody which is regressive in that its homage appears too complete, lacking the transforming power that would project it into the realm of future fiction. Progressive parody, on the other hand, in attempting to aggressively expand the premises of its pre-text, may not succeed in its project, and may thus lose even the generous reception which homage tends to inspire in the reader, who in any parody poses as the earlier author's alter ego.

An evaluation of regressive or progressive contemporary parody is difficult because it is uncertain whether the author gains or loses by his respective attitude. Yet, insofar as the parodying attitude has become part of the narrative structure of those texts, at least their historical place can be defined. Both regressive and progressive parody are responses provided by contemporary fiction to formation of an intertextual aesthetic. By inscribing his or her own parodic attitude into the text, the author substantiates the text: he or she can then treat the other text as a whole body that—just as a narcissistic mirror image—will reveal the identity of its challenger. Thus, the "death of the author" can be successfully circumvented if the contemporary author subscribes to parody.

On the literal level, contemporary erotic parody is ultimately paradoxical. While converting parody's diachronic features into supposed synchrony by treating its model as a contemporary text, it nevertheless repeats the diachronic "mistake" (as seen from an intertextual point of view) on another level. In negating the historic distance of the parodied model, contemporary parody implicitly dates itself—coming up as either regressive or progressive, prone either to self-love or self-hatred. Regressive parody, in reverting towards the canonized text, seems to grant its author the joy of identification with his own text, whereas progressive parody subjects its author to the pain of jealousy towards further versions of the parodied text. However, to the extent that the erotic form of regressive identification fails to distinguish between life and art, it must instill morality into art. Although moral fiction is not to be condemned out of hand, it still precludes a truly independent authorial attitude, since moral values depend upon established conventions. Progressive parody, on the other hand, while not without a concern for moral values, must subvert those that exist in order to enhance, rather than diminish, the difference between past and present texts, thus establishing between them a tension which serves to substantiate their separate identities. Progressive parody thus tends to instigate new fictional forms which must either be short-lived or gradually lose their progressive quality, since this quality depends not on social conditions, but on the self-perceived personality of the author. Although our predilections may lie with progressive parody, both forms, by synchronizing a diachronically oriented genre, are responses to the formation of intertextuality in a paradoxical attempt to overcome intertextuality in the name of, and for the sake of, the author.

Note

1. "Then a king's retainer, / A man proved of old, evoker of stories, / Who held in his memory multitude on multitude / Of the sagas of the dead, found now a new song / In words well linked: the man began again / To weave in his subtlety the exploit of Beowulf, / To recite with art the finished story, / To deploy his vocabulary." See *Beowulf: A Verse Translation into Modern English*, trans. Edwin Morgan (Berkeley and Los Angeles: University of California Press, 1966), 24.

Works Cited

Beowulf, with the Finnesburg Fragment. Edited by C. L. Wrenn. Rev. and enl. London: George G. Harrap, 1958.

Federman, Raymond. "Surfiction: Four Propositions in Form of an Introduction." In *Surfiction: Fiction Now and Tomorrow*, edited by Raymond Federman. 2d ed. Chicago: Swallow Press, 1981.

Ford, Ford Madox. *The Good Soldier: A Tale of Passion*. 1915. Reprint. Harmondsworth: Penguin, 1946.

Gardner, John. *Grendel*. New York: Ballantine, 1971.

Hawkes, John. *The Blood Oranges*. New York: New Directions, 1971.

Hutcheon, Linda. *A Theory of Parody: The Teachings of Twentieth-Century Art Forms*. London: Methuen, 1985.

The Ventriloquism of History

Voice, Parody, Dialogue

===

ALAN SINGER

> The higher a genre develops and the more complex its form,
> the better and more fully it remembers its past.
> —M. M. Bakhtin, *Problems of Dostoevsky's Poetics*

> The history of forms is one where subjectivity, the progenitor
> of forms, ends up being absorbed by them.
> —T. W. Adorno, *Aesthetic Theory*

Introduction: Novelistic History

The novel is our most prescient invocation of the past, of history. In *The Sense of an Ending* Frank Kermode reminds us of the truism that "novelty of itself implies the existence of what is not novel, a past" (117). Perhaps it follows that the novel is so inextricable from our experience of the past because, like history itself, the novel is formally a disjunctive moment expressed as a desire for conjunction. More conspicuously than other genres, the novel seeks its unity through heterogeneity. For it speaks obliquely, and nowhere more obliquely than in the convention of voice itself. Voice, the dominant metaphor for the totalizing power of novelistic form, is the genre's locus of subjectivity. But as such it is uniquely problematic, since novelistic voice is inherently and notoriously multiple: no *one* speaks in the novel. In its ineluctable multiplicity, novelistic voice subverts the unitary imperative of the very metaphor of human speech which otherwise endows its rhetorical aptitude. Novelistic voice is the annunciation of an intertextuality that shatters the subject who speaks of it.

Accordingly, recent theorists of the novel who want to assert its perspicuous historicity see the problematic of voice as precisely the touchstone of the genre's conceptual richness. Contemporary narrative theorists distinguish the novel from other literary genres according to the extremity of the problematic of voice.[1] For in novelistic voice, they argue, the human subject has manifestly experienced the vicissitudes of a crisis of self-knowledge that the genres of epic and lyric escape by their vicarious ahistoricality. By invidious comparison with the novel, epic and lyric are deemed to be

72

mouthpieces for a monologic subject—whether authorial or characterological—which is disguised to itself by the single-mindedness (single-voicedness) of its representations. According to this account, the paradox of voice in the novel is precisely what has made the genre a more rigorously philosophical enterprise than lyric or epic. The philosophical shadow cast longest on literary aesthetics in the twentieth century is that of Cartesian idealism; the idealist tradition has designated the subjective *cogito*, as a voice tragically divided from the world it speaks about, to be the insurmountable obstacle to its own historical self-realization. For post-Lukacsian theory this is the fate of the self which the novel has been bound to narrate by its formal complicity with such historical fatalism.

The recent currency of the theoretical writings of Mikhail Bakhtin gives new urgency to the idea that the novel is a vital confluence of history and subjectivity.[2] The force of Bakhtin's argument is carried in his assertion that the concept of voice is indistinguishable from the concept of dialogue. For Bakhtin, dialogical meaning in the novel is always articulated across the barrier of an intractable otherness: author vs. character, character point of view vs. character point of view. Speech gains intelligibility from neither the systematic integrity of the language nor the rhetorical fulcrum of authorial intention. Rather, this intelligibility is emergent from the ratio of perspectives that instantiates any social speech situation. In other words, novelistic dialogue conspicuously recapitulates the conflict internal to the idealist cogito by virtue of its inescapable temporality, for time separates identity into otherness. Because novelistic voice mediates our knowledge through differential relations rather than through the tropes of identity, Bakhtin maintains that the novel expresses the struggle of historical existence in human subjects with a lucidity unavailable to traditional paradigms of subjectivity. The intertextual imperative of the Bakhtinian novel thus comprehends the temporality of the subject without idealizing its historicity.

It is for this reason, I believe, that Bakhtin has been so enthusiastically appropriated by poststructuralist literary theory, which has sought to make history the new codex of literary value in order to subvert the hegemonic logocentrism of thematic and formalist criticism. Especially for those critics who identify themselves with "materialist" philosophy,[3] literary formalism, conducted under the sanction of the univocal or monologic subject, inhibits knowledge of how literature relates to the transformations of cultural life it is bound to reflect. This life it can only otherwise articulate in the unconscious gaps of its dogmatically ahistorical discourse. Thus for thinkers as diverse as Michel Foucault, Jacques Derrida, Paul de Man, Fredric Jameson, Louis Althusser, the category of history is posed against the classic values of the literary text: formal totality, self, ego, truth. History becomes the methodological pretext for dismantling the authority of the Cartesian cogito, for heralding an end to a homocentric *episteme*, for confronting our freedom by stripping off the hokey theatrical vestments of enshrined cultural identity.

In this essay I want to examine the use of the concept of history as a strategy for grounding literary value in the uniquely "critical" structures of subjectivity endowed by the novel. In this way I might specify the genre's general usefulness as a tool of speculative inquiry into the nature of human subjectivity. Nevertheless, while I will agree with Bakhtin that the category of history must be invoked to fend off the twin threats of formalist monism on the one hand and subjective relativism on the other, it will be necessary to specify the terms of dialogic history beyond the threshold of sheer otherness where Bakhtin leaves it. It will become clear, as I argue the benefits of situating his work in the context of T. W. Adorno's negative dialectic, that Bakhtin's history, articulated as unmediated difference, must be supplemented with a theory of contradiction and determinate negation if it is not to obscure the very process it is meant to reveal. Only in this way will history and subjectivity be brought into a conceptually productive relation to each other. Only a theory of contradiction will constrain us from departicularizing history in the guise of an autonomous transcendental subject or rendering the subject a threshold of relativity across which history is dispersed into infinite particularity. Indeed, only a reconciliation of contradiction and negation that is not a synthesis will account for an intertextuality that does not nullify its own historical determinations.

Furthermore, because Bakhtin's claim for the novel's unique powers to historicize converges upon the de-ontologizing postmodern scrutiny of organic form, I want to engage Bakhtin on the ground of the contemporary American novel. My exemplar will be William Gaddis, in whose work, I will argue, novelistic historicity is made decisively intelligible by the trope of parody. Gaddis's recent novel, *Carpenter's Gothic*, compels us to see how history can be elucidated through the concept of parody, when we remember how parody belies the unity of experience it articulates by proliferating differences on a premise of identity. For this reason, I will argue in turn that parody is the exemplary case of Bakhtinian dialogue. I want to test the validity of Bakhtin's attempt to re-ground formal study of the novel in dialogue and history. But more importantly, I want to show how in Bakhtin, any notion of history as a corollary of formal totality must entail a model of the subject that is assimilable to the concepts of transformation and transition; these concepts elucidate the experience of contradiction without mitigating its disjunctive and therefore vital temporality. Such, I believe, is the burden dialogue gives to parody in the dialogic imagination.

With this proviso, and contrary to the prevailing post-structuralist dogma, I want to insist that the dialectical path of the Bakhtinian novel in general, and Gaddis's novel in particular, does not lead us to a reckless dismantling of subjectivity, but to a redefining of subjectivity under the valid materialist constraint that refuses to allow interpretation to rest outside the tumult of historical changes it gives voice to. By refusing interpretation any extralocality in relation to historical change, the materialist subject is the irrepressible parodist of idealist notions of history. It is for this reason that Bakhtin himself specifically elides parody with history as a textual substrate of dialogue. Dialogic voice renders the individual voice indistinguishable from many voices insofar as it is specifically a function of social exchange—thus a counter of temporality. So history, within the expressive scope of the Bakhtinian novel, is a kind of parodic ventriloquism that speaks through the temporal contradictions it engenders, that is, the intrinsic intertextuality of the subject.

The Subject of Dialogue

Of course, if we are to hear the dialogic voice of history in all its subtly audible multiples of self, Bakhtin admonishes us to listen for it under the deceptively peaceful murmurings of the dominant ideology. By contrast with dialogue, ideological discourse enchants us into a stupor of uncritical reflection. It seduces us to the delusive harmonies of identity-based (rather than differentially based) language systems. Bakhtin judges ideological discourse to be too one-sided for the historical scope aspired to in dialogue because ideology is specifically not amenable to the exigencies of time. Therefore in the Bakhtinian novel we pious fathers of history must first be the skeptical children of ideology.

With this proposition we can begin to appreciate the usefulness of the Bakhtinian aesthetic as a fulcrum of ideological critique. Nevertheless, we must realize that if Bakhtin's dialogue is (on the basis of its powerful historicity) to benefit by invidious comparison with ideological discourse, it must further enable us to conceptualize the subject of history as an agent of historical change better than ideology. Above all, it must be able to specify the mediational terms of subjectivity precisely as ideological discourse does, but without reifying them in the modes of ideological production. In other words, if dialogue is to reveal its unique grasp of change better than ideological discourse, then the concept of dialogue must be reconciled with the perennial paradox of subject-object relations upon which every social or aesthetic totality produced within ideology rests. Yet it must do so, we will see, by proposing a subjective agency comparable to what Julia Kristeva has called a "subject-in-process." That is to say it requires an agency that is not subsumed within the deductive imperatives of its own telos. Indeed, Kristeva's portentous opening of the intertextual scene in contemporary criticism conspicuously defers to Bakhtinian dialogue as an imperative of change upon which subjectivity must converge in any self-understanding that does not preemptively reduce itself to a metaphysical reflection. Just as Kristeva says of intertextuality in general, that "it requires a new articulation of the thetic" (59–60; translation mine), so it may be said of dialogue specifically that its telos is continually assimilated to the agency which articulates it.

It follows that parody is arguably Bakhtin's most representative case of dialogue precisely because it so strongly intimates a subject-in-process as "a new articulation of the thetic." Parody is technically the appropriation of the voice of another twisted to new motives.[4] But Bakhtin's exposition preempts our construing an overly facile Nietzschean will to power by this gesture. On the contrary, because dialogic voice is so exclusively constituted on the threshold of otherness, whether it is the voice of self or other, parody in Bakhtin's special context eschews the teleological traps of intentionality and univocal meaning. Significantly, Bakhtin chooses the term *utterance* instead of *word* to designate the generative locus of meaning in parody. Utterance invokes the nonverbal imperatives of speech acts (intonation, scene, time, etc.).[5] The manifest overdetermination of the speech act designated in the term *utterance* requires a more dialectical notion of subjective agency than any intentional-teleological model of interpretation has yet offered. In any case, utterance, as Bakhtin defines it, is mediated too diversely to sustain the unity of the transcendental Cartesian subject presupposed in it.

The dialectical imperative of utterance impels us all the more strongly toward embracing the concept of a subject-in-process when we consider the dynamics of the social scene out of which dialogue and parody arise, according to Bakhtin. Though dialogue has its textual roots in the rhetorical forms of Menippean satire, Socratic irony, diatribe, and the seriocomic, its life spark is the social situation, the public *agora* wherein one's (authorial) meaning is necessarily mediated by the intentions of others. Bakhtin locates the originary scene of such mediations in the ritual armature of medieval carnival: the ceremonies of crowning and decrowning. The crowning and decrowning of a king is the essential carnivalistic act of Saturnalia, European carnival, etc. The emphasis on movement, transformation, transition, which is intrinsic to the ritual of crowning and decrowning, celebrates, as Bakhtin says, "the shift itself, the very process of replaceability" (*Problems* 125). In this regard, Bakhtin points out that the crowning/decrowning rituals in medieval carnival are analogous to the key tropes of Menippean and Socratic irony: anacrisis and syncrisis (the rhetorical triggers of classical parody) which progress by disjuncture. These tropes, by proposing communication across a brazen contradiction of styles, require a unique agency of transition in order to mediate differences without nullifying the differential play, the parodic spirit that animates them.

Furthermore, it is important to observe that the threshold of otherness by the cultural texts of carnival, parody, and dialogue (all roughly homologous in this perspective) is sharply distinguished by Bakhtin from what he considers to be the insufficiently dialectical mediations of merely "stylized" discourses. In the genre of stylized discourse, arising from a contradictory opposition of forms, meaning is expressed too simply in terms of a resolution of difference. Thus, transition is vitiated as an aspect of meaning, and the mobility of the subject presupposed in transition is rendered discursively inert. Bakhtin's insistence on the distinction between stylized and dialogical discourse compels our attention because it bears out his pragmatic stake in the mobility of the subject, in transition as a mode of intelligibility, whereby dialogism must be anchored in determinate moments but not confined to them in its way of articulating them.

With this preliminary understanding we are obliged to see that the warrant for Bakhtin's privileging of dialogue and parody requires him to demonstrate how, in these genres, otherness articulates difference over time without losing its historical specificity. Otherness itself must be reconciled with subjective agency. As if to meet this demand head-on, Bakhtin, from his earliest "Architectonics of Answerability," [6] elides dialogic/parodic meaning with the concept of action. Action definitively entails a change of state, a transitional moment. Dialogic discourse is deemed, above all else, to be an "activity," by virtue of its transitional recursiveness: that is, because the meaning of a word in dialogue is determined in the interpretation of "an other," the further dialectical entailment of intersubjective conflict is necessarily part of that interpretation. Michael Holquist summarizes this fundamental principle of dialogue: "Discourse does not reflect a situation; it is a situation" (204). The transitional movement valorized in the crowning and decrowning ritual is thus reflected under this principle with the implicit proviso that the resolution of "situations" in dialogue may never be abstracted from the conditions of their utterance.

Unfortunately, when Bakhtin attempts to elaborate the terms of otherness that would elucidate the analogy of parody/dialogue to action and thus render it a plausible site for historical specificity, his exposition attenuates to a set of conspicuously undialogical abstractions. Dialogue is profoundly mystified in the universalizing trajectory of phrases such as "joyful relativity" or "carnival sense of the world." Such characterizations imply that the only relevant "situation" of dialogue is the universality of difference or sheer alterity itself. Within the conceptual miasma of such abstraction, it would appear as if the historical "other" were indistinguishable from an ontological "other*ness*." That is to say, Bakhtin appears to open a methodologically unbridgeable gap between dialogism and dialogue.

Furthermore, Bakhtin's attempts to clarify the meaning of dialogic "activity" by stipulating the relation of self to other, such that one is not lost or subsumed in the other, result only in an apparently irrational juxtaposition of contradictory motives: on the one hand, the threshold of otherness is deemed to be intentional so as to preserve its historical specificity; on the other, the threshold of otherness is deemed to be universal so as to transcend the teleological boundaries of intentionality and the subject–object dichotomy which imposes them. Indeed, the tropological roots of dialogue, anacrisis and syncrisis, which as I've already mentioned go deeply into the Menippean bedrock of dialogue, already adumbrate the contradictory imperative of this thought. Syncrisis, "the juxtaposition of various points of view on an object," presumes upon a threshold of unmotivated difference; anacrisis, "a means for eliciting and provoking one's interlocutor," denotes a threshold of intentional difference (*Problems* 110). Precisely because both tropes are sedimented at the same level in Bakhtin's archeology of dialogue, he fails to articulate the contradiction between them as a meaningful exigency of the literary practice he wants to valorize.

To make matters worse, Bakhtin's most sympathetic commentators conspicuously founder on the contradictory coordinates of his theory by ignoring them. For example, in his enthusiastic preface to *Problems of Dostoevsky's Poetics*, Wayne Booth is driven to conflate intentional with differential imperatives in dialogue, in order to transcend the necessity of a logical transition between them. The result is that Booth confuses the dialogic moment with temporal immediacy. From that rhetorical springboard, Booth is obliged to make the dangerous leap into an airy (because conceptually empty) sublime, asserting that dialogue is unspecifiable except in terms of what Longinus called "a sublimity of freed perspectives" (xx).

Quite to the contrary, Bakhtin himself is adamant that sublimity, as a definitive measure of the mind's inability to particularize its experience (and hence its inability to historicize), subsists exclusively in a monologic negation of nature. More importantly, the abstraction that obtains in sublimity, through its negation of historical immediacy, eschews the very subjective mobility that gives an ethical burden to carnival in the first place. Indeed, this degree of abstraction vitiates any concept of authorial will or formal totality by which we would be able to designate some texts as dialogic and others as not. Bakhtin thwarts all such logical purifications of his thought, finally, by unequivocally asserting that dialogic carnival

> is not: naked, absolute negation and destruction (absolute negation, like absolute affirmation is unknown to carnival). Moreover, precisely in this ritual of decrowning does there emerge with special clarity the carnival pathos of shifts and renewals, the image of constructive death . . . we repeat, crowning and decrowning are inseparable, they are dualistic and pass one into the other; in any absolute dissociation they would completely lose their carnivalistic sense. (*Problems* 125)

Clearly Bakhtin wants to sustain subjective mobility as reciprocally a condition and an end of dialogic intelligibility. For this enterprise he must be able to specify the historical particulars of the dialogic situation dialectically, but without precipitously resolving the dialectic in that gesture. This, I believe, is the methodological demand that dialogism makes upon itself, while it simultaneously denies itself the conceptual resources to answer.

Dialogue as Contradiction

We have arrived at an apparent impasse in Bakhtin's theory. We can see that the concept of dialogue is precisely what makes Bakhtin's theory of language transpersonal and therefore conducive to the critique of idealism so pervasive in contemporary literary theory. But now we must acknowledge that his novel concept also manifestly fails to account for the specific agency of its own unique mediation of difference through transition, such that it can elude the solipsistic nominalism of intentionalist (Cartesian) subjectivity on the one hand and resist the pull of sheer relativity or difference on the other.

For these reasons, I want to propose that the most constructive way to follow Bakhtin's arguments to their desired conclusion—that dialogue is a basis of aesthetic form in the novel (i.e., intentional) and a threshold of sociolinguistics that transcends literary form (i.e., relative)—might be to construe Bakhtin's "otherness" as contradiction per se. In other words, in order to transcend the contradiction between intentionalist and relativist imperatives at the heart of Bakhtin's theory of dialogue, parody, and the novel, we must construe contradiction itself as the methodological fulcrum of dialogic enterprise. Only by this means can we ascribe agency to the historical experience which Bakhtin is obliged to elucidate. Whereas in Bakhtin's lexicon dialogue is sometimes definable as a variable of intention and sometimes as a variable of free relativity, contradiction reciprocally expresses both the universality of difference and the specificity or determinateness of temporality and plot. After all, contradiction requires a structure of resemblance that is temporally prior to its articulations.

It is true that in *Problems of Dostoevsky's Poetics* there is a curious attempt by Bakhtin to distinguish dialogue and dialectic as if otherness could be divorced from time.[7] But in the Bakhtinian texts that give the fullest scope to dialogism, "Discourse in the Novel" and *Marxism and the Philosophy of Language*, the author seems to realize, as have all powerful theorists of mediation, that because contradiction depends on resemblance, as well as on difference, it preeminently marks the onset of time. Time, in other words, is the difference between contradiction and difference. My claim that Bakhtinian otherness entails contradiction rather than mere difference is buttressed by the fact that temporality is itself fundamentally articulated as contradiction in the speculative tradition which Bakhtin wants to continue. Contradictions are after all the propulsive moments of the Hegelian dialectic. Bakhtin seems to aspire to a Hegelian order of historical determinations in his much-touted pledge to restore the time of social reality to artistic language. But Bakhtin is plausibly even more radical than Hegel (and therefore even more congenial to recent materialist thinkers) precisely because his dialogue does not ultimately render the threshold of contradiction timeless (through *geist*), but effectively proliferates historically determinate moments by insisting upon the absolute irreducibility of their contradictions. Or at least Bakhtin points out this epistemological path by foregrounding the intrinsic recursiveness of the social exchange upon which dialogue is premised. If the dialogic voice can only be intelligible in terms of the response it gets, we might justifiably surmise that the meaning of the whole "utterance" can only be clarified as a deliberate proliferation of contextual contingencies upon which interpretation will thereafter subsist.

The importance of this point is best observed when we recall that a popular straw man in Bakhtinian argument is Saussure, who privileged the systematic (synchronic) and thus timeless aspect of language over the temporally bounded performance (diachrony) of individual speakers. Saussure's aim was precisely to escape the "unscientific" contingencies of *parole*. Bakhtin evokes a striking contrast with the Saussurean stance in *Marxism and the Philosophy of Language*, where he observes that dialogic utterance is fundamentally a "value judgment" generated out of the contradiction between two aspects of the word: theme, which designates the historical instant of utterance, and meaning, which designates the parts of utterance that are repeatable, the self-identical components of systematic language. The relationship between theme and meaning is necessarily expressed as contradiction, but it becomes quite clear that contradiction may be said here to be constitutive of utterance precisely insofar as utterance (meaning) is recursive for theme. Bakhtin specifically elaborates this point:

> There is nothing in the structure of signification that could be said to transcend the generative process, to be independent of the dialectical expansion of social purview. Society in process of generation expands its perception of the generative process of existence. There is nothing in this that could be said to be absolutely fixed. And this is how it happens that meaning—an abstract self-identical element—is subsumed under theme and *torn apart by theme's living contradictions* so as to return in the shape of a new meaning with a fixity and self-identity only for the while, just as it had before [emphasis added]. (Volosinov 106)

Because theme is articulated in the instant of speech and is thus, by definition, unreproducible, the contradictions it embodies are not expressible except as theme is differentially related to the contingencies of its expression. Theme may only be said to be "torn apart by living contradictions," as Bakhtin claims, if we acknowl-

81

edge that such contradictions constitute a return of meaning, that is, the transformation of the relations between theme and meaning, self and other. Bakhtin generalizes that value, issuing from this threshold of contradiction, always depends on an "evaluative orientation," with the proviso that "a change in meaning is essentially always a reevaluation: the transposition of some particular word from one evaluative context to another." We must appreciate how Bakhtin's notion of "evaluative orientation" here explicitly recalls and reemphasizes the transitional moment of ritual crowning and decrowning in carnival which is central to the conceptual efficacy of dialogue. We will recall that such a moment always redounds to a transformation of the terms which articulate it. Its intelligibility, then, is intrinsic to its recursiveness, and its recursiveness is a proliferation of its contingencies. We may now adopt the viewpoint that it is precisely the contingencies of expression which dialogue preeminently expresses, rather than the mere fact of its own intrinsic otherness. Thus, dialogism would no longer float free as a term designating the radical otherness of "joyful relativity." It would be more meaningfully anchored in the determinations that change it; transition would be assimilable to formal/social totality. If, in dialogue, contingencies are proliferated through contradiction, we could say that contradiction is revealed rather than resolved through a mode of representation that, as a result, entails the temporality of reflection. This mode of representation follows the original epistemological path of dialogue, which was intended to move language towards the status of act. Following this deduction, I believe we can more confidently conceptualize dialogue, along with Bakhtin, as a mediation that preserves its own historical particularity but nonetheless transcends the idealism of intentional consciousness through which we first objectified it.

Negative Dialogue: Bakhtin and Adorno

Even Bakhtin's most enthusiastic recent commentators have ignored the line of argument I am pursuing here, in part, I believe, because it is not congenial with the more radical poststructuralist purge of subjectivity. For example, Paul de Man, in his professedly appreciative overview of Bakhtin's achievement (in *The Resistance to Theory*), observes a metaphysical *impensé* in Bakhtin's exposition of dialogue. This, he argues, mitigates its lucidity with respect to the exigencies of textual interpretation. De Man's diagnostic finger points to "Discourse in the Novel" as Bakhtin's most symptomatic text. Here, says de Man, Bakhtin posits the absolute discontinuity between intentionalist discourse (de Man calls it tropological) and dialogic discourse, while ignoring the contradiction that binary opposition is itself tropological, which is to say (intentional) nondialogical. In this analysis, de Man rightly sees what we have also noted, that Bakhtin needs to assimilate the notion of agency to otherness in order to realize the fullest conceptual potential of the dialogic principle—but that he cannot specify terms for such a conceptualization that do not devolve to a devastating self-contradiction: "The ideologies of otherness and of hermeneutic understanding are not compatible, and therefore their relationship is not a dialogical but simply a contradictory one. It is not a foregone conclusion whether Bakhtin's discourse is itself dialogical or simply contradictory" (de Man 112). I would suggest that de Man does not see how the move from dialogism to dialogue can take place in Bakhtinian theory precisely because he does not see contradiction as intrinsic to dialogic discourse. In this essay, de Man, like many poststructuralists, will not conceive of otherness except as radical otherness, sheer alterity. Therefore, he cannot construe otherness as an aspect of temporality or a motor of transition. By contrast, Bakhtin is emphatic (in the very text that de Man cites) that the historical reality disclosed in dialogue renders otherness indistinguishable from the process of historical change: "Historical reality is an arena for the disclosure and unfolding of human characters—nothing more" (Bakhtin, *Dialogic Imagination* 114). The significant assertion here is that the determinateness of history is now predicated on a concept of totality, the disclosure of which is its transformation and the result of which is its narrative momentum.

So despite his professed enthusiasm for Bakhtin, de Man might make us doubt the much-touted affinity between dialogism and the timeless, subjectless, relativistic drift of poststructuralist ideology. On the contrary, if there is a continuity between Bakhtin and contemporary theory, I would argue that we should look for it in the belated and therefore even more profoundly historical influence of the Frankfurt school. In particular, we should look to the work of T. W. Adorno, for whom contradiction as a mediating term that grounds historicizing consciousness suggests precisely the possibility (contra de Man) that otherness (nonidentity) and hermeneutic understanding can be compatible.

The success of Adorno's effort to salvage Hegelian negation for a historical hermeneutic rests on the term *nonidentity*. Nonidentity stipulates an otherness which does not pass away within the negating consciousness (it becomes instead a constitutive contingency of the agency expressed or represented in it). Adorno vehemently distinguishes this agency from the Hegelian "negation of the negation." Specifically, it is not subsumed by a Hegelian *geist*. It is true that both Hegel's and Adorno's models of mediation seem to present an equally striking complement to Bakhtinian dialogue (one that is even more specifically grounded in contradiction than Bakhtin's, whether it is the contradiction between *begriff* and *sache* [Hegel] or between mental and manual labor [Adorno]). Furthermore, the constitutive moment of the subject in both Hegel and Adorno is marked on a threshold of otherness whereupon the subject adapts to the contours of its object, thus adumbrating the paradigm of Bakhtinian dialogue. But, as I have already hinted, Adorno radically departs from the Hegelian course and calls Bakhtin more exclusively to mind at precisely that point where he faults Hegel for subsuming the tension between subject and object within the negative moment rather than redeploying that tension as the generative structure of its own reflection.

Adorno's attack on the Hegelians is sharpest in the charge that "they hope to conceal mediations instead of reflecting them" (70). Here the echoes of Bakhtin's insistence on the ineluctability of the generative process of dialogue (hence its relation to historical reality) suggest that Adorno and Bakhtin share a commitment to the materiality of the moment, to the realm of temporality which reveals no inner essences. The Hegelian negation, in Adorno's view, abandons the proper task of philosophy, which is to recover to thought (reflection) the content that subsuming judgment has eliminated, thus preserving in the nonidentity of the reflective moment the dialectical movement of history—what he calls "determinate negation." Bakhtin's dialogic novel satisfies the dialectical requirements of Adorno's determinate negation by similarly resisting any easy conflation of self and other, author and character, part and whole. More important, however, Adorno's negative dialectic suggests how the otherness of dialogue might be specifically conducive to hermeneutic enterprise insofar as it (otherness) entails a return to the differences which instantiated it. For the negated (or in Bakhtin's terms, the dialogized) other necessarily makes the negating subject different from itself, that is, temporalizes it or interprets it rather than making it abstract. For Adorno, the moment negated emphatically preserves its historicity when it is interpreted according to the first nature that passed away within it. Once again he contrasts his thinking with Hegel's: "In forgetting . . . at each new dialectical stage the right of the preceding one, Hegel produces the very image of what he takes abstract negation to task for:

abstract positivity dependent on subjective arbitrariness for its con-firmation" (Adorno 162). Insofar as Adorno persuades us that the fruits of negation are inextricable from the interpretive (critical) activity which produces them, that is, from the hermeneutic task, I believe that we have grounds to discount Bakhtin's loose pheno-menalizing of dialogue as "pure relativity" or "becoming," which likewise eludes any hermeneutic determination.[8] On the contrary, we have a greater warrant to emphasize instead those theoretical moments in Bakhtin that are committed to making history *livable* in dialogue. For in this regard Bakhtin's conceptual ends share more with Adorno than his methodological means might seem to distinguish him.

Indeed, at this crossroads of argument, Adorno's usefulness for clarifying the mediational imperatives of dialogic discourse be-comes even more compelling, since Adorno's thinking is worked out in relief against the philosophy of his influential mentor and friend, Walter Benjamin. Adorno observes in Benjamin a self-contradictory desire to negate the world while eschewing any ground of determination beyond the negation itself. The resem-blance with Bakhtin's desire to historicize without a methodology whereby he can distinguish historical moments provides an occa-sion to reemphasize Bakhtin's need for a more dialectical concept of mediation (despite Bakhtin's repudiation of dialectic in *Problems* 36) than he is inclined towards in his most influential discoursings upon the dialogic imagination. In his critique of Benjamin's es-say "The Work of Art in Its Age of Mechanical Reproduction," Adorno finds his most decisive occasion for speculating in the di-rection of more dialectical mediations. His argument is all the more pertinent to the issues raised by Bakhtin, because it specifically de-fends the formal autonomy of the work of art. Thus, it is especially congenial to Bakhtin's project of elaborating a theory of history through the form of the novel. Benjamin had repudiated the au-tonomous work of art on purportedly "materialist" grounds in *The Origin of the German Tragic Theater*. He had long held that historical meaning could be derived from the mediations of consciousness only through a "discontinuous finitude" exemplified by the form of allegory. Allegory guaranteed a discontinuous finitude in its ob-trusion of an insuperable otherness (presented by the tropological figure itself). In fact, Benjamin's rich notion of allegory as a work that expresses the nonidentical relation of mind to nature followed suit with Adorno's own conviction that the mediation of subject and object was substantial, and historically anchored only insofar as it was a mediation by the social totality in all its concreteness. For

Adorno, the detotalizing overdeterminations of the social totality opened upon the process of historical change. Adorno's initial enthusiasm for Benjamin's work on allegory led him (in *Die Idee der Naturageschichte*) to declare that the "theme of the allegorical is decisively history" (Buck-Morss 358). Allegory facilitated the demolition of the false appearance of totality given by unreflective images of history. Indeed, the myth of history as a structured totality (which is the rhetorical complement of Bakhtin's monologic discourse) was critiqued by both Adorno and Benjamin for its appearance of self-sufficiency.

Nevertheless, when Benjamin went further to analogize mythic history to the aura of self-sufficiency presented by the formal/aesthetic rules of the artwork, he inexplicably ignored what Adorno took to be the most compelling aspect of the artwork: its mediation of the artist and his material exclusively according to the technical laws of its own construction/tradition. Adorno accused Benjamin of disregarding an elementary experience embodied by the work of art: "That precisely the utmost consistency in the pursuit of the technical laws of autonomous art *changes* this art, and instead of rendering it into a taboo or fetish, approximates it to the state of freedom, as something that can be produced and made consciously" (Buck-Morss 13; emphasis added). Adorno argued that art did not present an impenetrable totalization in its formal integrity; instead, Adorno postulated art's transformative power, hence its historicality, as brought about by the dialectical relation between the artist and the historically developed techniques of the artwork, a relation that he felt was already epitomized in Benjamin's allegory.

The negative moment of the artwork is never empty of historical particulars for Adorno, because the irreducible facticity of technical laws, vis-à-vis praxis, entails the automatic recursiveness of the concept expressed in the work's technique. The artwork exemplifies what Adorno called "the riddle character" of interpretation, which necessitates a transformation of the artistic image. This transformation is catalyzed by the discrepancy between praxis and technical laws, which obtains as the very condition of its occurrence. Just as every negation of a primary nature entails not simply a secondary nature but its "interpretation," so the artistic image, in the necessity it occasions for interpreting technical rules (by executing them), changes those rules determinately. By comparison, Adorno saw that Benjamin's blind negation of aesthetic rules themselves was historically empty, particularly when Benjamin postulated the negative potency of the artwork as an inverse proportion of the alienating technologies of modern art production. Within this perspective Adorno realized that the work of art could never get beyond the negative moment itself. The negation of the work of art, unreflected in the rules of aesthetic form, would result only in an irrational fragmentation of mental experience, verging on a historically retrograde mysticism. We can hardly forget that the same charge is hurled against Bakhtin when, conjuring the aura of a "joyful relativity," he loses his methodological grasp of the particular concrete historical determinants of dialogic otherness.

In Bakhtin's *The Formal Method in Literary Scholarship*, however, there is a notable complement to Adorno's criticism of Benjamin, which will bring us back to the issue of contradiction, where we left off our consideration of literary form proper. It will at the same time reassert the value of juxtaposing Bakhtin with a more methodologically rigorous thinker such as Adorno in order to unlock the richest potential of dialogue. Adorno's investment in aesthetic form is especially pertinent for the purposes of any literary critic who wants to exploit Bakhtinian theory for literary study, since Bakhtin posits the aesthetic form of the novel as prior to the possibility of any meaningful sociolinguistics. In *The Formal Method* Bakhtin attacks Russian formalism for privileging the literary device over thematic material exclusively in terms of its negation of that thematic material, rather than, to borrow Adorno's term, the further *interpretation* of the negation. Bakhtin conceives the possibility of salvaging the concepts of motive and device (which are crucial to the description of artistic form and which he believes the formalists have rendered abstract beyond usefulness) only by attending to a specific quality of artistic structure itself; this he takes as preliminary to any meaningful judgment of artistic validity:

> We are only provided with a real criterion for a decision when there is an obvious *contradiction* between the artistic plan and its fulfillment, i.e, when the work is immanently unsuccessful. Only such a work contains elements which are superfluous to the construction and only function to introduce others. Other than this, only caprice and crude subjectivism are able to make a differentiation between motivation and device a part of the interpretation of the poetic structure. (116)

Here literary form may be productively engaged by the critic insofar as the form itself is discerned in the self-transformative capacity of its own articulations. Here I believe we can listen for an echo of Adorno, who would say that the contradiction between artistic plan and its fulfillment is immanent to the plan, and that this is the link between the "immanently unsuccessful" and the principle of transformation that animates the riddle character of interpretation. According to the analysis he performs here, we can imagine that Bakhtin's ideal dialogic text would now acquire the historical density of a more determinate mediation (as Adorno proposes) than he indicates in other phases of argument, owing chiefly to the new emphasis he places on contradiction. For contradiction in this passage would seem to be indistinguishable from a proliferation of contextual contingencies marked in "elements which are superfluous . . . and function only to introduce others." In other words, it is contradiction which, for Bakhtin as for Adorno, would make an immanent critique uniquely possible without relapse into crude subjectivism on the one hand or mysticism on the other.

The Dialogic Novel as an Agency of Reflection: The Example of William Gaddis

I have already suggested that a useful way of construing parody, as the exemplary dialogic discourse, is to understand it as a proliferation of contingencies within an apparent resemblance. In this way, it neither reifies or absorbs the otherness by which it articulates its meaning. So, standing once again on the threshold of contradiction (which depends upon the contradictory appearance of a resemblance within a difference) and now able to see how contradiction can be the motor of a dialectic that does not elude historical particulars, we may return to the parodic impetus of the novel proper. We are now prepared to discuss the novel's aptness as a model of human subjectivity which can, as Bakhtin intimates, redeem historical subjects to a more productive relation with their social totality.

My particular argument that parody is the best representative case of dialogue/novel depends, as we have seen, on a modification of Bakhtinian dialogue so as to reconcile radical otherness with the temporal constraints of transition and determinate negation. As Bakhtin chose Dostoevsky to be the famous exemplar of novelistic dialogue, I have chosen William Gaddis to be an exemplar for the modifications I am working on Bakhtinian theory. By looking at the enabling conditions of Gaddis's rhetoric in *Carpenter's Gothic*, I hope to give further warrant for the need to take Bakhtin into serious account, thus inversely making Bakhtin's formulation yield a more serious account of temporality as a determining aspect of literary form. Gaddis is most conspicuously a novelist of dialogue because his novels are written pervasively in dialogue, but even more significantly because his dialogue is wrought with such syntactical "otherness" as to epitomize the distinction between the Bakhtinian nuance of the term and its conventional referent. In Gaddis's characteristic dialogue, rendered as it is without secure pronomial markers or linear punctuation, voice crosses the syntactical boundaries of person and theme. The conventional totalizing power of voice is denied by a syntactical fluidity which precludes a lucid thematization. Thus the distinction between the critique of the subject and its most naive embodiments, so potent in Bakhtin's sense of dialogue, emphatically becomes the crux of narrative development in this fiction.

Bakhtin said of Dostoevsky that, above all, his dialogic novels do what parodists have done from classical times: they call unified language into question. Gaddis's polyphonic prose gives an eloquent gloss on this characterization of the premier dialogist, but without indulging the attendant banalities of leaving the "question" open-ended in a relativistic drift of meaning. By denying himself a fixed place in relation to his language, by *enacting* intertextuality, and by making voice a shifting horizon of perspective, Gaddis confers on his prose the character of mediation that specifically mitigates the inside/outside distinction that makes any thematic abstraction originally possible. I believe it is this distinction, insofar as it serves as the basis of the theme–form dichotomy, which Bakhtin himself sought to discredit in his most generalized definition of the novel as any expression within a linguistic system that acknowledges its own limits.[9] We shall see that despite its seemingly unbounded voices, Gaddis's writing is not reducible even to a thematic of sheer otherness precisely because it inhibits thematic knowledge per se by articulating it at the limit of its intelligibility.

This argument is already underway in the self-mocking reflexivity of Gaddis's title. *Carpenter's Gothic* specifically refers to a Hudson River style of architecture which mimes the stonework of European medieval stone gothic in wood. The exterior appearance of large graciously proportioned rooms is belied by an interior without a plan. The craftsmen worked from design books of European facades, not from the sculptural exigencies of stone and wrought iron. Indeed, because the builders were interested only in outward appearance, the interiors were, of necessity, an irrational patchwork. By definition, theme is incompatible with form in the hallmarks of this style. The thematic depth inferred from the bold facade returns the gaze abruptly to the material surface. One confronts the self-contradiction of this style like walking into a mirror. By its facelessness, the inside renders the outside more conspicuously a facade, but one which cannot be detached to be revealed. Mr. McCandless, the character in *Carpenter's Gothic* who reflects on these facts most self-consciously, is prompted to see in this architectural *trope* l'oeil, a reflection of the inside of his own head. Mc-Candless's mind is aptly proffered as a cerebral core of the book, a thematic recess, the "voice" of the book's truth. But because Mc-Candless's mind is inextricable from the epistemic problems of the architectural model it reflects, his voice comes under a scrutiny that it cannot bear without revealing its insubstantiality to be its only infrastructure. More specifically, it will become clear that the formal elements of Gaddis's novel mediate the thematic content of voice so as to make thematic meaning—as Bakhtin suggests in *Marxism and the Philosophy of Language*—a contingency of historical development rather than to make history a contingency of theme.

I am proposing that in order to appreciate the formal innovation of Gaddis's novel, we must read it as a critique of the form of the genre conceived under the metaphor of voice. I believe this was Bakhtin's chief impetus in showing how voice is inherently double and so irrecuperable to any thematic gloss that is not itself subject to the temporal exigencies of form (once again mitigating the distinction between inside and outside). Above all, we must understand that despite its omnipresence in a novel of dialogue, in Gaddis's fiction voice is meant only to be an ever more provisional category of intelligibility.

Parody is a particularly apt tool in this undertaking because, as I have defined it in Bakhtinian terms, it productively entails the time that thematic closure typically reduces to the timeless unity of voice. In Aristotelian narrative plot, closure confers the identity of voice through the elimination of temporality as an ungovernable contingency. In the subordination of voice to plot, the reader of conventional narrative enjoys a spectacular simplification of time, whereby the contemplative activity of reading is spatialized by the mesmerizing contours of scenic spectacle. We recognize time to be Gaddis's parodic object in *Carpenter's Gothic* because here time is deliberately complicated (rather than simplified) by voice, producing a ruthless de-realization of scenic spectacle. Specifically, as I have already indicated, in *Carpenter's Gothic* the proliferation of voices without clear syntactic or pronominal distinctions makes temporality irreducible to voice. By using voice to subvert the stable temporality of conventional plot, Gaddis is revealing the secret complicity of voice with plot and theme in all the monologisitic modes of conventional fiction. By contrast, the urgency of Gaddis's dialogism relates to our incipient freedom from the thematic constraints of voice, and thus to the disclosure of the parodic potential of all plot, which is time. Time, the knowledge of which monologic plot eclipses behind the fatalistic tropes of closure, is here found mugging in the mirror of plot's most sobering mimesis.

We can capture the best reflection of time's parodic countenance in Gaddis's prose by juxtaposing the syntactic rigors of a representative passage with the unifying imperative of the novel's would-be theme: the tragicomic return of all of the characters in *Carpenter's Gothic* to the primal Gregory Rift in Africa, where human time began. The return to the rift portends the ultimate thematization of dramatic plot, which is to say, the ultimate dream of historical fulfillment—for in the origin of time is its proverbial negation. All of Gaddis's characters are seeking to resolve the contradictions of a history that has cheated them of identity. They are drawn towards the rift as towards a threshold of self-redemption. Yet the consummation of the thematic return to the rift is most spectacularly abortive in *Carpenter's Gothic* insofar as the theme of the rift itself punningly echoes the very rhetorical mediations of Gaddis's prose, which preempt (at least for the reader) any such interpretive return to monologistic bliss: such is the syntactical rift between voice and person that makes the contingencies of self-presentation the sole constraint of thematization in *Carpenter's Gothic*.

I want to insist nevertheless that the perspectival drift in the rifted syntax cannot be read thematically as loss of meaning or the nostalgia for an Edenic permanence, even proffered as it is here in the guise of an archeological site which can be, albeit laboriously, dug up. Neither can the rifted syntax be generalized as the tragedy of history. History made into a metaphor for loss would be too perversely departicularized in the very access to time which is otherwise nothing but particular in its mediations of human fate. On the contrary, I would say that this novel is preoccupied with the impossibility of loss where there is no object to recover from the shifting rifts of perspective. Gaddis's concern is with the mediation of the experience of loss, not the experience of loss itself. As is the case in Adorno's precept that negation entails interpretation for its most decisive knowledge, I believe that in the apparent loss of syntactical perspectives by which Gaddis's novel progresses, there arises a conspicuous structure of interpretation, possessing its own temporal determinations. In other words, the rift of perspective itself becomes a reflective ground in Gaddis's prose, which, insofar as it obtrudes its own particulars, resists thematic generalization without surrendering its thematic rationality.

The complex mediation valorized here, insofar as it preserves the particulars of its agency in the course of transformation, has no more dialogic exemplification than in a passage where Liz Booth, Gaddis's Dickensian heroine, is caught up in the doubly duplicitous act of composing/plagiarizing a line of fiction. Appropriately, by mirroring the project of Gaddis's multiple-voiced novel, the passage makes the parody of authorship its most eloquent expression of authorial agency:

> Knees drawn up she pulled the towel round her bared shoulders and a shiver sent breath through her, staring at that page till she seized the pencil to draw it heavily through his still, sinewed hands, irregular features, the cool disinterested calm of his eyes and a bare moment's pause bearing down with the pencil on his hands, disjointed, rust spotted, his crumbled features dulled and worn as the bill collector he might have been mistaken for, the desolate loss in his eyes belying, belying . . . The towel went to the floor in a heap and she was up naked, legs planted wide broached by scissors wielded murderously on the screen where she dug past it for the rag of a book its cover gone, the first twenty odd pages gone in fact, so that it opened full on the line she sought coming down with the pencil on belying a sense that he was still a part of all that he could have been (95).

The rifted syntax, inaugurating the paragraph with an unpunctuated dependency, epitomizes the problem presented by Gaddis's prose in its apparent dismemberment of what it seeks to unify. At the same time, such syntax portends a succinct elucidation of this problem. For the run-on of the dangling or dismembered part "knees drawn up" with the full predication of "she pulled the towel" explicitly entails contradiction as a threshold of its formal reconstitution. Its reconstitution as a scenic/grammatical whole wherein the knees can be integrated with the rest of Liz's body and the dependency is integrated with a complete predicate is an inescapable imperative of its composition here. Simply because the dangling clause is so emphatically a part before it is a whole, temporality conspicuously obtrudes in its representation. Such is the case with the rest of the paragraph, where all our attempts at assembling parts devolve to a transitional movement between apparently mutually exclusive scenic gestalts. For example, the knees and the hands of the author are jumbled with those of her character. The diction of the text "belying" authorial presence is transposed with the diction of narrative itself, which calls attention to itself belying authentic inspiration. Furthermore, the natural subsumption of verbal particulars to thematic wholes (signaled in this familiar problematic of parts and wholes), is frustrated by the increasing abstraction of the verbal parts themselves. As the verbal parts are more and more atomized by rifted syntax, and as it is increasingly difficult to parse the integrative functions of words/phrases in this paragraph, we realize how their functions (because they are so insistently mediated by contradiction) may be reciprocal for contradictory contexts: Liz's hands bearing down on the pencil "bear" the hands "disjointed, rust spotted" of the character in her manuscript without bridging the contexts between them.

As we have discussed already, contradiction, founded on resemblance, represents the temporal shift that sheer difference, by its deferral of the representational moment, must restrict to metaphysical intuitions. Thus we may generalize that in this paragraph, the more atomistic the parts, the more their differentials come to be reflected in them as a structure through which they change, effectively rendering the parts recursive for the whole. For example, the "bare shoulders" "bearing down" are only construable "parts" of a totalizing metaphoric intuition when they "belie" their metonymic succession. But the succession itself is contrived so that it articulates itself more fully through the metaphoric structure superinduced upon it. This reciprocal determination of parts is even more conclusive in the deliberate shuffling of scenic frames that propels the narrative exposition in this passage. An implicit prepositional ambiguity hovers over the entire passage as the agency of transposition: there are the hands represented on/in the manuscript page of Liz's novel, the scissors wielded in/against the "legs planted wide" and the rag of a book located in/beyond the television screen where the reaching hands are illuminated by it. The apparent superimposition of scenic coordinates occasioned in this prepositional ambiguity is a result of the elided transitions between discontinuous contextual frames. Paradoxically, this is to make transition (in space but necessarily in time) the most pervasive aspect of the text, since every contextual frame would seem to open spontaneously onto another contextual frame without a definitive revelation of its contents.

Finally, the fact that the paragraph culminates in a highly theatricalized plagiarism (where, by definition, contextual frames are indistinguishable from what they frame) tempts us to abstract the diverse formal parts to the integrative thematic whole which this prose has resisted so powerfully from the start. Indeed, the juxtaposition of the concept of plagiarism with the scenic ambiguities of the prose taunts a fashionable thematization in terms of the metafictional regress of rational perspectives, wherein fact is revealed to be indeterminately relative to fiction. Such, after all, is always the

ALAN SINGER

epistemological taunt of plagiarism. I believe that above all else, however, the distinction of Gaddis's fiction is that here, the act of plagiarism remains profoundly "a part of all [it] could have been," in such a way that form and theme decisively do not coincide. Gaddis refuses the invidious choice of plagiarism versus authenticity, fact versus fiction. In doing so he insists that the relative values of each scenic particular of the paragraph can only be said to claim significance in relation to the whole as they elaborate the problem of scenic construal rather than solving it. Indeed, the "he" in the last line may now be said to be interpreted (in Adorno's sense) rather than thematized, by the conflation of past tense with the conditional future perfect that articulates his presence. The inherently contradictory reference of the pronoun (he) to an antecedent that is already temporalized in two directions (was/could have been) is an eloquent summary of the conditions of reading Gaddis, wherein every statement must be reconsidered in terms of the conditions of its utterance, which changes those conditions determinately. All that is "belied" in the "he" of this passage is inextricably "a part of what he has become"; it indisputably lies revealed in the proliferation of contingencies that animates our reading at this point. In this effect, "he" might appreciate how vividly Gaddis's prose recalls the promise of Bakhtinian dialogue: to give us access to a discursive reality which is temporalized without being thematized, where transition becomes a mode of recognition, where the novel is interpreted under the sign of parody as a rethinking through contradiction. The novel is history-making, with the proviso that history remains an activity of mind which can be reflected only through the juxtaposition of irreconcilably distinct moments. This is the experience of time par excellence.

In *Carpenter's Gothic* the contradictoriness of a syntax that unifies by proliferating the contingencies of consciousness fatefully redounds to a displacement of the person (Liz) from the activity of reflective mind which otherwise personifies human agency. Indeed, this consciousness of time reconceived as the condition of consciousness obtrudes most momentously in *Carpenter's Gothic* at the profoundly ambiguous moment of Liz's death, when time proverbially ceases to be a credible object of representation.

Significantly, the displacement of character which we saw "figured" in Liz's act of plagiarism is, at the moment of her demise, both echoed and complemented by the abrupt displacement of the reader from normal gestures of readerly competence. Gaddis orchestrates a drama of misreading which conspicuously coincides with the unfolding of the dramatic episode. Here, what purports

94

to be the climactic action of the novel, an apparent murder, turns out not to be an action at all but a cerebral stroke, an involuntary seizure, the revealed absence of a presumable subject for the deed of murder which mitigates the deed as act. Having set up the action by placing Liz in a room that is melodramatically charged with the notice that "the front door hadn't closed," Gaddis lets a spectral intruder interpose "himself" in an ambiguous perspective which slips from the reader's grasp just as the reader establishes himself or herself within it:

> The front door hadn't closed, and through its glass panels the bare shadows of branches in the streetlight rose and fell on the black road out there in a wind scarce as the gentle rise and fall of breathing in exhausted sleep. For a moment longer she [Liz] held tight to the newel as though secured against the faint dappled movement of the light coming right into the room here and then suddenly she turned back for the kitchen where she rushed into the darkness as though she'd forgotten something, a hand out for the corner of the table caught in a glance at her temple as she went down. (253)

The "hand out for the corner of the table" reaches from a profoundly ambiguous space; an ambiguity deepened by our inability to tell the agency of the action. Does Liz glance at what she'd forgotten—the open door, the intruder's presence caught in time to rescue the autonomy of her subjective gaze? Or is *she* caught in the glance of another's consciousness which portends her victimization? Indeed the trajectories of the other conspicuously agitated verbal constructions in this passage ("coming right into the room . . . she turned back . . . she rushed into the darkness") are similarly elusive. Misreading is compelled by such ambiguity in inverse proportion to the manifest intransitivity of the action. Specifically, the ironic juxtaposition of the overdetermined moment of misreading (prompted by the illusion of an intruding subject) with the moment of Liz's death (death as the quintessential identity out of time) offers the clearest elucidation of Gaddis's purpose as a narrative artist concerned with history. Because here the time of interpretation conspicuously becomes the variable of scenic projection, the very success of which, in orthodox thematic narrative, would contrastingly devolve upon the cathartic death of readerly time— wherein the perspectives of reader and writer always coincide. The syntactic ambiguity of the word "glance" in this passage is aptly the pivot of this understanding, just as pronominal mobility was in the earlier passage. Here the glance is made to serve as a counter for the autonomy of the subject's position as putative agent, while serving to position the temporalized subject (bound as it is to locate itself only outside itself) in contingency. The abrupt disappearance of the subject (as a specific agent) behind the readerly "glance" (at the table) coincides with the materiality of the glance (the blow to the head) which must detonate the readerly consciousness first in the shock of rereading. In other words, subject and object in this scene coalesce in a verbal density as concussive/concatenating for the reader as the corner of the table is for Liz's consciousness at the moment it is extinguished: at that moment, consciousness proceeds along a trajectory that always "returns" to the circumstances of its own projection by transforming them.

Such is the curiously selfless experience of time adumbrated by McCandless in his most eloquent critique of the modern world, which is tragically oblivious to its own historical inertia, and, therefore, blind to the self-limiting imperatives of the naively totalizing self. Towards the middle of the novel, McCandless entertains his most self-consuming conception of human subjectivity by imagining a telescope so distant from earth that "you could see history, Agincourt, Omdurman, Crecy . . . [so strong] that you could see the back of your own head [or] set up a mirror on Alpha Centauri, then you'd see yourself four, about four and half years ago" (153). I have tried to show how history is the resolving focus of that telescope in *Carpenter's Gothic*. It is space mediated by time, a space crossed only by contradiction. Liz, the character to whom McCandless is speaking here, aptly takes his remarks as a mockery of her own credulity, as a parody of her desires, a gap in her understanding—for Liz has mistaken Agincourt, a battle, for the name of a planet or "constellation." Yet the fulcrum of parody here is not her ignorance, not her misconstrual of the relevant constellation of concepts. Rather, it resides obliquely in the concept of constellation itself, if we remember that both Adorno and Benjamin used the term *constellation* to designate the most potent methodological weapon of the allegorist. The allegorist strips away the false appearance of totality by rendering meaning in a "juxtaposition of extremes," that is, a conjunction of image/concept whose rationality is produced by the separation of concept and object which it exhibits. Liz's mistake instantiates such a conjunction by virtue of the inverse logical reciprocity of "battles" (Agincourt) and constellations, which asserts its own contextual imperative here. The interpretive proposition is in fact not very different from the mythological constellations captured by the astronomer's telescope, which are of course only "reflections" of the naked eye itself, refracted through the desire for its own objectification. The telescope embraces the contradiction between the two realms that it pretends to unify, the earthly and the unearthly: it is a juxtaposition of extremes. McCandless's desire to see the back of his own head with the telescope is a similar juxtaposition of extremes, whereby lucidity does not escape the threshold of contradiction because, once again, it entails transition and change. It reformulates the conventional wisdom of character and reader alike, such that the undeluded reflection of human subjectivity can only credibly appear in the parodic two-way glass of nonidentical relations between subjects and objects.

Finally, parody is decisively revealed here as that discursive genre which gains intelligibility as it proliferates contingencies (in nonidentity) rather than resolving them. It simulates the most rigorous rhetorical structure of intertextuality. The novelist must, in effect, ventriloquize his own voice to achieve a philosophical eloquence. Indeed, like the ventriloquist's displaced voice, which problematizes the inside/outside structure of thematic certainty and formal stability, Gaddis's parodic/dialogic fiction fulfills a philosophical imperative in the guise of a "carnival" entertainment; he makes theme intelligible as structure, voice intelligible as vocal agency, and temporality intelligible as time. Only in this way does carnival culture become more consequentially what Bakhtin aspires to but cannot attain in his more mystically-minded expositions of dialogue: an active place of reflection rather than a moribund reflection of our place in history.

Notes

1. The influential texts in this regard belong to Derrida, who has so notoriously problematized speech as a locus of meaning. I take the key disseminators of a narratology focused on the problematic of voice, Genette, Culler, Chatman, Greimas, et al. to be working directly out of or at least presuming upon fundamentally Derridean assumptions.

2. The Bakhtin revival can be credited in large measure to Caryl Emerson and Michael Holquist's translation of *The Dialogic Imagination*, which led to the reissue of a broad range of Bakhtinian texts dealing directly with the question of the subject: *The Formal Method of Literary Scholarship, Marxism and the Philosophy of Language, Problems of Dostoevsky's Poetics*, and, most recently, *Speech Genres and Other Late Essays*. The recent publication of Clark and Holquist's *Mikhail Bakhtin* and Todorov's *Mikhail Bakhtin: The Dialogic Principle* have brought this question even more starkly into the foreground of Bakhtinian theory.

3. This group includes theorists of the novel, such as Lukacs and Mach-

erey, historical Marxists such as Althusser and Jameson and narratologists working within the poststructuralist paradigm.

4. Bakhtin's discussion of parody in *Problems of Dostoevsky's Poetics* is particularly noteworthy, insofar as it abandons the structural crux of mimicry and broadens the scope of the term to include the reciprocity of all social significations, thus precluding any idealizing "fusion of voices": "In carnival, parodying was employed very widely in diverse forms and degrees: various images . . . parodied one another variously and from various points of view; it was like an entire system of crooked mirrors, elongating, diminishing, distorting in various directions to various degrees" (127).

5. See especially the discussions of utterance in Bakhtin's *The Formal Method* for their bearing on the analysis of ideological representations.

6. This title is given by Clark and Holquist to a set of fragments (written between 1918–1924) in which Bakhtin initially posed the problem of the relations between self and other. Clark and Holquist characterize it as "a treatise on ethics in the world of everyday experience, a kind of pragmatic axiology. Ethical activity is conceived as a deed" (62).

7. See *Problems in Dostoevsky's Poetics* 30.

8. Rosen gives an excellent account of the conceptual grounds for my extrapolation of Adorno's critique of Hegel to the problem of mediation in Bakhtin.

9. See *Problems* 36.

Works Cited

Adorno, T. W. *Negative Dialectics*. New York: Seabury Press, 1973.

Bakhtin, Mikhail. *The Dialogic Imagination: Four Essays*. Edited by Michael Holquist. Translated by Caryl Emerson and Michael Holquist. Austin: University of Texas Press, 1981.

———. *The Formal Method in Literary Scholarship*. Translated by Albert J. Wehble. Cambridge: Harvard University Press, 1985.

———. *Problems of Dostoevsky's Poetics*. Edited and translated by Caryl Emerson. Introduction by Wayne Booth. Minneapolis: University of Minnesota Press, 1985.

Benjamin, Walter. *The Origin of the German Tragic Theater*. London: New Left Books, 1977.

Buck-Morss, Susan. *The Origin of Negative Dialectics: Theodor W. Adorno, Walter Benjamin, and the Frankfurt Institute*. New York: Free Press, 1968.

Clark, Katerina, and Holquist, Michael. *Mikhail Bakhtin*. Cambridge: Harvard University Press, 1984.

de Man, Paul. *The Resistance to Theory*. Minneapolis: University of Minnesota Press, 1986.

Gaddis, William. *Carpenter's Gothic*. New York: Viking, 1985.

Kermode, Frank. *The Sense of an Ending*. London: Oxford University Press, 1967.

Kristeva, Julia. *La Révolution du language poétique*. Paris: Seuil, 1974.

Rosen, Michael. *Hegel's Dialectic and Its Criticism*. Cambridge: Cambridge University Press, 1984.

Todorov, Tzvetan. *Mikhail Bakhtin: The Dialogic Principle*. Translated by Wlad Godzich. Theory and History of Literature, vol. 13. Minneapolis: University of Minnesota Press, 1984.

Volosinov, V. N. *Marxism and the Philosophy of Language*. Translated by Ladislav Matejka and I. R. Titunik. Cambridge: Harvard University Press, 1986.

REVISIONARY INTERTEXTUALITY

Portrait Narration

Generals James and Stein

===

CHARLES CARAMELLO

I

In the early 1930s, Gertrude Stein began an intertextual portrayal of Henry James in relation to herself; it starts at the beginning of *The Autobiography of Alice B. Toklas* (1933). Stein introduces James into the *Autobiography* in paragraph four, as someone Toklas early admired, and then immediately introduces herself in paragraph five (3–4). Stein later tells us, through Toklas's voice, of course, that she had not had an early interest in James but now admires him greatly and considers him "quite definitely as her forerunner, he being the only nineteenth century writer who being an american felt the method of the twentieth century"; and, again, that she now thinks James "the first person in literature to find the way to the literary methods of the twentieth century," but did not read him during her "formative period" probably because "one is always naturally antagonistic to one's parents" (96–97). In this first work of her later phase, then, Stein identified Henry James as her "forerunner" and composed her opening passage to exemplify his priority.

Stein continued this portrayal in her subsequent theoretical writing. In *Lectures in America* (1935), she discusses at length James's having brought the paragraph to the point of its "having been completely become"; this, Stein adds, left her "to do more with the paragraph than ever had been done" (47–54). Some pages later, while discussing what she had done with the sentence in *The Making of Americans* (composed ca. 1906–8, published 1926), Stein speculates that "Henry James in his later writing had had a dim feeling that this was what he knew he should do" (225). In *Narration* (1935), Stein discusses an increasing autonomy of the word "in the American writing" and cites as exemplars of the practice eight American authors since Emerson, with herself immediately preceding Sherwood Anderson and succeeding James (10). Finally, in her so-called "Transatlantic Interview" (1946), Stein discusses at length the Cézannean and Flaubertian influences on "decenterment" in her composition. Although she claims that no one had previously "used that idea of composition in literature," she allows that "Henry James had a slight inkling of it and was in some senses a forerunner" (15). Some lines later, in a discussion of characterization, she credits James with having anticipated her own strategy of not "making the people real" in the manner of nineteenth-century realism but of locating "the essence or, as a painter would call it, value" (16).

These citations reveal three aspects of Stein's portrayal of James and herself. First, Stein claimed that her starting to read James with "interest"—a highly charged word in her vocabulary—coincided with her starting the work of her later phase. In the work of this phase she began to refer regularly to James. Second, Stein discussed James over a period of years with specific reference not only to paragraphs, sentences, and words, but also to composition and characterization. She credited James with having brought to fruition the nineteenth-century practice of each element, and, so, with having pointed the way to a twentieth-century practice. Third, Stein coolly transformed this tribute to James's prescience into an aggrandizement of James as *her* specific "forerunner." James "felt the method of," or "found the way to," or "had an inkling of," the twentieth-century way, but he could not arrive there; Stein, we are to see, could and did.

This portrayal reflects two of Stein's basic ideas about creativity and about progress in art. Stein clearly believed that the composition of a generation's way of living determines the general composition of its writing and painting. She would argue in *Picasso* (1938) that, as a result, "a creator is not in advance of his generation but he is the first of his contemporaries to be conscious of what is happening to his generation" (30). Stein also apparently believed that the composition of an artist's way of living determines a predisposition to such consciousness and determines also the specific composition of that artist's writing or painting. Stein would imply that she and James shared nationality, unconventional sexuality, and expatriation; but she would also imply that they differed in gender, in type of unconventional sexuality, and in place of expatriation. Stein would claim for herself and for James the consciousness of contemporaneity that marks the true creative genius, but she would stake her claim to succession on the aesthetic consequences of their generational and personal differences.

Stein characterized the work of her later phase as "portrait narration"; and she sought in this hybrid form to negotiate a tension *between* the immediate observation and spatial representation she identified with portraiture *and* the mediated observation and temporal representation she identified with narration. She would do so by fusing reference and autoreference. She would observe her biographical or autobiographical subject and would represent psychological or physical movement in that subject as a series of instants; simultaneously, she would observe herself observing that subject and would represent *her* observing and *her* representing as the processes that transformed those discrete instants into duration. When her subject was unavailable to direct observation, Stein would shift both operations to a more complex level of second-order discourse. She acknowledged that Henry James had been her forerunner in the general fusion of reference and autoreference. But she identified the specific means and ends of her practice of it with the conditions of her historical moment and, through analogy and metaphor, with her status as American, as woman, as lesbian, and as resident in France. In short, she adduced her practice of this fusion as further evidence for her succeeding James.

In doing so, Stein actually claimed to have succeeded James twice, first in her novels, then in her portrait narration. James had been among the first to recognize the superannuation of the Hawthornian romance as one of the things happening to his generation; Stein, so she implies, had been the first to recognize the superannuation of the Jamesian novel as one of the things happening to hers. She claims in *Lectures in America* that "the three novels written in [my] generation that are the important things written in this generation"—namely, *A la recherche du temps perdu*, *Ulysses*, and *The Making of Americans*—"do not tell a story" (184–85); obviously, James's novels do. But she also reports in her "Transatlantic Interview" that she eventually came to regard "the novel scheme" as "quite out of the question" in the twentieth century (22). In her later phase, she conjoined her portraiture, from which she expressly had excluded "story" (*Lectures in America* 121, 184–85), to biography and autobiography, narrative genres that presuppose "story," and she associated the portrait narration in which she did so with her reading of James's own later-phase experiments in autobiography.

Not surprisingly, then, Stein chose portrait narration for her one sustained treatment of Henry James, and also not surprisingly, she reserved this treatment for her study of creativity in Americans, *Four in America* (composed 1931–34, published posthumously 1947). In this book Stein advances counterfactual hypotheses about her four biographical subjects: she envisions Ulysses S. Grant as a religious leader, Wilbur Wright as a painter, Henry James as a general, and George Washington as a novelist. And she develops these hypotheses within a complex thematics that refers to the nature of American democracy and to the nature of the relationships it fosters between winning and losing and between religion, war and aesthetics. Attending to this referential dimension, one contemporary reviewer noted that Stein meant "to show how each of her representative Americans would have expressed his genius if he had been in some very different relation to the problems of human experience" (Gray 30). Another concluded that the book's "ultimate symbol of creativity" is the novel (Pearson 745). If we look more closely at its autoreferential dimension, we will see that *Four in America* shows how Gertrude Stein is expressing *her* creative genius in writing. It advances as its covert thesis Stein's centrality in twentieth-century art, and it offers as its symbol of creativity *not* the novel—not even the Jamesian novel—but itself as portrait narration.

II

Stein introduces *Four in America* with four hypothetical questions, the third of which reads: "If Henry James had been a general what would he have had to do." I would propose three sources for the conceit. Stein is first alluding to James's memoirs, *A Small Boy and Others* (1913), *Notes of a Son and Brother* (1914), and *The Middle Years* (composed 1914, published posthumously 1917), in which James reveals a distinct fondness for generals from Napoleon to Winfield Scott to U. S. Grant. She is also applying to James a common analogy between warfare and writing: James plans his works with the care of a strategist and devises literary tactics to assure the success of his strategy, but can improvise tactics when faced in the heat of composition with unforeseen contingencies. Finally, she is employing an etymological pun about which José Ortega y Gasset had earlier written: "The poet aggrandizes the world by adding to reality, which is there by itself, the continents of his imagination. Author derives from *auctor*, he who augments. It was the title Rome bestowed upon her generals when they had conquered new territory for the City" (31).[1] Stein, then, is moving from a specific allusion to James's memoirs, through a common analogy implicit in the allusion, to an etymological pun inherent in the terms of the analogy.

Stein's basic conceit thus not only refers to James but also forms a reflexive wordplay: it names its own movement from the specific to the general. In so doing, moreover, it suggests the systemic wordplay of Stein's composition. The key to this wordplay lies in Stein's brief poem, "James Is Nervous" (1918). There Stein had written: "James is not nervous. / Any more. / Indeed he is general" (*Bee Time Vine and Other Pieces* 208). Now James is both *a* general and *general*. James is a general because he identifies himself with generals, because he composes his work in the way that generals conduct battles, and because he is an *auctor*; James is general because James the individual memoirist comes to represent a general type of autobiographical writer for his reader, Stein. In her composition, Stein will coordinate James's being a general with his being general, and she will explore James's method of composition in his memoirs in relation to her own reading of them.

Stein will also explore, simultaneously, her own method of composition, a method she will present as a variation of James's method and as a legitimation for her regarding herself as a successful general in the aesthetic wars of the twentieth century. Stein's constructing James as a general and as general thus suggests, in a further wordplay, that Stein will exemplify in her composition general principles about writing that she has derived from her reading of James's memoirs. Stein, then, will represent the autobiographically mediated James who acted in deed *like* a general, she will present a textual James who *is* a general precisely because Stein constructs him according to that analogy, and she will compose her text as an *exemplification* of general principles formulated by James and developed with appropriate variations by Stein, herself an *auctor*.

Stein, however, actually opens her "Henry James," her forty-one page treatment of James in *Four in America*, with seemingly irrelevant propositions about the difference between Shakespeare's plays and Shakespeare's sonnets and about Stein's having "found out the difference" either by "accident" or by "coincidence" (119). In the twenty-one page "Duet" that follows, Stein elaborates that difference. More important, she connects Shakespeare and herself through the "coincidence" that led her to discover it: "The coincidence is with Before the Flowers of Friendship Faded Friendship Faded," that is, with Stein's translation, published under that title in 1931, of Georges Hugnet's poem "*Enfances*." Stein argues that Shakespeare's sonnets and her *Before the Flowers* "were not as if they were being written but as if they were going to be written," whereas Shakespeare's "plays were written as they were written" (119–20). She then establishes the general principle, derived from her writing of *Before the Flowers* and her remembering of Shakespeare, which will govern her analysis of James: there are two ways of writing, "writing what you are writing" and "writing what you are going to be writing" (122).

James first appears on the tenth page of this "Duet," where Stein interjects that "nobody has forgotten Henry James," presents a set of permutations on James's being a general and winning an army in order to win a battle or a war, and charges herself and, apparently, her reader to "remember how Henry James was or was not a general" (128). Stein now connects Shakespeare and James through her principle about the two ways of writing: Shakespeare "wrote both ways" but did so in two distinct genres—plays and sonnets; James, by contrast, "saw he could write both ways at once" (133), and, in so seeing and in so doing, did what he would have had to do had he been a general. As Stein explains her figuration, James "came not to begin but to have begun," he "came to do this" (137), and, she concludes this "Duet," "you must remember that in a battle or a war everything has been prepared which is what has been called begun and then everything happens at once which is what is called done and then a battle or a war is either not or won" (139).

It turns out that Stein's opening propositions and her elaborating "Duet" together constitute only "Volume 1" of her James composition; its remaining twenty pages comprise passages of varying lengths individually labeled volumes 2 through 34. As Stein's parodic mode of labeling suggests, these "volumes" present a "life" of Henry James, and they are, indeed, replete with such biographical facts as James "was not married in any way" (141), and James "did not prepare for flight" (151). At once perfectly literal and studiously figurative, such facts signal the presence in this composition of more than one Henry James: the autobiographically mediated James who was *like* a general; Stein's textual James who *is* a general; and Stein's text itself, simply titled "Henry James," which concretely *exemplifies* general principles of writing. It is the "life" of this third "Henry James" that Stein is telling in detail, and, as she indicates in a purposeful pronominal shift, "Henry James is a combination of the two ways of writing and that makes *him* a general a general who does something. Listen to *it*" (137; emphasis added).

The reader who attends closely to this third "Henry James" will find a cubist composition whose intricate simultaneity of reference and autoreference admits only clumsy paraphrase. On one plane, Stein triangulates the Stein–Shakespeare connection and the Shakespeare–James connection, thereby suggesting the central Stein–James connection. She first explains the process by which her writing of *Before the Flowers* and her remembering of Shakespeare's sonnets had brought her to her knowledge of the "two ways of writing"; she then explains the process by which her reading of James's memoirs and her current writing of "Henry James" are bringing her to her knowledge of writing "both ways at once." On an intersecting plane, Stein unfolds the process of writing "both ways at once" that James used in his memoirs to represent his life and to analyze his representation; she thus suggests the process she herself is using to construct her simultaneity of three "lives." Through a cryptic discussion of "the three Jameses" (139–43), that is, she refers to the complex form of James's memoirs, in which (one) the elderly writer creates (two) a highly self-conscious persona through whom he strives to apprehend (three) himself as a boy, youth, and young man. She then implicitly renders those (three) Jameses analogous to the three Jameses whose "lives" she is telling.

The two planes intersect, as it were, by "coincidence." Stein defines coincidence in her opening propositions as "when a thing is going to happen and does" (119). She later adds that "a coincidence is having done so" (130), and that "the way to find this out all this out is to do likewise, not to do it alike but to do it likewise" (134). Shakespeare's sonnets and Stein's *Before the Flowers* are literally "coincidental": they are texts with only an accidental, or noncausal, relationship. But they are also coincidental in the sense of an etymological pun: they are texts that "happen together" in Stein's mind because writing *Before the Flowers* caused her to remember the sonnets. Shakespeare had done something in his sonnets, Stein had done "likewise" in *Before the Flowers*, Stein had kenned the similarity; Stein had thereby come to her present knowledge of the "two ways of writing." Coincidentally, moreover, Stein *happened* to be reading James *while* she was writing *Before the Flowers*. Her reading of James caused her not only to *re*consider the "two ways of writing" but to *consider* for the first time the dynamics of writing "both ways at once"—the dynamics of being an *auctor* and a general. The memorial relationship between *Before the Flowers* and Shakespeare's sonnets thus differs from that between Stein's "Henry James" and James's memoirs. Nonetheless, Stein could come to her present knowledge of writing "both ways at once" only by doing "likewise" in her James composition. Once she has done so, she will have become a winning general.

Stein still will have left herself, however, with the problem of claiming succession. She needed to remember James's compositional method in order to do "likewise" and thereby to reach her knowledge of writing "both ways at once," but she also needs to forget James's compositional method in order to find the method appropriate to her historical moment. Stein had begun by noting that neither she nor her reader "has forgotten" Henry James or the way in which he "was or was not a general." Stein's imagined James may now comment to her—while she comments to herself and to her reader—that "I understand you undertake to overthrow my undertaking" (150); and Stein may, nonetheless, "commence to cover the ground" (157). But in this cubist conflation of two distinct metaphors, Stein acknowledges James simultaneously as one dead "parent" not easily interred and as one general not easily outmaneuvered, no matter how much ground Stein "likewise" takes for the City. In order to succeed Henry James, Stein would need to be "doing something" in her "Henry James" that establishes her not only as a winning general but as the winning general of her generation. She is, indeed, doing two such things.

III

The clues to the first appear after the fact, and they concern *The Autobiography of Alice B. Toklas*. While discussing in *Lectures in America* her work during the 1920s, Stein reports having then gone on to do "an entirely different something" in the *Autobiography*, something that "came out of" her writing of *Before the Flowers* (204–5). She explains that she had "told what happened as it had happened" in the *Autobiography*, observes that "there is something much more exciting than anything that happens and now and always I am writing the portrait of that," and concludes that she has "been writing the portraits of Four in America, trying to write Grant, and Wilbur Wright and Henry James and Washington do other things than they did do" (205–6). Several years later, in her "Transatlantic Interview," she adds: "I did a tour de force with the *Autobiography of Alice Toklas* . . . But still I had done what I saw, what you do in translation or in a narrative. I had recreated the point of view of somebody else" (19).

In the portrait narration of the *Autobiography*, Stein had begun her later phase of experiments with voice and with perspective— as marked, for example, by her complex and celebrated re-creation of Toklas's autobiographical point of view. Such complexity, however, seems to mark no significant advance upon James, the acknowledged master of such re-creations, and especially not upon James's memoirs, in the second volume of which, *Notes of a Son and Brother*, he had by editing and arranging their correspondence re-created the points of view of his father, his three male siblings, and his cousin, Minnie Temple. But Stein had begun something less obvious with these experiments, something that she developed fully in the particular form of writing "both ways at once" she practiced in *Four in America*.

The two central personae of the Toklas/Stein *Autobiography* form a relationship whose significance Stein elsewhere glossed. While speaking in *Lectures in America* about the relationship between *Before the Flowers* and the *Autobiography*, Stein says "that for the first time in writing, I felt something outside me while I was writing, hitherto I had always had nothing but what was inside me while I was writing" (205). This dichotomy of outside/inside encapsulates three relationships that Stein was rendering analogous in her work of the 1930s: reader (or "audience")/writer, translator/writer, and writer as self-observer/writer as self-observed.[2] Although Stein is speaking in this passage specifically of "audience," her references to *Before the Flowers* and to the *Autobiography* suggest outside texts to be translated and outside points of view to be re-created and imply a dynamics of self-observation in writing. In *Narration* Stein proceeds to characterize similar writing, that in which "the outside and the inside flow together without interrupting," that which is "a diffusion but not a confusing," as "really a kind of an imitation of marrying of two being one, and yet being two and presumably two as much as anything" (55).

Given that Stein often used the term *marriage* to describe her relationship with Toklas, we can infer three things about the *Autobiography*. First, Stein realized while writing *Before the Flowers* that she could translate a poem by another person, Hugnet, in a way that would produce two distinct voices, Hugnet's and her own, which would remain intimately related as a dyadic vocalization of one poem. Second, she realized that she could recreate the point of view of another person, Toklas, in a way that would produce two distinct points of view, Toklas's and her own, which would remain intimately related within the one dyadic perspectivalism of the *Autobiography*. Third, she realized that these compositional methods would be the linguistic equivalent of the emotional and erotic movement of the Toklas/Stein marital relationship as she experienced and directly observed it—outside and inside flowing together, voices and points of view becoming one while maintaining their duality.

Stein connects this relationship, as manifested in the composition of the *Autobiography*, to the dynamics of her James composition. Volume 27 of "Henry James" begins: "A narrative of Henry James told by one who listened to some one else telling about some one entirely different from Henry James" (155). Stein then alludes specifically to the *Autobiography* in her gloss, thus implying that she has expanded a doubly dyadic compositional relationship into a doubly triadic one. The vocal and perspectival sources in the James composition, that is, are three—James in his memoirs, Stein reading

James, and Stein's reader reading Stein. More important, each participant enters a relationship not only with the others but with himself or herself *as other*. Stein is signaling an advance from the *Autobiography*, in which two interpenetrating voices present two intersecting points of view, to "Henry James" itself, in which "Duet" serves only as a procedural model for constructing a *multi*vocal and *multi*perspectival composition.

Volume 27 exemplifies the complexity of the composition. It invites us to refer the three "ones" of the passage to Stein, Toklas, and another woman, *or* to Stein, Toklas, and Stein at an earlier point in time. But it also prevents our reducing this passage to even that degree of ambiguous reference. This constellation of three "ones" shifts and slides with an indeterminacy that admits several permutations of relationship between three persons or two persons and, in addition, does not prohibit the three "ones" from being, in turn, three aspects of any one of three persons. Stein employs the lure of autobiographical allegory, in sum, to bring into the foreground an allegory of reading and writing that is rendered concrete in the text that presents it. She multiplies possibilities of voice and perspective through a compositional method that remains indebted to James's while differing from his, one in which Stein both remembers and forgets his method.

Stein acknowledges that James could write "both ways at once" in several senses: he could, like a good general, plan and improvise; he could tell "what happened [to him] as it had happened" and could tell the more "exciting" story of what did not happen but might have; he could represent an extratextual reality while reflecting upon his process of representation. In his memoirs, he translates the felt experience of his life, he re-creates points of view of others and of himself as other, he anticipates readerly interventions; and he also tells a metanarrative about his doing all three. Stein, herself, has reenacted James's achievement: she, too, plans and improvises; she tells what happened to James as he reports it and tells the more "exciting" hypothetical story of James as a general; she represents James's memoirs while reflecting upon her process of representation. In her "Henry James," she translates the felt experience of her reading of James, she re-creates the points of view of James and of herself as the reading other who preceded the self now writing, she anticipates readerly interventions; and she also tells a metanarrative about doing all three.

That James "was not married in any way," however, now assumes its considerable significance. Just as James never married in life, Stein seems to suggest, so did he never effect the marriage of voices and of points of view that Stein claims to have begun in *The Auto-biography of Alice B. Toklas.* In the centerpiece of his memoirs, *Notes of a Son and Brother,* James details his filial relationship with his father, his fraternal relationship with his brothers, and his tenuous relationship with Minnie Temple, whom, significantly, he did not marry, although one gathers that he wishes he could have. Throughout these memoirs, moreover, James strives to retain control over voice and point of view, to keep his composition centered upon himself, and, with his endlessly qualifying periodic sentences, to contain and to order every possible nuance of meaning. Stein uses a metaphor of celibacy implied by bachelorhood to connect the content to the form of James's memoirs and to reject the model of autobiographical writing those memoirs suggest. She implicitly treats them as a narrative of celibate heteroerotic relations and vaguely incestuous and rival homoerotic relations—a narrative told within the essentially autoerotic narration of James creating a persona through whom to apprehend himself as a boy, youth, and young man. James's memoirs serve Stein as a model of repressed desire seeking an impossible closure in the realm of remembrance.

Stein, however, offers a different model toward a different end. She conflates narrative and metanarrative in the cubist structure of her composition. She constructs a portrait that represents the movement of James's memoirs as being read by her; simultaneously, she constructs a narrative that tells, *in precisely the same words,* a story about that portrait's being written by Stein and being read by her reader. She does so with a multivocalism and a multiperspectivalism that opens her text to James's and, more particularly, to her reader's interventions. Stein thus extends the compositional method of the *Autobiography* that she had analogized with marriage. She relinquishes considerable control over voice and over point of view, decenters her composition with respect to content and form, and allows her indeterminate linguistic surface to proliferate a multiplicity of contesting meanings. Using a metaphor of sexuality implied by "marital relations" in the broadest acceptation, she projects a model of (auto)biographical writing as necessarily—and joyfully—free from the closure of remembrance, a model that can be said to anticipate more recent manifestations of "feminine writing."[3]

My reading of Stein's erotics of writing, however, requires us to regard her as attributing repression to James; we must recall that she elsewhere specified James's "disembodied way of disconnecting something from anything and anything from something" *not* as "repression" but as "a lack of connection, of there being no connection with living and daily living because there is none, that makes American writing what it always has been and what it will continue to become" (*Lectures in America* 53–54). The problem of disconnection, then, would seem to extend to herself as a practitioner of the American writing. Stein apparently concluded that she could replace James's negative disconnection with a positive decenterment through her erotics of writing but that she would need to do so as a general, notwithstanding that rank's masculine and, perhaps, repressive associations. Thus Toklas/Stein reports in the *Autobiography* that "I [Toklas] often teased her [Stein], calling her a general, a civil war general of either or both sides" (19). And thus Stein employs her biographies of four Americans to construct *Four in America* as an autobiographical portrait narration of her own generalship—a generalship in which she did a second thing different from James.

IV

The clues to that thing also appear after the fact, this time in *Picasso*, Stein's "life" of the painter, which tells the history of cubism in painting as the history of Picasso's struggles. Early in this book, Stein speaks of Picasso's beginning to "struggle" in 1909 with problems of cubist portraiture (13), specifically, the problems of trying to "express things seen not as one knows them but as they are when one sees them without remembering having looked at them" (15). Stein adds that "I was alone at this time in understanding him, perhaps because I was expressing the same thing in literature, perhaps because I was an American and, as I say, Spaniards and Americans have a kind of understanding of things which is the same" (16). She then interjects that "we are now still in the history of the beginning of that struggle" (16), referring with this polysemous remark to the events she is narrating, to the narration in *Picasso* of those events, and to the composing of *Picasso* and similar texts as an event occurring in the mid-thirties. Stein is speaking, in short, of the continuing history, begun in 1909, of her and Picasso's analogous struggles to "express things" directly in portraiture. Her struggles had led to the cubist portrait narration of *Four in America*.

We first regard *Four in America* as a serial polyptych comprising four panels of apparently equal importance. Its two outer panels are clearly symmetrical. The left-hand panel treats a general, Grant, who lived wholly in the nineteenth century and who commanded the victorious army in the Civil War, the war which reunited the United States of America and which, so Stein believed, initiated America into the twentieth century (see *Autobiography* 96). The right-hand panel treats a general, Washington, who lived wholly in the eighteenth century and who commanded the victorious army in the Revolutionary War, the war which founded the United States of America, the nation that would eventually be the first to enter the twentieth century. For the import of these panels, we must recall Stein's theory that wars only confirm a new reality for "everybody," that "the entire change has been accomplished and the war is only something which forces everybody to recognise it." Wars, moreover, force the public to recognize the "creator who has seen the change which has been accomplished before a war and which has been expressed by the war," the creator, again, who is not in "advance" of his or her generation but who is the first to perceive the conditions of its lived composition and to practice successfully the aesthetic composition appropriate to them (see *Picasso* 30).

The asymmetrical central panels of *Four in America* treat two such creators in Wilbur Wright and Henry James, nineteenth-century figures who lived into the twentieth century and who saw before everybody else the new movement that defined their generation's lived composition. Wright, more precisely, was *not* such a creator, but he indirectly anticipated one by inventing a technology that anticipated, in a different realm, the technique of cubism. Wright invented the controlled powered flight (of heavier-than-air machines) whose form of movement Stein saw as defining the twentieth century and as affording it the shifting perspectivalism that Picasso independently discovered in cubism (see *Picasso* 50). Had Wright been a painter, as Stein hypothesizes him, he might have been a direct precursor of cubism, a Cézanne. James *was* such a creator, but the fact that he "did not prepare for flight" now assumes its considerable significance. James was not prepared to accept the consequences of controlled powered flight either for the conditions of the lived composition or for the aesthetic composition appropriate to them. James, however, directly anticipated Stein and, with Cézanne, specifically prepared the way for Stein's cubist decenterment in composition, a decenterment that Stein felt the Civil War had initiated in the composition of living but that only World War I had brought to full expression.

We can now see that Stein's serial polyptych comprising four panels of equal importance actually forms a decentered triptych. Two symmetrical outer panels thematically support a central panel "decentered" by *its* bifurcation into two asymmetrical subjects: Wright and James. And each half of this central panel accrues meaning when we supply the associations and identifications we have derived intertextually: those linking Wright to Picasso and those linking James to Stein. These two halves, then, together allow the tryptych's real subject to emerge dialectically: Stein's development of cubist portrait narration.

The overall design of the triptych is this: Washington and Grant were the victorious generals in the political wars that first founded and then reunited the country that was the first to enter the twentieth century, the country of Stein's origin; Wright invented controlled powered flight and indirectly anticipated Picasso's invention of painting in the twentieth century, cubism; James developed fully the elements of nineteenth-century narration and directly anticipated Stein's development of writing in the twentieth century, also cubism. *Four in America* thus foreshadows Stein's *Picasso*, in which she argues that Spain and America "were the natural founders of the twentieth century" (12), and which she opens with the claim that "painting in the nineteenth century was only done in France and by Frenchmen," but "in the twentieth century it was done in France but by Spaniards" (1). The implication, clearly, is that writing in the twentieth century is done in France but by Americans, that is, by Gertrude Stein. *Four in America*, in a crucial sense, looks backward to *The Autobiography of Alice B. Toklas and* forward to *Picasso*. Stein conjoins her marital relationship with Toklas to her sibling relationship with Picasso; and just as she used the former to suggest the feminist aspect of her advance upon James, so does she use the latter to suggest the cubist aspect of her advance upon this "parent" to whom she was "naturally antagonistic."

Stein has left herself, however, with another problem. The simultaneous development of cubism in painting and in writing had happened in the first decade of the century, years before the writing of *Four in America*. World War I had subsequently revealed cubism as the appropriate expression for the composition of prewar life, but the changed conditions of postwar life required an aesthetic expression appropriate to them (see *Picasso* 11). In the 1930s, Stein obviously believed that she needed to correct the former bifurcation of cubism into the distinct genres of painting and writing, however metaphorically, in order to shape that expression: just as she had to practice a feminist "diffusion" of masculinist narration to assume her generalship and win her army, so she had to write the two cubisms "both at once" to win her battle in the war of aesthetics. It follows that Stein could not simply narrate the history of cubist portrait narration as the history of her struggles; she had to use the form that her struggles were revealing to her as the appropriate one. Living in France, where Wilbur Wright pursued his program of flight and Picasso his program of cubism, Stein would use this form to point in *Four in America* to a "foreign America" whose exemplars of creativity, especially Henry James, she had succeeded if not quite forgotten.

V

Stein deployed her portrait narration, then, as part of her larger project in the 1930s. She treated James, her textualized James, and her text "Henry James" simultaneously, using a method that commingled the points of view of James, herself, and her reader. With this method, she implied, she met the aesthetic challenge posed by her "forerunner," demonstrated her response to that challenge, and successfully established herself as the true successor. Throughout this period, she treated nearly *every* subject as a composite of the primary subject, her observation of it, and her representation of that observation, and, in order to do so, defined a method of writing characterized by the plural perspectives of cubism and the plural voices of lyric drama. By defining that method systematically, moreover, she produced a highly programmatic body of work; with that corpus, in turn, she advanced an evolving theory of aesthetics and an evolving portrait of herself as the true creative genius for her generation. She produced, in short, a precise, horizontal intertext.

She also extended that intertext into the verticality of history. In *Four in America*, as in her other work of this period, she treated her composite subject as also including *public* representations of the primary subject. She composed "Henry James," for example, within an intertext comprising not only companion texts in the same volume (those on Grant, Wright, and Washington) and contemporaneous texts in her corpus (such as *The Autobiography of Alice B. Toklas*), but also prior texts in the literary tradition (principally James's own work) and, least obviously but most pointedly, a cultural text collectively produced: namely, the American iconography of genius.[4] This extension into history explains the otherwise odd incongruity in her basic mode of representation. On the one hand, she treated James and her other Americans as real people, artists, and argued that creative Americans, especially James, had led to herself and her portrait narration; on the other hand, she treated James and her other Americans as repositories of cultural values, icons, and argued that the American iconography of genius included them but excluded her.

Obviously, Stein did not write *Four in America* just to solve an aesthetic problem, to reconcile the observational aspects of portraiture and self-portraiture with the memorial and narrational aspects of biography. She wrote it to construct the premises on which she could claim for herself the status of genius and, necessarily, to deconstruct the premises on which American culture had conceived that status and assigned it to others. She defined general, husband, and *auctor* from feminist–lesbian and cubist perspectives, and then assumed those roles. She freed those roles from militaristic, partriarchal definition, and thus subverted the conventional values they had represented. She confounds us, then, if we try to decide whether her purpose was self-promotion and *Four in America* a case study in the anxiety of influence, or whether her purpose was cultural analysis and her book a critique of a militarist patriarchy and its criteria for value. Her self-promotion *was*, intrinsically, cultural critique.

Stein responded to her historical moment by pressing the "two ways of writing" to a point at which portraiture and narration, in effect, became textualism and intertextualism. Although she had shifted from the referential to the autoreferential, that is, she then shifted again from a highly textualized form of autoreference to a highly intertextualized form of reference: ultimately, she *was* composing *Four in America* as a study of American success and American failure. She was addressing not only what it meant to fail or to succeed artistically, but also what it meant to be represented by a culture as having failed or succeeded. She staked her claim to success (and to the James succession) on her method of writing "both ways at once," and she staked her claim to true contemporaneity on that success. She used that method, moreover, to portray how and why Americans of her generation rejected her claims and, in the process, actually suggested why many Americans of our generation accept them: Stein clearly saw how her culture used an iconography to validate its norms and how she could exploit the same iconography to subvert those norms. Therein lies her genius and her success.[5]

Notes

The present essay adapts and redirects material from my longer essay, "Reading Gertrude Stein Reading Henry James, or Eros Is Eros Is Eros Is Eros," *The Henry James Review* 6, no. 3 (1985): 182–203.

To my knowledge, Stein first used the phrase "portrait narration" in "A

Transatlantic Interview": "After the *Four Saints* [1927] the portrait narration began, and I went back to the form of narration" (19).

1. Assuming Stein is employing this pun, she may have arrived at it independently, or she may have derived it from Ortega's essay, first published in Spanish in 1925. I think the former more likely. Despite Stein's extended visits to Spain (1912) and to Spain and Mallorca (1915), I find no evidence that she read Spanish.

2. See Neuman 34. See, also, Neuman's succinct bio-bibliographical account of the circumstances surrounding *Before the Flowers* (14).

3. Stein is playing a complicated and ambiguous verbal game with James's predilection for marriage as a metaphor for the fusion of form and content in literature. See, for example, James, *The Art of the Novel*: "They ['substance and form in a really wrought work of art'] are separate before the fact, but the sacrament of execution indissolubly marries them, and the marriage, like any other marriage, has only to be a 'true' one for the scandal of a breach not to show. The thing 'done,' artistically, is a fusion, or it has not *been* done" (115–16). As preoccupied with proper relations between form and content as were James and her fellow post-Jamesians, Stein introduces into her art the alternative marital model she practiced in her life; what James sees as "scandal" Stein sees as ideal relationship, sexually and textually: not "fusion" but, as she puns, purposeful "diffusion." Stein is advocating, sexually and textually, alternatives and experimentation—not promiscuity.

For an account of the Stein–Toklas marriage, see Stimpson 122–39. For accounts of Stein in relation to *l'écriture féminine*, see Gibbs 281–93, and DeKoven.

4. These prior representations include four on which Stein seems specifically to have based her compositions: Grant's *Personal Memoirs*; the Wilbur Wright memorial at Le Mans; James's memoirs, *A Small Boy and Others*, *Notes of a Son and Brother*, and *The Middle Years*; and Henry Lee's *Funeral Oration on the Death of General Washington*, also published as *A Funeral Oration, in Honour of the Memory of George Washington*.

5. Were I to play a parlor-game of naming Stein's true successors, I would choose neither the novelists nor the poets who claim her as predecessor but, rather, the Laurie Anderson of *United States: Parts I–IV*, and the Robert Wilson of *The CIVIL warS: a tree is best measured when it is down*.

Works Cited

DeKoven, Marianne. *A Different Language: Gertrude Stein's Experimental Writing*. Madison: University of Wisconsin Press, 1983.

Gibbs, Anna. "Hélène Cixous and Gertrude Stein: New Directions in Feminist Criticism." *Meanjin* 38 (1979): 281–93.

Gray, James. Review of *Four in America*, by Gertrude Stein. *Saturday Review of Literature*, 22 November 1947, 30.

James, Henry. *The Art of the Novel: Critical Prefaces.* New York: Charles Scribner's, 1934.

Neuman, S. C. *Gertrude Stein: Autobiography and the Problem of Narration.* ELS Monograph Series, no. 18. Victoria, B.C.: University of Victoria Press, 1979.

Ortega y Gasset, José. *The Dehumanization of Art and Other Essays on Art, Culture, and Literature.* Princeton: Princeton University Press, 1968.

Pearson, Norman Holmes. "Gertrude Stein." Review of *Four in America*, by Gertrude Stein. *The Yale Review* 37 (1948):745.

Stein, Gertrude. *The Autobiography of Alice B. Toklas.* New York: Harcourt, Brace & Co. 1933.

———. *Lectures in America.* New York: Random House, 1935.

———. *Picasso.* 1938. Reprint. New York: Scribner's, 1939.

———. *Four in America.* New Haven: Yale University Press, 1947.

———. *Bee Time Vine and Other Pieces.* In *The Yale Edition of the Unpublished Writings of Gertrude Stein*, vol. 3. New Haven: Yale University Press, 1953.

———. *Narration.* 1935. Reprint. Chicago: University of Chicago Press, 1969.

———. "A Transatlantic Interview." An excerpt from "Gertrude Stein Talking—A Transatlantic Interview." In *A Primer for the Gradual Understanding of Gertrude Stein*, edited by Robert Bartlett Haas. Los Angeles: Black Sparrow Press, 1971.

Stimpson, Catherine R. "Gertrice/Altrude: Stein, Toklas, and the Paradox of the Happy Marriage." In *Mothering the Mind: Twelve Essays of Writers and Their Silent Partners*, edited by Ruth Perry and Martine Watson Brownley. London: Holmes & Meier, 1984.

American Violence

Dreiser, Mailer, and the Nature
of Intertextuality

===

RONALD SCHLEIFER

No writer succeeded in doing the single great work which
would clarify a nation's vision of itself as Tolstoy had done
perhaps with *War and Peace* or *Anna Karenina*, and Stendhal
with *The Red and the Black*, no one novel came along which
was grand and daring and comprehensive and detailed, able
to give sustenance to the adventurer and merriment to the
rich, leave compassion in the icechambers of the upper class
and energy as alms for the poor. . . . Dreiser came as close as
any, and never got close at all, for he could not capture the
moment, and no country in history has lived perhaps so
much for the moment as America. After his failure, American literature was isolated—it was necessary to give courses
in American literature to Americans, either because they
would not otherwise read it, or because reading it, they could
not understand it.
—Norman Mailer, *Cannibals and Christians*

About a third of the way through *Cannibals and Christians* Norman
Mailer reproduces a talk he gave at the Modern Language Association (MLA) meeting some time in the early sixties. This talk can
function as the starting place for what will be the focus of my essay,
an examination of the nature of intertextuality. In this lecture
Mailer presents an "intertextual" understanding of American literature by opposing two different ways of understanding American letters, one based upon literary categories (figured as "Dreiser"
and "Wharton") and another based upon class conflict (figured as
"cannibals" and "Christians"). This double presentation will help
me to offer an intertextual reading of Mailer's great book, *The Executioner's Song*, in relation to another remarkably ambitious American novel, Theodore Dreiser's *An American Tragedy*; at the same
time, it will help me to define both Mailer and Dreiser in a more
radically intertextual position, that of a claimed *absolute* difference
from the novel of manners in America. This absolute difference,
in turn, will situate a particular American intertextuality as a kind
of violent understanding of literature and experience altogether.

In his MLA talk Mailer imagines himself presenting a twenty-minute lecture dealing with "The Dynamic of American Letters." Immediately, then, Mailer creates a context of citation in his talk, a discourse that is simultaneously direct and indirect. In this presented and imagined lecture he presents "my first sentence as lecturer: 'There has been a war at the center of American letters for a long time'" (*Cannibals* 96). That war, he notes, is class war: war between a literature of the upper middle class looking for "a refinement of itself to prepare a shift to the aristocratic" and "a counter-literature whose roots were found in poverty, industrial society, and the emergence of a new class" (96). Mailer goes on to define this war in literary terms—"naturalism versus the Genteel Tradition it has been called" (98)—and to figure the warfare as that between Edith Wharton (and her avatar Truman Capote [*Cannibals* 100; see McCord 68–77]) and Theodore Dreiser. But after the failure of Dreiser, Mailer suggests, the warfare itself degenerates into the opposition between cannibals and Christians, the "Camp" discourse of Terry Southern and the morality of Saul Bellow: "Literature was down to the earnest novel and the perfect novel, to moral seriousness and Camp. Herzog and Candy had become the protagonists" (100).

The Christians themselves, Mailer concludes, degenerate further than Herzog. "American consciousness," he writes, "in the absence of a great tradition in the novel ended by being developed by the bootlicking pieties of small-town newspaper editors and small-town educators, by the worst of organized religion" (102) while the sons of immigrants, motivated by resentment and disappointment, "took over the cities" and plundered them as

> cannibals selling Christianity to Christians, and because they despised the message and mocked at it in their own heart, they succeeded in selling something else, a virus perhaps . . .
> Yes, the cannibal sons of the immigrants had become Christians, and the formless form they had evolved for their mass-media, the hypocritical empty and tasteless taste of the television arts they beamed across the land encountered the formless form and the all but tasteless taste of the small-town tit-eating cannibal mind at its worst, and the collision produced schizophrenia in the land. (102–3)

The warfare between cannibals and Christians could stand for the conflicts that inhabit, in their different ways, Dreiser's *American Tragedy* and Mailer's *Executioner's Song*. Dreiser, after all, situates Clyde Griffith's early life within the "worst of organized religion" in the Griffith ministry, and Mailer situates Gary Gilmore's early life in the schizophrenic Mormon world of Utah, with no seeming alternative between the wholesome life of Max Jensen, the young Mormon Gilmore kills, and the life of bikers and incest that Gilmore's nineteen-year-old lover, Nicole, inhabits. Moreover, both books articulate the distinction between cannibals and Christians in terms of the American geography of East versus West, and Mailer even divides *Executioner's Song* into two global sections, "Western Voices," and "Eastern Voices," (with the latter, apparently, including the voices of California).

But more to my point is the fact that the "dynamic" of American Letters Mailer describes is an intertextual dynamic in two important ways. It describes the relationship between particular texts— *Herzog* and *Candy*, for instance—and it also describes the relationship of literary texts to the discursive network of American culture, the culture of immigrants and aristocrats, of class struggle and class warfare. Thus, it articulates both the weak and strong forms of intertextuality that Jonathan Culler discusses. These two understandings of intertextuality are, at one extreme, the precise intertextuality of reference to "a single anterior action which serves as origin and moment of plenitude" (Culler 110)—reference, that is, to some *preceding* text which, at the extreme, becomes the "influence" study of traditional intertextual readings—and, at the other extreme, the intertextuality of discourse as such, the intertextuality of the diacritical generation of signification in the Saussurean tradition.

The first extreme of this analysis, as John Frow describes it, is *particular* in historical as well as textual terms. It is exemplified in Hans Robert Jauss's model of "the situation of the text in relation to a unified horizon of expectations which is not purely literary but which forms a homogeneous structure determining the production and reception of new texts" (125)—structures which, like the mindless clichés of the immigrant media moguls Mailer portrays, include literary genres and, more specifically, particular previous literary texts. The other extreme is exemplified in Julia Kristeva's "concept of the intertextual relations between literary discourse and its raw material"—the "general discursive field" (Frow 127). In this instance, Frow notes, "instead of the social *determination* of the literary norm, we have the social text as *content* of the literary text" (127), the book about "a nation's vision of itself" as Mailer describes it (*Cannibals* 98).

This double view of intertextuality is somewhat self-contradictory. It is simultaneously *external* and *internal*. External intertextuality describes the interrelationship with preexisting social "texts," including both particular literary works (*The Red and the Black, In Cold Blood*) and social forms (genres, the economics of publishing, the literacy of readers, etc.); internal intertextuality describes the diacritical discursive interrelationships that generate meaning altogether (the binary oppositions between "cannibals" and "Christians," "East" and "West," "text" and "text"). Frow goes on to argue that "intertextuality is always in the first place a relation to the literary canon (to the 'specifically literary' function and authority of an element) and only *through* this a relation to the general discursive field" (128), but if this is true of Dreiser (or, at least, of Mailer's reading of Dreiser's opposition to the novels of manners of Wharton and James), Mailer himself, as I shall argue, achieves a more thorough intertextuality *between* these conceptions and approaches.

These two conceptions are subtly changed in Mailer's double argument about American culture and American literature—in the dynamics that run across these two accounts of the "Dynamic of American Letters." America, Mailer says, lacks the "external" tradition of particular "national" works that creates a literature outside the assignments of the classroom, a "useful" literature that can teach its citizens how to live. And in that lack America creates its own virtually impossible "internal" discourse—a dynamic discourse born out of the dynamic of American letters. This internal American discourse is the energy of the continent figured in its living "for the moment," a relation to time that destroys all tradition and, specifically, the European tradition of letters which it assumes as its own literary model. Such a discourse is different from either intertextuality as Culler and Frow describe it, the external intertextuality of Jauss's reading or the "internal" cacophonous play of voices without a stable content or center in which to ground itself. Rather, these two intertextual forces are at play in Mailer's work to create his own version of the "nation's vision of itself" in *Executioner's Song*. I will figure them in the *particular* novel of Dreiser, *An American Tragedy*, and in the general comments about novels that Gustave Flaubert makes to help define a late-nineteenth-century literary tradition. But their presence in Mailer delimits another kind of interplay—a postmodern intertextuality played against the violence of the energetic version of American intertextuality, the discourse of the moment.

That is, in *Executioner's Song*, written fifteen years after he presented his MLA talk, Mailer himself joined (or really rejoined) the war at the center of American letters by answering the gentility of

Capote's *In Cold Blood*—which he specifically mentions in his lecture—with his own attempt at clarifying the nation's vision of itself.
Mailer's book, like any such American visionary attempt, is itself
intertextual in both of the senses I have outlined. It is, I believe, a
rewriting and resituating of Dreiser's *An American Tragedy*, but like
that earlier book in Mailer's estimation, it is also an attempt to give
sustenance to Americans by capturing the moment of another intertextuality in the warfare between the voices of small-town Christians (like Jauss) and urban cannibals (like Kristeva), between the
West and the East. Such warfare, as Mailer notes, is best figured in
the reduction of intertextuality to schizophrenia and the reduction
of discourse to television. The "momentary" vision of America that
Executioner's Song offers is a television event, a public execution,
which articulates what I will describe as a kind of intertextual
overload. As such, it can help us to read and reread Dreiser's
achievement in *An American Tragedy* and the intertextual dynamic
of American letters altogether.

A Book about Something

So let us say the war was between Dreiser and Edith Wharton, Dreiser all strategy, no tactics; and Wharton all tactics.
Marvelous tactics they were—a jewel of a writer and stingy
as a person—she needed no strategy.
—Norman Mailer, *Cannibals and Christians* (98)

The two traditions in American literature Mailer describes, figured
in the persons of Dreiser and Wharton, can help us to understand
Mailer's attempt to do what he thought Dreiser could not do,
namely, to present America with a vision of itself. What Mailer
achieves in *Executioner's Song* is a book that captures the modernity—
or really the postmodernity—of American culture by presenting
what Dreiser called an American *tragedy* as a media event. That is,
Executioner's Song rewrites the tragedy of Clyde Griffith's American
life in the form of what Flaubert called "a book about nothing," a
book whose events, finally, are *inconsequential* because its protagonists and its events are so thoroughly ordinary. "There are in me,"
Flaubert wrote in 1852, in his famous letter to Louise Colet,

literally speaking, two distinct persons: one who is infatuated with
bombast, lyricism, eagle flights, sonorities of phrase and the high
points of ideas; and another who digs and burrows into the truth
as deeply as he can . . .
What seems beautiful to me, what I should like to write, is
a book about nothing, a book dependent on nothing external,

which would be held together by the strength of its style ... a book which would have almost no subject, or at least in which the subject would be almost invisible, if such a thing is possible. The finest works are those that contain the least matter; the closer expression comes to thought, the closer language comes to coinciding and merging with it, the finer the result. (154)

Dreiser, throughout his work, but especially in *An American Tragedy*, is a person of the first type Flaubert describes. More than anything else, he wants to achieve a book about something, what Mailer describes as "a nation's vision of itself," in the bombastic ambition of his fiction rather than the "finer" stylistic achievement Flaubert describes. For Dreiser, as for Mailer, the energy of vision is more important than its discrimination.

For a book about nothing, like the recent turn in literary studies from interpretation to examining the *conditions* of interpretation (including *intertextuality* as a condition of interpretation in which language and "thought" merge and coincide), is a turn from subject matter to the exquisite intelligence that *reads* the minute signs that govern and condition social life. Thus, Wharton ends *The Age of Innocence*, for instance, without action and in the silent "reading" of events. At the end of the novel Newland Archer sits before his aging lover's house and refuses to act. Instead, he "reads" the servant's closing of the shutters "as if it had been a signal he waited for" (361), and then he leaves. Similar to Flaubert's *Sentimental Education*, what Wharton offers instead of bombast is the "making sense" of an accidental gesture, creating a semiotic reading out of the "nothing" of a habitual action. This is what Saussure calls the "zero sign" in the intertextual interplay of linguistic and semiotic elements, where "a material sign is not necessary for the expression of an idea; language is satisfied with the opposition between something and nothing" (86). In a book about nothing, "nothing," meaningless gestures, the absence of action, are so situated within a semiotic system that "nothing" takes its place within a system of meaning to convey possible significance. The "style" of linguistic interplay between something and nothing creates the condition of possible meaning. It creates the semiotic possibility that "nothing" can come to signify.

A book about something, on the other hand, takes experience to be more than the interplay of signs, more than the intertextuality of all meaning in the second definition of intertextuality I have offered. It takes experience to be the positive effects of such interplay, the "sonorities of phrase and high point of ideas" Flaubert speaks of, the bombast that infatuates him. Such bombast is that of asserted interpretation, rather than the silent recognition of the semiosis that conditions and is internal to all discursive tactics and formations. *An American Tragedy*, like much of Mailer before *The Executioner's Song*, is such a bombastic discourse. For this reason Clarence Darrow describes the experience of reading it not as the feeling of reading a story, but rather "that of a series of terrible physical impacts that have relentlessly shocked every sensitive nerve in the body" (5), an experience which, as Irving Howe says, "pulls one, muttering and bruised, into the arena of [Dreiser's] imagination" (820). And H. L. Mencken describes Dreiser's style as "wholly devoid of what may be called literary tact," containing writing he calls "dreadful bilge" (13, 15).

In these terms, there are two novels in Dreiser, just as there are in Flaubert, which play against one another unconsciously, diacritically, intertextually. When Dreiser plots inarticulate experience, he achieves, as Mailer says, a kind of power of vision. But when he seeks to explain his vision, to articulate its "truth"—when he aspires to the understanding of Wharton or the intelligent sensitivity of James in a novelistic discourse that, in Mailer's terms, could "reason out" how things work—he cannot pass on the knowledge he has gained. Dreiser, Mailer writes, is "like some heroic tragic entrepreneur who has reasoned out through his own fatigue and travail very much how everything works in the iron mills of life, but is damned because he cannot pass on the knowledge to his children" (*Cannibals* 97). Dreiser, he says, cannot pass on his vision to the "cannibals" for whom he wrote because since he had "no eye for the deadly important manners of the rich, he was obliged to call a rich girl 'charming'; he could not make her charming when she spoke, as Fitzgerald could" (97). Dreiser cannot articulate the semiosis of "charm," the interplay of language that creates the meaning-effect /charm/. Instead, he "commodifies" (Jameson) or "substantifies" (Greimas) it in the "necromancy" of bombastic attribution. In this way, he fails to bring intelligence and understanding to the events, the plot, of his novel.

But the *quality* of that bombast—what makes Dreiser, for Mailer, superior to Wharton—is precisely the fact that he doesn't dig or burrow into the conditions of silent understanding by presenting, without action, the scene of recognition. Rather, he presents the force of events to be recognized and attempts to articulate explanations of these events that are proportionate to their power and energy. In this is the central paradox of Dreiser, whom Jameson calls "our greatest novelist" (161): his verbal understanding never coincides with the events it attempts to understand. Jameson describes this as "a strange and alien bodily speech . . . interwoven with the linguistic junk of commodified language" (160–61). But it is the *interplay* of these two languages—the "bodily speech" absent from Wharton's centers of consciousness and recognition and the "commodification" of understanding making the subtle semiotic interplay of meaning into objective, "substantified" discourse—that creates Dreiser's (and America's) particular intertextual power.

That is, Dreiser expresses the *energy* of "eagle flights," rather than the discriminations of truth, intelligence, or semiosis, precisely in the central unintelligibility, the essential indiscriminate "commodified" explanations of his discourse. Thus, Mencken goes on to assert that Dreiser "regards himself as an adept at the Freudian necromancy." He "frequently uses its terms, and seems to take its fundamental doctrines very seriously but he is actually a behaviorist of the most advanced wing. What interests him primarily is not what people think, but what they do. He is full of a sense of their helplessness" (16). That is, Dreiser creates a bombastic discourse within which exists not truth or semiotic play or exquisite readers of truth and semiotic play, but rather the play of events beyond intelligence. The gesture of explanation without intelligibility—in a word, the gesture of necromancy aping authors of the novel of manners such as Wharton—generates the power of his discourse, the meaning-effect of power beyond intelligence.

For all the bombastic examples of explanation in *An American Tragedy*, for all the bombast of a rational discourse shading into a ludicrous parody of a Whartonian exploration of motives and the conditions of action, such discovered jewels of explanation are not what interests Dreiser in the way they interest the "Eastern" (i.e., Californian) voice of Barry Farrell in *Executioner's Song* when he discovers the significance of Gary Gilmore's eyes (827–29). Rather, as Julian Markels notes in a remarkably insightful study of *An American Tragedy*,

> When Dreiser locates the drowning two-thirds through the 800-page novel, having told in minute detail the grim story of his hero's life beginning at age twelve, critics on the scent of naturalism assume that he has been spending his time building up a great weight of environmental forces that are to crush Clyde and explain the murder. But none of the mountainous information about Clyde's early life is even relevant to explain the murder. (49)

The information is not relevant because Dreiser does not aim at explanation. He seeks instead to articulate characters who are, as Markels says, "so to speak, below the threshold of consciousness"

(51); that is, "by his characteristic arrangement of episodes, Dreiser creates a firm pattern for the inscrutable, patternless drift of experience" (50).

The failure of explanation is the vehicle of signification in Dreiser, its own kind of "zero sign" conveying randomness rather than pattern, not a semiotic unconsciousness to be read, as Freud reads it, in slips and stutters, but the utter unconsciousness of accident. It is precisely the inarticulateness of his explanations—precisely the lack of proportion between events and understanding—that presents, bombastically, the energy of Dreiser's vision. In other words, Dreiser himself offers in the interplay of event and explanation that can never encompass the event itself a form of bombast that does not clarify but does present and enact the nation's vision of itself. The very fact that Dreiser fails at intelligence is part of his power and a condition of his strength.

Virtually every chapter in *An American Tragedy* begins with some kind of explanation or necromancy and, more often than not, they seem to be the kind of "bilge" Mencken speaks of. In fact, the problem with the novel—its dullness and pretentiousness—might well be a problem with chapters, with what linguistics calls the *segmentation* of its discourse. Chapters begin by attempting to understand and explain what is going on—to summarize the preceding chapter or proleptically to summarize what will come—and it is precisely these attempts that make Dreiser seem such an inept Wharton. One can randomly open the novel to such explanations. For instance, chapter 45 of book 2 begins with notably inept figures:

> There are moments when in connection with the sensitively imaginative or morbidly anachronistic—the mentality assailed and the same not of any great strength and the problem confronting it of sufficient force and complexity—the reason not actually toppling from its throne, still totters or is warped or shaken—the mind befuddled to the extent that for the time being, at least, unreason or disorder and mistaken or erroneous counsel would appear to hold against all else. In such instances the will and the courage confronted by some great difficulty which it can neither master nor endure, appears in some to recede in precipitate flight, leaving only panic and temporary unreason in its wake. (463)

Leaving aside the strong sense, when reading this passage in isolation, that Dreiser seems to be describing the difficulty of the novelist's task—or, at least, the difficulty of the novel of explanation and manners he apes in such passages, the novel that attempts constantly the tactics of a metalanguage to explain and understand the behavior and relationships of its characters—we still are presented with an almost unreadable passage, a parody of explanation.

Such a passage is comparable to the kinds of explanations Clyde Griffith (or Dennis Boaz in his "California" discourse of synchronicity in *The Executioner's Song*) might give himself, a kind of aping of what popular culture validates as appropriate explanation. Thus Clyde describes Sondra, in a passage written in ambiguous indirect discourse, as "in her small, intense way, a seeking Aphrodite, eager to prove to any who were sufficiently attractive the destroying power of her charm" (320). And in a passage from *The Executioner's Song* that is more clearly Boaz's indirect discourse he "began to ponder the tougher side of Gary. Macho to a certain extent. Of course, he had to use a gun to prove his power. Lived in ultimates. Must have been a very sensitive child" (527). Dreiser's explanation of Clyde's behavior, like Clyde's perception of Sondra's "charm" and Boaz's perception of Gilmore's "macho" side, is the second kind of intertextuality I mentioned at the beginning of this study, that between a text and the diacritical system of invested values in which it is embedded. In the opening to chapter 65, Dreiser simultaneously assumes the conceptual framework of Freudian necromancy and the discourse of allegory (reminiscent of some of Poe's psychical figures in "The Fall of the House of Usher") to find a language to articulate Clyde's inarticulate experience. The fact is, Clyde is less intelligent than a character in James or Wharton, less aware of the discourses that control his consciousness, less conscious of the kind of global intertextuality that Kristeva describes. And Dreiser shares this limitation with his character. The novel of manners is the novel of semiotics, an "intertextual" model in which characters read, more or less, the intertextual condition of signmaking that governs their behavior and their environment. Dreiser apes this novel in his explanations, his necromancy, his attempts to transform the accident of Clyde's life not into a sign, but into a positive event, a commodity, a tragedy.

Yet despite the constant gesture towards explanation—the constant *model* of the novel of manners which Dreiser apes with ludicrously bad results—this novelistic project is, as I have said, not the strength of his vision. That strength is the very bombast of his writing, which demonstrates, seemingly beyond Dreiser's own understanding, the power of events beyond understanding. Like the power of Dreiser's novel, the tragedy of Clyde's life is not in the explanation, but stems from the palpable fact that explanations cannot sufficiently explain the unbreachable gap between the energy of Clyde's desire and the poverty of his understanding. In

other words, the very attempt to encompass the inarticulate movement of events within some intelligible framework functions, seemingly beyond Dreiser's own intention, as its own "zero sign," which
creates the effect of energy and desire that is unconscious to characters and apparently to Dreiser himself.

Chapter 65, for instance, goes on to describe Clyde's "inner conflict" in a heavy-handed way. Dreiser's description of Clyde's mind
is representative of his attempt to comprehend inarticulateness, to
situate "nothing" as a positive content. "The center or mentating
section of his brain," he writes:

> at the time might well have been compared to a sealed and silent
> hall in which alone and undisturbed, and that in spite of himself,
> he now sat thinking on the mystic or evil and terrifying desires or
> advice of some darker or primordial and unregenerate nature of
> his own, and without the power to drive the same forth or him-
> self to decamp, and yet also without the courage to act upon any-
> thing. (464)

Yet for all the awkwardness of this conceit, it finally asserts in its
crude way not simply the reality of the inner conflict that Clyde
undergoes (surely Wharton could have presented this more effectively) but the reality of Clyde's being overwhelmed by events which
language cannot encompass or control. Manners cannot stem this
desire in the way they stem the desire of Newland Archer; manners, reading, semiotics, social life simply do not have the resources
even to articulate the "Giant Efrit" that whispers to Clyde, telling
him to "whisper, whisper—let your language be soft, your tone
tender, loving, even. It must be if you are to win her to your will
now. So the Efrit of his own darker self" (472).

Mailer's Song

I hear America singing, the varied carols I hear, . . .
Each singing what belongs to him or her and to none else,
The day what belongs to the day—at night the party of
    young fellows, robust, friendly,
Singing with open mouths their strong melodious songs.
—Walt Whitman, "I Hear America Singing"

Although Mailer perceived in 1966 the strength of Dreiser's achievement, he could only discover an intertextual understanding of
Dreiser after he embarked on *Executioner's Song* in 1979 and gave
up, in that work at least, his own bombast. Thus he answers the
bombastic poem in *Cannibals and Christians* entitled "The Executioner's Song"—a poem, first published in the magazine *Fuck You*,

which describes killing, gravedigging, and bowel movements—with his own quiet and seemingly anonymous *old prison song* as the epigraph to his book about Gilmore (see *Executioner's Song* 1052). Even in *Cannibals and Christians* he notes that his desire to write a long novel

> may be here again, and if that is so, I will have yet to submit to the prescription laid down by the great physician Dr. James Joyce—"silence, exile, and cunning," he said. Well, one hopes not; the patient is too gregarious for the prescription. (5)

The patient did prove too gregarious for cunning, and America too exciting for exile, but Mailer learned a kind of "silence" in which to let the American "noise," with its own "momentary" bombast, articulate itself.

In American culture Mailer discovered, as Dreiser never did with European and Jamesian models standing before him, that he was dealing with a subject which did not lend itself to cunning explanation; he found that there were, in fact, aspects of human and social life that were not susceptible to intelligent responses. What the story—not the tragedy—of love and death in Gary Gilmore's life, and more generally in American life, demonstrated to Mailer was the poverty of intelligence and the necessity of a kind of silent listening even if the noise he heard did not make sense. As he told William Buckley on the television program *Firing Line*,

> This material made me begin to look at ten or 20 serious questions in an altogether new fashion, and it made me humble in that I just didn't know the answers. I mean, I've had the habit for years of feeling that I could dominate any question pretty quickly—it's been my vanity. And it was an exceptional experience to spend all these months and find that gently but inevitably, I was finding myself in more profound—not confusion—but doubt about my ability to answer to give definite answers to these questions. But what I had instead is that I was collecting materials that I would think about for the rest of my life. In other words, I was getting new experience. I thought it might be very nice for once just to write a book which doesn't have answers, but poses delicate questions with a great deal of evidence and a great deal of material and let people argue over it. (Quoted in Hellmann 60)

What Mailer discovered was that a vision of America, unlike a vision of Russia or France, cannot produce answers and explanations. This is the knowledge which Mailer sees that Dreiser, writing above all a book about "something," lacks.

In this way, then, *Executioner's Song* situates itself against the interplay between energy and semiosis, between something and nothing. It situates itself against precisely what *An American Tragedy*, for all its ambition, could not accommodate: the momentary dynamic in American letters between Wharton's "tactics" and Dreiser's "strategy." *The Executioner's Song*, in an important way, is a book about nothing—a book about Gary Gilmore's own attempt to create significance in the face of overwhelming pain through the accidental murder of strangers. These murders are accidental in a sense very different from Clyde Griffith's murder. In Dreiser's novel it seems clear that Clyde murders Roberta without intentionally (i.e., consciously) choosing to do so. In Mailer's book Gilmore clearly kills Jensen and Bushnell intentionally, but it is equally clear that any particular people would have served his purpose just as any "material sign"—including the "zero sign"—will serve semiosis. Gilmore's murders are embodiments of the arbitrary nature of the sign.

For Mailer the sign is arbitrary in the way it is arbitrary for Wharton but not for Dreiser. The remarkable thing about Mailer's book is that more than in Wharton, more than in even Flaubert, more than in Joyce (who claimed to have memorized the whole of *Sentimental Education*), one can open *Executioner's Song* to any page and discover there a sign that can constitute the interpretive center of the book as a whole. That is, *Executioner's Song* maintains a network of internal intertextuality. For instance, in describing the love between Nicole and Gary, Mailer offers this paragraph early in his book:

> All she wanted was more hours with him. She had always appreciated any minute she had to herself, but now she would get impatient with wanting him to be back. When five o'clock rolled around and he was there, the day was made. She loved opening that first beer for him. (86)

As in Joyce and Flaubert, here is a kind of apotheosis of free indirect discourse, a discourse, unlike that of Dreiser (and like that of Wharton), which presents but does not authorize interpretation. There is no bombast in the assertion of the symbolic force of opening the beer, yet one can read in this signifier—if one is sensitive enough—the sign of the relationship between Nicole and Gary, their class and sexual situation, and the limitations of what they can imagine for themselves.

Yet more than in Wharton, this arbitrariness is temporal as well as spatial; it embodies the accidental nature of what Mailer calls America's relation to the moment. *The Age of Innocence*, as a book

133

about nothing, narrates the failure to seize the moment, Archer's repeated failure in youth and age. In this it follows the pattern of Flaubert, of Joyce's Dubliners, even of the patience and passivity of Austen's heroines. In other words, the novel of manners, like structuralism itself, conceives of the diacritical intertextual play constituting semiosis as primarily spatial: semiosis is *situated* in a "center of consciousness" which reads (or learns to read) the world's signs. *An American Tragedy*, a book about something, narrates a similar moment's failure, but it is a failure in action and the timing of action rather than a failure determined by intelligence and reading. Dreiser brings intelligence to bear on the tragedy he narrates; he apes the situated tactical reading of experience by drawing, as Mencken notes, on contemporary "received" understandings of behavior. His novel, however, is not about such tactics, but rather about a larger comprehension of America: it does not relate the tactics of a situated class, but the strategic warfare between classes.

In *Executioner's Song* the moment is a determinant in every sign— every sign asserts meaning in the face of the accidents of time— even though, as in Dreiser, the signs are not local readings of experience, but attempts at global understandings. Nicole's beer is thus significantly different from Archer's hesitation: it is situated at the end of the workday for working-class people not by the intelligence of its perceiver but by a *commercial* sign-system, what Jean Baudrillard calls the "commodity as system" (92). In *Executioner's Song* every sign is arbitrary because it is commodified in the assertions, conscious or unconscious, of its users. As such an asserted sign, it both exists outside of any temporal pattern and exists as a sign of its own moment. By means of such signs—again consciously or unconsciously—all the characters of *Executioner's Song* seek to flee temporal determination through semiotic acts, just as Clyde Griffith seeks to flee the accidental determination of his birth through the bombastic act of murder while Dreiser himself attempts to present a universal, tragic vision of America in his own "commodified" language. The main characters of *Executioner's Song*, the "Western" Gilmore and the "Eastern" Schiller, pursue semiotic repetition (re-presentation) with as much energy as Clyde pursues social promotion. Gilmore, like Gatsby, wants to live over the past life he lost in prison; he dates girls fifteen years younger than himself, and he imagines a metaphysics of reincarnation to allow the actions of life to be repeated. Schiller sees the Gilmore story as the opportunity to remake himself as a writer, to overcome the image of an ambulance chaser he has acquired, just as he sees his upcoming second marriage as a way to remake the pattern of his personal life. But all the characters of *Executioner's Song*—both Eastern and Western Americans—seek to comprehend experience by understanding the moment as a spot of time susceptible to spatialization. Boaz constantly understands experience in terms of "synchronicity," while Farrell seeks to understand Gilmore as a type of "Harry Truman, mediocrity enlarged by history" (828); the Mormons see marriage as itself simultaneously earthly and heavenly, while Dr. Woods, Gilmore's psychiatrist, seeks to understand him in terms of the drug Prolixin: "Whole fields of the soul could be defoliated and never leave a trace" (400).

These are examples of intertextuality as a kind of commodification of discourse. To read Nicole's beer as I have as a sign of the narrative is an internal intertextuality taking its place metaphorically, interplaying with the many beers, usually stolen (and thus usually functioning as a kind of synecdoche), that Gilmore consumes. Yet it is also external, an embodiment of American culture at a particular moment, where beer commercials repeatedly commodify leisure and relaxation under the sign of "beer." In a way, *Executioner's Song*, like other postmodern works such as Robert Coover's "The Babysitter," is an implicit manifestation of a television culture. As Arthur Kroker and David Cook note in *The Postmodern Scene*, "the *language of signification* and its surrealistic reversals is the basic codex of the real world of television culture. Cars *are* horses; computers *are* galaxies, tombstones or heartbeats; beer *is* friendship" (275). Nicole's very understanding—the repetitious/spatial understanding as a sign in relation to something else, something *not there*—is governed by the moment of commodification, not the action of semiosis.

Here, I think, is the significance of the special status of indirect discourse in *Executioner's Song* and the often noticed spacing of its paragraphs. "The trick," Phyllis McCord has noted,

> is that the narrator is himself fragmented into these points of view, for he does not make connections; only the character or the reader does. Rather than the usual seamless web of omniscient historical narration, there are only gaps between the discourses. A "visible" reminder of this is in fact invisible: the white space between paragraphs or short groups of paragraphs on nearly every page of the novel. (73; see also Hellmann 62)

Unlike *An American Tragedy*, whose narrator constantly attempts to make the "connections" his characters cannot make, Mailer's enormous book is made of small sections typographically separated from one another by spaces. In this it enacts a kind of intertextuality, even going so far as to have some chapters virtually comprised of juxtaposed texts: newspaper accounts, Gilmore's letters, interview transcripts (see Anderson 121). In the same way that Dreiser uses his chapters to offer summarizing global understandings of the overwhelming activity of American life, so Mailer uses spaces to offer the innumerable *asserted* interpretations that comprise his vision of America. Every paragraph in *Executioner's Song* offers a sign by which to read the life of Gary Gilmore: a can of beer, a senseless murder, an apple tree, all are readings of his life.

But they are signs to be read in "voices," in the indirect discourse of the characters who inhabit *Executioner's Song*. Here Mailer follows Dr. Joyce's prescription of silence. But it is a noisy and cacophonous silence of many voices speaking simultaneously, comparable to the constant din of background noise Gilmore complains about in prison. As McCord notes, "there is no such omniscient narrator in Mailer's masterpiece; all the news comes through an intervening consciousness or viewpoint, and the text thus enacts through its form the idea that there is no unmediated experience, no world except that created by consciousness and language" (71). The text thus enacts its own intertextuality, what McCord later describes as the "competing discourses" (78) of Mailer's internal intertextuality. What competes, however, are different interpretations of experience, different moments, as dialectical philosophy describes it, of understanding. These philosophical moments attempt to do what Dreiser attempts, to capture the frenzied moments of American life in strategies of intelligent action. Mailer said that he had planned to call his book *American Virtue* because, as John Hellmann summarizes his explanation, "he discovered in writing it that a concern with doing 'the right thing,' however varying the concept of what that might entail, was the trait most characteristic of Americans" (59). Hellmann goes on to note that Mailer gave up this title because he was convinced that it would be misinterpreted as sardonic. But what is most striking about this explanation is that it focuses on cliché—"the right thing" (like "the right stuff")—just the kind of "received ideas" that Flaubert suggests constitute "nothing." That is, while Dreiser uses—often quite unconsciously—the necromancy of received ideas to make sense out of experience, Mailer presents a *"true life story"* that represents that semiotic process on every page, in every paragraph, and in various moments indirectly, through its class-determined characters' manners of understanding. This representation is still semiotically conceived, but it is situated in the very commodification of junk that Dreiser articulates, situated in the difference or interplay between human energies and desires and junk meanings.

136

The Executioner's Song presents a structure of texts defining "the right thing," yet those things themselves are arbitrary to the extent of inviting without authorizing their intertextual reading. Take, for instance, the "apple tree" of the book's first sentences: "Brenda was six when she fell out of the apple tree. She climbed to the top and the limb with the good apples broke off. Gary caught her as the branch came scraping down. They were scared" (5). This beginning seems to resonate with other texts—the Bible, Faulkner perhaps, even the ambiguous apple tree in the backyard of Joyce's "Araby." It does so precisely because of its *textual* situation at the beginning of the book. But the style, like that of Joyce, simply does not authorize any particular connection. Here an absolute paratactic discourse creates no hierarchies of meaning, calls attention to none of its elements. It is as if the tree is simply a tree, and the great anxiety of this beginning is to make sense out of it. But *Executioner's Song* never authorizes a way of understanding its indirect discourse. Moreover, as Chris Anderson notes,

> the language continues in this vein for over a thousand pages, rarely varying in tone or emphasis, and this is the key to its effect. With a minimum organization and intervention, Mailer takes us from one point in Gilmore's life up to the end, relentlessly recording all the trivia, all the meaningless details of his experience, reproducing the texture of his life without making it meaningful or giving it a literary shape . . . The obvious flatness of the language mirrors the randomness of detail. (119)

The "momentary" quality of the indirect discourse of *Executioner's Song* is most unnerving in its randomness. Gossip and voyeurism carry the text along, and it is, I suspect, the nonfictional status of this "*true life story*," as Mailer calls it in the afterword (1053), that sustains it in the face of its own trivia. Mailer hears America singing in *Executioner's Song*, but the momentary indirect discourse he hears never quite achieves melody beyond its individual voices, its indirect moments.

The Discourse of the Moment

> The siren song turns into the maddening noise of promotional culture: all emotional primitivism on the one hand, and the artificial intelligence of a serial culture under the sign of quantum technology on the other.
> —Kroker and Cook, *The Postmodern Scene* (16)

In *Executioner's Song* Mailer hears America singing, but it is as if the songs he hears are the programmed clichés of television jingles, as if, as Kroker and Cook say, the siren song of America singing has turned promotional. For *Executioner's Song* is a novel about "promotion" in a very different sense from Clyde's quest for promotions in his work and life. Schiller and Gilmore, Boaz and Farrell, even Mailer himself—author of *Advertisements for Myself*—are all engaged in self-promotion. Moreover, the book itself grows out of television and its own maddening promotional noise: Schiller pursues the story which he finally sells to Mailer as a possible television mini-series, one which was eventually aired. In this, the book presents intertextuality with a vengeance, what Arthur Kroker calls the "hysterical semiology" of the postmodern scene (79). Such postmodern semiology "functions," as Kroker says, "on the basis of a transformation of the *real* into an empty 'sign system'" (100); it is "a technology of hyper-symbolization . . . which functions by processing culture and economy into a sign-system (a *radical* structuralism) endlessly deployable in its rhetoric and always circular in its movement" (75), a sign-system "which refracts its 'fictitious' *terms* in a ceaseless process of lateral referentiality" (108). As such, hysterical semiology is "a pure sign-system: it cannot be embedded in a chain of finalities because . . . [it] signifies the cancellation of vertical being" (79).

Here is an intertextuality which is all surface and no depth, the discourse of the moment: the interplay among its voices is like the ceaseless changing of channels on a television set, the ceaseless interchangeability of elements, the temporal arbitrariness of signs. In this way, as Kroker says,

> the new information of the electronic mass media is directly destructive of meaning and signification, or neutralizes it. Information, far from producing an "accelerated circulation" of meaning, a plus-value of meaning homologous to the economic plus-value which results from the accelerated rotation of capital, implies the destruction of *any* coherent meaning-system. (176–77)

Such hysterical semiology—Kroker might have termed it "panic semiosis"—is what he calls "the death of the social and the triumph of signifying culture . . . the indefinite reversibility and self-liquidation of all the foundational *recits* of contemporary culture" (26). It is a semiological overload which destroys the social basis of sign systems by multiplying the moments of discourse in its varied voices beyond coherence.

Thus, if the characters' indirect voices in *Executioner's Song* ape the sensitivity of Wharton in her attempt to read signs of social life everywhere, they also ape Dreiser's interpretive strategies, his attempt to control the uncontrollable energy of American ambition.

The plenitude of signs overwhelms the reader of *Executioner's Song* very much like the plenitude of power overwhelms the reader of *An American Tragedy*, until semiosis itself explodes under its own fullness. As Dreiser says in the passage I have quoted, "the will and the courage . . . recede in precipitate flight, leaving only panic and temporary unreason in its wake" (463). Gilmore, in willing his own death and using it as a media event, is the very *signifier* of such semiotic explosion. Here Mailer is attempting to counter the genteel semiotic tradition not with positive tragic events, but with overload, with panic semiosis.

It is this panic that controls not only Dreiser, in his rush to make sense and tragedy out of the accidental experience of Clyde Griffith, but also Mailer's commentators. Thus, Chris Anderson immediately transforms the experience of *Executioner's Song* into a significatory system. In this understanding Gary Gilmore is a kind of zero sign since, as Anderson amply demonstrates, Gilmore himself resists any kind of explanation of his behavior: "'What I do,' he says, 'is the absence of thought'" (800), void of content, motive. Anderson goes on to cite Gilmore's description of himself as "slightly less than bland" and notes that "as he struggles to understand Gilmore's personality and feeling, Schiller comes to realize that the murders express a deep and even terrifying void" (126).

All this, however, leads Anderson to the conclusion that there is an important *figurative* signification here: "Textuality figures superficiality," he asserts (127). That is,

> on a second reading stylistic traces of Mailer's earlier voice begin to emerge, examples of a language that could only come from Mailer himself as author behind the silent poses, and these serve to direct the flow and meaning of the text, rendering its very flatness and superficiality figurative. A voice emerges which gives us the key to reading the voice of the recorder as ironic, a way of disclosing Mailer's sense that the Gilmore story is fundamentally meaningless, representative of a void. (122)

Here is semiosis with a vengeance, the discovery of a figurative sign in the absence of signs, transforming nothing into something. Such a figurative sign functions by means of premature closure, of making a pattern of moments, in an attempt to understand Gilmore's story in ways that Mailer, posing questions that cannot be answered, never attempts.

In other words, this is an example of the broadest sense of intertextuality imaginable: the *textualization* of experience so that one can make sense, any kind of sense. If meaning is textual and intertex-

tual, if it depends upon the diacritical play between elements—phonemes, lexemes, different texts themselves—then "making sense"
of experience, transforming accident into tragedy, pain into a motive for action (murder), is a kind of unavoidable necromancy, an
hysterical semiosis. Jacques Derrida addresses this very procedure
of textualization throughout his work. Textualization—including
the appropriations of the *intertextual*—is always violent, in a violence that Jacques Lacan figures as "murder" (104). Yet such violence, Derrida argues, responds to an even greater violence in a
kind of panic, a hysterical rush to meaning. "Discourse," Derrida
writes,

> if it is originally violent, can only *do itself violence*, can only negate
> itself in order to affirm itself, make war upon the war which insti-
> tutes it without ever *being able* to reappropriate this negativity, to
> the extent that it is discourse. *Necessarily* without reappropriating
> it, for if it did so, the horizon of peace would disappear into the
> night (worst violence as previolence). This secondary war, as the
> avowal of violence, is the least possible violence, the only way to
> repress the worst violence, the violence of primitive and prelogical
> silence, of an unimaginable night which would not even be the
> opposite of day, an absolute violence which would not even be the
> opposite of nonviolence: nothingness or pure non-sense. Thus
> discourse chooses itself violently in opposition to nothingness or
> pure non-sense. (130)

Here Derrida is describing the choice of intertextuality over discourse without discursive (that is to say, "meaningful") contexts, a
discourse of the moment. For Dreiser *not* to see Clyde Griffith's life
as a tragedy, not to articulate his motives as a kind of rational dialogue, not to discover in the accident of his life the sign of America
itself would plunge the world into panic and horror worse than the
unintelligibility of his explanations. This is another intertextuality,
a *radical* intertextuality between random, momentary events and
the order of discourse.

It is not the same for Wharton. The motive behind Newland
Archer's refusal to act is solely tactical: he never acknowledges, as
Wharton herself never acknowledges, the possibility that the sensibility that has governed his life might be a strategic act of violence,
that the semiotic forms that situate him in a privileged position in
his world might articulate a violence against the world that responds to the greater violence of accident and nothingness.

I cannot say, as Archer can, and Anderson can, and Truman
Capote can, what the "experience" of *Executioner's Song* figures,
what "beer" in that book, for instance, figures, whether the fall

from the apple tree at the beginning is a meaningful sign existing in an intertextual network that constitutes it as a sign or whether it is a random and momentary event. In these cases the book enacts the simultaneous struggle between semiosis and silence (which Wharton engages in) and semiosis and noise (which Dreiser engages in), the prescriptions of Dr. Joyce and Dr. Mailer. In them, I suspect, Mailer is attempting to articulate the energy of America as a kind of virtue.

But he does so in an intertextual discourse—a postmodern American discourse—which, while engaging both external texts and genre and the internal interplay of textuality itself, also engages in its quiet hysteria the absolute violence behind its text and behind Griffith, Gilmore, and the cacophony of America's random and momentary voices. *The Executioner's Song* offers a figure for this *radical* intertextuality in its description of Pete Galovan's prayer:

> He prayed that the Lord have mercy on Nicole and Gary, and bless them, and that Gary get some control of himself. Pete didn't remember all the things he said in the prayer, or even if he held her hand while he prayed. One was not supposed to remember what was said in prayers. It was a sacred moment, and not really to be repeated. (133)

Prayer, in this passage, can stand for the trivia and tedium of Gary's life and Mailer's narrative of his life. But more important, I think, it describes the discourse of the moment. Prayer, here, addresses God at a particular moment in particular circumstances. It cannot be repeated because it is a response to the world rather than an understanding of it. Such an act can be understood as a figure of a situation in the semiosis of synecdoche. But more importantly, it is an unrepeatable act, essentially random, violent, *without the possibility of semiotic assimilation*, without any intertextual status. This prayer, like television, implies the destruction of *any* coherent meaning-system.

Here is a "discourse" radically about nothing, about inconsequential and random events, including language-events. In it, event is conceived, as Kroker and Cook describe the "panic philosophy" of postmodern culture, as meaningless and contextless, America singing a Coke commercial: "The postmodern scene," they write, "is a panic site, just for the fun of it" (27). Paul de Man, in what I take to be his darkest statement, articulates such a "panicked" vision of the interplay between event and discourse. Such interplay, as I have suggested, can lead to the reduction of event to semiosis or to the reductive commodification of language. But de

Man describes it as simply random interplay. Shelley's *The Triumph of Life*, he writes,

> warns us that nothing, whether deed, word, thought or text, ever happens in relation, positive or negative, to anything that precedes, follows or exists elsewhere, but only as a random event whose power, like the power of death, is due to the randomness of its occurrence. (69; see Schleifer 222)

Dreiser and Mailer present two kinds of randomness in *An American Tragedy* and *Executioner's Song*. Both are in opposition to the world of Wharton—and the world of Sondra Finchley—where only tactics are necessary because the social order makes sense. Dreiser's is the randomness of unconscious motivation; Mailer's is the randomness of the arbitrary nature of the sign. But the sign for both is murder and violence, and for both the signs are only achieved through the play of texts.

Mailer, as he says, achieves what Dreiser cannot achieve, a sense of America living for the moment. Such a sense destroys the possibility of discourse by destroying intertextual spaces and voices. The moments—"Miller Time," as the commercials say, or the speed with which headaches go away—commodify experience and commodify discourse. *The Executioner's Song*, however, uses such commodified discourse as an element of play in its own intertextual strategies, both internal, in the play of voices throughout the book, and external, in relation to Dreiser's book and in relation to the violence of random and meaningless American language. In so doing, Mailer achieves a book that is simultaneously about nothing and something, babble and song—a book that can clarify the nation's vision of itself, including the "vision" of earlier texts.

Works Cited

Anderson, Chris. *Style as Argument*. Carbondale: Southern Illinois University Press, 1987.

Baudrillard, Jean. *For a Critique of the Political Economy of the Sign*. Translated by C. Levin. St. Louis: Telos Press, 1981.

Culler, Jonathan. "Presupposition and Intertextuality." In *The Pursuit of Signs*, 100–118. Ithaca, N.Y.: Cornell University Press, 1981.

Darrow, Clarence. "Touching a Terrible Tragedy." In Salzman 5–9.

de Man, Paul. "Shelley Disfigured." In *Deconstruction and Criticism*, edited by Harold Bloom et al., 39–74. New York: Continuum, 1979.

Derrida, Jacques. "Violence and Metaphysics: An Essay on the Thought of Emmanuel Levinas." In *Writing and Difference*, translated by Alan Bass, 79–153. Chicago: University of Chicago Press, 1978.

Dreiser, Theodore. *An American Tragedy.* 1925. Reprint. New York: Signet, 1964.

Flaubert, Gustave. *The Letters of Gustave Flaubert: 1830–1857.* Translated and edited by Francis Steegmuller. Cambridge: Harvard University Press, 1980.

Frow, John. *Marxism and Literary History.* Cambridge: Harvard University Press, 1986.

Greimas, A. J. "Du Sens." In *Du Sens,* 7–17. Paris: Seuil, 1970.

Hellmann, John. *Fables of Fact: The New Journalism as New Fiction.* Urbana: University of Illinois Press, 1981.

Howe, Irving. Afterword to *An American Tragedy,* by Theodore Dreiser. In Dreiser, 815–28.

Jameson, Fredric. *The Political Unconscious: Narrative as a Socially Symbolic Act.* Ithaca, N.Y.: Cornell University Press, 1981.

Jauss, Hans Robert. *Towards an Aesthetic of Reception.* Translated by Timothy Bahti. Minneapolis: University of Minnesota Press, 1982.

Kristeva, Julia. "Word, Dialogue, and Novel." In *Desire in Language,* translated by Thomas Gora, Alice Jardine, and Leon S. Roudiez, 64–91. New York: Columbia University Press, 1980.

Kroker, Arthur, and David Cook. *The Postmodern Scene.* New York: St. Martin's, 1986.

Lacan, Jacques. *Ecrits: A Selection.* Translated by Alan Sheridan. New York: Norton, 1977.

McCord, Phyllis. "The Ideology of Form: The Nonfiction Novel." *Genre* 19 (1986):59–79.

Mailer, Norman. *Cannibals and Christians.* New York: Dial, 1966.

———. *The Executioner's Song.* Boston: Little, Brown, 1979.

Markels, Julian. "Dreiser and the Plotting on Inarticulate Experience." In Salzman, 45–55.

Mencken, H. L. "Dreiser in 840 Pages." In Salzman, 12–17.

Salzman, Jack, ed. *Studies in* An American Tragedy. Columbus, Ohio: Charles E. Merrill, 1971.

Saussure, Ferdinand de. *Course in General Linguistics.* Translated by Wade Baskin. 1959. Reprint. New York: McGraw-Hill, 1966.

Schleifer, Ronald. "The Anxiety of Allegory: De Man, Greimas, and the Problem of Referentiality." In *Rhetoric and Form: Deconstruction at Yale,* edited by Robert Con Davis and Ronald Schleifer, 215–37. Norman: University of Oklahoma Press, 1985.

Wharton, Edith. *The Age of Innocence.* 1920. Reprint. New York: Scribner's, 1968.

Color Me Zora

Alice Walker's (Re)Writing
of the Speakerly Text

====

HENRY LOUIS GATES, JR.

> O, write my name, O write my name:
> O write my name . . .
> Write my name when-a you get home . . .
> Yes, write my name in the book of life . . .
> The Angels in heav'n going-to write my name.
> —Spiritual Underground Railroad

> My spirit leans in joyousness tow'rd thine,
> My gifted sister, as with gladdened heart
> My vision flies along the "speaking pages."
> —Ada, "A Young Woman of Color," 1836

> I am only a pen in His Hand.
> —Rebecca Cox Jackson

> I'm just a link in a chain.
> —Aretha Franklin, "Chain of Fools"

For just over two hundred years, the concern to depict the quest of the black speaking subject finding his or her voice has been a repeated *topos* of the black tradition and perhaps has been its most central trope. As theme, as revised trope, as a "double-voiced" narrative strategy, the representation of characters and texts "finding a voice" has functioned as a sign both of the formal unity of the Afro-American literary tradition and of the integrity of the black subjects depicted in this literature.

Throughout this tradition, one finds at work in the patterns of revision from text to text unifying metaphors that reflect the problematic identity of the speaking subject. The Anglo-African narrators published between 1770 and 1850 placed themselves in a line of descent through the successive revision of one trope—a sacred text, a "talking book"—that refuses to speak to its would-be black auditors. Later in the tradition, Zora Neale Hurston depicts her protagonist's ultimate moment of self-awareness in her ability to name her own consciousness, divided between speaking and writing. As a thematic element and as a highly accomplished rhetorical strategy that depends for its effect upon the "bi-vocality" of free indirect discourse, this "voicing" of a divided consciousness (another topos of the tradition), has been transformed in Ishmael Reed's *Mumbo Jumbo* into a remarkably self-reflexive representation of the ironies of writing a text in which two foregrounded voices compete with each other for control of narration itself. Whereas the development of the tradition to the publication of Hurston's *Their Eyes Were Watching God* seems to have been preoccupied with the mimetic possibilities of the *speaking* voice, black fiction after *Their Eyes* seems more concerned to explore the implications of doubled voices upon strategies of *writing*.

Strategies as effective as Hurston's innovative use of free indirect discourse and Reed's bifurcated narrative voice lead one to wonder how a rhetorical strategy could possibly extend, or signify upon, the notions of voice at play in these major texts of the black tradition. How could a text possibly trope the extended strategies of voicing in *Their Eyes* and *Mumbo Jumbo*? To signify upon both Hurston's and Reed's strategies of narration would seem to demand a form of the novel that, at once, breaks with this intertextual tradition yet revises those salient features which define its formal unity.

Just as Hurston's and Reed's novels present seemingly immovable obstacles to an equally telling revision of the tradition's trope of voicing, so too does Ralph Ellison's *Invisible Man*. The first-person narration of *Invisible Man*, the valorization of oral narration in *Their Eyes*, and the italicized interface of showing and telling in *Mumbo Jumbo*, taken together, would seem to leave little space in which narrative innovation could be attempted. Alice Walker's revisions of *Their Eyes Were Watching God* and Rebecca Cox Jackson's *Gifts of Power*, however, have defined a new mode of representation in the black quest to make the text speak.

Rebecca Cox Jackson was a free black woman who lived between 1795 and 1871. A fascinating religious leader and feminist, Jackson founded a Shaker "sisterhood" in Philadelphia in 1857 after a difficult struggle with her family, her original religious denomination, and even the Shakers. Her extensive autobiographical writings (1830–1864) were collected and edited by Jean McMahon Humez and published in 1981; they were reviewed by Alice Walker in that same year (*Gardens* 73–75).[1] The reconstitution of Jackson's texts is one of the major scholarly achievements in Afro-American literature, both because of the richness of her texts and because the writings of black women in antebellum America are painfully scarce, especially when compared to the large body of writings by black men.

Jackson, like her contemporary black ex-slave writers, gives a prominent place in her texts to her own literacy training. Writing between 1830 and 1832, Jackson refigures such antecedent texts as the autobiography of the slave John Jea, and in particular, Jea's depiction of a divine scene of instruction. Jea's odd revision of the familiar scene of "the talking book" serves to "erase" the figurative potential of this traditional instructional trope for slave narrators who followed him. After Jea, these narrators imagined the scene of illumination or divine instruction in terms of reading and (re)writing the divine text, rather than making it "speak."[2] Jackson's refiguration of this supernatural event is specifically cast within a sexual opposition between male and female. Whereas her antecedents used the trope to define the initial sense of difference between slave and free, African and European, Jackson's revision charts the liberation of a (black) woman from a (black) man over the letter of the text. I bracket "black" because, as we shall see, Jackson freed herself from her brother's domination over her literacy and her capacity to interpret the words of the text, while supplanting him with a mythical white male interpreter.

Jackson, recalling Jea, writes that "After I received the blessing of God, I had a great desire to read the Bible." Lamenting the fact that "I am the only child of my mother that had not learning," she seeks out her brother to "give me one hour's lesson at night after supper or before we went to bed" (Jackson 107). Her brother, a prominent clergyman in the Bethel African Methodist Episcopal Church, was often "so tired when he would come home that he had not [the] power so to do," a situation, Jackson tells us, which "would grieve me." But the situation that grieved Jackson even more was her brother's penchant to "rewrite" her words, to revise her dictation—one supposes, to make her writing more "presentable." Jackson takes great care to describe her frustration in the fight with her brother to control her flow of words:

> So I went to get my brother to write my letters and to read them. I told him what to put in. Then I asked him to read. He did. I said, "Thee has put in more than I told thee." This he done several times. I then said, "I don't want thee to *word* my letter. I only want thee to *write* it." Then he said, "Sister, thee is the hardest one I ever wrote for!" These words, together with the manner that he had wrote my letter, pierced my soul like a sword . . . I could not keep from crying. (Jackson 107)

Jackson's brother, "tired" from his arduous work for the Lord, cannot be relied upon to train his sister to read. When she compromises by asking him to serve as her amanuensis, he "words" her letters, as Jackson puts it, rather than simply translating her words (in their correct order, as narrated) from spoken to written form. This contest over her wording is not merely the anxiety that the author experiences when edited or rewritten; rather, we eventually learn that his sister Rebecca's rather individual mode of belief not only comes to threaten the minister-brother, but leads ultimately to a severance of the kinship bond. The brother-sister conflict over the "word" of the letter, then, prefigures an even more profound conflict over the Word and Letter of God's will.

God, however, takes sides. He comforts the grieving Rebecca with a divine message: "And these words were spoken in my heart, 'Be faithful, and the time shall come when you can write.' These words were spoken in my heart as though a tender father spoke them. My tears were gone in a moment" (Jackson 107–8). God was as good as His promise. Just as He had done for His servant, John Jea, the Lord taught Jackson how to read:

> One day I was sitting finishing a dress in haste and in prayer. [Jackson sustained herself by dressmaking.] This word was spoken in my mind, "Who learned the first man on earth?" "Why, God." "He is unchangeable, and if He learned the first man to read, He can learn you." I laid down my dress, picked up my Bible, ran upstairs, opened it, and kneeled down with it pressed to my breast, prayed earnestly to Almighty God if it was consisting to His holy will, to learn me to read His holy word. And when I looked on the word, I began to read. And when I found I was reading, I was frightened—then I could not read one word. So I done, until I read the Chapter . . . So I tried, took my Bible daily and praying and read until I could read anywhere. The first chapter that I read I never could know it after that day. I only knowed it was in James, but what chapter I never can tell. (Jackson 108)

When confronted with the news, Rebecca's incredulous husband, Samuel, challenges her claim: "Woman, you are agoing crazy!" Jackson, undaunted, reads to him: "Down I sat and read through. And it was in James. So Samuel praised the Lord with me." Similarly, her brother accuses her merely of memorizing passages overheard being read by "his" children: "Thee has heard the children read, till thee has got it by heart" (108).

When challenged by her doubting brother, Jackson tells us, "I did not speak," allowing her husband to speak in her defense. At the end of her long description of this miracle of literacy, this "gift of power," she summarizes the event as the "unspeakable gift of Almighty God to me." It is this double representation of *unspeakability* that connects Jackson's miracle of literacy to Alice Walker's strategies of narration in *The Color Purple*. Walker makes much of this scene in her essay on Jackson, underscoring the fact that "Jackson *was* taught to read and write by the spirit within her" (*Gardens* 73). When Walker dedicates *The Color Purple* "To the Spirit," it is *this* "spirit" which taught Rebecca Jackson how to read. It is the representation of the unfolding of this gift of "the spirit within her," an "unspeakable gift," through which Walker represents the thoroughly dynamic development of her protagonist's consciousness within the unspeakable medium of an epistolary novel comprised of letters *written* but never *said*, indeed, of letters written but never read. For Celie's only Reader, and Rebecca's only literary teacher, is God.

Rather than representing the name of God as unspeakable, Walker represents Celie's words, her letters addressed to God, as unspeakable. God is Celie's silent Auditor, the Addressee of most of her letters, written but never sent. This device, as Robert Stepto has suggested to me, is an echo of the first line of W.E.B. Du Bois's well-known "After-Thought" to *The Souls of Black Folk*: "Hear my cry, O God the Reader." But, more important to my analysis of Walker's revisions of *Their Eyes Were Watching God*, Celie's written voice to God, her Reader, tropes the written-yet-never-uttered voice of free indirect discourse which is the predominant vehicle of narrative commentary in Hurston's novel.

Specifically, Hurston draws upon free indirect discourse as a written voice masked as a speakerly voice—as, in Hurston's phrase, "an oral hieroglyphic." The double voice of *Their Eyes*, which conveys the illusion of a (writing) narrative presence that records the actual words of a (speaking) subject, is best exemplified in passages such as this one, where both voices speak/write at once:

> They sat there in the fresh young darkness close together. Phoeby eager to feel and do through Janie, but hating to show her zest for fear it might be thought mere curiosity. Janie full of that oldest human longing—self-revelation. Phoeby held her tongue for a long time, but she couldn't help moving her feet. So Janie spoke.
> "They don't need to worry about me and my overhalls as long as Ah still got nine hundred dollars in de bank. Tea Cake got me into wearing 'em—following behind him. Tea Cake ain't wasted up no money of mine, and he ain't left me for no young gal, neither. He give me every consolation in de world. He'd tell 'em so, if he was here. If he wasn't gone."
> Phoeby dilated over all with eagerness, "Tea Cake gone?"
> "Yeah Phoeby, Tea Cake is gone. And dat's de only reason you see me back here—cause Ah ain't got nothing to make me happy

no more where Ah was at. Down in the Everglades there, down on the muck."

"It's hard for me to understand what you mean, de way you tell it. And then again Ah'm hard of understandin' at times."

"Naw, 'taint nothin' lak you might think. So 'taint no use in me telling you somethin' unless Ah give you do understandin' to go 'long wid it. Unless you see de fur, a mink skin ain't no different from a coon hide. Loka heah, Phoeby, is Sam waitin' on you for his supper?"

"It's all ready and waitin'. If he ain't got sense enough to eat it, dat's his hard luck."

"Well then, we can set right where we is and talk. Ah got the house all opened up to let dis breeze get a little catchin."

"Phoeby, we been kissin' friends for twenty years, so Ah depend on you for a good thought. And Ah'm talking to you from dat standpoint."

Time makes everything old so the kissing, young darkness becomes a monstropolous old thing while Janie talked. (*Their Eyes* 18–19)

Here, where it is bordered by the prosaic voice of the narrator, "speech" appears as spoken (black) dialect *within* the framework of formal writing or "official discourse." Phoeby and Janie are speaking about talking and understanding, but this speech must be modified by the voice of the narrator who formulates a written commentary upon the nature of the intimacy their speech represents. Thus their voices are "written over," or, rather, Janie (re)writes, as she represents, her own speech.

Celie's voice in *The Color Purple*, on the other hand, is a spoken or mimetic voice, cast in dialect, yet masked as a written one—a mimetic voice disguised as a diegetic voice, but also a diegetic voice disguised as a mimetic one. If mimesis is a showing of the fact of telling, then Celie's letters are visual representations that attempt to tell the fact of showing. Whereas Hurston represents Janie's discovery of her voice as the enunciation of her own doubled self through a free indirect "narrative of division," Walker represents Celie's growth of self-consciousness as an *act of writing*. Janie, and her narrator, speak themselves into being; Celie, in her letters, writes herself into being. Walker signifies upon Hurston by troping the concept of voice that unfolds in *Their Eyes Were Watching God*. Janie's movement from object to subject begins with her failure to recognize an image of her colored self in a photograph, precisely at a point in her childhood when she is merely known as "Alphabet" (a figure for all names, and none), but Celie's ultimate movement of self-negation is her self-description in her first letter to

God: "I am." Celie, like Janie, is an erased presence. Celie, more-over, writes in "Janie's voice," on a level of diction and within an idiom similar to that which Janie speaks. Celie, on the other hand, never "speaks"; rather, she *writes* her speaking voice and that of everyone who speaks to her.

This remarkably self-conscious signifyin(g) strategy places *The Color Purple* in a direct line of descent from *Their Eyes Were Watching God*, in an act of literary bonding quite unlike anything that has ever happened within the Afro-American tradition. I have always found it difficult to identify this bond textually, by which I mean that I have not found Hurston's literal presence in Walker's texts. In *The Color Purple*, however, Walker rewrites Hurston's narrative strategy, in an act of ancestral bonding that is rare in black letters, especially since black writers have tended to trace their origins to white male parents.[3]

In a tradition replete with publication of letters, Walker has, in effect, written a letter of love to her authority figure, Zora Neale Hurston. Ignatius Sancho's *Letters* were published in London in 1782, and Phillis Wheatley's letters to Arbour Tanner were so well-known by 1830 that they could be parodied in a broadside. Even the device of locating Celie's sister in Africa, writing letters home to her troubled sister, has a precedent in the tradition in Amanda Berry Smith's diary-like entries of her African missionary work, published in her *Autobiography* (1893).[4] Despite these precedents, we do not have, before *The Color Purple*, an example of the episto-lary novel in the black tradition of which I am aware. We must first ask, then, why Walker turns to the novel of letters to revise *Their Eyes Were Watching God*.

The Color Purple is comprised of letters written by two sisters, Celie and Nettie. Celie addresses her letters first to God and then to Nettie, while Nettie, off in the wilds of Africa as a missionary, writes her letters to Celie. Her letters are intercepted by Celie's hus-band, stashed away in a trunk, and finally read by Celie and her friend, companion, and lover, Shug Avery. Nettie's unreceived let-ters to Celie suddenly appear almost at the center of the text (112), and continue in what we might think of as the text's middle passage (162), with the "interruptions," as it were, of three letters of Celie's addressed to God. After page 163, Celie's addressee is Nettie, until she writes her final letter (249–51), which is addressed to God (twice), and to the stars, trees, the sky, "peoples," and to "Every-thing." While I do not wish to diminish the importance of the nov-el's plot, or its several echoes of moments in Hurston's novel, I am more interested here in suggesting the formal relationship that obtains between the intertextual strategies of narration of *Their Eyes* and *The Color Purple*. Like Janie, Celie is married to a man who would imprison her, indeed brutalize her. Unlike Janie, however, Celie is liberated by her love for Shug Avery, the "bodaciously" strong singer with whom she shares the love that Janie shares with Tea Cake. It is Shug Avery, I shall argue, who stands in this text as Alice Walker's figure for Zora Neale Hurston herself. Perhaps it will suffice to note that this is Celie's text, a text of becoming, as is *Their Eyes*, but a becoming with a signal difference.

Of what does this difference consist? The most obvious difference between the two texts is that Celie *writes* herself into being before our very eyes. Whereas Janie's moment of consciousness is figured as a ritual speech-act, for Celie the written voice is her vehicle for self-expression and self-revelation. We read the letters of the text, as it were, over Celie's shoulder, just as in *Their Eyes* we "overhear" Janie telling her story to Phoeby as they sit on Janie's back porch. Whereas Janie-and-the-narrator do most of Janie's speaking (in an idiomatic free indirect discourse), in *The Color Purple* two of the novel's three principal characters do all of the writing. Celie is her own author, in a manner that Janie could not possibly be, given the third-person form of narration of *Their Eyes*. To remind the reader that we are rereading letters, the lower border of each page of *The Color Purple* is demarcated by a solid black line, an imitation of how the border of a photoduplicated letter might look if bound in hardcovers.

What is the text's motivation for the writing of letters? Nettie writes to Celie because she is far away in Africa. Celie writes to God for reasons that Nettie recapitulates in one of her letters:

> I remember one time you said your life made you feel so ashamed you couldn't even talk about it to God, you had to write it, bad as you thought your writing was. Well, now I know what you meant. And whether God will read letters or no, I know you will go on writing them; which is guidance enough for me. Anyway, when I don't write to you I feel as bad as I do when I don't pray, locked up in myself and choking on my own heart. I am so *lonely*, Celie. (122)

The italicized command that opens the novel—"*You better not never tell nobody but God. It'd kill your mammy.*"—which we assume has been uttered by Celie's stepfather, is responded to literally by Celie. Celie writes to God for the same reason that Nettie writes to Celie, so that each may read the text of their lives, almost *exactly*, or *simultaneously*, as events unfold.

This is the text's justification of its own representation of writing.

151

But what are *Walker's* motivations? As I suggested above, Celie writes herself into being as a text, a text we are privileged to read over her shoulder. Whereas we are free to wonder aloud about the ironies of self-presentation in a double-voiced free indirect discourse, the epistolary strategy eliminates this aspect of reader-response from the start. Celie writes her own story, and writes everyone else's tale in the text except Nettie's. Celie writes her text, and *is* a text, standing in discrete and episodic letters, which we like voyeurs hurriedly read before the addressees (God, Nettie) interrupt our stolen pleasures. Celie is a text in the same way in which Langston Hughes wrote (in *The Big Sea*) that Hurston was a "book"—"a perfect book of entertainment in herself" (cited in Walker, *Gardens* 100). We read Celie "reading" her world and writing it into being, in one subtle discursive act. There is no battle of voices here, as we saw in *Their Eyes*, between a disembodied narrator and a protagonist; Celie speaks—or writes—for Celie, and of course, to survive for Nettie, then for Shug, and finally for Celie.

Ironically, one of the well-known effects of the epistolary narrative is to underscore the illusion of the "real," but also of the spontaneous (see Eagleton 25). The form allows for a maximum of identification with a character, precisely because the devices of empathy and distance, standard in third-person narration, no longer obtain. There is no apparent proprietary consciousness in the epistle, so readers must supply the interpretive coherence of the text themselves. Samuel Richardson understood this well:

> It is impossible that readers tho most attentive, can always enter into the views of the writer of a piece, written, as hoped, to Nature and the moment. A species of writing, too, that may be called new; and every one putting him and herself into the character they read, and judging of it by their own sensations. (cited in Eagleton 26)

Celie recounts events, seemingly as they unfold; her readers decide their meaning. Her readers piece together a text from the fragmented letters that Celie never mails, and from those which Celie, almost all at once, receives. But Walker escapes the lack of control over how we read Celie precisely by calling before us a writing style of such innocence that only the most hardened reader would fail to initially sympathize, and then eventually, empathize with it. By showing Celie as the most utterly dynamic of characters, who comes to know her world and to trust her readings of her world, and by enabling Celie to compel our compassion for the brutalities she is forced to suffer, followed triumphantly by Celie's assertion of control (experiential control that we learn of through her ever-increasing written control of her letters), Walker manipulates our responses to Celie without even once revealing a voice in the text that Celie, or Nettie, does not narrate, or repeat, or edit.

How is this different from first-person narration in a fluid, or linear, narrative? Again, a remarkably self-conscious Richardson tells us in *Clarissa*:

> Such a sweetness of temper, so much patience and resignation, as she seems to be mistress of; yet writing of and in the midst of *present* distresses! How *much more* lively and affecting, for that reason, must her style be; her mind tortured by the pangs of uncertainty (the events then hidden in the womb of fate) *than* the dry, narrative, unanimated style of persons, relating difficulties and dangers surmounted; the relator perfectly at ease; and if himself unmoved by his own story, not likely greatly to affect the reader! (cited in Eagleton 26)

Unlike the framed tales of Janie in *Their Eyes* or of the nameless protagonist of *Invisible Man*, the reader of a novel of letters does not, indeed cannot, know the outcome of Celie's tale until its writing ceases. The two voices that narrate Ishmael Reed's "anti-detective" novel, for instance, are troped in *The Color Purple* almost by a pun that turns upon this fact: whereas a topos of *Mumbo Jumbo* is a supraforce searching for its text, for its "writing," as Reed puts it, Celie emerges as a force, a presence, by writing all-too-short letters which her readers weave or "stitch" together as both the text of *The Color Purple* and the autobiographical "text" of Celie's life and times, her bondage and her freedom. Celie charts her growth of consciousness day-to-day, or letter-by-letter. By the end of the novel, we know that Celie, like Reed's silent character, "jes' grew." Celie, moreover, "jes' grew" by writing her text of herself. Whereas Reed's "Jes' Grew" disappears, as it were, we are left at the end of *The Color Purple* holding Celie's text of herself in our hands. It is we who complete or close the circle or chain of Jes' Grew's Carriers in an act of closure that Jes' Grew's enemies disrupt in *Mumbo Jumbo*. When Nettie inevitably gets around to asking Celie how she managed to change so much, Celie quite probably could respond that "I jes' grew, I 'spose," precisely because the "tyranny" of the narrative present can only be overthrown by a linear reading of her letters, from first to last. Celie does not recapitulate her growth, as does Ellison's narrator, or Hurston's Janie; only her readers have the leisure to reread Celie's text of development, the text of her becoming. Celie "exists" letter-to-letter; her readers supply the in-

153

tertextual coherence necessary to speak of a precisely chartable growth, one measured by comparing or compiling all of the fragments of experience and feeling that Celie has selected to write.

Let us consider this matter of what I have called the tyranny of the narrative present. Celie, as narrator, or author, presents herself to us, letter-to-letter, in a continuous "written present." The time of writing is Celie's narrative present. We see this even more clearly when Celie introduces Nettie's "first" letter, which Celie and Shug have recovered from the attic trunk:

> Dear God,
> This is the letter I have been holding in my hand. (112)

The text of Nettie's letter follows, as an embedded narrative. This narrative present is comprised of (indeed, *can* be comprised of) only one event: the process of writing itself. All other events in *The Color Purple* are in the narrative past: no matter how near to the event Celie's account might be, the event is *past*, and it is this past about which Celie is writing.

We can see this clearly in Celie's first letter. The letter's opening paragraph both underscores the moment of writing and provides a frame for the past events that Celie is about to share with her addressee, God:

> Dear God,
> I am fourteen years old. ~~I am~~ I have always been a good girl. (11)

Celie places her present self ("I am") under erasure, a device that reminds us that she is writing and searching for her voice by selecting, then rejecting, word choice or word order: this also explains why Celie was once "a good girl," but no longer feels that she can make this claim before God. Because "a good girl," especially at the age of fourteen, connotes the avoidance of sex, we expect her fall from grace to be a fall of sensual pleasure. Celie tells us that we were right in this suspicion, but also wrong: there has been no pleasure involved in her fall. As her account of the recent past explains:

> Last spring after little Lucious come I heard them fussing. He was pulling on her arm. She say It too soon, Fonso, I ain't well. Finally he leave her alone. A week go by, he pulling on her arm again. She say, Naw, I ain't gonna. Can't you see I'm already half dead, an all of these children.
>
> She went to visit her sister doctor over Macon. Left me to see after the others. He never had a kine word to say to me. Just say

You gonna do what your mammy wouldn't. First he put his thing
gainst my hip and sort of wiggle it around. Then he grab hold my
titties. Then he push his thing inside my pussy. When that hurt, I
cry. He start to choke me, saying You better shut up and git used
to it.

But I don't never git used to it. And now I feels sick every time
I be the one to cook. My mama she fuss at me an look at me. She
happy, cause he good to her *now*. But too sick to last long. (11;
emphasis added)

Celie has been raped by the man she knows as her father. Her
tale of woe has begun. Celie's first letter commences in a narrative
present, shifts to a narrative past, then in the letter's penultimate
sentence, returns to a narrative present signified by "now." Pro-
phetically, she even predicts the future, her mother's imminent
death. In the narrative past, Celie develops, in fact controls, the
representation of character and event. In the narrative present,
Celie reveals to us that hers is the proprietary consciousness which
we encounter in third-person narration, rendered in an epistle in
a first-person narrative present. Celie, as author of her letters to
God, might not be able to know what course events shall take, but
the past belongs to her, salient detail by salient detail. We only
know of Celie's life and times by her recounting of their significance and meaning, rendered in Celie's own word-order. In this
epistolary novel, the narrator of Celie's tale is identical with the
author of Celie's letters. Because there is no gap here, as there is in
Their Eyes between the text's narrator and Janie, there would seem
to be no need to bridge this gap through free indirect discourse.

This, however, is not the case in *The Color Purple*. While the gap
between past and present is not obliterated, the gap between who
sees and who speaks is obliterated by Celie's curious method of reporting discourse. The epistolary form's *necessary* shift between the
narrative present and the narrative past creates the very space in
which free indirect discourse dwells in Celie's narrative. It is in her
representation of free indirect discourse that Walker undertakes
her most remarkable revision of *Their Eyes Were Watching God*.

The Color Purple is replete with free indirect discourse. The
double-voiced discourse of *Their Eyes* returns in the text of Celie's
letters. Celie, as I have said, is the narrator and author of her letters. The narrator's voice, accordingly, is the voice of the protagonist. This protagonist, moreover, is "divided" into two parts: Celie,
the character whose past actions we see represented in letters (an
active but initially dominated and undereducated adolescent) and
that "other" Celie, who—despite her use of written dialect—we

155

soon understand to be a remarkably reflective and sensitive teller, or writer, of a tale, of her own tale. Because of the curious interplay of the narrative past (in which Celie is a character) and a narrative present (in which Celie is the author), Celie emerges as *both* the subject and the object of narration. The subject-object split, or reconciliation, appears as the central rhetorical device by which Celie's self-consciousness is represented in her own capacity to write a progressively better-structured story of herself.

Whereas Hurston represents her protagonist's emergent self in the shifting level of diction in the narrator's commentary and in a black-speech informed indirect discourse, Walker represents Celie's dynamism in her ability to control her own narrative voice (that is, her own style of writing) but also in her remarkable ability to control all other voices spoken to Celie, which we encounter only in Celie's representation of them. It is Celie's voice that is always a presence whenever anyone in her world is represented as having spoken. We can therefore never be certain whether a would-be report, or mimesis, of dialogue is Celie's or the character's whose words we are overhearing, or more precisely, *reading* over Celie's shoulder.

Let me be clear: no one "speaks" in this novel. Rather, two sisters correspond to each other, through letters which one never receives (Celie's) and which the other receives almost all at once (Nettie's). There is no true mimesis, then, in *The Color Purple*, only diegesis. But, through Celie's mode of apparently reporting speech, underscored dramatically by her written dialect voice of narration, we logically assume that we are being shown discourse, when all along, we never actually are. Celie only *tells* us what people have said to her; she never *shows* us their words in direct quotation. Precisely because her written dialect voice is identical in diction and idiom to the supposedly spoken words that pepper her letters, we believe that we are overhearing people speak, just as Celie did when the words were in fact uttered. We are not, however. Indeed, we can never be certain whether Celie is, as it were, showing us a telling, or telling us a showing, as awkward as this sounds. In the "speeches" of her characters, Celie's voice and a character's merge into one. In these passages from *The Color Purple*, the distinction between mimesis and diegesis is apparently obliterated: the opposition between them has collapsed.

This innovation, it seems to me, is Walker's most brilliant stroke, her most telling signifyin(g) move on Hurston's text. Let us examine just a few of scores of examples. The first is Celie's account of Mr. ——'s sisters, named Carrie and Kate, as one of Walker's signifyin(g) gestures toward Jean Toomer's *Cane*, where Carrie Kate appears as a central character in "Kabnis."[5] (Walker, incidentally, loves *Cane* almost as much as she does *Their Eyes*, as she writes in "Zora Neale Hurston: A Cautionary Tale and a Partisan View.")[6] Celie's depiction of Carrie and Kate's discourse follows:

> Well, that's no excuse, say the first one, Her name Carrie, other one name Kate. When a woman marry she spose to keep a decent house and a clean family. Why, wasn't nothing to come here in the winter time and all these children have colds, they have flue, they have direar, they have newmonya, they have worms, they have the chill and fever. They hungry. They hair ain't comb. They too nasty to touch. (27)

Who is speaking in these passages: Carrie and Kate, or Celie, or all three? All three are speaking; or, more properly, no one is speaking, because Celie has merged whatever was actually said with her own voice and written it out for us, in a narrative form that aspires to the spoken, but which never represents or reports anyone else's speech but Celie's, on one hand, and Celie-cum-characters', on the other. Celie is in control of her narration, even to the point of controlling everyone else's speech, which her readers cannot encounter without hearing their words merged with Celie's.

We can see Celie's free indirect discourse in another example, which reveals how sophisticated an editor Celie becomes, precisely as she grows in self-awareness.[7] Celie is introducing, as it were, or framing, one of Nettie's letters, in a narrative present:

> It's hot here, Celie, she write. Hotter than July. Hotter than August *and* July. Hot like cooking dinner on a big stove in a little kitchen in August and July. Hot. (138)

Who said, or wrote, these words, words which echo both the Southern expression, "a cold day in August," and Stevie Wonder's album *Hotter Than July*? Stevie Wonder? Nettie? Celie? All three, and no one. These are Celie's words, merged with Nettie's, in a written imitation of the merged voices of free indirect discourse— an exceptionally rare form in that, here, even the illusion of mimesis is dispelled.

What are we to make of Walker's remarkable innovation upon Hurston's free indirect discourse? We can assume safely that one of Hurston's purposes in the narrative strategies at play in *Their Eyes* was to show James Weldon Johnson and Countee Cullen, and just about everyone else in the new Negro Renaissance, that dialect not only was not limited to two stops, humor and pathos, but was fully capable of being used as a literary language even to write a novel. Dialect, or black English vernacular and its idiom, as a literary device was not merely a figure of spoken speech; rather, for Hurston, it was storehouse of figures. As if in a coda to the writing of *Their Eyes*, Hurston even published a short story entirely in the vernacular, entitled "Story in Harlem Slang" (1942), complete with a glossary as an appendix. Yet, just as Johnson had edited or interpreted the language of the black vernacular in his rendition of the "Seven Sermons in Verse" that comprise *God's Trombones* (1927), so too had Hurston merged dialect and standard English in the idiom of the free indirect discourse that gradually overtakes the narrative commentary in *Their Eyes*. Hurston showed the tradition just how dialect could *blend* with standard English to create a new voice, a voice exactly as "black" as it is "white." (Johnson, of course, had "translated" from the vernacular into standard English.) Walker's signifyin(g) riff on Hurston was to seize upon the device of free indirect discourse, as practiced in *Their Eyes*, but to avoid standard English almost totally in Celie's narration. Walker has written a novel in dialect, in the black vernacular. The initial impression that we have of Celie's naiveté slowly reveals how one can write an entire novel in dialect. This, we must realize, is as important an intertextual troping of *Their Eyes* as is the page-by-page representation of Celie's *writing* of her own tale. If Hurston's writing aspired to the speakerly, then Walker's apparently speaking characters turn out to have been *written*.

There are other parallels between the two texts which provide evidence of their intertextual relation. Whereas, in *Their Eyes*, Janie's sign of self-awareness is represented as her ability to tell Phoeby her own version of events, Walker matches this gesture by having Celie first write her own texts, then discover her sister's purloined letters, arrange them with Shug in a chronological order, then read them, so that a second narrative unfolds that both completes and implicitly comments upon Celie's narrative, which has preceded it by 106 of the text's pages. This newly recovered narrative is a "parallel" text. The cache of unreceived letters functions as a frame tale within Celie's tale, as do Nettie's subsequently received letters, recapitulating events and providing key details absent from Celie's story. Nettie's letters are written in standard English, not only to contrast her character with Celie's, but also to provide some relief from Celie's language. But Celie controls even this narrative, by ordering the reading of the letters and especially by "introducing" them, within her letters, with her own commentary. Nettie's letters function as a second narrative of the past, echoing the shift from present to past that we see within the time-shifts of Celie's letters. We recognize a new Celie once Nettie's letters have been read. Celie's last letter to God reads:

Dear God,
    That's it, say Shug. Pack your stuff. You coming back to Tennessee with me.
    But I feels daze.
    My daddy lynch. My mama crazy. All my little half-brothers and sisters no kin to me. My children not my sister and brother. Pa not pa.
    You must be sleep. (163)

Order has been restored, the incest taboo has not been violated, Celie is confused, but free and moving.

Janie's declaration of independence in *Their Eyes*, read in the starkest of terms to her husband, Joe, is repeated in *The Color Purple*. As Celie is about to leave with Shug, this exchange occurs between Celie and her husband:

    Celie is coming with us, say Shug. Mr. ——'s head swivel back straight.
    Say what? he ast.
    Celie is coming to Memphis with me.
    Over my dead body, Mr. —— say, . . . what wrong now?
    You a lowdown dog is what's wrong, I say. It's time to leave you and enter into the Creation. And your body just the welcome mat I need.
    Say what? he ast. Shock.
    All round the table folkses mouths be dropping open . . .
    Mr. —— start to sputter. ButButButButBut. Sound like some kind of motor. (181)

This marvelous exchange refigures that between Janie and Joe. Celie's newly found voice makes "folkses mouths" drop open, and Mr. ——'s voice is inarticulate and dehumanized, "like some kind of motor." A bit later, Celie continues, in triumph, to curse her oppressor:

    Any more letter come? I ast.
    He say, What?
    You heard me, I say. Any more letters from Nettie come?
    If they did, he say, I wouldn't give 'em to you. You two of a kind, he say. A man try to be nice to you, you fly in his face.
    I curse you, I say.
    What that mean? he say.
    I say, Until you do right be me, everything you touch will crumble. (175–76)

This quasi-Hoodoo curse reads like one of Hurston's recipes for revenge that she published in her classic work on *Vaudou*, entitled *Tell My Horse* (1938). Significantly, these exchanges, Celie's first open defiance of her husband, Albert, are repeated or written in Celie's first two letters addressed to Nettie, rather than God. Celie's husband's weak response follows:

> He laugh. Who you think you is? he say. You can't curse nobody. Look at you. You black, you pore, you ugly, you a woman. Goddam, he say, you nothing at all. (187)

But Albert no longer has the power of the word over Celie, just as Joe cannot recoup from Janie's signifyin(g) on his manhood in public, in *Their Eyes*. This exchange continues:

> Until you do right by me, I say, everything you even dream about will fail. I give it to him straight, just like it come to me. And it seem to come to me from the trees.
>
> Whoever heard of such a thing, say Mr. ——. I probably didn't whup your ass enough.
>
> Every lick you hit me you will suffer twice, I say. Then I say, You better stop talking because all I'm telling you ain't coming just from me. Look like when I open my mouth the air rush in and shape words.
>
> Shit, he say. I should have lock you up. Just let you out to work.
>
> The jail you plan for me is the one in which you will rot, I say . . .
>
> I'll fix her wagon! Say Mr. ——, and spring toward me.
>
> A dust devil flew up on the porch between us, fill my mouth dirt. The dirt say, Anything you do to me, already done to you.
>
> Then I feel Shug shake me. Celie, she say. And I come to myself.
>
> I'm pore, I'm black, I may be ugly and can't cook, a voice say to everything listening. But I'm here.
>
> Amen, say Shug. Amen, amen. (187)

Celie has, at last, issued her liberating (and liberated) call, while her friend Shug, like any black audience, provides the proper ritual response to a masterful performance: "Amen, say Shug. Amen, amen." Celie speaks herself free, as did Janie, but in a speaking we know only by its writing, in a letter to Nettie. Celie has conquered her foe, Albert, and the silence in her self, by representing an act of speech in the written word, in which she turns Albert's harsh curses back upon him, masterfully.

Just as this scene of instruction echoes Janie's, so too is *The Color Purple* full of other thematic echoes of *Their Eyes Were Watching God*.

Houses confine in *The Color Purple*, just as they do in *Their Eyes*, but Celie, Nettie, Shug, and Janie all find a freedom in houses in which there are no men: Nettie's hut in Africa and Shug's mansion in Tennessee. The home that Nettie and Celie inherit will include men, but men respectful of the inherent strength and equality of women. Celie and Nettie own this home, and the possession of property seems to preclude the domination of men.

Shug would seem to be a refugee from *Their Eyes*. It is Shug who teaches Celie that God is not an "old white man," that he is Nature and love and even sex, that he is a sublime feeling:

> Here's the thing, say Shug. The thing I believe. God is inside you and inside everybody else. You come into the world with God. But only them that search for it inside find it. And sometimes it just manifest itself even if you not looking, or don't know what you looking for. Trouble do it for most folks, I think. Sorrow, lord. Feeling like shit.
>
> It? I ast.
>
> Yeah, It. God ain't a he or a she, but a It.
>
> But what do it look like? I ast.
>
> Don't look like nothing, she say. It ain't a picture show. It ain't something you can look at apart from anything else, including yourself. I believe God is everything, say Shug. Everything that is or ever was or ever will be. And when you can feel that, and be happy to feel that, you've found It. (177–78)

But it is also Shug who teaches Celie about Janie's lyrical language of the trees, a language of Nature in which God speaks in the same metaphors in which He spoke to Janie, a divine utterance which led Janie to enjoy her first orgasm, an experience that Shug tells Celie is God's ultimate sign of presence:

> She say, My first step from the old white man was trees. Then air. Then birds. Then other people. But one day when I was sitting quiet and feeling like a motherless child, which I was, it come to me: that feeling of being part of everything, not separate at all. I knew that if I cut a tree, my arm would bleed. And I laughed and I cried and I run all round the house. I knew just what it was. In fact, when it happen, you can't miss it. It sort of like you know what, she say, grinning and rubbing high up on my thigh.
>
> *Shug*! I say.
>
> Oh, she say. God love all them feelings. That's some of the best stuff God did. And when you know God loves 'em you enjoys 'em a lot more. You can just relax, go with everything that's going, and praise God by liking what you like.
>
> God don't think it dirty? I ast. (178)

And if we miss Shug's connection with Janie, Walker first describes Shug in the same terms she has used to describe Zora Neale Hurston:

> She do more than that. She git a picture. The first one of a real person I ever seen. She say Mr. —— was taking somethin out of his billfold to show Pa and it fell out and slid under the table. Shug Avery was a woman. The most beautiful woman I ever saw. She more pretty than my mama. She bout ten thousand times more prettier than me. I see her there in furs. Her face rouge. Her hair like somethin tail. She grinning with her foot up on somebody motocar. Her eyes serious tho. Sad some. (16)

Compare that description with Walker's description of Hurston:

> she loved to wear hats, tilted over one eye, and pants and boots. (I have a photograph of [Zora Neale, writes Walker] in pants, boots, and broadbrim that was given to me by her brother, Everette. She has her foot up on the running board of a car—presumably hers, and bright red—and looks racy (Walker, *Gardens* 88)

Celie's voice, when she first speaks out against the will of Mr. ——, "seem to come to me from the trees" (176) just as Janie's inner voice manifests itself under the pear tree. Celie, like Janie, describes herself as a "motherless child" (167). Key metaphors repeat: Hurston's figure of nature mirroring Janie's emotions—"the rose of the world was breathing out smell" (23)—becomes Shug and Celie's scene in which Shug teaches Celie to masturbate, using a mirror to watch herself:

> I stand there with the mirror.
> She say, What, too shame even to go off and look at yourself? And you look so cute too, she say, laughing. All dressed up for Harpo's smelling good and everything, but scared to look at your own pussy . . .
> I lie back on the bed and haul up my dress. Yank down my bloomers. Stick the looking glass tween my legs. Ugh. All that hair. Then my pussy lips be black. Then inside look like a wet rose.
> It a lot prettier than you thought, ain't it? she say from the door. (79)

Later, in her first letter to Nettie, Celie uses the figure of the rose again in a simile: "Shug a beautiful something, let me tell you. She frown a little, look out cross the yard, lean back in her chair, look like a big rose." (178)

In the same way that Walker extends to the literal Hurston's figure of "the rose of the world breathing out smell," she also erases the figurative aspect of Janie's metaphor for her narration to Phoebe ("'mah tongue is in my friend's mouf'") by making Shug and Celie literal "kissin' friends," or lovers. That which is implicit in Hurston's figures, Walker makes explicit. In addition, Walker often reverses Hurston's tropes: whereas *Their Eyes* accounts for the orgasm she experiences under the pear tree by saying, in free indirect discourse, "So this was a marriage!" (24), Celie writes that when Mr. —— beats her, she turns herself into a tree:

> He beat me like he beat the children. Cept he don't never hardly beat them. He say, Celie, git the belt. The children be outside the room peeking through the cracks. It all I can do not to cry. I make myself wood. I say to myself, Celie, you a tree. That's how come I know trees fear man. (30)

The circular narration of *Their Eyes*, in which the end is the beginning and the beginning the end, is troped in *The Color Purple* by linear narration.

Walker has *signified upon* Zora Neale Hurston, in what must be the most loving revision, and claim to title, that we have seen in the tradition. Walker has turned to a black antecedent text to claim literary ancestry, or motherhood, not only for content, but for structure. Walker's turn to Hurston for form (and to, of all things, the topoi of medieval romance known as "The Incestuous Father" and "The Exchanged Letter" for plot structure), openly disrupts the patterns of revision (white form, black content) that characterize many of the intertextual relations of Afro-American literature to this point (see Schlauch 63–69). Even the representation of Celie's writing in dialect echoes Hurston's definition of an "oral hieroglyphic," and her ironic use of speakerly language, which no man can even speak, but which can exist only in a written text. This, too, Walker tropes, by a trick of figuration, people who speak dialect think that they are saying standard English words; when they write the words that they speak as "dis" or "dat," therefore, they spell "this" and "that." Walker, like Hurston, masters the illusion of the black vernacular by its writing, in a masterful exemplification of the black trope of *stylin' out*.

Walker's revision of Hurston stands at the end of a chain of narration. Walker's text, like texts by Toni Morrison, Gloria Naylor, Leon Forrest, Ernest Gaines, and John Wideman, affords subsequent writers tropes and topoi to be revised. Endings, then, imply beginnings. After Walker and Reed, however, black authors can increasingly turn even more explicitly to black antecedent texts

both for form and content. The tradition of Afro-American literature, a tradition of grounded repetition and difference, is a tradition characterized by its urge to start over, to begin again, but always to begin on a well-structured foundation. Our narrators, our
signifiers, are links in an extended ebony chain of discourse, which
we, as critics, protect and encase. As Martin Buber puts the relation
in *The Legend of Baal-Shem*:

> I have told it anew as one who was born later. I bear in me the
> blood and spirit of those who created it, and out of my blood and
> spirit it has become new. I stand in the chain of narrators, a link
> between links; I tell once again the old stories, and if they sound
> new, it is because the new already lay dormant in them when they
> were told for the first time. (x)

We can observe the canonical implications of this new succession
by casting back once again, beyond the principal silent second text
of *The Color Purple* to Rebecca Cox Jackson's narrative. While the
principal silent second text of *The Color Purple* is *Their Eyes Were
Watching God*, Walker's critique of Celie's initial conception of God,
and especially its anthropomorphism, revises a key figure in Rebecca
Cox Jackson's narrative which surfaces as a parable for the so-called
non-canonical critic.

Just after Celie and Shug have discovered, arranged, and read
Nettie's purloined letters, Celie writes this to Nettie:

> Dear Nettie,
>   I don't write to God no more, I write to you.
>   What happen to God? ast Shug.
>   Who that? I say.
>   . . . What God do for me? I ast.
>   She say, Celie! Like she shock. He gave you life, good health,
> and a good woman that love you to death.
>   Yeah, I say, and he give me a lynched daddy, a crazy mama, a
> lowdown dog of a step pa and a sister I probably won't ever see
> again. Anyhow, I say, the God I been praying and writing to is a
> man. And act just like all the other mens I know. Trifling, forgit-
> ful, and lowdown. (175)

A few pages later, Shug describes to Celie the necessity of escaping
the boundaries caused by the anthropomorphism of God, and calls
this concept that of "the old white man" (176). This, Celie confesses, is difficult: "Well, us talk and talk bout God, but I'm still
adrift. Trying to chase that old white man out of my head" (179).
Shug responds that the problem is not only "the old white man,"
but all men:

Still, it is like Shug say, You have got to git man off your eyeball, before you can see anything a'tall.

Man corrup everything, say Shug. He on your box of grits, in your hand, and all over the road. He try to make you think he everywhere. Soon as you think he everywhere, you think he God. But he ain't. Whenever you trying to pray, and man plop himself on the other end of it, tell him to git lost, say Shug. Conjure up flowers, wind, water, a big rock. (179)

This passage, most certainly, constitutes an important feminist critique of the complex fiction of male domination. But it also recalls a curious scene in Rebecca Cox Jackson's text. Indeed, Walker's text signifies upon it. Jackson was careful to show that God's gracious act of instruction freed her from her minister-brother's attempts to dominate and determine her words (their order, their meaning); by rearranging her words he had sought to control their sense. Jackson became free, and freely interprets the Word of God in her own, often idiosyncratic, way. But is Jackson's a truly liberating gesture, a fundamental gesture of a nascent feminism?

Jackson substitutes a mystical "white man," the image of whom Shug and Celie seek to dispel, for the interpretive role of the male represented as the relation of truth to understanding, of sound to sense. Her account is strikingly vivid:

A white man took me by my right hand and led me on the north side of the room, where sat a square table. On it lay a book open. And he said to me, "Thou shall be instructed in this book, from Genesis to Revelations." And then he took me on the west side, where stood a table. And it looked like the first. And said, "Yea, thou shall be instructed from the beginning of creation to the end of time." And then he took me on the east side of the room also, where stood a table and book like the two first, and said, "I will instruct thee—yea, thou shall be instructed from the beginning of all things to the end of all things. Yea, thou shall be well instructed. I will instruct."

When Samuel handed me to this man at my own back door, he turned away. I never saw him any more. When this man took me by the hand, his hand was soft like down. He was dressed all in light drab. He was bareheaded. His countenance was serene and solemn and divine. There was a father and a brother's countenance to be seen in his face.

And then I awoke, and I saw him as plain as I did in my dream. And after that he taught me daily. And when I would be reading and come to a hard word, I would see him standing by my side and he would teach me the word right. And often, when I would be in meditation and looking into things which was hard to understand, I would find him by me, teaching and giving me understanding. And oh, his labor and care which he had with me often caused me to weep bitterly, when I would see my great ignorance and the great trouble he had to make me understand eternal things. For I was so buried in the depth of the tradition of my forefathers, that it did seem as if I never could be dug up. (146–47)

Jackson contrasts the "white man" who would "teach me the word right," he who would stand "by me, teaching and giving me understanding," with the delineation of understanding imposed by her brother, and, curiously enough, by "the depth of the tradition of my forefathers." So oppressive was the latter that, she admits, "it did seem as if I never could be dug up."

Shug and Celie's conception of God signifies upon these passages from Jackson. Jackson's "white man" and Celie's, the speaking interpreter and the silent Reader, are identical until Celie, with Shug's help, manages to "git man off your eyeball." Whereas Jackson suffocates under the burden of tradition, "buried in the depth" as she puts it, Walker's text points to a new model for a self-defined, or an internally defined, notion of tradition, one black and female. The first step toward such an end, she tells us, was to eliminate the "white men" to whom we turn for "teaching" and the "giving [of] understanding." This parable of interpretation is Walker's boldest claim about the nature and function of the black tradition and its interpretation. To turn away from, to step outside of the white hermeneutical circle and into the black is the challenge issued by Walker's critique of Jackson's vision, and by her echoing revision of Zora Neale Hurston's voice.

Notes

1. Walker's review first appeared in the November–December 1981 issue of *Black Scholar*. Walker has informed me in a letter that Jackson's book "was the first book I read (I read almost nothing while writing *The Color Purple*) and reviewed *after* I finished. I took it as a sign that I was on the right track." The uncanny resemblances between key figures in Jackson's and Walker's texts suggest that forms of tradition and patterns of revision can be remarkably complex, indeed *cultural*.

2. For further discussion of Jea's autobiography and its refigurations of traditional metaphors of instruction, see chapter 4 of my *The Signifying Monkey*.

3. For her explicit comments on Hurston, see Walker, *Gardens* 83–119.

4. I wish to thank Mary Helen Washington for pointing this out to me.

5. Walker informs me that "All names in *Purple* are *family* or Eatonton, Georgia, community names. Kate was my father's mother. In real life she was the model for Aunt Julia (in the novel), my grandfather's 'illegitimate' daughter (who in the novel is the wife, but who in real life is the granddaughter of Albert who in the novel is her father). It was *she*, Kate, my grandmother, who was murdered by her lover (he shot her) when my dad was eleven. Carrie was an aunt. But [your] version is nice, too, and my version is so confusing. For instance, the germ for Celie is Rachel, my stepgrandmother: she of the poem 'Burial' in *Revolutionary Petunias*."

6. Walker writes, "*There is no book more important to this one* (including Toomer's *Cane*, which comes close, but from what I recognize is a more perilous direction)" [*Gardens* 86]. See also "The Divided Life of Jean Toomer" in *Gardens* 60–66.

7. Kate Nickerson points this out in "'From Listening to the Rest'" 57.

Works Cited

Buber, Martin. *The Legend of Baal-Shem*. Translated by Maurice Friedman. New York: Harper & Brothers, 1955.

Eagleton, Terry. *The Rape of Clarissa: Writing, Sexuality, and Class Struggle in Samuel Richardson*. Minneapolis: University of Minnesota Press, 1982.

Gates, Henry Louis, Jr. *The Signifying Monkey*. New York: Oxford University Press, 1988.

Hurston, Zora Neale. "Story in Harlem Slang." *The American Mercury* 45 (July 1942): 84–96.

———. *Their Eyes Were Watching God*. 1937. Reprint. London: Virago, 1986.

Jackson, Rebecca. *Gifts of Power: The Writings of Rebecca Jackson, Black Visionary, Shaker Eldress*. Edited by Jean McMahon Humez. Amherst: University of Massachusetts Press, 1981.

Nickerson, Kate. "'From Listening to the Rest': On Literary Discourse between Zora Neale Hurston and Alice Walker." Unpublished manuscript.

Schlauch, Margaret. *Chaucer's Constance and Accused Queens*. New York: New York University Press, 1927.

Smith, Amanda. *An Autobiography: The Story of the Lord's Dealings With Mrs. Amanda Smith, the Colored Evangelist; Containing an Account of Her Life Work of Faith, and Her Travels in America, England, Ireland, Scotland, India, and Africa, as an Independent Missionary*. 1893. Reprint. Chicago: Christian Witness Co., 1921.

Walker, Alice. *In Search of Our Mothers' Gardens*. New York: Harcourt Brace Jovanovich, 1983.

———. *The Color Purple*. 1982. Reprint. New York: Washington Square Press, 1983.

INTERTEXTUALITY AND THE
POSTMODERN SUBJECT

Transgressing Genre

Kathy Acker's Intertext

===

KATHLEEN HULLEY

If there is any realism left . . . it is a "realism" which is meant
to derive from the shock . . . of slowly becoming aware of a
new and original historical situation in which we are condemned to seek history by way of our own pop images and
simulacra of that history, which itself remains forever out of
reach.
—Fredric Jameson

Modern patriarchy has a way of assimilating any number of
potentially subversive gestures into the "mainstream," where
whatever subversive energy they may have possessed becomes neutralized.
—Susan Suleiman

Perverse Practices: Displacements

Pray you, undo this button
—*King Lear*, 5.3

In the passage to modernism, Marshall McLuhan traces in King
Lear's division of his kingdom a metaphor for the breakdown of
the hierarchic, ordered succession of both power and the physical
senses. For McLuhan, that breakdown was predicted by the tele-
scopic triumph of sight over the other senses and the subsequent
visualization of space into mapped territories.[1] But Lear's breakdown marks an equally disorienting parallel between a new bourgeois set of economic relations and a father's overweening desire
for the unconditional love of his daughters. Lear's blind desire to
freeze Cordelia's love at a regressive state of dependency pits the
stable laws of feudal succession against a culture whose "lousy material conditions" (Acker, *Algeria* 4) provide the objective correlative for the new forms of subjectivity territorialized desire demands.

At the postmodern end of Lear's blind insight, punk artist Kathy
Acker works to undo and make visible the intricate buttoning of
incest and politics we inherit from that awesome renaissance. In
her undoing, she explicitly transforms current conventions of feminist and political content by articulating the ways in which sexuality and the contradictory liberation movements of our time are

171

predicated on a social construction whose political unconscious is embedded in textually sanctioned father/daughter incest. In modernist literature that unconscious has been disguised under biography as content and under realism as form, but the politics of incest has remained a subtext which authorized pursuits of textuality have successfully displaced. In the Derridean sense that "writing" precedes speech, then, ideology precedes text.[2]

It is therefore important to refute or, at the very least, to acknowledge a trap in the craftiness of the discourse which reconstitutes intertextuality as the (phallic) quest for influences and origins. Instead, intertextuality as a strategy of feminist interpretation must be pursued in those interstices where writing acknowledges that *all* literary precedent is plagiarized, not simply from literary works but from the cultural codes which determine the contemporary versions of reality literature constructs. To avoid phallic enticements, I select only those strategies of intertextual interpretation that most fruitfully uncover the suppressed metaphoric systems that authorized textual relations mask. In her contribution to this collection, Thaïs Morgan defines intertextuality as the "opening up [of] an apparently infinite play of relationships with other texts." Mikhail Bakhtin, for example, claims the novel as a polyphonic "carnivalization of literature" which is, for Morgan, "a complex of cultural behaviors" characterized by "its carnivalistic attitude to reigning ideologies and the authoritarian institutions that enforce them" (248–49). Morgan cites Bakhtin's description of the novel as a multi-tongued "heteroglossia" of "systematic connections that can be analyzed among literary and *nonliterary* discourses" (my italics), and compares this to Derrida's idea that "every text, every utterance, is an 'interweaving' or a 'textile' of signifiers whose signifieds are by definition intertextually determined by other discourses" (255). Finally, for Morgan, Julia Kristeva demonstrates that subjectivity is itself a linguistic practice constituted by "a complex 'procès de rejet multipliant la position du langage et du sujet'" (259). The crucial points here are the anti-institutional, nonliterary nature of an intertextuality that speaks *among* cultural behaviors and various discursive levels and Kristeva's insistence that subjectivity itself is a textual construct.

Acker relies on five disjunctive practices to wedge into the heteroglossic sub-texts of behavioral, literary, and nonliterary voices speaking between the cracks in authorized textuality. First, she mixes genres so randomly that what begins as a fiction turns quickly to autobiography, play, essay, poem, commentary, theory, graphic art. Languages emerge—English, Persian, French, Spanish; narrators change gender, locale, person, each proliferating and infecting one another so that no generic distinction can possibly take hold. Against the diachronic process of generic evolution—epic, tragedy, realism—she posits a synchronic critique of political content as constituted by conventional form. Our own fussy attempts to discriminate between the canonic and the kitsch merely expose our complicity with the ethos linking the two. In place of that ethos, Acker transmits a dis-ease whose contagion signals and depends upon epidemic dangers in historical contexts *external* to their textual intercourse.

Her second strategy of disjunction is to allow abrupt shifts in plot, character, theme, story—motivated less by signifying chains than by shifts in emotional tone. She steals randomly and promiscuously from Shakespeare, de Sade, Dickens, Jean Genet, *Cosmopolitan Magazine*, Pauline Réage, Harlequin romances, Cervantes, bathroom walls, Sylvere Lotringer, the *Koran*, *Newsweek*, Dick and Jane, even from "Kathy Acker." The trouble is—third disjunction— that although these predecessors are evoked indirectly by titles, style, or names, when we read the text subsumed under the authorized signature, we find a flood of obscene, disgusting language and images stolen as much from an "unspoken" popular culture as from authorized Literature:

> The old actress isn't good anymore . . . Her legs are grotesque: FLABBY. Above, hidden within the folds of skin, there's an ugly cunt. Two long flaps of white skin spreckled by black hairs like a pig's cock flesh hang down to the knees. There's no feeling in them. Between these two flaps of skin the meat is red folds and drips a white slime that poisons whatever it touches. Just one drop burns a hole into anything. An odor of garbage infested by maggots floats out of this cunt. One wants to vomit. The meat is so red it looks like some one hacked a body to bits with a cleaver or like the bright red lines under the purple lines on the translucent skin of a woman's body found dead three days ago. This red leads to a hole, a hole of redness, round and round, black nausea. The old actress is black nausea because she reminds us of death . . . Glory be to those humans who are absolutely NOTHING for the opinions of other humans: they are the true owners of illusions, transformations and themselves. (Acker, *New York City*)

This is not pornographic, and it surpasses the obscene. This is language scraping as close as possible to an unspeakable, and obliterating "Real." At the same time, it is utterly artificial, suggestive somehow of those seductive supermarket headlines, "Ninety-year-old woman gives birth to two-headed child." Perverse and tacky, there's something obtusely fascinating in its grotesque promise to provide a glimpse of some unspoken physical horror repressed by voguish enticements of eternal youth and beauty. More to the point, this passage portrays the way in which the scope and organization of post-renaissance literature colludes in fragmenting the commodified body. Acker returns repeatedly to contemporary simulacra of our *constituted* others to show us how the Imaginary produces the politics of the Real through the discourse of the unspeakable. "Madame Bovary, c'est moi!" confesses Flaubert, because behind Emma Bovary's romantic illusions lies the inevitable fall into the NOTHING literature masks. But straddle-legged and obscene, Acker shows us modernism's "old bitch gone in the teeth," that gross reality to which the modernist obsessively returns only to fondle his private superiority to the culture he despises.

This open, pathetic body is one aspect of Acker's muse: its disequilibriums shape Acker's final disjunction, already present in her generic, narrative, and semantic revolt. But this last strategy is purely linguistic, a voiding of any textual ground where bourgeois identity might construct its Self. At one level all her plagiarism and disdain for genre displaces those spatial and temporal perspectives which inscribe a unified subject both in and out of the text. But it is in her sentence structure that Acker most decenters the textual subject. She alternates wildly between the present tense, which situates the narrator inside the linguistic process—and, therefore, at the mercy of her narration—and the past tense, which constructs a narrator who is always already written not simply because she is (sometimes) inscribed in the illusory mastery of the preterite, but because narrative control is riddled with ideology. The deictic conventions distinguishing *énoncé* from *énonciation* slide precariously from one sentence to the next, destroying all perspectival assurance for both writer and reader. For Acker, the locale of power *is* inscription, so that, defined by charted territories, even "Acker" becomes merely the nomenclature of a constituted boundary between ideology and text, a mere deictic shifter fixed neither outside the writing in the place of an author nor inside the text in the place of a narrator. The flickering subject dreams the cultural fiction that she can live outside the discourse she mimics. But as the subject disappears before our eyes, Acker drops her audience abruptly into an abyss where the polyvalent dependences of meaning slide ceaselessly, one against the other.

Acker's isomorphic and obsessive reiteration of the same motifs surpasses the demands of the storyteller's design to describe an individual life. All her treatment is obsessional: father/daughter incest, unmitigated female masochism, the colonized body. Every narrative circles around a mother who commits suicide, an incestuous and promiscuous father, a sexually victimized daughter desperately seeking love along limited channels of possibility. In her work, we are in the presence of that abject and terrifying realm of desire so insatiable that its invasions and betrayals reveal themselves as a frantic reconstruction of a fictional self that returns us only to the scene of our own obliteration. Acker's work is a direct encounter with the recursive return of the repressed.

But while her obsessive themes gradually acquire tentative acceptance, her disjunctive style does not. For example, in his review of Acker's *Don Quixote*, Tom LeClair, who likes her work, complains that her writing is "much too frequently composed of banal language, [and] stilted and formulaic high-school passion . . . How to separate the trash compactor from the trash?" (30). But in fact, Acker's stilted, formulaic language is crucial to her displacement of authority, not simply as an anti-aesthetic strategy, but as the insistent erasure of her own discursive mastery. "I write," Acker explains, "by using other written texts rather than by expressing 'reality,' which is what most novelists do . . . Our reality . . . *is* other texts" (Miller 30). This is important to Acker, since if all experience is indeed textual, then there is the possibility that its hierarchies of desire can be transformed by language. When we attempt to separate the trash from the trash compactor we repress, once again, Acker's enraged transformation of Man's centrality. All her work strains against the Promethean distance romantically inscribed for the artist; for her, the artist is no more than a copyist who finds materials in the excrement of the already written. Her place in the hierarchy of cultural range is determined, then, by an excremental circulation: first nourishment, then shit. In one sense, it is all a matter of a point of view; in another, it is a matter of words.

Trash, therefore, constructs a model of intertextuality too dirty for conventional metaphors of weaving. Acker's intertextuality invades, seeping into vulnerable areas where tidy immunities break down. Trash leaks, smells, offends, as if the servants had hauled in the offal of supper amidst the elegant meal. What offends most is not the mess, but that we have to acknowledge the class distinctions inherent in the barrier between where we eat and where we throw the rejects. Acker doesn't simply want to offend us; she wants to spread dis-ease. She swerves towards a cultural transformation which drives straight through apocalyptic visions of rapturous ascent into the internal corruption transforming lived bodies. Her "banality" strips the skin from a chaotic metastasis spreading through the body politic, thus leading us to deeper etiologies of contagion. She clogs the proper systems of cleanliness, decorum, ownership, and class by forcing open new channels of flow—as if by churning up the filth she can exacerbate the symptoms hidden in our post-renaissance body, bringing them to the surface where those habitual inoculations upon which cultural "discriminations" rely can be unmasked as no more than illusory placebos. Acker hauls in the trash so that the modernist prophylactic of decorum can no longer sheathe the symptoms of its disease.

Since 1973, then, Acker has written about a dozen works, each of which blurs any generic distinctions between fiction, theater, lyric, autobiography, history, and graphic art. Her works include *The Childlike Life of the Black Tarantula, I Dreamt I Was a Nymphomaniac! Imagine, The Adult Life of Toulouse-Lautrec, Kathy Goes to Haiti, Blood and Guts in High School, Great Expectations, My Death My Life by Pier Paolo Pasolini*, the libretto for *The Birth of the Poet*, and most recently *Don Quixote: which was a dream*. Aside from writing, she has been a teacher at the California School of Fine Arts and she illustrates her own books. Now living in London, she continues to be a painter, a linguist, and a writer of fiction, drama, film, biography, and autobiography. Perusing this impossibly random list, we see the extent of her resistance to any formal categories.

Genre must be transgressed for Acker because it is a mapping of territories for possession, for signature, and for authority. Acker discerns a dialectics of balances and nostalgia in the modernist aesthetic that begs for violation. Naturally she obliges by exposing modernism in its most abject postures of longing. Behind the posture of nostalgia for a lost mythic perfection Acker shows the workings of a disingenuous narrative strategy which supports the prevailing distributions of power. Both the romantic and realistic conventions constitute earlier modes of literature as mirrors of a more cohesive reality in order to signify opposing modes of literature as the mere detritus of culture, its rejects, its garbage, its junk. For Acker, however, the difference between junk and art is neither transcendent nor eternal; it is a matter of market forces. Once literature is cut up into generic distinctions, it becomes an artifact in the network of semiotic signs that determine class affiliation. Since the history of genre mirrors the history of class relations, the novelistic themes of Cervantes' emptied world and Dickens' codified family politics simply authorize a world parceled out into distinct, isolated units.

Precisely in those gaps where the generic codes and conventions of modernist identity achieve distinction—lyric, not myth; literature, not junk; writing, not painting; above all, art, not politics—Acker locates the aesthetic superstructure inscribed within an incestuous ideology of the modern nuclear family. Genre has served the Law of the Father by occulting behind the rules of linguistic and narrative property the elaboration of his desire. If Hegel's master/slave interchange is indeed the motor of history, Acker wants to disengage literature from the model of eroticism on which the dialectic rests. In other words, for Acker the metonymic signs of exploitation spewed out by the apparently contrary modes of high and low cultural production turn upon the insight initiated when Lear links bourgeois remappings to the father's demand of his daughters' undivided love.

To explore these links, Acker exploits abjection as an image which exposes the return of the repressed determined by those external politics which infect family and economic relations. Against the nostalgic balance of modernism, Acker relentlessly juxtaposes images of the open, unclosable body that undermines nostalgia and shows it up for its oppressiveness. The paragraph following that horrifying image of the old actress reads:

> old people have to go either to children or most often into rest homes where they're shunted into wheel chairs and made as fast as possible into zombies cause it's easier to handle a zombie, if you have to handle anything, than a human. (Acker, *New York City*)

As quantity becomes quality, so abjection is a contemporary social content becoming deadly form. Those naked displays of what seem undigested personal anguish—the sordid details of a private degradation, untransformed by artistic control or distance—transport us to tyrannical postures which reimpose, if not the patriarch's laws of modesty and genre, then certain feminist laws of positivism. But in that repulsion we come up against our oedipal limitations. Modernist solipsism, turned outside its formal limits, screams at a world drained of meaning by its own despairing version of history as a dialectic of master/slave recognitions.

Acker's graffiti make epidemic a new relation to self, culture, and history after their disarticulation by the contemporary technological modes of production and communication. By codifying desire as nymphomania, body as cunt, love as fucking, Acker scribbles across the bounds of desire and censorship the temporary appropriation of an anonymous space where her scribble, too, is subject to erasure. Defacing walls whenever she finds them, she trespasses against conventions of private property or cohesive form. In the place of genre, she poses street art—random, ugly, lyric, anonymous, temporary; not an inscription, but the performance of an inscription. When she steals from canonized authors, she doesn't simply appropriate, she obliterates, scrawling another text across the original, blurring its outlines, assumptions, themes. At the same time, merely by evoking these absent texts, she allows their ideologies to loom visibly through contemporary obscenities. It is as if the obscenity emerges from within the canonic, the dirty secret hidden beneath its elaborately mythologized calligraphy. All that dirty talk is more than disobedience, however; those forbidden words trap Acker's reader as complicit voyeur in the ob-scenity of writing. Naturally, however, "dirty" words, too, are thick with connotation, for as "graffiti" they inevitably provoke those class and canonic distinctions they would defy.

In a sense, then, any critical attention to Acker resists her anti-oedipal pressure, for as her work gains critical attention it loses its force as graffiti. It ceases to be the anonymous, communal and traditional reconstitution of the present tense of its writing and becomes, instead, personal, private, conventional, and fixed in the preterite of the institution. Legitimized by the Brooklyn Academy of Music, or the *New York Times Book Review* or The Johns Hopkins University Press, Acker's bewildering scribble risks assimilation into that very ethos of getting-at-the-truth whose authority she subverts. But that is the power of abjection: Acker can only be appropriated; her critics can only acknowledge their violations of her hopelessly open body. And so a sly perversity unifies our texts in the guilty and unsavory sublime of the market forces which determine our textual intercourse.

Despite Acker's resistance to paternal succession, it is expedient then (for the critic) to acknowledge those "predecessors" who have influenced her. For with Acker's insistence on the abject, the obscene, the irrational, and the provocations of black humor (which takes its own abjection as an object for abuse), one cannot avoid tracing a perverse path through Dadaism, surrealism, Céline's grotesque parodies of family life, de Sade's revolutionary sado/masochism, Bataille's ecstatic violence, and Genet's sexual politics. The Dadaist tradition can be perceived in her montage of styles, her deformation of language, and her desire to shock. Surrealistic techniques of hysteria and exaggeration sexualize the political unconscious and demystify the ways in which the New Morality links nationalism to religion by encoding the body as irrational. Perhaps Acker's deepest affinities are with Céline, whose exacerbated degradation permits her to stage every posture of political and sexual abjection through images of our darkest, most terrorizing "other."[3] For Acker, these images are the veiled and victimized force of female desire which juxtapose, on the one hand, images of the incestuous daughter over against, on the other, media reflections of the third-world terrorist who, with the force of suppressed desire, shatters the benign surface of ordinary life to reveal the limits of our tenuous control. Genet, of course, stamps final authorization on a vision which claims abject sexuality and third-world colonization as mutually interchangeable vehicle and tenor, each undoing the structural exchange of need and repression at the base of political power. What Fredric Jameson has called "the underside of culture . . . blood, torture, death and horror" (57), Acker renders explicit in abject postures of obsessive submission.

Acker's uncanny recognition of the complicity between sexuality and territoriality bears witness to the force with which current events have dispersed Western borders so that they can no longer be cured, owned, or closed. On the other hand, or rather, on the other side of the page, where her readers desperately try to reestablish frontiers, or at least to hide their increasing vulnerability, a different scenario is played out. Since, for Acker, contemporary politics is a text of abjection, the process of habitual reading must, itself, be put on trial. Acker's graffiti pervert the occulted sadism of narrative exchange by scrawling all their secrets in the open: "I love" for Acker equals "I hate you" in an immediate unmasking of the disavowed hostility of the romance. It is not, exactly, that the reader is violated by Acker's anti-story, but rather that there are too many gaps for the narrative to fill. Plots, narrators, genres, subject, and themes proliferate randomly, spreading throughout the eroticized body of the text, inviting entry everywhere yet opening elsewhere as the reader's desire for closure multiplies. We expose our own affinities with those master/slave alterities which for Acker have transformed "woman" and "Arab" into the wholly imaginary signifiers of the Real. As putative origins recede forever out of reach, we fall in love with the subject of our own castration or with those exhausted erections which would "fill" the proliferating displacements of Acker's narrative holes.

To return, then, to origins, whatever clarity King Lear achieves by the end of Shakespeare's play is isolated and merely personal. But its biographical form masks its deeper cultural affect in shifting from formal cosmologies of social obligation to that unencoded and, in fact, uncontrollable dimension of personal tragedy. Lear is tragic not because he is flawed but because his time is out of joint and no amount of personal suffering can put it right. It is no wonder, then, that when woman returns speaking of the void, she no longer exposes the reified codes of succession but screams instead the gaping abyss of that break.

In and Out of the CUNT: Readings

Levi Strauss: Meaning depends on rules.
Is rules. That's the nature of language.
Acker, *Algeria* 19

In Acker's work, the isomorphic interplay of abjection and politics traverses so many layers—both formal and thematic—that her fictions and plays demand enormous attention both to the ways their multiple surfaces and voices interact and to her varied decentering strategies. Further, because abject woman is the figure through which Acker explores other modes of territorialization, it seems appropriate to examine a work which makes that link explicit. Thus, I will now focus on one of Acker's works, in which various modes of female subjection are juxtaposed against colonized Islam: the piece (story? play? political tract?) *Algeria*.

Algeria tells two stories: one, set in New York, is about THE CUNT, Omar—sometimes signified as male, sometimes female, but always a hole; the other retells "The Battle of Algiers," where, to resist the colonizer, THE CUNT disguises herself under various veils which, depending upon who controls the gaze, signify her otherness. The work has seven major sections—some narrated, some dramatized, some apparently in the form of a direct address from author to reader—each punctuated by headlines staging their own scene of writing as an obscene metatextual performance of "intentionality." Each of these headlines signals a shift in setting between New York and Algeria, or from performance to spectacle, master to victim, male to female, writer to written.

Algeria undoes a putative history of literary hierarchies—romanticism, Victorianism, pop-culture—unraveling each as an infinitely receding reflection in a mirror of circulating codes. It opens in "New York," where THE CUNT represents its "fear of intimacy" as a montage of images and texts borrowed from the seeming opposites of popular women's magazines and pornographic journals: "Whenever a cock enters me every night three nights in a row," she confesses, "I ask myself regardless of who the cock belongs to should I let my SELF depend on this person, or should I remain a closed entity. I say: I'm beginning to love you I don't want to see you again. The man thinks I'm crazy so he wants nothing to do with me" (3). The text ends by juxtaposing a live sex show against a parody of that Arnoldian isolation at the base of modernity, "we are forced together even though we hate each other because we are so lonely frightened unsure defensive because we have to survive" (29). There's something humorous about this—as if we are over-hearing the Victorian crisis in meaning as heartfelt, banal conver-sation. Its immediate effect is to drain our literary tradition of its already encoded passions by foregrounding the hollow potency of that tradition's ideological function.

Before we even open *Algeria*, our gaze is drawn into a series of iterative penetrations by a picture postcard on its cover which shows a winding pedestrian alley. Our view is increasingly nar-rowed by low buildings which curve inward as the street recedes to dark, impenetrable shadows. Trapped at various spots between those enclosures stand five women, each veiled, each turning as if caught unawares by an anonymous, candid camera that gazes at them from beyond the page through an arch which frames its en-closed openings like a pair of labia. Triply veiled, then, by street, clothes, and custom, the postcard signifies a series of CUNT, both in its form and in its content, but CUNT as obsessively repressed. Secret and secretive, the faceless women are nothing but nameless inscrip-tions of someone else's text. Yet their veiling is analogous to lan-guage which can never say what it means and is inadequate to represent:

> All Algerian women wear the veil . . . There is no such thing as a woman. Henceforth a woman is a CUNT. A CUNT can see. It cannot be seen . . . The Frenchmen who say they want cunt find real CUNTS frustrating. (5)

Transparency is impossible. All CUNT are the same; only language makes distinctions. Yet language invokes only the father's "rule-governed" discourse. No matter how perverse, language can al-ways be recuperated. The enemy is always elsewhere—not where we look but in the very tools of looking, caught in the eye of its inquisition.

Strangely, the veiled and anonymous CUNT reveals a series of vio-lent reversals, which name the unnameable conventions by which desire is enslaved to an otherness that works itself into language only through repulsion. Perhaps what is most frightening about CUNTS is their power to see without being seen: in Derrida's apho-rism, "Woman is the untruth of truth;" CUNT is nothing but a signifier, taboo because "real cunts" figure the (w)hole meaning while the naked *word* hides the secret weapons by which it seduces its colonizer. CUNTS made visible are blinding.

Algeria's title page reiterates the obsessive veiling of its cover by opening on a double obversion, white on black, which reads:

ALGERIA

A Series of Invocations
Because Nothing Else Works

by

KATHY ACKER

The other side of this page, also white on black, reads:

The Land in Algeria
is pink
Life in this America stinks

CUNT

In 1979, right before
the Algerian revolution
begins, the city
is cold and dank . . .

This doubled entitlement is printed so that CUNT is "Kathy Acker's" obverse side: pink, stinky, cold, and dank. Nineteen seventy-nine is the year of Acker's Algerian revolution, a private year of revolt and oppression whose insistently slippery signification operates as a temporal catechresis without erasing history as process. By situating the question of difference within the imaginary locale of the abject, impenetrable Other of colonized Islam, Acker reproduces a correlative energy for the obscenity of the unsayable in Western discourse: the female, the woman, the CUNT. Shadowing one another, Algeria/Kathy Acker/CUNT, each signifies spaces inhabited by the topology of their unseen, verso other.

In this process, *Algeria* veils CUNT, giving title to a text organized around the figure of veiled woman as a trope for the oedipal evasions of materiality itself. CUNT is a forbidden word whose insistent capitals insinuate a symmetrical relation to the symbolic force of phallic propriety. The shock of the language—both its obscenity and its conventional power to diminish—are overwhelmed by the physicality they inscribe in the text where they appear. CUNT, as Jane Gallop points out, is con-centric, the metonymic lure to closure; yet its display as CUNT "gives us an immediate contact with the language" (31). The Real is the hole in meaning which the CUNT fetishizes, veils, and fills. But iterated in literature, THE abysmal CUNT overwhelms any potentially encoded romance of phallic proportion and unveils instead the mediating function of romantic repression. Stolen from a phallic discourse which diminishes female sexuality, CUNT reinscribes woman as unreclaimable, dirty, and out of bounds.

The first section of *Algeria* is entitled "1. THE STUD ENEMY." It seems to portray a love story about a man named Kader who lives in Toronto, and a woman, named Omar, in New York. The section opens in the middle of a love scene which quickly displays the way subject/sexual positions are written:

> I am fucking you and you are coming you have a hard time coming you breathe hard you have periods when you strain to come then your cock withers you strain to come again. (1)

The missing punctuation not only defies the rules of grammar but makes "I" the grammatical subject of a sentence in which "you" is the subject of the action, "you strain . . . you wither." "Separation from Kader," Omar continues, "makes me have to fill that separation with nothing," because separation from Kader is a matter of punctuation. They exist as alternating textual entities: "Kader and I write each other," writes Omar, "I have to make Kader here even if he isn't here" (5). She writes, of course, not only because Kader exists when written, but also because both "Kader and I" *are* writing and exist only as linguistic positions: "I have to fuck I have to fuck I have to fuck I" (5) [*sic*].

Into the midst of these opening violations Acker inserts the plot of "The Battle of Algiers," the Algerian revolution of May 8, 1945. As Acker tells it, this revolt began at the end of World War II during a putative anti-Nazi celebration which was intended to mask its anticolonial message to Algeria's French occupiers. In the aftermath of Hitler's theatrics, we have learned that for the politics of power bodies and words are mutually dependent: torture and "information" are bound together. Hence, when during that celebration of "freedom" a French policeman, confused by his desire to "fuck up the ass" a beautiful Algerian boy, shoots the boy in the stomach, the body on which power inscribes its message is inevitably sexualized precisely because it can be killed. The power of possession and the power of desire are intimately twined; or, as a character in Thomas Pynchon's *V.* says, "all political events; wars, governments, and uprisings, have the desire to get laid at their roots; because history unfolds according to economic forces and the only reason anybody wants to get rich is so he can get laid steadily, with whomever he chooses" (198). Desire, of course, is a function of the world's resistance to that wish; on the other hand, absolute power contains the compelling, possessive eroticism of torture and death.

Strewn across a geography of shifting political boundaries, the personal and the political become mutually exclusive objective correlatives for one another in a performance that fragments the symbol as that which both constitutes and represents meaning. "The Battle of Algiers" tells the story of an Algerian woman who, like her sisters, has first taken up the veil as a symbol of resistance to French colonization, then abdicates the veil to engage in terrorist resistance, then veils herself again at the end of the Algerian war as a symbol of restored cultural identity. As the veil flickers between two discourses, it marks the locale where surfaces touch. Signifying both woman's colonization by the Algerian male and Algeria's resistance to colonization by an exterior force, the veil itself becomes a text whose function depends upon the politics of those who hold the power to control the meaning of semiotic systems. Because it depends for its meaning on position, the veil is a mediating sign of both repression and of liberation. Thus, putting on and taking off the veil as signifier of female anonymity is a symptomatic recovery of the colonized subject for which woman, as CUNT, has been the sign.

CUNT ironically opposes any transcendent signifier, for THE CUNT is always already an absence. Directly connected to a gendered body, it permeates every linguistic encounter, odiferous, pungent, ubiquitous. If writing has traditionally been imaged as male violation of the feminine blank by the erect pen, Acker reverses these terms, speaking as the empty signifier, the open wound of female desire, throbbing, flayed, screaming its rage, anguish, and terror before the void which writing produces. CUNT becomes the overdetermined return of our desire to encode and control the discourse. Its repetitions obliterate generic safety and void *woman* of any conventional placement, making the term itself operate as the black hole through which meaning leaks—the place where the signifier reveals its slippery dependency.

The "woman" in love with Kader, Omar, is sometimes male, sometimes female, sometimes in New York, sometimes Algiers. Unlike CUNT, whose sign is everywhere, Omar's signifying function slides, as if the bar no longer functions and signifier and signified now leak into one another. Gender, setting, identity lose their fix;

the veil is in place, but we keep passing from one side to the other. When Omar pretends to be what he/she is not by uncovering what he/she is, the otherness which Algeria/CUNT struggles to signify is disarmed. Omar represents only the blind desire the Other wants to see. Thus revealed, Omar implodes the foundations of colonized identity by turning it inward toward the scopic fetishization of its own impotence. He/she remains *Algeria*'s protagonist only insofar as "Omar" is a signifier which occupies all settings, appears in all plots, and can be designated by either gender. He/she loves Kader, is engaged to Ali, is betrayed in Algeria by his/her desire for a CUNT, and makes love on stage with Hacene. At the center of these juxtapositions of writing and "The Battle of Algiers" is CUNT's own story:

2. CUNT
"This is the way THE CUNT my mother committed suicide"

Here comes the story that blows *Algeria* off the page—the untranslatable double of a script whose intelligibility can only be trans-lated by another story:

> THE CUNT ate at the most expensive restaurants in New York City. It purchased five copies of every expensive piece of clothing it liked. It bought needlepoint designs at $300 a piece. It rode in taxis and hired limousines. THE CUNT ran through $300,000 of its husband's life insurance money and the money THE CUNT its mother gave it in two years. The closer THE CUNT came to no money, the more frenzily it spent. It stole money and jewelry from THE CUNT its mother. . .
>
> THE CUNT was one who came the closest to successful suicide by blowing money . . .
>
> Its empty hole was arising. (5–6)

The cruelty of this analysis links the Mother's sexuality to the obscenity of commodity while its brutality drains "Mother" of all sentimentality. As a result, "mother" becomes the nomenclature of all textual gaps. Figured as ubiquitous CUNT, the mother is analogous to that earlier horror; here, it clothes its potency behind an accumulating list of things which render it harmless not because they cover the hole, but because the clothes themselves are com-modified: "skirts, sweater, a pair of black patent leather shoes, a nightie, a bathrobe, two pairs of nylon underpants" (6). THE CUNT produces no action but is, rather, transported through a series of commercial sites: Bloomingdale's, the Museum of Modern Art, the New York Hilton. Each of these sites is covered by the dead father's money which becomes increasingly abstracted from the hole it too represents: first paper, then an expired Master Charge card, and finally a bad check which exchanges an empty value for a series of symbolic values, none of which have any worth beyond their function to veil the void they represent. This CUNT, this dead mother, unlocks Algeria's blind alleys. We've already seen her spraddle-legged, that slimy mess from which Bloomingdale's—that icon of American freedom—distracts us. Woman commits suicide first by buying, then by dying, obligingly, before we have to recognize the void of her origins.

On the face of things, the two settings of New York and Algiers seem to explore almost wholly separate issues. New York locates the text as personal: Mother-as-suicide, middle-class marriage, and the nuclear family. In this setting, Omar variously confesses his/her failure to love, his/her responsibility for the mother's suicide, his/her pleasure at performing in a live sex show that dramatizes THE CUNT as a center for scopic fascinations. But in Algeria similar patterns of failure and betrayal are made explicitly political. As alternatively, or even simultaneously, male and female, Omar is a device for exploring the way disguise constructs gender as a mise-en-scène of colonization.

Woman's body, then, is the metonymic sign of domination, not the mirror of history, but an inscription of the present crisis in historicity itself which, according to Jameson, returns the past to us only "by way of our own pop images and simulacra of that history which . . . remains forever out of reach" (71). By working from within those simulacra, "Acker" herself becomes nothing more than a series of images learned from literature and television. What is erased is not "woman" or "Algerian" but the illusion that either is any more than the reflection of a phallic imaginary. Thus, "woman" is obliterated not because she is erased, but because she is duplicated everywhere *as* erased.

CUNT and Algeria function as interchangeable vehicle and tenor of a metaphor which signifies the infection of the oedipal desire that blind representation duplicates. First fathers seduce daughters, then they desert them for other women. Acker resists this invasion by stealing the Father's s(t)ex(ts) and reinjecting their poison as a homeopathic doubling of the phallic discourse, not in order to erase the disease, but to make its functioning visible; this is a kind of anti-immunization which forces to the surface of ideology the cancerous and waiting diseases swathed beneath the benign codes of political correctness and modest reserve. When she discards the masks of depth, symbol, and transparency, she layers in their place shifting surfaces which reveal how language dons veils according

186

to the desires of the perceiver. Reading Acker, we are caught in an exchange without center. Desire is colonized, inhabited by the gaze of the Other in a mutual exchange where power can be blinded by showing what it says it wants to see.

In his critique of postmodern art and ideology, Hal Foster claims that "rarely does this [postmodern] art . . . expose the contextual contradictions of the styles upon which it draws" (30). The attraction of Acker's work is that it exposes everything, assuming its guilt of representational corruption and inscribing its theoretical impossibility. Acker links violence to a particular ethos of stylistic cohesion for which female sexuality is the repressed and disruptive sign. Thus, when she junks the modernist display of literary precedents and manly control, she reveals instead how that repression works at every level of language, metaphor, and formal constraint.

Acker writes in a moment when theory labors to restore what the aesthetics of representation have repressed: that the scopic privileging of linear meaning and isolate identity has a self-enclosed desire at its base. Her great expectations are born from an exhausted aesthetic which masks its narcissistic desires behind myths of transparency and thus divides language from history, economics, gender, politics, and, indeed, discourse itself. The aim of her isomorphic undoing of the "I" at the level of sentence structure, paragraph, chapter, and genre is to disarticulate those textually constructed modes of identity which mark the redundant slippage of absent cause. On top of Lear's narcissism, Acker scribbles a supplementarity—that "very little thing"—which is not the penis, but the already castrated body of the dead mother who represents identity as a hole constituted by the deictic interchange of texts. CUNT, dead mother, "Acker" each open the place where the "Real" reveals its function as the empty holding position in a triangulation of reader, text, and author.[4] For her, the Father is *not* dead, only incestuous and narcissistic. In his place the suicide-Mother constitutes meaning by voiding family hierarchies since she is always a series of already constituted texts, the third term of the dirty joke who, once exposed, deprives the modernist form of its exterior fulcrum in bourgeois irony.

Since the 1970s, questions of gender have become so thoroughly problematized that writing as "woman" can only be inescapably ironic, a self-miming doubling in which a person with female anatomy plays at being a woman. To read Acker as the story of female obliteration, then, is not to read her at all. CUNT, abjection, naked female desire—all are content becoming morselated form. When "Acker" assumes these abject roles—"woman," dog, knight,

Don Quixote, poet, artist, Pip, Omar, a stripper, a voyeur—each role is generated by a discourse in which all identity is performative, where genre, gender, and signature become mere masks that permit textual readings. Without these veils, no one can be seen or read.

Acker also reverses this process, making the veil of writing itself a kind of CUNT: repulsive, filthy, its lyric intensity and power producing a stink that transgresses not only what phallic proportion hides, but also overstepping the borders which authorize territorial possession. As a metonymy of desire, CUNT's part-iality reproduces the dependence of the writing subject on an overwhelming desire to transgress the limits of sense and to plunge into non-sense where identity evades the mappings which blind us to new senses. Extrinsic to constituted phallic power, THE CUNT's abjection provides accessibility to unlimited desire, to the hole which generates new "wholes." For Acker, CUNT is a sign that reverses the outside of ideology to the inside. Her writing of "woman" unclothes that abyss, that CUNT, whose four capitals replace the edifice of coherence, order, and potency, opening an intertextual dystopia without closure.

Notes

Once we conceive of intertextuality, it is impossible to stake any claims to originality. Thus, I would like to give a partial list of all the "authors" from whose works and discussions I have stolen: Louis Althusser, Roland Barthes, Homi Bhabha, Michael Beard, Jonathan Culler, Gale Davy, Jacques Derrida, Elizabeth Ermarth, Elinor Fuchs, Hal Foster, Jean Genet, Barbara Harlow, Fredric Jameson, Julia Kristeva, Jacques Lacan, Georg Lukács, John MacCanles, Oscar Manoni, Marshall McLuhan, Sheryl O'Donnell, Gerald Rabkin, Edward Said, William Shakespeare, Mary Shelley, Kaja Silverman, George Styan, Gayatri Spivak.

1. In *The Gutenberg Galaxy*, Marshall McLuhan writes, "The new patterns of power and organization which had been discussed during the preceding century were now, in the early seventeenth century, being felt at all levels of social and private life. *King Lear* is a presentation of a new strategy of culture and power as it affects the state, the family, and the individual psyche. . . . More important, the map brings forward at once a principal theme of *King Lear*, namely the isolation of the visual scene as a kind of blindness" (1).

2. I use here Louis Althusser's definition of ideology as "a representation of the Imaginary relations of individuals to their Real conditions of existence" (162). This is similar to the sense in which Barthes uses "myth" to mean depoliticized and dehistoricized speech.

3. Perhaps nothing is more symptomatic of how intertextuality infects

popular culture than the fact that when I wrote this article, I had not yet seen Julia Kristeva's moving study of abjection in *The Powers of Horror*. The editors of this collection, however, suggested that I ought, in all honesty, to acknowledge Kristeva's influence on my piece. Since then I have read Kristeva and confront in her work an uncanny mirroring of language, interpretation, tone. There is no place I could have stolen that vocabulary except from the general air of popular discourse which surrounds feminist, Marxist, and psychoanalytic studies. Somehow, what I am most sorry I missed is Kristeva's insight that unlike most cultural constructions of otherness, "the abject has only one quality of object—that of being opposed to *I*" (1). The abject for Kristeva is pure WANT, incapable even of desire. However, there is a difference in emphasis between Kristeva's inquiry into the abject and my own. While hers *implies* the politics of abjection, she is more interested in the mystical force of that unclosed psychic wound. I have ignored Acker's mystical insights (which are important) in order to probe the ways she opens the abject wound to political interpretation by juxtaposing its force against legitimized forms of political oppression.

4. George Styan, for example, in *The Elements of Drama*, points out that the person playing Hamlet is "Hamlet" only by a convention. "Hamlet" never exists except when the triangulation of audience, actor, and staging coincide. Thus, the stage and the semiotic systems which traverse it are always empty.

Works Cited

Acker, Kathy. *Great Expectations*. New York: Open Book, 1983.

———. *Algeria: A Series of Invocations Because Nothing Else Works*. London: Aloes Books, 1984.

———. *Blood and Guts in High School*. New York: Grove Books, 1984.

———. *Don Quixote: which was a dream*. London: Paladin Grafton Books, 1986.

———. *New York City in 1979*. Top Stories 9. New York: Top Stories, n.d.

Althusser, Louis. *Aesthetics and Politics*. London: New Left Books, 1977.

Barthes, Roland. *Mythologies*. Translated by Annette Lavers. New York: Hill & Wang, 1972.

Foster, Hal. *Recodings: Art, Spectacle, Cultural Politics*. Port Townsend Wash.: Bay Press, 1985.

Gallop, Jane. *The Daughter's Seduction: Feminism and Psychoanalysis*. Ithaca, N.Y.: Cornell University Press, 1982.

Jameson, Fredric. "Postmodernism, or the Cultural Logic of Late Capitalism." *New Left Review* 146 (1983): 53–92.

LeClair, Tom. "The Lord of La Mancha and Her Abortion." *New York Times Book Review*, 30 November 1986, 10.

McLuhan, Marshall. *The Gutenberg Galaxy*. Toronto: University of Toronto Press, 1966.

Miller, Lori. "In the Tradition of Cervantes, Sort Of." *New York Times Book Review*, 30 November 1986, 10.

Pynchon, Thomas. *V.* New York: Bantam, 1963.

Styan, George. *The Elements of Drama.* London: Cambridge University Press, 1960.

Suleiman, Susan, ed. *The Female Body in Western Culture: Contemporary Perspectives.* Cambridge: Harvard University Press, 1986.

Cyborgs and Cybernetic Intertexts:

On Postmodern Phantasms of Body and Mind

===

GABRIELE SCHWAB

Always two things
switching
Current runs through bodies
and then it doesn't
It was a language of sounds,
of noise,
of switching,
of signals.
   It was the language of the rabbit,
                  the caribou,
                  the penguin,
                  the beaver.

A language of the past.
Current runs through bodies
and then it doesn't.
On again.
Off again.
Always two things
switching.
One thing instantly replaces
another.

It was the language
Of the Future.
—Laurie Anderson, "The Language of the Future"

The language of Laurie Anderson's capitalized Future is a language of cyborgs with current running through bodies and "always two things switching." It is at the same time a language of the past, because the electronic sounds—the noises, the switching and the signals—recall an archaic language of sounds: the primordial sound-signals of the animal world. If one were to experience what Laurie Anderson poetically evokes, one would have to listen simultaneously, in the present, to the language of the past and to the language of the future. The language of the present would, in other words, condense past, present, and future time. To experience this synchronicity between the "high-tech lingo" of computerese and the primordial animal sounds, one would need a synchronistic sound perception, not unlike the "horizontal hearing"

191

required to understand polyphonic music (see Ehrenzweig 26–28; 75–76; 159–60). One would need a cyborg who has stored the past in its memory in order to display it instantly on the screen of a current experience. This cyborg, moreover, would be able to read the future in the present, to project a holistic notion of a temporal synchronicity of all times, as it could be stored in a computer or in the human brain.

A quarter of a century ago, N. Clyne and M. Klynes published their book *Drugs, Space, and Cybernetics: Evolution to Cyborg*. The authors projected a utopian cyborg, a product of the technocybernetic evolution of the human organism. Eyes would be improved by implanting optical cells, livers and kidneys activated with technological stimulants, and artificial elements would replace specific parts of the head. The authors fantasized jaws made from "vitallium" and containing nylon dentures with plastic teeth. Polyethylene would provide plastic arteries, nylon a new aorta, inorganic joints and hips would be substituted for organic ones. The human skeleton would be supported by an exoskeleton, moved by electromotors—an image that could very easily be taken as a bodily representation of the Lacanian fortress that symbolizes the human ego.

In 1966, the Polish science-fiction writer Stanislav Lem supplemented his *Summa technologiae* with an essay entitled "The Production of Cyborgs."[1] He outlined a similar scientific project, a reconstruction of man that would allow the human organism to adapt to changing cosmological environments. The reconstructed humanoid, a cybernetic organization, could provide an "ecological shelter" for surviving an ecological catastrophe or an atomic war. The elimination of the digestive system, for example, would make jaw muscles and teeth superfluous. Solving the problem of communication by way of telecommunication would ultimately make the mouth dispensable as well. Lem's cyborg, however, still retained a series of biological elements: a skeleton, muscles, skin, and a brain. In contrast to our body's unconscious steering of most of its internal functions, the brain, supported by artificial means, would steer all bodily functions consciously. Osmotic pumps, connected to the body, would provide food, activating substances, medication, hormones, and stimulants. Since the body would continue to have living cells as its basis, the reconstructed parts would not, however, be genetically encoded. A genetically encoded simulacrum of man would require a different project, that of genetic engineering.

In his novel *If on a Winter's Night a Traveler*, Italo Calvino has even depicted the postmodern reader as a cyborg:

In New York, in the control room, the reader is soldered to the chair at the wrists, with pressure manometers and a stethoscopic belt, her temples beneath their crown of hair held fast by the serpentine wires of the encephalogram that mark the intensity of her concentration and the frequency of stimuli. All our work depends on the sensitivity of the subject at our disposal for the control tests: and it must, moreover, be a person of strong eyesight and nerves, to be subjected to the uninterrupted reading of novels and variants of novels as they are turned out by the computer. If reading attention reaches certain highs with a certain continuity, the product is viable and can be launched on the market; if attention, on the contrary, relaxes and shifts, the combination is rejected and its elements are broken up and used again in other contexts. (Calvino 127)

This and related thought experiments that fantasize about a technological reconstruction of the human sphere by reconceptualizing body and mind have captured our imaginations during the postmodern era: Samuel Beckett's experimental bodies, Thomas Pynchon's cybernetic organisms, Laurie Anderson's high-tech mutants, David Byrne's techno-citizens, and the organless bodies and disjunctive minds in Deleuze and Guattari's *Anti-Oedipus*—all exemplify our fascination with the conversion of organisms into machines. Meanwhile these fantasies have also begun to assume more and more reality in our quotidian lives. The United States is the leading country in technologizing and "cybernetifying" the human realm, a process that affects practically all social spheres.

These fantasies of fragmented and cybernetically reorganized bodies challenge familiar notions of the body and the text. The boundaries of each, as well as the boundaries between subjectivity and textuality, have become fluid and flexible. Units are broken up, new associations are established. Fragmentation and reorganization are privileged operations of what critics have called "the postmodern mind." But these operations of fragmentation and reorganization are no longer confined to the mind. The body has become a new focus of interest in literature and the arts, in theory, science, and in a flourishing industry of body culture. While the reorganization of the body and the transgression of its limits are at stake in such different areas as medicine (from organ transplants to cosmetic surgery), bioengineering, gerontology, psychobiology, and related disciplines, a new interest in the fragmented or even the grotesque and carnivalesque body has captured the cultural imagination at large. In the field of literature and literary criticism, this interest is linked to a preoccupation with the "fragmented text," that is, with intertextuality as a textual production in which the same operation of fragmentation and reorganization prevails. The current interest that literature and literary criticism take in both intertextuality and the fragmented or grotesque body belongs to the same phenomenon of a larger cultural and epistemological change affecting body and mind, subject and text.

In what follows, I will be concerned with the phantasmatic aspects of the technological imagination, with the ways in which it expresses fears and desires that are derived not so much from technology per se as from deeper psychic sources. From this perspective, technology is not viewed in the context of its concrete implications, be they utopian or dystopian. Instead, I hope to shift the focus toward the psychohistorical dynamic that expresses itself in the ways in which technology becomes a field of cathexis, an imaginary screen onto which psychic energies from the most archaic to the most current may be projected. I am interested, in other words, in the ways in which technology is used to rewrite the human body as a phantasmatic body—even in contexts as "real" as those of medicine or genetics.

The body, from this perspective, becomes more than an organic body. It becomes a text, a screen onto which cultural fantasies, desires, fears, anxieties, hopes, and utopias are projected. Cybernetic organisms inspire such projections because they are products of a technological, or artificial, manipulation of the body. A great deal of the fascination with such technological manipulations stems from the fact that the manipulated bodies are, on an unconscious level, also perceived as phantasms of the fragmented body. If we take a close look at them and visualize their organic reality we tend to experience them as grotesque or uncanny. The grotesque body has always lived through its proximity to phantasms of the fragmented body. It might, in fact, be seen as a way of aesthetically coping with or working through an uncanny and potentially dangerous fascination with bodily fragmentation.

This might be one reason why the grotesque body plays such a preeminent role in postmodern culture. In the grotesque body the underlying phantasms of the fragmented body are domesticated. Under the harmless aesthetic form or the distance of an aesthetic response, however, lurks the dark side of the phantasm. Cybernetic organisms as such are, of course, not necessarily grotesque. Rather, I think that our tendency to perceive them as grotesque, that is, from an aesthetic distance, already involves a defense mechanism against their inherent threatening qualities. The same holds true for the ways in which literature and the media present cyborgs as grotesque organisms. We still seem to need such defense mechanisms because we are not yet familiar enough with cyborgs and therefore see the technological manipulation of the body as a transgression of its boundaries. This is why we can experience the cultural production of cybernetic organisms as a carnival of grotesque bodies, because cybernetic organisms are transgressive bodies that outgrow the organic body and challenge its limits. Even if these new bodies are not publicly staged as carnival (though very often the media willingly or unwillingly contribute to such a staging), their grotesque realism invites us to invest them with all sorts of unconscious images of the body. This is why the cyborg may, in the most diverse cultural spheres, become the object of complex semiotic performances and the locus of postmodern phantasms of body and mind.

On this imaginary level of cultural body politics the different spheres interact with each other because the phantasmatic cathexis of the cyborg establishes a common frame of reference. We can, in fact, observe a network of intertextual links not only between cybernetic fictions in literature and the media but also, more generally, between cultural representations of the body and social practices involving the body (like medicine or education) or other forms of body politics. As I will show with the following observations, this intertextuality is often not established by direct intertextual references but by shared images connected with similar fantasies and fears. This phantasmatic intertextuality is particularly intense in a postmodern culture where everything, from the most private dreams to the most public affairs, is filtered through or even controlled by the media or other cybernetic systems. Thus, the production of cyborgs does not necessarily presuppose an invasive technological manipulation, like the artificial reconstruction of the body. There is also a way in which a television culture establishes an interconnectedness with others that constantly blurs the boundaries between the real and the imaginary, which may be enough to produce a culture of cyborgs.

The imaginary "cyborgization" starts in infancy with the socialization of the child through television and technological toys. It comes as no surprise that the latter are highly gendered and, to a considerable extent, directed toward boys, socializing them into the role of imaginary soldiers, or "Masters of the Universe." Thus, the role and behavior models of American boys are plastic cyborgs, soldiers that transform into guns, cars that convert into robots, voice-transformers that change the human voice into a robot voice, or even, as we know from Laurie Anderson, a female into a male voice. There is also an increasingly sophisticated market-oriented interplay between toys and television programs. The fact that one needs expensive technological gadgets to tune into "interactive" television games creates a class system among children, based on a technologically controlled body politics of inclusion and exclusion. Only if you can tune your body into the screen will it be able to respond with its own sensory signals.

At school, the "magic writing pad," used by Freud as a metaphor for the unconscious because its wax board contains invisible traces of whatever has been written on its erasable surface, is replaced by high-tech computer games which help train various skills without leaving any individual trace on the software memory. Memory, instead of becoming internalized (as, for example, through the memorizing of poems), is externalized and stored in the artificial memory of the computer. Children learn, for instance, to "write their own stories" on a computer with "Kidwriter," a program which provides them with stencilled phrases and prefabricated gaps where they can fill in phrases that they have semiotically internalized from television cartoons and commercials. The intertextuality of the thus-produced texts is preprogrammed and even the filling of the gaps is highly predictable—although the children enjoy subverting the expected plots by producing nonsense-stories. This fragmentation of the child's creative imagination is supplemented with phantasms of the fragmented body. "Captain Cosmo," to choose one of a whole world of imaginary characters, is a plastic figure whose white and red body can be taken apart and rebuilt in various forms. The children can substitute a leg for the head, an arm for the leg, the head for the arm, and most important, shoot parts of the body off into space. Finally, they can also "transplant" the limbs of fellow characters into Captain Cosmo's body in endless variations.

The practice of children acting out phantasms of the fragmented body is, of course, not new and, in principle, there is no need for a sophisticated technological imagination to engender it. New, however, is the way in which and the extent to which joint ventures of the toy and media industries increasingly explore, market, and manipulate the imaginations of children by exploiting and fashioning such psychic dispositions as the fascination with the fragmented body. The glorification of war and warlike activities, the paranoid obsession with enemies and invaders, the self-aggrandizing fantasies of dominating other living beings as well as nature, space, time, and mortality are clearly the outstanding features of current models of a boy's world-making. The imaginary and socially sanctioned cyborgization is, as far as childhood culture is concerned, a predominantly male enterprise in the most traditional sense.

This is clearly demonstrated by a comparison with the equally conventional role models for girls. Mothering as a social institution is reenforced, for example, in the imaginary world of the Cabbage-Patch Kids, which brought about the 1983 American Cabbage-Patch craze, a media-promoted hysteria about imaginary mothering that degenerated into frantic adult consumers mutilating real children while trying to snatch their Cabbage-Patch babies from the little girls' arms.

Perhaps phenomena like the Cabbage-Patch hysteria indicate a surfacing of the cultural unconscious, a specific dark side of the status of children in postmodern American culture. This hypothesis seems to be supported by a reactive "intertextual" phenomenon, namely the parodistic exploitation of the Cabbage-Patch hysteria in the production of the so-called Garbage-Pail Kids. Garbage-Pail Kids are pictures of violently attacked or abused cyborg paper dolls. Their market and exchange value among children again reveals a cultural obsession with phantasms of the fragmented body. The Garbage Pail travesties are traded on the margins of commercial toy culture under the desks of schoolchildren, because adults obviously dislike being confronted with the dark side of their culture's imagination of children. Or, to quote a nine-year-old boy, "Parents and teachers think they're gross but we think they're rad." Garbage-Pail Kids come as little square pictures with a certain type of bubble gum. They obviously appeal to children by presenting them with images of sadistic phantasms of the body, while training their cybernetic as well as their semiotic imagination. Most often they are inspired by punning on names—for example, "Greta Garbage," "Salvatore Dolly" "Hy Gene," and "Frank N. Stein." Naming becomes an act of aggression, because beneath every normal name is a mutilated one. When I interviewed a couple of nine-year-olds about their Garbage-Pail craze, one of them said: "They are so creative because you can invent more and more of them and you can tease kids by giving them Garbage-Pail names." These little cyborg horror creatures are all technologically or otherwise mutilated as, for example: Geeky Gary, whose face emerges from hundreds of television screens as from a whirlpool; or Melba Toast, the bread-shaped roasted boy, who pops out of a toaster; Frying Bra-in, the kid from jail with his post-Derridean name, who wears a bowl on his head with electrical cords connected to a lever with the sign "full power." Among the (of course) less high-tech girls, we find two black cyborg-doubles, Jean Machine and Iron Jaw Erin, whose iron jaws are full of nails, screws, and nuts. And finally—how could he be missing from this American crew of postmodern kids?—there is Adam Bomb, the tough guy with a joystick and the crucial button he must just have pressed, because pieces of fragmented bodies and severed limbs are flying all over the place.

As adults, those who enjoyed Cosmo or the Garbage-Pail Kids might use their well-trained cybernetic imagination in bioengineering, a field that is at least equally exciting as far as the phantasms of body and mind are concerned. This most important sphere of "cybernation" gradually proceeds toward the willful steering of the evolution of our species along with that of other organisms on this planet. For one interested in the phantasmatic side of genetic engineering, the clones provide the best objects of desire. Once scientists become able to read the genetic code, they have also learned how to manipulate it. Thus, they can obtain an optimal definition of the genotype, and even conceive a parthogenetic insemination which would allow them to reproduce endlessly one and the same initial model. The old dream (and fear) of an exact double has become scientifically and technologically feasible. The radical implications of this feasibility reach from the "question of the subject and its boundaries" to that of the existential status of a clone and the ethics of biogenetic doubling. The clone has long become a new mythological figure at the horizon of postmodern imagination. He or she (or do I have to say "it"?) is invested with fantasies of immortality, doubling, endless mirroring, and phantasmatic redefinitions of death. The boundaries between life and death seem shaken or shifted. As Gena Corea has pointed out in *The Mother Machine*, the phantasmatic interest in the clone can be linked with two archetypal desires: the "patriarchal urge to self-generate" and the "desire to control death" (Corea 260, 270). As far as the phantasm of male parenthood or creation of life is concerned, the clone is a descendant of Frankenstein. The important technological progress lies in the fact that man can virtually produce a replica of himself as well as, ultimately, control *who* has the right to be born—a new form of embryonical eugenics.[2] The two desires of self-generation and immortality are closely linked. By reproducing an identical heir one could, in a way, become one's own father again and again—eternally.

> In reading literature on any of the reproductive technologies, not just cloning, one sees that desire for immortality expressed time and again. The cycle of birth, growth and death in nature, a cycle

venerated in the Goddess religion and epitomized by a woman bearing a child is one against which patriarchal man has long railed. He does not want to die. He does not want to return to the dark womb of the earth. The inevitability of his death is an affront to him. He dreams of resisting death by cannibalizing clones or transplanting organs or building himself a body out of rustproof steel, or manipulating cells to stop the aging process. He fantasizes about constructing a steel womb—with a glass porthole to let the light in—for the gestation of his clones. His desire to control birth through the reproductive technologies, then, is also a desire to control death. (Corea 262)

Fantasies of cloning show how intricately linked certain theories and practices of human reproduction are with literary and especially science-fictional fantasies. The first narrative about a clone to engender a worldwide discussion was, interestingly enough, a hybrid between a scientific and a fictional narrative, an undeclared "science fiction," so to speak, with a pretense to reality. *In His Image* (1978), a male technological family romance by David Rorvik (who also wrote a book with the title *A Man Becomes Machine: Evolution to Cyborg*) tells the story of Max, a rich, elderly businessman desperate for a male heir and his own immortality. He uses a "pretty virgin" to bear his clone. While the fantasy leaves the "boundaries of the subjects," the father and his son, intact, its implications challenge those very boundaries. Who is the fantasized clone? Is he, for the character Max, a different subject from the original? The dreams of immortality signal that, at least phantasmatically, the clone is supposed to be the same. The idea of the "self" is extended beyond the original body and its death into another body and a subsequent life history.

If one generalizes the structure of the phantasm of the clone in connection with certain trends in contemporary science, one can see a new order of the whole and its parts emerging, inspired by a kind of holographic model or a holonomy of the subject. This model is paradigmatically represented by the cell or, more precisely, by the fact that every cell in a living organism begins with all the genes necessary for the development of a complete being:

> The assumption on which rests the possibility of human cloning is . . . that the nucleus of every cell of every tissue in our bodies contains within it a full blueprint for the development of the complete organism. It is not just the sperm and egg cells that have these vital genes. No matter how cells have differentiated into specialized organs—eye, liver, fingernail—they all contain the latent potential for reproducing a complete adult. (Corea 265)

199

Most intriguing, and therefore a major object for phantasmatic cathexis, is the fact that a clone could potentially be produced in any phase of a human being, not only from embryonic tissue. An adult could thus realize his phantasm of immortality by having a clone produced out of his cells.

The most terrifying counterpart to these fantasies of producing endless copies of oneself in the form of clones who nourish an illusion of immortality is, of course, the simultaneous self-aggrandizing fantasy that humankind is, for the first time in history, able to destroy all forms of life on this planet. The desire to have power over life and death produces the questionable utopia of nuclear transplantation and artificial reproduction at a time when all life is potentially threatened by nuclear holocaust. The dreams of a technologically induced artificial immortality complement the nightmares engendered by Star Wars as a military technological program. Omnipotent fantasies of the destruction of our whole planet are the drive underlying this new American Dream— not without, of course, also providing the necessary survival fantasy in the form of an "ecological shelter," an artificial human biosphere in space, a postmodern ark which will preserve the human species and the organic life of this planet in the face of postmodern Apocalypse. This sphere is projected as a closed system destined to outlive the menacing nuclear catastrophe. At the same time it provides, uncannily, the phantasmatic justification for the nuclear holocaust.

Numerous technological or cybernetic fantasies have already assumed political and practical reality, and they seem at times to exceed whatever can be imagined by the most daring literary imagination. What interests me here is the impact of such "cultural fantasies" on the postmodern imagination in general and, especially, on the conception and production of a postmodern subjectivity. Because of the interplay of different cultural spheres, this subjectivity is produced by a phantasmatic intertextuality. The latter does not, as one could too hastily conclude, replace subjectivity. It rather produces a new type of subjectivity that can no longer be seen separately from the cultural spheres that enter into its production.

In literature and art the cyborg is a descendant of the human automaton, also brought into this world in an artificial "birth" fabricated by male technology. While the latter was a product of the mechanical age, the cyborg is a product of the new age of electronic technologies and computers.[3] The human automaton and the cyborg can be seen as collective fantasies used to symbolize a transition in the historical formation of subjectivity. "The human automaton, which symbolized the transition between romantic and modern subjectivity, is replaced by the cyborg, which symbolizes the transition between modern and postmodern subjectivity. The human automaton was created as a centered organism and as such served to compensate for the uncontrollable forces of the unconscious at the price of a shift to the inanimate" (Schwab 10). The cyborg, on the other hand, is "decentered" in a new way. Its psychological decenteredness is supplemented by a social one to the extent to which cyborgs are preprogrammed by transindividual semiotic and cybernetic systems. This programming extends so far as to reach and shape even their phantasmatic desires. The interaction between different cultural spheres on a phantasmatic level is a postmodern form of cultural intertextuality which has been discussed as simulacrum or as society as spectacle. The cyborg, born out of this cultural intertextuality, is then more than a new literary figure. Constituted by transgressive intertextual plays and boundary-crossings, she or he is no longer a cultural object in the narrow sense. More important is the transgression of boundaries between the human (body) and the technological.

At this point technology and desire interpenetrate. A "Technological Eros" is created and used to transform technology into "second nature." This transformation is often mediated by technological phantasms of the fragmented body—phantasms which indicate a breakdown of the cultural boundaries of subjectivity. The idea of a cybernetic reconstruction of the human organism by far exceeds the futuristic reconception of the human body. It signals how and to what extent the alien bodies of technology have already invaded our minds and taken part in shaping the boundaries of subjectivity. This process involves a good deal of violence against the "old organic body," and perhaps it is significant that in the United States, where postmodern technology, science, and medicine are most advanced, we also witness an invasion of shared cultural phantasms of fragmented bodies and cybernetic organisms disseminated through the media and the arts.

Postmodern medicine, with its spectacular organ transplants, engenders proliferating speculations about the physical and metaphysical boundaries of the subject. These speculations have increased dramatically with the first heart transplants and the technological feasibility of brain transplants, because the heart and the brain have long symbolized the soul and the mind, and seem to contain the "essence" of the subject—be it only phantasmatically. Beginning with the invention of the very first tools, mankind has always used technology to work toward the extension and perfection of the human body. Today, technology has reached a stage in which what started out as a struggle for survival verges on phantasms of omnipotence and immortality. As early as 1930 Freud discussed the ambivalence of these phantasms of a cyborg:

> Man has, as it were, become a kind of prosthetic God. When he puts on his auxiliary organs he is truly magnificent; but those organs have not grown on to him and they still give him much trouble at times. (Freud 43)

The various attempts to "increase man's likeness to God" (Freud) by technological means always express, among other things, the relationship of a specific culture to death. In his recent article, enigmatically entitled "Freud and the Technical Media: The Road Belong Cargo," Laurence Rickels even goes so far as to argue that the postmodern technical media hold the place of a missing death cult in our culture (14). It is not astonishing, then, that heart transplant patients are celebrated in the media as the new stars on the stage of postmodern medicine. Mr. Schroeder and Baby Fay become collective symbols, imaginary characters who carry a whole nation's phantasmatic desire to be granted a second life with a new heart. Organ transplants also nourish quite uncanny fantasies of the body surviving one's own death. In 1985, for example, the *New York Times* interviewed a woman whose daughter had died in a car accident. This mother confessed how happy she was to see her daughter live on through her eyes, her kidneys, and her liver that had been donated to different human recipients.

The publicity surrounding issues of health and medicine and, as a result, the phantasmatic cathexis of the technomedical manipulation of the body make a decisive cultural difference between the old and the new world. A striking example is the phantasmatic interest within the United States in President Reagan's cancers of the colon and the nose. The media mimicked the surgical intrusion into the president's body—displaying his inner organs, the size of his tumors, and the surgical incisions to the public gaze. This was followed by a cathartic reconstruction—the malicious alien cells were located, cut out, and destroyed, the surface of the body restored. After a couple of days, even the president's nose looked just as it did before. The fearful fantasies of mutilation and fragmentation were relieved by wishful fantasies of invincibility and technological superiority which had made possible the destruction of the invader, the malignant cancer cells. The publicity surrounding the intrusion into the president's body and the cutting into his nose represents something important in postmodern American culture.

This publicity brings a whole nation close to (if not phantasmatically inside) its president, while at the same time demonstrating technological control and superiority.

The nose, on the other hand, has always been a favorite organ for phantasmatic cathexis—as we know from literature as well as from Mikhail Bakhtin's reflections on carnivalization, and, of course, from Wilhelm Fliess's famous psychoanalytic "nose-mysticism." The phantasmatic interest in the nose and its expression in numerous forms of nose-mysticism has been so obsessive that Laurence Sterne could "carnivalize" it in continuous references to and even whole chapters on the nose in *Tristram Shandy* (1760), only to have his narrator insist ironically on the fact that a nose is a nose is a nose: "For by the word *Nose*, throughout all this long chapter of noses, and in every other part of my work, where the word *Nose* occurs—I declare by that word I mean a nose, and nothing more or less." (166). Tristram Shandy's father, on the other hand, reading *Erasmus*, tries to "study the mystic and the allegorick sense" and, in fact, to "mend the sense" of the nose by scratching the printed word from the page in order to get behind the technology of print to "the real thing" (16).

There is a long intertextual history of cut-off or missing noses from Gogol's *The Nose* to Beckett's *The Unnamable*, who muses "Why should I have a sex, who have no longer a nose?" (23). Finally there is Woody Allen's *Sleeper*, interesting in the context of this paper because this film plays with the fantasy of a biogenetic reconstruction of a president's body out of his nose. After a bomb attack, all that is left of Allen's fictitious president *is* his nose. The latter becomes the object of a meeting of bioengineers and medical scientists, who discuss the possibility of reconstructing the president out of the genetic material contained in his nose. By feeding this material into a special computer program containing the complete genetic code of the president, they hope to be able to rebuild the whole from the part. As we have seen earlier, this is not so far-fetched, because bioengineers are already able to realize this process with plants and project the same for human beings. Woody Allen carnivalizes this fantasy of reconstructing the whole from a part, which is closely related to that of cloning.

The possibility of the reconstruction of the whole human subject from any one of his or her parts would, as I have said earlier, lead to a "holonomy of the subject," meant here in the sense of a storage of the complete information of this subject in all of his or her parts—just like the storage of the complete information on a holograph in all of its parts. One could easily imagine techniques for freezing cells that would allow for an eternal storage with the possibility of eternal and multifold revivals of the very same object. The crucial question that remains is whether we would be willing to say that these new objects are still the same "subject."

The exuberant proliferation of cyborgs in contemporary literature, as well as the phantasmatic interest in cyborgs that we can witness in the most different cultural spheres, gives evidence of a cultural shift of the boundaries between the natural and the technological that already has a deep impact on the human use of body and mind. These fantasies of cyborgs seem to suggest that there is a dimension of postmodern subjectivity which can only be accounted for with categories able to grasp the intrusion of technology into or even the technologizing of body, mind, and soul.

In this context the idea of a holonomy of the subject merits further consideration. I have thus far used it to describe the impact which the readability of the genetic code has had on the contemporary imagination of subjectivity, and especially on some phantasmatic aspects of this imagination. But the idea of a holonomy of the subject also has implications that exceed the realm of the purely imaginary; I would even go so far as to say that the cyborg as a postmodern mythological figure may symbolize a transition to a new notion of the subject that is in a much more general way linked to what I have heuristically called holonomy of the subject. I now want to develop some implications of this idea.

When Erwin Schrödinger lectured in 1943 on the readability of the genetic code, he introduced the idea of a holographic writing to describe how the complete potential of the future development of the organism is contained in the chromosomes of a cell. The relation of each cell to the whole organism can be compared to the relation of each element of a three-dimensional holographic picture to the whole holograph. The whole can then be reproduced from the part because each cell stores in itself the information for the complete body. Moreover, the holonomy metaphor has recently been used by David Bohm in contemporary brain research to describe the functioning of human memory. If the brain can indeed be compared to a hologram, then the cyborg can be taken as a positive model for a "holonomy of the mind." He or she would then not only stand for a science-fictional utopia (or dystopia) of a technological reconstruction of the human body, but also for a new holistic concept of subjectivity. The "body as text" means more here than a mere metaphor to describe cultural "readings" of the body. It means that the biological body itself, its genetic material, is organized like a text. As this bodily text is not linear but holonomic, its intertextual relations are holistic. Any new "text" (information) is stored and assimilated into a new "whole." Changes in the code lead to irreversible mutations because there are no boundaries left between text and intertext.

Since it is based on a holistic model of thought, the idea of the cyborg representing a holonomy of the subject would feed into a more general paradigm shift induced by the cybernetification of the human realm. This paradigm shift is itself supported by the increasing sophistication and dissemination of computer technologies. Its basic characteristic could be described as a cultural tendency to recuperate holistic perspectives. Theoreticians from different areas of specialization—for example, Marshall McLuhan, André Leroi-Gourhan, David Bohm, Gregory Bateson, and Walter J. Ong—have all developed some sense of a new holism. More than twenty years ago, Marshall McLuhan argued in *Understanding Media: The Extensions of Man* (1964) that "the electric age is recovering the unity of plastic and iconic space" (166). Similarly, André Leroi-Gourhan speculated in *Le geste et la parole*, which appeared in the same year, that computer technologies might, in the long run, induce a drastic shift in our forms of thinking from print-oriented linearity to screen-oriented simultaneity and multidimensionality.[4] Since the only available model for the required multidimensional thinking is the preverbal holistic perception of the child, Leroi-Gourhan concludes that a reactivation of these primary modes of thinking will be necessary. Walter J. Ong, in *Orality and Literacy* (1982), thinks along similar lines when he describes the emergence of a "secondary orality" induced by the electronic transformation of verbal expression. He rightly insists, however, on the crucial difference between this new mode and the earlier orality:

> This new orality has striking resemblances to the old in its participatory mystique, its fostering of a communal sense, its concentration on the present moment, and even its use of formulas. But it is essentially a more deliberate and self-conscious orality, based permanently on the use of writing and print, which are essential for the manufacture and operation of the equipment and for its use as well. (136)

Here it becomes relevant that contemporary literature presents subjectivity as a form of intertextuality. Modern and postmodern literary texts experiment not only with a "new orality" in Ong's sense but also with holistic perspectives and with new notions of the subject and of the text. Marshall McLuhan and Quentin Fiore have, for example, taken Joyce's *Finnegans Wake* as a paradigm for a new use of writing and print that produces a new orality. And Joyce himself plays throughout his whole text with the idea of a scriptural hologram, the great Letter, which contains the whole text, and which, in turn, contains all other texts and ultimately the whole universe. In a different way, Samuel Beckett plays with cybernetic modes of presentation and communication and with the notion of closed systems and the entropy of the subject. Thomas Pynchon, on the other hand, displays cyborg characters whose bodies have been chemically conditioned or technologically reconstructed and whose minds are obsessed with technological myths of transcendence. The literary cyborg, then, is not restricted to the technologizing of the body as we know it from science fiction. She or he is rather a product of a much more generalized technologizing of the word and particularly of the ways in which writers incorporate contemporary notions of cybernetics or field and systems theories. The literary cyborg could thus be seen as an experimental literary subject under the effects of cybernetics and technology. She or he is, in this respect, also a product of an intertextual coupling between literature, technology, and theory.

The holistic perspective could also become important for the discussion of intertextuality. Instead of emphasizing the process of fragmentation, the breaking up of textual units, the boundary-crossings between texts and the contamination of texts by other texts, a holistic perspective would emphasize the complementary process of reorganization as well as the new "flexible unit" that is presented to the reader. Such a perspective would ultimately contribute to the discussion of new types of reading as envisioned not only by theoreticians, such as Leroi-Gourhan, but also by writers, such as Joyce, whose *Finnegans Wake* contains numerous textual reflections of a holistic and simultaneous reading.[5]

In her book *The Cosmic Web: Scientific Field Models and Literary Strategies in the Twentieth Century*, Katherine Hayles reads contemporary fiction with the premise "that well-known developments in the modern novel are part of a larger paradigm shift within the culture to the field concept" (24). This premise is crucial, because the various scientific field models she refers to are all based on a holistic model of thought. The problems of an intertextual influence, that is, of a transference of such models to the realm of language, literature, or subjectivity are obvious. Katherine Hayles asks "can the representation of a holistic field be accomplished within the linear flow of words, or is the attempt inherently limited by the fragmentation of the medium?" (25). Hayles interprets some of the experimental forms in postmodern literature in terms of a struggle to reach a holistic perspective through language. The philosophical and epistemological implications of such a perspective require a new concept of both the text and the subject. In this context, the notion of the cyborg gains a dimension that I indicated earlier. The cyborg appears in these experimental literary texts not in his or her phantasmatic function as a postmodern myth of transition, as a "prosthetic God" aiming at omnipotence and immortality; instead, the literary cyborg becomes an imaginary representation of those new concepts of subjectivity that have emerged in contemporary thought at large. The holonomy of the subject, metaphorically derived from the holism of a hologram, serves as a heuristic model, which, apart from postmodern technology, also takes into account the above-mentioned general shift of paradigm in contemporary thought toward holistic models.[6]

I would like to conclude by giving some special attention to a particular area in which the problem of the body intersects in a special way with that of the text: the functioning of memory. Memory seems to be especially affected by the technologically induced changing of the subject. Memory is thus a crucial issue for the paradigmatic value of the cyborg as a positive model for a changing subjectivity. But how does technology affect memory? Can we, for example, use the relation of the cell to the whole organism, or of parts of the brain to the whole brain, as a model for the cyborg's mind? How does the metaphor of the holism of the subject relate to memory, be it the individual memory or the collective memory stored in cultural objects and transmitted through chains or networks of intertextual and intercultural relations? Is there a reconception of memory that can be linked to the more general paradigm shift referred to earlier? Doubtless there is a trend toward the totalization of memory through archives and computer memories. But this leads to an externalization of memory which does not, as such, empower the subject by extending its boundaries. One might even go so far as to consider this externalization of memory a weakening of the subject—a move that would recall Plato's critique of the technologies of script and writing. Plato argued that these facilitating devices destroy or weaken rather than extend memory understood as a capacity of the subject. There is, of course, also an extension of memory, but it requires a different frame. The storage of memory is indeed increased as far as memory alone is concerned. We then consider the whole system, which consists of the individual subject and the external archives at his disposition. Memory seen as a function of the whole system, subject and archive, can then be extended, whereas the memory of the subject considered separately might be impoverished. (Clyne and Klynes' idea of an exoskeleton might be seen as an organic equivalent. While it is supposed to support the body better than the vulnerable human skeleton, it will in the long run contribute to the degeneration of the organic skeleton.)

With the facilitated technological means, memory, or the storage of knowledge and information, has nearly become a cultural obsession. The ultimate aim seems to be to create a new type of collective memory which would make it possible for one to gain access to the totality of available knowledge of all times by simply pressing the right buttons on a computer. Jean Baudrillard points to the cultural mania of burying the world in microfilm and archives: "To archivate the whole world in order to have it rediscovered by some future civilization—a freezing of total knowledge until its resurrection—a transition of the totality of knowledge as value/sign into immortality."[7]

This may remind one of the desire to control death and the dream of an artificial immortality which turned out to be so prominent in the phantasmatic cathexis of the cyborg. Can we perhaps detect, as Baudrillard seems to suggest, a similar although displaced motivation behind the technologies we use as double-edged crutches or extensions of our memory? How do these extensions— the computer, the media, the microfilm archives—affect the memory of a culture and the individual memories of its subjects? The immortality evoked by Baudrillard is based on "dead memory." How do all those postmodern vaults of dead memories, the archives, in conjunction with the speaking memories of the media, build the memories of those who use them as technological extensions? How are processes of cultural memorization determined by the technological memories?

Freud's "prosthetic man" has found his postmodern version. Technological ghosts hover over our dead bodies: our photographic and filmic reproductions are the media that form the memories of those who survive us, obliterating more and more of the original image (as illusory as it may be); but there are also technological ghosts like the dead but still radiating nuclear reactors with our technological waste, our legacy for future generations. They will contaminate their memory of us, including their genetic memory stored in a mutilated and mutating genetic code. Our materialized and totalized knowledge, storable in the memories of computers, microfilms, and even in old-fashioned books, will, in the predictable future, be extended to include the genetic memories of clones, frozen and preserved in the data banks of the industries of reproductive technology.

This vision evokes the dark side of a culture of cyborgs. Technology, meant to extend our organs and our senses or even to support our phantasms of immortality and transcendence, seems to threaten what we wanted to preserve by destroying us as the subjects we thought ourselves to be when we took refuge in technological projects and dreams. Is the postmodern transmutation into cyborgs based on an identification with the aggressor? Do we, by internalizing technology, lose ourselves as the "subjects" of our culture? Such a conclusion would conflate the potential of technology with a specific cultural use of it. It is true that the present use of technology in postmodern culture does not allow for a great deal of optimism. The reason for this, however, lies not in technology as such but in the fact that the use of technology follows the overall dynamic of culture and its patterns of what Bateson calls "culture contact," which are, at the present moment, to a large extent governed by the concerns of a war culture. This is what Pynchon's *Gravity's Rainbow*, for example, shows in connection with the text's central object: the Rocket as a deadly weapon which serves, at the same time, as a technological myth of transcendence, thus concealing its destructive functions. For the characters in *Gravity's Rainbow*, this myth serves, among other things, to repress the reality of war and death.

The link between technology and repression or, better, the possibility of semiotizing technology for purposes of repression, seems to be rooted in a very general structure of memory. Memorization as a symbolic process presupposes the absence if not destruction of the remembered object and its revitalization as memory. This unavoidable absence haunts Derrida's notion of the impossibility of mourning in "Mnemosyne"—an impossibility that seems to be radicalized in the postmodern techniques of memorization, the freezing of memories or the covering of death by the technical media.

In "The Work of Art in the Age of Mechanical Reproduction," Walter Benjamin writes about the "loss of aura." The loss of the aura, of unique and finite personhood, individuality, or textuality, turns the dead into a death which cannot be mourned. The uncountable dead that we have become accustomed to seeing in the news as well as in war and crime movies will remain unaccounted for. We may thus arrive at "unmournable death." The "incapacity for mourning" has been analyzed critically by Alexander and Margarete Mitscherlich as an inability of the German war generation to deal with the Nazi past and its consequences. In the case of postmodern technologies the incapacity for mourning loses its character of individual repression, rejection, or forgetfulness. Instead, the media help to establish and maintain a cultural repression in the Freudian sense of a "structural repression." This is why the modern technical media replace and obliterate collective practices of mourning without providing a substitute for them. The incapacity for mourning has become technologically institutionalized.

One has again to insist that this repression is not an intrinsic function of the technical media but the result of their specific cultural use. Poets of all time have known how to use the technologies of writing and print against the codifying force inherent in them. As we have seen, some experimental postmodern writers and performance artists have liberated the cyborg from his or her original role, defined by the *American Heritage Dictionary* as a "human individual who has some of its vital bodily processes controlled by cybernetically operated devices." Instead they explore how cybernetics, that is, the knowledge of control processes in electronic, mechanical, and biological systems, and especially of the flow of information in such systems, affects semiotic systems. Or, seen from the perspective of the creative process, these artists use the cultural impact of cybernetics and field theories in order to create not only new types of literary subjects but also new types of texts informed by these theories. In a similar way, postmodern media artists can use the flow of information in the media against the grain, for example, against the inherent dynamic of a structural repression of memory.

Throughout the history of film, filmmakers have explored numerous ways in which to represent and reactivate memory and to affect the memory of the spectator. They have, in other words, used specific technologies to extend the memory in more than a simply mechanical way. Interview films such as Marcel Ophuls' *The Sorrow and the Pity* or Claude Lanzmann's *Shoah*, for example, have self-reflexively used the double-edgedness of technologically reproduced memories and worked with the specific effects an audience experiences when exposed to the recorded memories on the screen of a movie theater. These films have also escaped the "loss of aura" and perhaps one could even go so far as to say that they have re-created an aura, allowing thus for the reactivation of formerly repressed memories. They work through the incapacity of mourning or even re-create mournable death. It is, then, not the technical media as such, but the cultural tendency to mistake the order of the media for the order of things, which creates the simulacra of postmodern existence.

Being both body and text, cyborgs have a double-edged reality. They lead the phantasmatic lives of postmodern simulacra, but at the same time, they carry a memory that reaches beyond their

210

imaginary realm back to the past and "back to the future." If we learn to listen to the current that runs through their bodies, their dance of electricity, then we will hear, in Laurie Anderson's words, a song of entropy in negentropic voices: "We are going down. We are all going down, together . . . It was the language of the Future."[8]

Notes

1. For the relevance of the cyborg in contemporary literature and culture, see also Woodward, "Cybernetic Modeling," Haraway, Hayles, and Porush.

2. I deliberately say "himself" because, as Corea has argued, literature about cloning hardly ever talks about cloning women, and if it does so, then it talks about men cloning women such as Raquel Welch.

3. See Woodward, "Art and Technics," where she writes: "electrical-electronic technologies make a genuinely new phase in the scientific-technological revolution because they have increased the degree of artificiality in man's environment significantly, and have thereby generated new, non-natural needs" (174–75).

4. See also Derrida, *De la grammatologie*, 129 ff.

5. For the further development of such a holistic perspective and its implications for a theory of contemporary fiction, see Schwab, *Entgrenzungen und Entgrenzungsmythen*.

6. If primary modes of thinking are holistic and syncretistic (in the sense of Jean Piaget's "syncretistic vision"), this does not mean that they are organicist in the traditional sense. They are, on the contrary, seen in constant tension to secondary analytic modes of thinking; the "new holism" presupposes a dynamic tension between the two modes. What the new holistic model shares with organicist models is the idea of a certain balance between parts and whole. The whole, however, is not an isolated object but a kind of perspective whole, a heuristic construct used as an organizational device in varying cultural contexts. It belongs to a systems theory model founded by an ecological notion of system and environment as described by Gregory Bateson and others. Its boundaries are flexible and open to continuous change.

7. Baudrillard 281. Translation mine.

8. A first and considerably shorter version of this essay, with a different thematic focus, was published as "Cyborgs: Postmodern Phantasms of Body and Mind," *Discourse* 9 (Summer, 1987).

Works Cited

Anderson, Laurie. "The Language of the Future," in *United States*. New York: Harper & Row, 1984.

Baudrillard, Jean. *L'Echange symbolique et la mort*. Paris: Gallimard, 1976.

Beckett, Samuel. *The Unnamable*. New York: Grove Press, 1958.

Benjamin, Walter. "The Work of Art in the Age of Mechanical Reproduction." In *Illuminations*, 217–51. New York: Schocken, 1969.

Bohm, David. *Wholeness and the Implicate Order*. London: Routledge & Kegan Paul, 1980.

Calvino, Italo. *If on a Winter's Night a Traveler*. New York: Harcourt Brace Jovanovich, 1979.

Clyne, N., and M. Klynes. *Drugs, Space, and Cybernetics: Evolution to Cyborg*. New York: Columbia University Press, 1961.

Corea, Gena. *The Mother Machine: Reproductive Technologies for Artificial Insemination to Artificial Wombs*. New York: Harper & Row, 1986.

Derrida, Jacques. *De la grammatologie*. Paris: Minuit, 1967.

———. "Mnemosyne." In *Memoires for Paul de Man*, translated by Cecile Lindsay, Jonathan Culler, and Eduardo Cadava, 1–43. New York: Columbia University Press, 1986.

Ehrenzweig, Anton. *The Hidden Order of Art: A Study in the Psychology of the Artistic Imagination*. Berkeley and Los Angeles: University of California Press, 1967.

Freud, Sigmund. *Civilization and its Discontents*. London: Hogarth Press, 1940–1952; New York: Norton, 1961.

Haraway, Donna. "A Manifesto of Cyborgs: Science, Technology, and Socialist Feminism in the 1980s." *Socialist Review* 80 (1984): 65–107.

Hayles, Katherine. *The Cosmic Web: Scientific Field Models and Literary Strategies in the Twentieth Century*. Ithaca, N.Y.: Cornell University Press, 1986.

Lem, Stanislav. *Summa technologiae*. Krakow: Wydawnictwo Literackie, 1964.

Leroi-Gourhan, André. *Le geste et la parole*. Paris: A. Michel, 1984.

McLuhan, Marshall. *Understanding Media: The Extensions of Man*. New York: New American Library, 1964.

Mitscherlich, Alexander, and Margarete Mitscherlich. *Die Unfahigket zu trauern: Grundlagen kollektiven Verhaltens*. Munich: R. Piper & Co., 1967.

Ong, Walter J. *Orality and Literacy: The Technologizing of the Word*. London: Methuen, 1982.

Porush, David. *The Soft Machine: Cybernetic Fictions*. London: Methuen, 1985.

Rickels, Laurence. "Freud and the Technical Media: The Road Belong Cargo." Unpublished manuscript.

Rorvik, David. *In His Image: The Cloning of Man*. Philadelphia: Lippincott, 1978.

Schwab, Gabriele. "Creative Paranoia and Frost Patterns of White Words: Making Sense in and of Thomas Pynchon's *Gravity's Rainbow*." Working Paper No. 4, The Center for Twentieth-Century Studies at the University of Wisconsin–Milwaukee, Fall 1985.

———. *Entgrenzungen und Entgrenzungsmythen: Zur Subjektivitat im modernan Roman*. Stuttgart: Franz Steiner Verlag, 1987.

Sterne, Laurence. *Tristram Shandy*. 1760. London: Everyman, 1967.

Woodward, Kathleen. "Art and Technics: John Cage, Electronics and World Improvement." In *The Myths of Information: Technology and Post-industrial Culture*, edited by Kathleen Woodward. Center for Twentieth-Century Studies, Theories of Contemporary Culture, vol. 2. Madison, Wis.: Coda Press, 1980.

————. "Cybernetic Modeling in Recent American Writing: A Critique." *North Dakota Quarterly* 51 (1983): 57–73.

Metavideo

Fictionality and Mass Culture in a
Postmodern Economy

====

JOHN CARLOS ROWE

> What was projected psychologically and mentally, what used
> to be lived out on earth as metaphor, as mental or metaphori-
> cal scene, is henceforth projected into reality, without any
> metaphor at all, into an absolute space which is also that of
> simulation.
> —Jean Baudrillard, "The Ecstasy of Communication"

There are two reasons why poststructuralists have had trouble
dealing with popular media in contemporary Western societies.
First and foremost, these media have been theorized in terms that
apply best to industrial economies, in which relatively clear distinctions can be made between basic modes of production and the
ideological strategies by which economic practices are justified. Second, mass media in our postindustrial Western economies depend
for their very survival on the adaptation of methods and styles that
often have striking similarities with those we recognize as deconstructive. Among the chief methods and styles of the contemporary
popular media are those that fit remarkably well the academic definitions of *intertextuality*, polysemousness, and dissemination. In the
case of the first problem, poststructuralists may be criticized for
having failed to take into account the significant semiotic changes
occasioned by the shift from industrial to postindustrial production
in the West; this is a blindness they share with Frankfurt School
theorists, who pioneered critical studies of the media in the 1920s
and 1930s. At worst, poststructuralists can be charged in this regard simply with being out-of-date, drawing as they often do on
a nineteenth-century economic model. In the case of the second
problem, however, poststructuralist naiveté is more willful and
defensive. Like postmodern literary experimenters, deconstructive critics are often unwilling to acknowledge the self-conscious
rhetorical strategies of the mass media precisely because such
strategies pose a genuine challenge to the claims for ideological
critique made by both postmodern writers and deconstructionists.
Indeed, the self-consciousness of contemporary media is so perva-

sive and powerful, albeit serving the very different purposes I will try to illustrate, that it virtually negates the deconstructionist's claim to the special authority of *demystification* as a critical practice. In this postmodern and postindustrial *economy*, demystification is already a conventional rhetorical device, which contributes significantly to the commercial success of these media as well as to the maintenance of certain normative values.

In "Requiem for the Media" in *For a Critique of the Political Economy of the Sign* (1972), Jean Baudrillard criticizes Hans Magnus Enzensberger's "optimistic and offensive position" with regard to the popular media (168). Baudrillard argues that Enzensberger's attempt (in "Constituents of a Theory of the Media") to theorize the media as parts of "a simple 'medium of distribution'" ignores the fact that in a postindustrial economy the popular media are themselves vital modes of *production* (168). Enzensberger's notions of the "consciousness industry" and "the industrialization of the mind" betray his assumption that mass media are primarily off-shoots, by-products, of a familiar industrialism.[1] As a consequence, Enzensberger can imagine rather optimistically the relatively un-problematic transformation of this "medium of distribution" into "a true medium of communication" (Baudrillard, 168). Still imag-ining that the mass media might be employed by the Left as "popu-lar media," as Brecht had hoped in *Theory of Radio* (1932), Enzens-berger reaffirms the materialist distinctions between production and distribution, between economy and ideology. For Baudrillard, Brecht and Enzensberger merely demonstrate how inapplicable classical Marxism is to postmodern capitalism, in which "the media are not *coefficients*, but *effectors* of ideology" (169).

As Jean-François Lyotard has argued, "knowledge" in postmod-ern society is a function or effect of its primary "product": infor-mation. Evaluative criteria for "performative efficiency" by which such information is judged and knowledge constituted are part of the language games that determine production as surely as the machinery of industrialism.[2] *Information, service, postindustrial*, and *technological* products, as crude as these terms are at this stage of analysis, share a common feature: whatever materiality may be in-volved (computer hardware, telematic machinery, offices and ve-hicles for services) is subordinate to the essential *immateriality* of the product.[3] Marketing firms, consulting agencies, computer analysts and programmers, and the like may be supported by elaborate and seemingly indispensable hardware and technicians, but these rec-ognizably material tools and skills are subordinate to the a priori law of postmodern capitalism: the immateriality of production (or the production of immateriality). "Getting results," "increasing production," "maximizing profits" no longer refer as clearly and simply as they once did (did they *ever?*) to the increased numbers of objects manufactured and sold. The production of immaterial goods such as information and services depends not so much on the simple volume of such goods as on the potential of such goods for subsequent production. In this view, the classical Marxist conception of surplus value would have to be redefined, perhaps incorporating the differential becoming and heterogeneity so prized by countercultural critics from William James to Jacques Derrida, from James's pluralistic, "unfinished" universe to the Derridean supplement and dissemination.[4]

Mass media typify this mode of immaterial production. The signifying system of these media relies upon the total subsumption of use-value to exchange-value. Whereas Marxists claim to demystify the elaborate ideological strategies by which capitalism naturalizes such practices as the exchange of money for labor-power, the length of the workday, and the organization of the nuclear family, postmodern economic practices are in no way justified by any appeal to external reality or "nature." The gradual subsumption of use-value by exchange-value under industrial capitalism is no longer an issue in such an economy, since the very terms of such immaterial production transform use into a function or by-product of exchange. The popular media image simply has no other possible use except its exchange. Whatever use-value the immaterial image might appear to possess is merely the effect of the repression of the exchange-value (i.e., the potential for exchange and circulation) that constitutes the image.

For the Frankfurt School theorists and subsequent cultural critics who have followed their pioneering work, mass media served the interests of basic capitalist economic practices by distributing both its products and its values. And the relatively simple model of the mass media as secondary effects of more fundamental productive processes made it possible to imagine "popular culture," often linked closely with vanishing folkloric conventions, as a possible resistance to and subversion of the secondary exploitation of workers by mass media. Even in the work of Mikhail Bakhtin, such concepts as the "carnivalesque," the novel's "dialogic" structure, and the essential heteroglossia of language itself depend in large part on a significant distinction between the rhetoric of ideology and some critical discourse that might expose ideology's "monologic" forms of mystification.[5] Yet, once we theorize the media as involved in the basic modes of production in the immaterial economy of the postmodern age, the distinction between "mass" and "popular" media becomes difficult to sustain. And before we rush to answer the by-now familiar question—How is *any* resistance possible?—we need to examine the practical consequences of media representations that are in and of themselves (in their inherently intertextual modes of production) producers not only of money but of that even more troubling surplus value: social and psychic behaviors, in both their apparently willed and automatized modes.

The electronic media have their own internal histories, in which the transvaluation of the customs of Marshall McLuhan's "print-culture" took place gradually (even amid the notorious acceleration of the postmodern age) and amid significant contradictions. I cannot hope to reproduce that history with any thoroughness in this essay, so I shall simulate a kind of figurative history by looking briefly at the metafictional assumptions of various popular television programs from the 1950s to the early 1980s. In that period, significant changes occur in the attitudes and values of popular television with respect to its own medium. In the 1950s, television projects itself variously as a fragile artifice (an extension of theatrical unreality, requiring our suspension of disbelief) or as merely an extension of everyday life (a sort of studied and strained "realism," according to nineteenth-century definitions of the term). By the 1960s, however, popular television imagines itself in terms of a power over the immaterial that is sometimes compensatory (for what the viewer cannot have) and at other times competitive (offering the viewer genuine power). By the 1970s, television bids for genuine social and political power, in keeping with its own claims that power in contemporary America depends fundamentally on control and manipulation of the image. By the 1970s, then, television may claim a special kind of realism, drastically different from the realism of 1950s television, and recognizable as *postmodern realism*, in which the authority of the immaterial, the figurative, and the metamorphic is increasingly accepted by the viewer as part of his or her reality-principle. These changes, I would add, cast deconstructive conceptions of intertextuality and avant-garde claims for literary self-consciousness in an extremely different light.

In *The Honeymooners* (1955–1956), Ralph Kramden (Jackie Gleason) and Ed Norton (Art Carney) quite consistently express the wistful yearning of the exploited working class for the magical powers of the capitalist.[6] Ralph, in particular, falls for every get-rich-quick scheme that wafts through the tenement window, despite Alice's (Audrey Meadows) insistence that he has a "good job." Norton takes particular pride in his technical expertise as a sewer worker for the Department of Sanitation, but Ralph is disgusted with such stupidity and usually convinces Norton to share the enthusiasm, expense, and folly of his various enterprises. The conclusion of a typical episode is paradigmatic: Alice and/or Norton help Ralph cut his losses, get his job back as a driver for the Gotham Bus Company, and restore his self-esteem. It is Ralph's surviving pride, of course, in his abilities to rise above his working-class conditions that allows the complications of the next episode to follow, so it is fair to say that Ed and Alice (as well as Ed's wife, Trixie) serve quite directly the interests of capitalist exploitation of the working-class imagination. In keeping with the basic structure of the situation comedy, *The Honeymooners* solves problems for the sake of reproducing them in subsequent programs.

Ralph's problem, besides his working-class situation, is his failure to distinguish between a legitimate businessman and a con-man. Even so, there are many examples of benign businessmen in this series, many of whom (such as Ralph's boss) help extricate him from his various problems. Businessmen and bosses have their idiosyncrasies, but they are recognizable in their patronizing understanding of the follies of the working class.[7] Dressed in sober suits, balding and elderly, they help negotiate the often vast distance separating their knowledge of the worker's abilities and his desires.

The representation of the media, however, is altogether a different matter in *The Honeymooners*. Some of Ralph's most fantastic schemes involve him and Norton in television and film ventures. Directors and producers resemble more closely the sleazy con-men who exploit Ralph and Ed than the kindly businessmen and government officials who help extricate them from their problems. Caricatures, these agents of the media appear dressed in berets, wearing scarves, smoking cigarettes in long holders, and otherwise fulfilling the working class's suspicions of those who openly trade in illusion. Even so, Ralph is particularly drawn to the fabled riches of the mass media, and he is even willing to mime the effete dress and mannerisms of these *artistes* for the sake of his dreams of power and authority.

The consequences of Ralph's pudd'nheaded behavior in the television and film studios are quite different from his other escapades. Whereas Ralph and Norton never threaten the stability of legitimate business for more than a brief moment, both of them often create utter havoc in the world of the media. In one famous episode, "The Chef of the Future," Ralph and Norton stumble on the opportunity to do television commercials for a multipurpose kitchen tool: the fabled slicer/dicer/ricer of 1950s advertising.[8] As Norton demonstrates the time-consuming process of coring an apple with a paring knife or opening a can with a conventional opener, Ralph is supposed to follow each of Norton's laborious tasks with a swift demonstration of the kitchen gadget's labor-saving efficiency. The result is perfectly predictable: Norton pares the apple in one swift motion, while Ralph fumbles and bumbles, drops the apple, trips on it, and freezes in complete and utter stage fright (Norton, of course, continuing to talk and perform with the bravura of a television chef). In the various efforts by director, stagehands, and Norton to save this live-television commercial, they push and nudge Ralph back into action, but this time he weaves drunkenly across the set, waving the kitchen gadget menacingly, and crashes into the plywood kitchen counter, sink, and appliances. The false kitchen begins to come apart until Ralph and Norton, wrestling maniacally with each other, topple into the very walls of the set. As the director screams desperately, "Cut! Cut!," the commercial ends with a shot of the heap of plywood and dust to which Ralph and Norton have reduced this world of illusion.

The real world for working-class men like Ralph and Norton is the industrial world, even though the Great Depression has caused both of them to be employed in the growing service industries of the postmodern age.[9] The working-class identity of both characters is perfectly compatible with that of the nineteenth-century industrial worker. As an increasing number of working-class people entered service industries in America in this period, they could identify with characters like Ralph and Norton, who still do work that dirties the hands and exhausts the body. It is thus not difficult to understand why *The Honeymooners* consistently portrays its own medium in such frivolous ways and as composed of such fragile illusions. Hollywood and Madison Avenue aren't real for the viewers, and they are explicitly contrasted with the more substantial character of everyday labor, which now includes those public services without which urban production would be impossible.

Postmodern television is more thoroughly prefigured, however, in shows like *The George Burns and Gracie Allen Show* (1950–1958) and *I Love Lucy* (1951–1957), in which theatricality, celebrity, and performance are the central concerns of form and content. In "Situation Comedy, Feminism, and Freud: Discourses of Gracie and Lucy," Patricia Mellencamp has shown convincingly how these two situation comedies employed their comedy to contain woman within the space of post–World War II domesticity: "In situation comedy, pacification of women occurred between 1950 and 1960 without a single critical mention that the genre's terrain had altered: the housewife, although still ruling the familial roost, changed from being a humorous rebel or well-dressed, wise-cracking, naive dissenter who wanted or had a paid job—from being out of control via language (Gracie) or body (Lucy)—to being a contented, if not blissfully happy, understanding homebody (Laura Petrie)" (81).

What Mellencamp terms "containment through laughter—a release which might have held women to their place, rather than 'liberating' them in the way Freud says jokes liberate their tellers and auditors"—depends crucially on the theatrical situations of both shows (87). George Burns plays "husband as television critic, solo stand-up comic, female psychologist, and tolerant parent/performer" to Gracie's unsettling non sequiturs and potentially subversive nonsense (83). Ricky Ricardo plays Cuban bandleader and professional entertainer to Lucy's always disastrous efforts to break into the "industry." Mellencamp concludes that the otherwise subversive gestures of Gracie's speech and Lucy's performances are allowed comic release in order to be controlled.

Mellencamp argues that the ideological effect of such containment is heightened considerably by the theatrical situation governing both domestic comedies: "Image/person/star are totally merged as 'himself,' the 'real' is a replayed image, a scene, a simulation—what Jean Baudrillard calls 'the hyperreal'" (88). Thus the equation of person, personality, and performer in George, Gracie, Lucy, and Ricky, for example, lends special legitimacy and even universality to the specific social circumstances of each show: "Living in suburban, affluent Beverly Hills[,] Gracie was certainly unlike TV's nurturing-yet-domineering mothers who dwelled in city apartments" (82). Gracie's upper-middle-class or Lucy's middle-class circumstances thus help repress the economic fact that after World War II, "[m]ost women over 35 remained in the paid work force; when allowed, instead of building battleships, they took other jobs" (81). The cliché of postwar American social history—reinforced by the recent nostalgia for the 1950s—has been that American women in this period are best defined by middle-class domesticity. Popular television not only delivered this message with a vengeance, it also employed the message to legitimate its own medium.

Mellencamp shows that the feminist issues cannot be separated from questions of race and class. "Lucy's resistance to patriarchy," for example, "might be more palatable because it is mediated by a racism which views Ricky as inferior" (90). I would add that the conflict between racism and feminism is complicated further by Ricky's status as a professional entertainer. Although the con-man and trickster still haunt the worlds of the nightclub, theater, and film, Ricky Ricardo's efforts to make his way in the industry as a Cuban bandleader follow the basic capitalist values of hard work, self-reliance, and initiative. Ambivalently poised between working-class immigrant and entertainment professional, Ricky uses the media to minimize the challenge he poses to working-class and middle-class viewers alike, at the same time that his character heightens interest in an otherwise conventional domestic sitcom. The role of Cuban bandleader satisfies the most obvious ethnocentric stereotypes, even as it allows him to pursue the American Dream within a profession that follows the presumed logic of popular attitudes toward "Latins."

The normality of Ricky's professional world, however, is what seems startling and still relatively contemporary to the rerun addict or television scholar. As *I Love Lucy* evolved into *The Lucille Ball– Desi Arnaz Show* (1958–1960), Ricky's job was used increasingly as the vehicle for introducing various celebrity guests.[10] On the one hand, Ricky is just a small businessman, who relies on his technical and organizational skills to confront the daily problems that are presumed to plague the bourgeois viewer: closing the deal, being on time for appointments, "networking," balancing the demands of work and family. At once an owner and a white-collar worker, an immigrant and a typical American husband, a slick musician (loose morals/fast living), and a devoted family man, Ricky seems to be a perfectly malleable and duplicitous character. Yet, in his professional life, the stress falls primarily on his consistent denial of clichés about slick-haired Latin lovers who hang out in nightclubs. Flashy clothes are "costumes"; Latin romance is an occasionally convenient pose. Above all, the fast times of the musician's life are much exaggerated, once the viewer is allowed to see behind the surfaces of the media's machinery for illusion-making. Entertainment is constantly justified as a necessary complement to the serious business of everyday work, and it quite clearly shares the values of "proper" work: discipline, motivation, self-reliance, initiative, talent—99 per cent perspiration and 1 per cent inspiration.

In *I Love Lucy*, Ricky thus works in the *prosaic* world of the nightclub. The fantastic qualities of the nightclub are normalized not only by Ricky's conventional work ethic, but also by their reflection in Lucy and Ricky's domestic lives. Without substantial property, living in an apartment owned by the kindly but befuddled landlord, Fred Mertz (William Frawley), and his wife, Ethel (Vivian Vance), Ricky and Lucy are on the make. In the early episodes, Fred and Ethel are both friends and surrogate parents to Ricky and

Lucy, thus offering the stability that property often confers in this period. Eventually, Ricky does indeed acquire property, but of the sort that expresses well the ambivalence of ownership in this transitional age. The Cuban bandleader at the Tropicana buys the place and renames it, The Ricky Ricardo Babalu Club.[11] The Cuban immigrant, anxious to be assimilated, has been accepted by American capitalism and its ethos of dedication and hard work. And when Ricky and Lucy really make it big, they move to California and buy a suburban house that appears to be just what it is: a television set. The move from New York to California, from apartment life to suburban ownership, is reflected in their relations with Fred and Ethel. In California, Fred and Ethel increasingly assume the roles of surrogate parents and grandparents to Ricky, Jr. (Desi Arnaz, Jr.). This extended family simulates a postmodern version of the oedipal transfer of power from father to son, bringing along with it all the patriarchal assumptions of oedipal triangulation. As Ricky succeeds, Fred not only ages visibly but also assumes a more domestic role that depends upon the celebrity of the Ricardos. The suburban homeliness of the family in California thinly disguises the aristocratic pretensions of the upwardly mobile Ricardos: Fred and Ethel increasingly play the roles of servants or faithful retainers. Yet, the estate of this new gentry is hardly equivalent to the landed aristocracy of the Victorian novel. The real property of the Ricardos belongs to the film studios; it is the real estate of the backlot. Ricky and Lucy assume their status as the new, postmodern aristocrats, prefiguring such economically powerful celebrities in our own decade as Bill Cosby and Michael Landon.[12] *I Love Lucy* and *The Lucille Ball–Desi Arnaz Show* trade openly on the ironic reversal of actual and theatrical roles. Every viewer knows that Desi Arnaz's success in show business was primarily the result of his marriage to Lucille Ball. (Anyone who doubts this should be forced to watch director Jean Yarborough's *Cuban Pete* [1946], in which Desi Arnaz plays himself.) Yet the situation in every episode of *I Love Lucy* and *The Lucille Ball–Desi Arnaz Show* depends upon Lucy's unsuccessful efforts to break into show business. Customarily assisted by the bumbling Ethel, Lucy dons disguises, hatches plots, hides in the wings of the nightclub or studio in hopes of being discovered. Lucy's weekly failures as a professional performer may be less a judgment of her lack of talent (she *is*, after all, obviously talented as Lucille Ball), but of her failure to *work at it*. For Lucy and Ethel, entertainment is adventure, romance, and fun; for Ricky, it is business.

Lucy and Ricky both represent the shift from material production to the immaterial production of a postmodern, postindustrial economy. And yet each character works to reproduce in our viewing experience the familiar distinctions we inherited from nineteenth-century industrialism: domestic woman/working man, privacy/publicity, family/world, Imaginary/Symbolic (to introduce here Lacanian concepts as psychoanalytic "headings" for sorting this list). Even as Lucy outperforms Ricky, she testifies to the fact that "real life" is even more fantastic and unpredictable than the most elaborate stage production or nightclub act. The incredulity that we experience in this simulated world of the everyday finally is less a function of a world out of joint than of *Lucy's* failings. Her comic resiliency encloses Lucy in the space of the home by demonstrating how incapable she is of inhabiting the serious world of work and discipline. As Ricky's success seems to teach us, illusion *is* serious business, best left to men.

By the last half of the 1960s, popular television had changed significantly its representation of gender and class in order to meet challenges and alternatives to the nuclear family. Once again, the medium's self-consciousness may be used as an index of such change as well as an indication of how far the immaterial had come to penetrate everyday life. In ABC's domestic comedy, *Bewitched* (1964–1972), Elizabeth Montgomery plays a witch, Samantha, struggling to escape her supernatural heritage and to find normality with Darrin Stevens (Dick York and later Dick Sargent), her utterly conventional, middle-class, ad-executive husband.[13] The condition of their marriage—that Samantha will not use her magical powers to affect their ordinary lives—is the repeatedly violated taboo in each episode. In virtually every program, Samantha *must* use her powers to resolve domestic problems no longer susceptible to mortal solutions. In most cases, "mortal" refers primarily to Darrin, who seems incapable of carrying out his customary duties as husband and wage-earner without extraordinary assistance from his wife. Although in some episodes it is Samantha's supernatural relatives who cause the problems—most often out of very mortal motives (bourgeois clichés about troubled relations between the husband and his in-laws are rehearsed again and again), most often Samantha saves Darrin from himself, his exploitative boss, Larry Tate (David White), or from unreasonable clients.

Samantha's powers are quite obviously the narrative occasions for technical special-effects designed to hold the viewer's interest in an otherwise shopworn format. The sitcom is a transparent spinoff of *I Married a Witch*, René Clair's popular 1942 film starring Fredric March and Veronica Lake. When Samantha makes chairs move, people disappear, doors open, dogs meow and cats bark, she is directing both literally and fictionally the representational medium of television. Lucy never quite breaks into show business; Samantha *is* show business. In episode after episode, her power over the representation of ordinary reality is presented as her compensation for an otherwise tedious, repetitive, and unrecognized life as housewife. Quite literally the woman behind the man, Samantha keeps the accident-prone Darrin from hurting himself or their marriage. By implication and repetition, *Bewitched* makes it clear that Samantha's magic is not much different from the imaginative feats required of the ordinary housewife trapped in a world of incompetent men.

In one especially explicit episode, Samantha is transported by one of her perverse relatives back to New Orleans in 1868, where she awakens to the ambivalent role of a postbellum Southern belle. In her conversations with her black servant, a black mother and child on the street, her imaginary relatives, and her aristocratic and domineering husband, she discovers an affinity between the continuing servitude of the recently emancipated Southern black and the dependency of the Southern belle. The Hollywood romance she desires and the viewer yawningly expects is thoroughly dismissed. Even after Samantha has returned with relief to Darrin, her daughter Tabitha, and her Westport, Connecticut tract house, she still notices uncanny traces of her dream in her bourgeois circumstances.

Samantha's witchcraft not only gives her a compensatory power, often employed as a form of revenge against her otherwise impotent social role, it is also a strategic self-consciousness. Whether wielded by Samantha or her kin, such supernatural power customarily reveals the unconscious of ordinary reality. That such an unconscious is, in its very essence, fantastic, magical, and unreal generally says less about magic in the modern age than it does about the primarily fantastic substructure of bourgeois life. Men are only apparently competent, authoritative, and responsible; in the reality of Samantha's supernatural world, such men reveal themselves as grasping, jealous, and incompetent buffoons. Women are only superficially dependent, emotional, romantically deluded, and sexually servile; in the logic of Samantha's magic, they can transcend their historical circumstances, author their destinies, and comprehend with a certain pity the frailty of mortal men.[14]

The fact that Samantha continues to play this game of appearance and reality by agreeing to suppress her magical powers for the sake of domestic normality tells us, of course, a good deal about the conscious purpose of *Bewitched* to legitimate bourgeois domestic relations at a particularly critical moment in the history of the American family. In *I Married a Witch*, Jennifer (Veronica Lake) commits herself to Wally Wooley (Fredric March) by promising "I'll try so hard to be a good wife, and I'll only use witchcraft to help you." In fact, Jennifer uses her powers to help Wooley win the race for Governor of New York.[15] In contrast, Samantha always returns to her family and reaffirms her marriage vows by pledging never again to use her powers to affect their lives (until the next episode, that is). Repressing her powers, Samantha assumes the role of the duplicitious woman, whose "witchcraft" consists of just this division between apparent domesticity and her secret will to power. The cultural consciousness of *Bewitched* betrays the growing consensus that the apparent normality of the bourgeois family is sustained by social customs that are at root fantastic and can be rendered acceptable only by the most elaborate magic. That such magic should be wielded by a woman diverts our attention from the wiles of both patriarchy and capitalism.

Samantha's supernatural powers *realize* Lucy's dream of the stage and the liberated performing self, and they transcend the servile magic of Jeannie (Barbara Eden) in the NBC competitor (from 1965–1970), *I Dream of Jeannie*. In that situation comedy, Jeannie's "master," Captain Tony Nelson (Larry Hagman), often undoes her magic, using his own technological skills as a NASA astronaut to counter her misguided wizardry. In the midst of the United States troop build-ups in Vietnam and Pentagon claims to a "quick" end to the war by virtue of American technological superiority, *I Dream of Jeannie* supports such foreign policies even as it utterly ignores the war itself. *Bewitched*'s Samantha is a decidedly more modern woman than Jeannie, whose cloying "Yes, Master" and bared midriff (the censors covered her navel in 1968) trade shamelessly on older stereotypes. Even so, Samantha is hardly a liberated woman, although her character is conceived in the spirit of television's efforts to incorporate such contemporary concerns. By locating the supernatural at the center of the American living room—both dramatically and in the viewing experience—*Bewitched* marks the historical transition from modern to postmodern America. To live in Samantha and Darrin's America, one must become a manipulator of the imagery that constitutes contemporary life.

Samantha is a producer and director; what attracts the viewer to her is her capacity to live comfortably with the fantastically meta-morphic qualities of postmodern life. Ralph and Ed are unhappy with the fantastic, even as they are deluded by impossible dreams. Lucy is unhappy, perhaps even schizophrenic, divided hopelessly between the dazzling reality of the theater and the tedious night-mare of the kitchen. Jeannie is a fragile anachronism, always liable to vanish at the will of the more powerful magic of American tech-nology. Samantha triumphs, pyrrhically of course, by adapting her powers to the work of the television.[16]

These interpretations confine themselves to the form of the do-mestic situation comedy, which certainly did dominate American popular television from 1950 to 1975. It is now enjoying a revival on *The Cosby Show*, *Family Ties*, *The Wonder Years*, *Growing Pains*, *Mr. Belvedere*, and many other shows that reaffirm the intrinsic values of the nuclear family. Still others, such as *Full House*, *thirtysomething*, *My Two Dads*, *The Golden Girls*, *Valerie's Family*, *Who's the Boss*, and *The Facts of Life*, play with virtually every new configuration of do-mestic arrangements in a nearly desperate effort to save the shat-tered dream of the bourgeois family. It may be premature, how-ever, to speak of any revival of the domestic situation comedy, since it has worked through its many ideological permutations from the beginning of television's popular history. American family life and television have been so intricately bonded in the last four decades that the new family shows of the 1980s may be simply the means by which network television reasserts a recognizable authority amid such new competitors as cable, video, and computerized games. Even so, the family room, even when it is on an Air Force base, as it is in *I Dream of Jeannie,* lingers on the border of the genuinely immaterial landscape of our postmodernity. The triumph of tele-vision's postmodern sublime could come only by translating domes-tic privacy's material privation into the positive immateriality of the city and its daily work. Drawing such crucial issues as gender relations into that circle, popular television could take dominion everywhere.

I thus select my final example in this short history in a relatively random and yet still strategic manner, shifting my focus from do-mestic comedy to the detective genre. As well as any popular series in the latter half of the 1970s, *The Rockford Files* (1974–1980) epito-mizes the fundamental *intertextuality* of network television.[17] The intertextuality of *Rockford Files* is as complicated as a sophisticated literary work, since the show trades parodically on most of the conventions of the private-eye narrative from Dashiell Hammett and Raymond Chandler to their early television imitations. James Garner's identification with the successful 1960s' series, *Maverick*, arguably the comic end to the television Western, helped establish his role as Jim Rockford, the engagingly ironic private investigator who is often amazed at the fantasy world of southern California. On the face of it, the detective or private-eye show seems a world apart from the domestic sitcom, but it is precisely the confusion of these two television genres that marks the postmodernity of the late 1970s.

A spin-off of *Harry-O*, a campy series about a marginal private eye (David Janssen) who also lives at the beach, *Rockford Files* weaves together recent television history with more venerable literary forms and types. Rockford is a reformed confidence man, in the best tradition of the American literary hero, who has served time for his crimes. We are never quite sure whether or not we are to believe Rockford that he was framed, so the original "crime" allows him to operate both inside and outside the formal legal structure. In many other ways, Rockford occupies the cultural margin so often crowded with rogues, madmen, and prophets in the western literary tradition. As a consequence, he possesses a certain insight into the nature of postmodern California, which is best expressed by his characteristic irony.

Rockford's wit is his saving grace in a world that has gone undeniably mad, and it is virtually identical to the playful irony that for some critics has been the impasse of the literary experimentalists of the late 1960s and early 1970s.[18] Always capable of telling a good story on himself, Rockford often verges on the brink of self-loathing, because he recognizes how intimately he is involved in the world he observes. Surrounded by the most meretricious extravagance and conspicuous consumption, which are clearly the symptoms of modern criminality, Rockford lives modestly in a rusting trailer on the beach in Malibu at Paradise Cove (an actual place). On the one hand, his domestic circumstances seem countercultural, an extension of the Youth Culture's rejection of bourgeois values for the sake of neo-ruralism. Rarely finding the time to fish from the pier or take a walk with a client/lover on the beach, Rockford dreams of escape from fantastic Los Angeles even as he knows that the city is his reality. Rockford's irony directly recalls that of Hammett's Nick Charles and Chandler's Philip Marlowe, but it also borrows from the ironic characters of the domestic sitcom, such as Lucy and Samantha. What Rockford's sordid underworld reveals is just what is repeatedly exposed and then repressed in the therapeutic narratives of those sitcoms: the contradictions of bourgeois, urban life.

His rebellion against middle-class life is not so much a rejection of his heritage as an ambivalent effort to rediscover his working-class roots. His father, Rocky (Noah Beery, Jr.), is a trucker who shares his son's love of fishing, cooking, and the outdoors. Rockford's nearly hopeless project is to convince his father that his profession as a private investigator is legitimate and deserves the respect that Rocky grants to material labor. For Rocky, Rockford is simply playing at life, as his mysterious work, messy trailer, and bachelor circumstances all seem to prove. In contrast, Rocky lives in a substantial Los Angeles bungalow, neatly and traditionally furnished, surrounded by mementos of his dead wife.[19]

In many ways, the character of Rockford is simply a television cliché, a variation on the good-hearted tough guy. Rocky and Rockford's clients (in cases involving female clients, Rockford's father almost always establishes a sympathetic relation, often hoping to match them with his son) are generally out of touch with reality, condemned to some twilight zone in which their commonsense values fail to accord with life as it must be lived in Los Angeles. Understanding as he does both worlds, Rockford mediates, serving as a kind of latter-day Marlowe to protect innocence with a strategic lie and still combat vigorously the deceptions that he knows constitute daily experience. There is, of course, nothing "postmodern" about such a narrative situation.

What *is* postmodern about *Rockford Files* is the decidedly textual quality of this new world of "experience," that domain so unfamiliar to Rocky and Rockford's clients. Each episode opens with the same photomontage of southern California's gaudy variety while a voice-over of Rockford's answering machine replays the messages of his day. Ordinary messages from irate bill collectors, jilted lovers, and neglected clients build to the message that establishes the plot. The ordinary and the extraordinary belong to the same textual reality, and technology only reinforces this association. The crimes that Rockford investigates are often quite conventional—missing person, homicide, extortion, blackmail—but Rockford's investigations *always* follow his postmodern modus operandi. Rockford gathers facts, and follows "leads" by way of strategic deception: posing as a state auditor to gain access to corporate records, playing the officious carpet cleaner to get into an office, disguising himself as a door-to-door salesman to enter a private home. In his car, Rockford keeps a portable printing press, where he turns out new business cards and documents according to his needs.

The series is called *The Rockford Files* because the stories are supposedly drawn from his professional records, but Rockford has no office, secretary, or bulging filing cabinets. Lacking even the grubby trappings of professionalism of a Philip Marlowe, Rockford relies on nothing but his metamorphic "character," his changeable personality as trickster, *homo ludens*. In his car or in his trailer, Rockford is southern Californian transience personified. His gold Firebird *is* his office, and each episode involves at least one choreographed car-chase scene, from which Rockford generally emerges triumphant. His car, his printing press, his masks, and his trailer are his best weapons.[20] Rockford is the consummate Hollywood actor, who prepares for his next scene in his trailer. When he "solves" the crime, he does so most often by changing the script he has been given and substituting his own text for that of his antagonist.

Living outside this world—fishing in the woods, settling down to a secure bourgeois existence—has its undeniable attractions for him, but he knows that to do so he would have to unmake himself, as well as reform completely this urban world. In the two-part episode "The House on Willis Avenue," Rockford discovers that the modest house of the title is actually the site for a complex computer system that his antagonist (Jackie Cooper) is using to develop an international information center for the political and economic control of the world's populations. Even Rocky's house is invaded regularly by murderers, gangsters, and various con-men. Rockford's girlfriend, Beth Davenport (Gretchen Corbett), is his lawyer, and both vow not to marry. It's not surprising, then, that Rockford's trailer is neither an office nor a home, but some unstable and temporary combination of the two. Although its shabbiness belies the comparison, his trailer prefigures the home office of the 1980s: that imaginary condo in Century City where the young tycoon does his business by phonemodem and FAX. Living in this world, Rockford must play the theatrical game better than his antagonist and "produce" a more convincing (marketable) product. Rocky trusts his working-class friends and extends this trust to the rest of the world, often at the risk of his son's career and life. Rockford trusts no one, rejecting at the very last even those innocent victims for whom he has battled. Least of all does he trust himself, for he knows himself to be nothing but a composition of all the characters he has experienced in this fantastic world. Thus Rockford's irony is not simply his final defense, but his form of self-consciousness, the way that he knows himself as nothing but the roles he is compelled to play.

Interpreting a television character like Jim Rockford in such decidedly ponderous ontological terms may appear at first absurd, but television shows in the 1970s seemed increasingly to make certain philosophical claims about the order of things and people. As television became the primary medium of social exchange, it also began to assume a certain philosophical authority. Like the artist-heroes of the high-modern novel, Rockford is an essentially classless figure, whose understanding of reality encompasses and transcends different classes and social groups. Nostalgically attracted to his working-class origins, fitfully entranced by middle-class respectability, and sympathetic with the youthful rebellion of the counterculture, Rockford actually aspires to the sort of power and authority that he combats each week.[21] Although he denies his criminal past, Rockford actually wants to become the sort of criminal who lives outside the law or who, better yet, *makes* the law while escaping its confinement.

The Rockford Files marks the historical moment in which television replaced the novel as a philosophical medium, just as the modernist novel had replaced formal philosophy and even lyric poetry as the cultural medium for introspection and abstract thought. I make such a hyperbolic claim (as impossibly "true" as Virginia Woolf's time and date for the beginning of modernism) without judging in any way the artistic qualities of *The Rockford Files* relative to *Absalom, Absalom!* or *The Great Gatsby*.[22] Putting aside for the moment such aesthetic criteria, forgetting even the crucial issue of audience, I would still contend that a show like *Rockford* marks a special turn in American cultural representation. Fully at home in a world of utter theatricality, Rockford makes no strenuous effort to expose the lies of this world, except in his struggle to make his own fictional production commercially successful and competitive.

As a consequence, *Rockford Files* encourages the viewer not only to accept the conditions of postmodern America—America remade in the image of southern California—but also to participate actively in this basic economy. Charmed by Rocky's quaint variations on the father's advice—"Get a *real* job!"—the viewer still sides with the son, who knows that a hard day's work in this world requires a good script. Ed Norton and Ralph Kramden bring the fragile walls of the sound stage tumbling down, but Lucy, Samantha, and Jeannie rebuild them more solidly to become the four walls of our family rooms. Jim Rockford builds the walls out further, until they assume the airy shapes of the postmodern city.

From the cult of show-business celebrity and the "talk-show" to the weekly sitcom, television history reveals the growing self-reflexivity of the medium. Peter Conrad explains Johnny Carson's success in terms of Carson's understanding of television's explicit appeal to its unreality: "Being on television is about being on television. If you forget the medium and its unreality, you fail" (16). As Conrad realizes, however, the medium's irony about its own illusion—an irony that could turn the "blooper" into a genre—hardly subverts or demystifies the medium. Rather, it increases its power by claiming for it a "hyperrealism" that fits well our postmodern situation. Unlike such high-cultural and avowedly countercultural forms as the "serious novel," television has not claimed such self-reflexivity as the unique and distinguishing characteristic of its medium. Instead, television has increasingly claimed that the fictionality and style of even its most extravagant programs merely follow the rhetoric of everyday life. Effacing itself, claiming a humble, albeit unfamiliar realism, popular television has aligned itself with the productive laws of a postmodern economy.

From the first half of the 1970s to the present, popular television has assumed an increasingly *serious* air even in its most frivolous productions. From *Rockford Files* to *Dallas*, television dramas and sitcoms have assumed a certain pedagogical mission—to teach us how to interpret our own personal relations to an irreducibly theatrical world. I am not referring here to the shallow bids for social relevance made by virtually every new television melodrama or to the host of documentaries, docudramas and "TV magazines" that crowd the pages of the bulging TV guides. Family shows and white papers, talk shows and interviews, civil rights sitcoms and feminist police shows are mere by-products of the deeper philosophical, hermeneutical, and economic authority of television. *Intertextuality* is no longer a term that can be used simply to identify an elementary characteristic of language that is ordinarily disguised, repressed, or erased by ideology. Intertextuality is itself the mode of production in our postmodern economy, and the "self-consciousness" (or metaliterariness) through which it has customarily been "recognized" as such must now be understood as the artificial unconscious that is the ultimate product of our postmodernity.

Notes

1. See in particular Enzensberger's essays, "The Industrialization of the Mind" and "Constituents of Theory" in his *Critical Essays*.
2. Lyotard writes that "power is not only good performativity, but also

effective verification and good verdicts . . . Now it is precisely this kind of context control that a generalized computerization of society may bring. The performativity of an utterance, be it denotative or prescriptive, increases proportionally to the amount of information about its referent one has at one's disposal. Thus the growth of power, and its self-legitimation, are now taking the route of data storage and accessibility, and the operativity of information."

3. The terms *immaterial* and *hyperreal* that I have borrowed from Baudrillard must be considered provisional at best, because they work by reference to *material* and *real*. Terminology remains a crucial issue in efforts to theorize our postmodern economy, and these inadequate terms reflect merely the primitive stage of the academic work thus far.

4. See my "Surplus Economies" for a more specific translation of Marx's surplus value into postmodern terms.

5. Bakhtin's vogue among contemporary theorists is yet another instance of poststructuralism's effort to distinguish clearly its own methods from those of ideology. See in particular Young's critical treatment of Bakhtin's popularity in "Back to Bakhtin."

6. *The Honeymooners* developed as a CBS series out of sketches that Gleason did on *The Cavalcade of Stars* (1949–1952). On his own show, *The Jackie Gleason Show* (1952–1955; 1956–1957; 1958–1961), Gleason also incorporates sketches involving the Kramdens and the Nortons. The independent series, *The Honeymooners*, lasted only one season (1955–1956), and was judged a television failure. It is difficult to judge whether such failure was a consequence of the show's political sentiments or simply its independent format or other unpredictables. That the sketches, when incorporated in the variety shows on early television that had evolved from vaudeville, were more successful may support my claim that the characters linger in the sociological limbo between industrial and postindustrial America. See Terrace 206.

7. As Terrace notes (206), Ralph entered the work force as a fourteen-year-old paperboy, but got his first adult job with the WPA during the Great Depression. Even though the "paperboy" is the clichéd prototype of the self-reliant modern American from Horatio Alger to Hollywood films of the thirties and forties, it also confirms that Ralph's "career" has been exclusively concerned with the media and public services, rather than explicitly industrial labor.

8. According to Terrace (206), "The Chef of the Future" was Art Carney's favorite episode.

9. Ralph owes both his job and his marriage to the WPA. He met Alice when she was distributing snow shovels to WPA workers. These details remind us of how the Great Depression changed the conditions of ordinary labor, as well as the presumably "free exchange" of labor power for wages between worker and capitalist. The employment of the unemployed on large-scale public works projects helped effect the transformation of American production from primarily material goods to "goods and services" and, ultimately, representations.

10. *The Lucille Ball–Desi Arnaz Show* ran on CBS from 1958 to 1960 and was directed by Desi Arnaz. Terrace (271) also provides a pertinent summary of the story line: "A continuation of *I Love Lucy*, wherein Lucy and Ricky Ricardo, and their friends Fred and Ethel Mertz, travel to various places and become involved with a different guest star in each episode."

11. Terrace 271. As first the orchestra leader at the Tropicana Club, Ricky owns the Ricky Ricardo Babalu Club by the end of *I Love Lucy*.

12. In 1987, the individual in the United States with the largest gross annual income was Bill Cosby. Corporate heads, like Lee Iacocca, barely made the top twenty, which was dominated by celebrities in television, film, and rock music. Bill Cosby and Michael Landon are good examples of the powerful entertainment celebrities anticipated by the sitcom in the 1950s and 1960s. Cosby "developed" from the Cold War spy in *I Spy* to the family comedian (both in his stand-up routines and on *The Bill Cosby Show*), just as Michael Landon "evolved" from the family-oriented Western, *Bonanza*, to starring roles in *Little House on the Prairie* and *Highway to Heaven*. The incredible success and influence of both Cosby and Landon has much to do with their abilities to combine acting with writing, producing, and directing.

13. *Bewitched* ran on ABC for 306 episodes, from September 17, 1964 to July 1, 1972 (Terrace 47–48).

14. Quite unsurprisingly, family relations among Samantha's supernatural relatives reproduce quite precisely "mortal" relations, suggesting that bourgeois family relations are, in fact, universal.

15. Although Jennifer's father is an 800,000-year-old warlock, Jennifer traces her origins to 1632 and Puritan America. Wooley's ancestors burned witches in the Bay Colony, which is why Jennifer and her father have returned to persecute him. In fact, the real "witch" in the movie is Wooley's fiancée, Miss Masterson, whose father is behind Wooley's candidacy for the governorship and who runs a powerful newspaper. In this 1942 film, the witchcraft is conventionally identified with the very mortal women, such as Miss Masterson, who reverse the customary roles of male dominance and feminine subservience. At her most seductive and yet wittily appealing in the role of the witch, Veronica Lake saves Wally Wooley from the castrating will of Miss Masterson. Transparent as the sexism of this film is, it anticipates the more complex ways that *Bewitched* will invest women with power in the 1960s.

16. Conrad notes that: "Samantha . . . is a technological maven who can do the housework by remote control, at the twitch of a nose not the flick of a switch. Actually, Elizabeth Montgomery on that show enjoyed the services of a troop of off-camera domestic servants, who performed the dirty work her magic affected to abolish" (26).

17. *The Rockford Files* ran on NBC from September 13, 1974 to July 25, 1980 (Terrace 352).

18. Newman contends that mass media are actually reactionary imitations of realist conventions: "The media, on the other hand, through the obsessive use of the very conventions Modernism discredited, endlessly

recirculates content, to produce an aura which makes the spectator experience an equally non-existent reality, employing all the conventions of Realism in the distortion of real life." Series like *Rockford*, however, demonstrate that modernist conventions are as influential in shaping popular television as realist devices. Irony, in particular, seems more pervasive in the story lines and styles of popular television in the 1980s than an unproblematic realism. Newman's trivialization of mass media, as well as the powerless academy, reflect his own lingering materialism in his extremely provocative analysis of postmodern America.

19. Even Rocky, however, is fascinated by the ways in which television confers "reality" on people and things. At the end of one episode, as Rockford and his father watch a client thank Rockford on the evening news, Rocky concludes: "I don't know much about all of this [Rockford's case and career], but I *do know* that it *means something* to hear my boy mentioned on TV!" The two-part episode thus concluded focused on a businessman (Jackie Cooper) trying to build a secret and international center for storing and processing information on the people of the world. Housed in an abandoned missile installation outside Los Angeles (where else?), the center would be used for geopolitical power.

20. Rockford is reluctant to use his gun, which he keeps in a cookie jar in the trailer. Although this trait may well be a survival from *Maverick*, whose protagonist preferred talking and playing to shooting, it still expresses the postmodern way Rockford "fights crime."

21. Rockford's sympathy with the counterculture never extends to the possibility of joining the movement. A veteran of the Korean War, Rockford knows that war is hell, so he understands antiwar activism and youthful efforts to explore alternative life-styles. Even so, he is a pragmatist of the fantastic, and he judges the idealism of youth to be merely a happy, foggy dream. In fact, most of the alternative lifestyles represented in the series are shown (generally by Rockford) to be secretly scripted by the rich and powerful. In "Quickie Nirvana," Rockford's sympathies for an aging hippie neighbor get him involved in her religious community, which is run by a pop-psychology guru who moonlights as a fast-living womanizer in Palm Springs. Rockford helps break his charge out of this community and straighten out her life in keeping with contemporary news stories of parents trying to "steal" their children from religious communes.

22. My literary examples are not entirely casual, of course. Like Sutpen's and Gatsby's, Rockford's dream of power is closer to that of the author than the merchant-prince.

Works Cited

Baudrillard, Jean. *For a Critique of the Political Economy of the Sign*. Translated by Charles Levin. St. Louis: Telos Press, 1981.

Conrad, Peter. *Television: The Medium and Its Manners*. Boston: Routledge & Kegan Paul, 1982.

Enzensberger, Hans Magnus. *Critical Essays.* Edited by Reinhold Grimm and Bruce Armstrong. The New German Library, vol. 98. New York: Continuum, 1982.

Lyotard, Jean-François. *The Postmodern Condition: A Report on Knowledge.* Translated by Geoff Bennington and Brian H. Massumi. Theory and History of Literature, vol. 10. Minneapolis: University of Minnesota Press, 1984.

Mellencamp, Patricia. "Situation Comedy, Feminism, and Freud: Discourses of Gracie and Lucy." In *Studies in Entertainment: Critical Approaches to Mass Culture*, edited by Tania Modeleski, vol. 7, 80–95. Bloomington: Indiana University Press, 1986.

Newman, Charles. *The Post-Modern Aura: The Act of Fiction in an Age of Inflation.* Evanston, Ill.: Northwestern University Press, 1985.

Rowe, John Carlos. "Surplus Economies: Deconstruction, Ideology, and the Humanities." In *The Aims of Representation*, edited by Murray Krieger, 131–58. New York: Columbia University Press, 1987.

Terrace, Vincent. *Encyclopedia of Television Series, Pilots, and Specials: 1937–1973.* Vol 1. New York: New York Zoetrope, 1986.

Young, Robert. "Back to Bakhtin." *Cultural Critique* 2 (1985): 75–92.

INTERTEXTUAL AFTERWORDS

The Space of Intertextuality

===

THAÏS MORGAN

Commenting on the problems confronting the theory of literature in the 1940s, René Wellek and Austin Warren challenge the predominance of influence studies since the nineteenth century. Historicism, or the assumption that a critic can reconstruct the author's intentions, the sources for his or her ideas, and the contemporary audience's response to his or her works, overlooks the dilemma that still concerns literary theorists today: "There are simply no data in literary history which are completely neutral 'facts'" (28). The very choice of texts to compare in investigating any literary relationship, and particularly influence, is fraught with "value judgments." Thus, to claim that author *B*'s poetry "derives" from author A's poetry already presupposes a complex series of inferences based on a detailed knowledge of each author's oeuvre as well as an almost encyclopedic knowledge of "the commonplaces of his period" (248). The problems are compounded when one tries to establish "parallels" between literature and the arts, or even between the humanities and the sciences, for not only do the modes of discourse and representation differ widely, but so do the implicit beliefs about truth and reality.

Intertextuality has been touted since the late 1960s as the panacea for many of the critical pitfalls involved in historically oriented approaches to literature and in New Criticism. As a structural analysis of texts in relation to the larger system of signifying practices or uses of signs in culture, intertextuality seems by definition to deliver us from old controversies over the psychology of individual authors and readers, the tracing of literary origins, and the relative value of imitation or originality. By shifting our attention from the triangle of author/work/tradition to that of text/discourse/culture, intertextuality replaces the evolutionary model of literary history with a structural or synchronic model of literature as sign system. The most salient effect of this strategic change is to free the literary text from psychological, sociological, and historical determinisms, opening it up to an apparently infinite play of relationships with other texts, or semiosis.

However, intertextuality is no more a value-free, innocent critical practice than historicism or New Criticism. It is no accident that

239

most of the best known theories of intertextuality to date come from the French: Roland Barthes, Julia Kristeva, Jacques Derrida, Gérard Genette, and Michael Riffaterre head the list. Indeed, the notion of intertextuality emerges from the cross-fertilization among several major European intellectual movements during the 1960s and 1970s, including Russian formalism, structural linguistics, psychoanalysis, Marxism, and deconstruction, at the least. Consequently, the Anglo-American literary critic must be wary of ideological axe-grinding when adopting one or more of the current theories of intertextuality for his or her own use. Without pretending to be exhaustive, then, this essay will discuss the major proponents of intertextuality and weigh their contributions to literary and interdisciplinary studies.

The Anxieties of Influence

"Influence" remains the most tenacious critical metaphor in the pedagogy and theory of literature today, despite the successive attacks mounted by New Criticism and structuralist poetics. Influence is what Max Black would call a "heuristic" metaphor, or a hypothetical equivalence between two disparate domains that has become the organizing principle or "model" for inquiry in the foregrounded domain (219–43). The metaphor of influence says that literary history is like the natural flow of water and that there is a unidirectional "current" or relationship between an anterior text and a posterior text. Text A influences text B when the critic can demonstrate that B has "borrowed" structure(s), theme(s), and/or image(s) from A or the "lender." Besides placing the burden of debt entirely on the more recent text, this model also valorizes text A more highly because it is the ur-text or "source" of certain features in text B. The long debate over the relative value of "imitation," or the apparently deliberate use of elements from text A by the author of text B, moves the metaphor of influence into the domain of aesthetics. A river is pure only at its source, and its flow becomes progressively muddier as it travels farther away from the origin; thus, this naturalistic model for literary art tends to judge an imitation or "derivation" to be inferior by definition.

But what about the revolutionary moments in literary history when new genres, styles, and motifs arise? The metaphor of influence is counterbalanced by another powerful heuristic figure: "inspiration." As a rival theory of literary origins, inspiration promotes the individual author and innovation in relation to previous authors and the canon or tradition of texts. Whether inspiration comes from outside the writer, as in the classical divine *adflatus* and the Christian revelation, or from inside the writer, as in the neo-classical emphasis on craftsmanship and the romantic celebration of genius, this model of literary history presupposes a dynamic, even discontinuous relationship between past and present texts. The resulting aesthetic judgment that "newer is better" is based on the same temporal model that grounds theories of influence, but the direction of textual relationships is reversed. Whereas the metaphor of influence is conservative and sees literary history as the continuity of a fixed set of norms over time, the metaphor of inspiration is progressive and regards later texts as positive advances over literature of the past. Consequently, influence studies stress the connections between literature and society or tradition, whereas theories of inspiration explore the connections between literature and psychology or the individual artist's development.

Given the incongruent presuppositions of these two models, it is not surprising that their point of unending dispute lies in that gray area which constitutes most of literature: those texts in which the author imitates or borrows features from an earlier text or set of texts, but in the process changes or transforms these features to suit the characteristics of his own previous work. In this situation, we have both influence, or what I would call a *positive intertextual relation* between two texts, such as in Joyce's use of the central episodes from Homer's *Odyssey* to structure the chapters in *Ulysses*, and inspiration, or a *negative intertextual relation,* for example, Joyce's ironic transformation of the epic hero in Bloom. It is important to note that neither influence nor inspiration takes into account a third factor cooperative in both types of intertextual relations: namely, the *intratextual relation* (potentially positive or negative) among earlier and later texts by the same author—for example, how the narrative and value structures in Joyce's *Portrait of the Artist as a Young Man* and *Stephen Hero* affect or are affected by those in *Ulysses*. But this is to anticipate the contribution of semiotics to literary criticism.

T. S. Eliot's essay "Tradition and the Individual Talent" is perhaps the most famous attempt to mediate between theories of influence and inspiration as well as between criticism and poetics. In order to break the stranglehold of the romantic cult of genius on modern literary critical judgments, Eliot returns to Matthew Arnold's reverence for the classical canon as an ethical as well as aesthetic norm. However, in deploying "tradition" against the fallacy of "individual talent," Eliot alters the essential definition of each term in the opposition—an interesting instance of his own theory of literary relationships, in which several texts are transformed by their encounter in and with the catalytic "mind of the poet" (54). Thus, Eliot locates the individuality of a poet neither in his innovativeness nor in his imitativeness, but in his ability to include all previous literature in his work so that past and present discourses *coexist*: "We shall often find that not only the best, but the most individual parts of his work may be those in which the dead poets, his ancestors, assert their immortality most vigorously" (48). This is a clever play on the critical metaphor of "filiation," another extension of the model of influence. Instead of using filiation to support the linear schema of literary history according to which the father is more worthy because closer to the origin than the son, Eliot reverses the implicit negativity of influence in favor of the son who acknowledges but also manipulates to his own ends the texts of his "ancestors." Likewise, Eliot treats tradition not as an inevitable burden of the past, but rather as a future goal, to be won only "by great labour" during each poet's study of literature (49).

What emerges from Eliot's critique of the metaphors of influence and inspiration is the concept of literature as a system of coequal, copresent texts. Although he certainly does not share the ideological premises of Roland Barthes or Julia Kristeva, Eliot's view of literary relationships as a network or structure rather than as an evolution or a family leads him to draw several conclusions found again in the theories of intertextuality proposed in *S/Z* and *Séméiotiké*, respectively. First of all, Eliot defines the "historical sense" necessary for the making of a poet in terms that balance diachrony and synchrony, or literature as history and literature as system. The poet must read the literature of the European tradition, the literature of his or her national tradition, and the works of contemporary writers in order to understand that all these texts have "a simultaneous existence and [compose] a simultaneous order" (49). Second, the systematicity of literature implies that "what happens when a new work of art is created is something that happens simultaneously to all the works of art which preceded it" (Eliot 49–50). Daringly, Eliot here reverses the directives of historicism and suggests the possibility that literature has no origins but exists only as open sets of transformations within a closed system—a paradox that will occupy the semiotics of intertextuality.

"Tradition and the Individual Talent" is remembered above all for Eliot's theory of the poet as "catalyst." However, it is precisely at this point of greatest insight that Eliot backs down before the deconstructive implications of his own argument and returns to an only slightly modified theory of inspiration. The problem begins with his assertion that "no artist," whether literary or otherwise, "has his complete meaning alone" because his works must be interpreted and evaluated in relation to the "*whole* existing order," or the system of literature (49–50). Just as the so-called originality of one text is lost in the vista of literature before and after it, so the so-called genius of the author becomes an incidental function of the intertexts of the past and contemporaneous literature that his works incorporate and transform. Yet, as a New Critical humanist, Eliot cannot accept the complete disappearance of the subject or individual author implied here. Even though he recommends with Flaubert and Pater "a continual extinction of personality" in the sense of "emotions," Eliot retains the presence of "the mind of the poet" which, acting as a unique "catalyst," can "digest and transmute" both experience and literature into "a new compound" (54–55). Despite his efforts to recuperate the status of the poet as creator, Eliot's metaphor of the catalyst finally does have the effect of dissolving the author as well as his work into the multiple chemical reaction of intertextuality. Although the poet's "mind" is like a "shred of platinum" that is absolutely necessary to set off the interaction between sulphur dioxide and oxygen, the catalyst leaves no trace of itself in the literary relationship(s) or "new compound" that it assists in forming. It is not far from Eliot's theory of the catalytic poet who is everywhere but nowhere and the simultaneity of all literature to Jacques Derrida's theory of writing ("*écriture*") in which the author's voice as well as the previous literature with which the author converses are "erased," leaving only ambiguous "traces" of themselves in the essentially intertextual text.

Among more recent efforts by Anglo-American critics to formulate a theory of literature that steers between the Scylla of source-hunting and the Charybdis of personality worship are Northrop Frye's *Anatomy of Criticism* (1957) and Harold Bloom's *The Anxiety of Influence* (1973). Frye and Bloom both appeal to theories of meaning outside the field of literature: the former to anthropology and Jungian psychology, the latter to Freudian psychoanalysis and modern philosophy. Frye and Bloom each begin with the assumption that literature is a system of interrelated texts, but neither is ultimately able to shake off the metaphors of influence and source and the teleology that the model of literary history implies.

Frye manages to sidestep the old debate over imitation and originality by insisting on the autonomy of the literary text as a structure of language in the "Polemical Introduction" to *Anatomy of Criticism*. The true critic must see literature as the "complication" as well as

243

the recurrence of "a relatively restricted and simple group of for-
mulas" that originate in "primitive culture" but continually reap-
pear "in the greatest classics" (17). Literary criticism of individual
texts and the theory of literature as a whole must be based on
"a conceptual framework derivable from an inductive survey" of
texts, and not from "an externally derived attitude." In order to
support the idea of literature as a system and its study as a "science," Frye identifies the organizing principles of literature with a
specific set of "modes," "symbols," "myths," and "genres." The
problem lies in the heterogeneity of these four main categories:
modes and genres put Frye into the formalist camp that runs from
Aristotle's *Poetics* through the New Critics and the structuralists,
whereas symbols and myths align Frye with the largely futile attempt to recover the primordial "archetypes" of language, behavior, and mind that characterizes early modern anthropology and
psychology. Thus, although his theory of literary patterns bears a
partial resemblance to the intertextual approach to literature and
culture, Frye's presuppositions still include an evolutionary model
of literary history that conflicts with the view of literature as a synchronic system of signs.

Interestingly, Bloom builds his theory of literary relations on the
very problem that historians and formalists alike shun: intentionality and the psychological connections among authors and texts,
both those written by others and their own.[1] At first, his project for
a typology of "intra-poetic relationships" in *The Anxiety of Influence*
seems a promising alternative to the usual source studies. Redefining "influence" as a "*misreading*" or "*creative correction*" of past authors, Bloom proposes "six revisionary ratios," or six stages in the
"life-cycle" of a poet's psychological development (30, 10, 14–16).
Every "strong" poet who does not wish merely to imitate his predecessors must—consciously and unconsciously—"distort" (*clinamen*), "antithetically complete" (*tessera*), "repeat" (*kenosis*), "convert"
(*daemonization*), "purge" (*askesis*), and finally gain "priority" over
(*aprophrades*) the poems written by his greatest "precursors." Bloom
emphasizes that these intra-poetic relationships are located primarily at the psychological level and have nothing to do with the "trans-
missions of ideas and images from earlier to later poets" which he
relegates to "source-hunters and biographers" (71).

In the bold "Interchapter: A Manifesto for Antithetical Criticism," Bloom pleads for a new "practical" criticism—pace I. A.
Richards—that will begin with the fundamental intertextuality of
all literature: "that the meaning of a poem can only be a poem, but
another poem—a poem not itself" (70). The critic must read poetry

exactly as it was written—as a "family romance," or the "dialectic" of "anxiety and desire" enacted among fathers and sons in the presence (or absence) of the maternal Muse (8, 57). Bloom even goes so far as to suggest that criticism and literature are two sides of the same coin, or the activity of creatively misreading the texts written by others—an idea about the intertextuality of literary theory developed at length by Roland Barthes.

Bearing in mind that the "precursor" whose "influence" causes "anxiety" in the later writer is often a "composite" of previous texts and their authors, we might ask if Bloom himself has reached that final stage of "priority" over the strong fathers of historicism and the equally powerful fathers of New Criticism. We might inquire especially closely into the reappearance of the dead, or *aprophrades,* indicated by the unmistakable echo of T. S. Eliot's voice in Bloom's heuristic use of the metaphor of filiation to describe literary relationships.[2] For, despite his iconoclasm, Bloom eventually bows down under the weight of the Anglo-American critical tradition, and in several ways. First, as Jonathan Culler comments in his introductory essay on intertextuality, Bloom's "shift from texts to persons" via Freud tends to reduce the potential variety of literary relations to "an oedipal confrontation" between an elite series of pre- and post-Romantic poets, all of whom have already been canonized as "classics" by more traditional methods (*The Pursuit of Signs* 108, 111). If the psychoanalytic terminology were removed, would Bloom's analysis of Milton and Shelley differ from Reuben Brower's study of "allusions" in Dryden and Pope? How far is the theory of the creative "swerve" (*clinamen*)—"the central working concept of the theory of Poetic influence" (Bloom 42)—from the study of "imitation," or "how [Pope] used the poetry of the past for his own expressive purposes" (Brower *viii*)? Significantly, both Brower and Bloom have difficulty proving the intentionality of literary borrowings and both are ambivalent when it comes to establishing whether the past or the present has the lion's share in a given poem. In the long run, Bloom's theory of intra-poetic relations does not decisively break with the teleology implicit in literary historicism, for tracing the evolution of a poet's psyche presupposes a temporal determinism. One might say that Bloom's heuristic metaphor of filiation (the "family romance" of poetry) betrays him into the anxieties of influence (the "flow" of critical tradition) as his parting words reveal: "The precursors *flood* us, and our imaginations can die by *drowning* in them, but no imaginative life is possible if such *inundation* is wholly evaded" (154; emphasis added).

Text/Culture Relations

The semiotics of intertextuality takes off where historicist and formalist approaches end: at the border between the literary text and its manifold relations to a broad spectrum of other texts, or culture. The distinguishing mark of a semiotic is perhaps less the concept of the "sign"—the principle that every unit of meaning can be analyzed into a signifier and a signified—than the systematicity of signs. Thus, signification depends upon the positioning of signs within rule-governed or "coded" structures.[3] The product of encoding signs or "semiosis" can be termed a "text," so that the text may be as small as a phrase or gesture, or as large as a novel or football game. With the view that any event—whether in verbal, visual, aural, or kinesic "discourse"—can be analyzed as a text, or a hierarchy of relations among codes and their constituent elements, the gateway is open to applying the concept of "intertextuality," defined generally as the structural relations among two or more texts, to any of the disciplines in the humanities and the social sciences.

We should be aware, however, that semiotics is also based on a heuristic metaphor. The assumption this time is that all signifying practices, whether verbal or otherwise, can be best understood on the model of language. Instead of the temporalization of authorial and literary relations in theories of influence and inspiration, semiotics proposes a spatialization of textual relations that subordinates diachronic developments to synchronic structuration of the field. Although temporal and material dimensions do enter into a semiotic analysis, the signs and codes in a text are presumed to be capable of interrelating in an unforeseeable number of ways, so that semiosis is always open, potentially infinite. Given that one text can connect significantly with a virtually unlimited set of other texts, just as a specific utterance (*parole*) can be located in numerous contexts within the system of language (*langue*), semiotics logically requires a theory of intertextuality. Indeed, *culture* itself, or the collection of signifying practices in a society, *is radically intertextual.* For instance, we cannot explain music except through verbal language, we probably use hand gestures to support our discourse about music, we wear clothes that affect our interlocutors' response to our discourse, and so on.

Ferdinand de Saussure's famous recommendation that "*semiology*," or the "*science that studies the life of signs within society*," be modelled on linguistics has not gone uncontested (16). Debate has also focused on whether or not the process of semiosis can be fully

246

formalized and the interpretation of significations made scientific. For present purposes we may place semioticians into two main camps around this issue of the limitability of meaning. One camp, abiding by the founding theories of structural linguistics in Saussure and Roman Jakobson, assumes that the signification of a text or corpus of texts can be contained and fully explicated by description of elementary units and their systematic or recurrent relations. The other camp, critical of this "structuralist" enterprise, emphasizes the ambiguity of the basic sign relation (signifier–signified) and the infinite regression or *mise en abîme* of signification. The theory and practice of intertextuality vary according to which position is adopted in this ongoing debate over the status of the sign, the text, and semiotics itself.

Juri Lotman's treatment of intertextuality in his work on the structure of aesthetic texts exemplifies the conservative, formalist school of semiotics. Taking for granted that any semiotic object is organized according to the linguistic model, Lotman defines art—verbal, visual, plastic, aural, or any combination—as a "secondary modelling system" whose units of value are complex because they build upon the primary signification system of language.[4] Since any artistic text is "multiply encoded," it can "enter into several contextual structures," taking on a different set of meanings for each relationship (*Structure of the Artistic Text* 59–60). Intertextuality, then, would be the normal situation for the artistic text because the "contextual structures" in question are not only the semantic and syntactic levels of the text(s), but also the new set of significant relations produced by the encounter between the texts: "New structures which enter into a text or the extra-textual background of a work of art (i.e., cultural information, itself encoded in a series of texts) do not cancel out the old meanings, but enter into semantic relations with them" (75).

When Lotman selects a poem by Pushkin, "Ruslan and Liudmila," as an example of literary intertextuality, his choice is calculated. The genre of poetry provides the favorite texts for structuralist poetics because it highlights the formal patterns of language, making arguments for overcoding as the sign of "literariness" both convenient and convincing (see Jakobson, "Closing Statement" and "Poetry of Grammar"). Moreover, Lotman relies on the most direct case of intertextuality—the quotation, in which "a fragment of another text" is introduced into the text under study. The intertextual citation is treated purely in terms of linguistic stylistics, as a deviation or "incompatibility" in the semantic structure of Pushkin's poem (*Analysis of the Poetic Text* 109). This approach strategically closes off the potential significations of the text by claiming to explain its "artistic effect" as the "*co-location*" of two heterogeneous sets of signs (*Analysis* 108). On the other hand, Lotman does recognize that the linguistic structures of text and intertext carry two different sets of cultural codes with disparate values. It is when he begins to speculate on how the reader of an intertextually marked poem is perforce drawn "into a particular system of ideological–cultural associations" that does not agree with the values presupposed by his or her own "'language'" that Lotman's theory becomes properly semiotic (*Analysis* 108).

Significantly, Lotman cites the work of Mikhail Bakhtin as the best available study of the artistic function of intertextuality. Likewise, the most recent analytical dictionary for semiotics awards Bakhtin the distinction of having "introduced" the concept—although not the term itself—of intertextuality as a "methodological replacement for the 'influence' theory upon which research in comparative literature" as well as national literatures "was based" (Greimas and Courtes 16). Yet Bakhtin's name appears neither in Terence Hawkes's introductory textbook, *Structuralism and Semiotics* (1977), nor in Jonathan Culler's widely read essay on "Presuppositions and Intertextuality" (1981). It is tempting to conclude that Bakhtin's uneven but growing reputation as a leading theorist of text/culture relations is due to his overtly polemical stance and to the radical implications of his literary semiotic.[5]

In his early study entitled *Problems of Dostoevsky's Poetics* (1963), Bakhtin roundly criticizes both historically oriented literary criticism and recent stylistics for their inadequate conceptions of language and of the aesthetic function of language in the novel in particular. It is impossible, Bakhtin argues, to read novels such as Dostoevsky's either as a homogeneous representation of reality, or as an expression of the author's personal opinions and psychology. These "*monological*" approaches cannot account for the variety of idiolects used by the characters, or for the presence of all sorts of extra-literary texts—newspaper articles, anecdotes, dirty jokes—in Dostoevsky's work. Breaking away from the tradition of European realism with its conservative, one-sided view of "reality," Dostoevsky challenges his readers to recognize what Bakhtin calls the "*polyphonic*" novel, or that type of narrative which insists on the "*coexistence* and interaction" of very different ways of using language and, hence, very different ways of evaluating "reality" (20–23).

Bakhtin supports his theory of the "polyphonic" novel with another thesis that has even more far-reaching implications: "the carnivalization of literature." Carnival is not originally a literary form, but a complex of cultural behaviors, a "*syncretic pageant*" with its own system of rituals and symbolism (*Problems* 100–108). Especially important is the carnival's global mixing and ironization of culturally sanctioned categories of action and discourse. The polyphonic novel is marked off from the realist novel by its carnivalistic attitude to reigning ideologies and the authoritarian institutions that enforce them. Consequently, parody and the polyphonic novel— itself largely parodistic in the sense that it proposes the "*jolly relativity* of every system" (102)—tend to flourish during periods of cultural crisis, as Dostoevsky's prerevolutionary novels and the conflict of medieval and Renaissance mores in Rabelais demonstrate (*Rabelais and His World*, 1965). The notion of the carnivalization of literature, then, is nothing less than a theory of intertextuality, or the systematic connection that can be analyzed among literary and nonliterary discourses. Bakhtin's admiring characterization of Dostoevsky's sensitivity to the dynamics of language and culture also serves as a definition of his own relativistic semiotic: "To orient oneself in the world meant for him to think of all its contents as being simultaneous and to *guess at their interrelationships in a single point in time*" (*Problems* 23).

The critical model of the "dialogue," or the continuous exchange of views without resolution, as well as the metaphor of the "polyphonic" novel as a musical "counterpoint" of different voices, derive from Bakhtin's intensely pragmatic approach to language. *Problems of Dostoevsky's Poetics* concludes with an exposé of the failure of linguistics and stylistics to account for the "*dialogical angle*" of discourse, or the ideological intention of the speaker as he both responds to previous utterances and anticipates future replies to his own speech (150). The very concept of the "text" hypostatizes the dialogism of language by fixing discourse into a hierarchy of levels of isolated units. Moreover, linguistic approaches to literature focus on the formal structure of the text as if it were an autonomous object, whereas in actual cultural life literature is inseparable from and indeed thrives on "extra-literary" and "symbolic phenomena" such as popular songs and visual "images of various art forms" (*Problems* 151–52). Bakhtin therefore proposes a supplementary "metalinguistics" whose major contribution is a typology of literary discourses based on the notion of the dialogized or "*double-voice word*" (*Problems* 153). Since most utterances, but above all literary utterances, are "oriented toward another person's word," discourse must be inspected for its "hidden internal polemic," or the way(s) in which language is used to argue with the "alien word" or others (*Problems* 164). Although Bakhtin himself does not suggest an interdisciplinary extension of this literary semiotic, the possibilities for an anthropologically or sociologically oriented theory of intertextuality as a distinctive feature of culture are there.

In the later essay entitled "Discourse on the Novel," Bakhtin gives a crucial twist to his theory of dialogism by promoting the novel as the intertextual genre par excellence, and hence the prime instigator of "indeterminacy" in the realm of literature (*The Dialogic Imagination* 7). The harmonious "polyphony" of Dostoevsky's novels now becomes the raucous "*heteroglossia*" not only of the iconoclastic novel, but of human cultural experience itself. Given the irreducible differences among sociolects, idiolects, and various ideological motivations of their speakers, language can never communicate just one denotative meaning or even the sole viewpoint of the speaker, for each utterance is always caught up in the crowded space of interdiscursivity: "But no living word relates to its object in a *singular* way: between the word and its object, between the word and the speaking subject, there exists an elastic environment of other, alien words about the same object, the same theme" (*Dialogic* 276). Although Bakhtin regards this situation of heteroglossia as a positive, creative opportunity for speakers to mold language to their own requirements, the very idea that every material object is "already as it were overlain with qualifications, open to dispute, charged with value, already enveloped in an obscuring mist—or, on the contrary, by the 'light' of alien words that have already been spoken about it" is sure to disturb those who hold a Saussurean view of "signification," as well as those who think that every text has a discoverable, fully explicable "meaning," be it thematic, psychological, symbolic, or historical. More specifically, for a theory of intertextuality, it is a far cry indeed from Lotman's reassuring description of the relationship between two poems as "the precipitation of crystals" caused by "an alien body falling into a supersaturated solution" (*Analysis* 109), to Bakhtin's radically destabilizing analogy between dialogism in literature and the modern theory of relativity: "It is as if varying systems of calculation were joined here in the complex unity of an Einsteinian universe" (*Problems* 12). The very indeterminacy of Bakhtin's metaphors for the dialogism produced by intertextuality—"mist" and "light"—casts doubt on the semiotic enterprise of formalizing the significations of texts and their multiple interrelationships.

Savage Bricolage or Savvy Deconstruction?

The wide cultural implications of the phenomenon of intertextuality have attracted the attention not only of literary scholars, but also of anthropologists and philosophers. Interestingly, some of the fundamental disagreements over the nature of signification, the status of the text, and the extent of semiotic relations among texts previously observed between Lotman and Bakhtin are replayed, with variations, between Claude Lévi-Strauss and Jacques Derrida. The notion of intertextuality apparently swings both ways: it can be used to support the claim that the "science of signs" adequately accounts for the structure and function of all sorts of texts, as in Lévi-Strauss, or it can furnish ammunition for an attack on the very idea of the sign by focusing our attention on the indeterminacy of meaning produced by the free play of signifiers among numerous texts, as in Derrida.

What I would call the constructive approach to intertextuality is exemplified by the structural anthropology of Lévi-Strauss. In the manifesto-like *The Savage Mind* (1962), Lévi-Strauss uses Saussure's theory of language and signification to refute the notion that "primitive" or oral cultures are intrinsically inferior to Western ones. So-called savage thought is equal to Western thought in its epistemological complexity, but the constitution of and operations for the sign in the two cultures differ. Whereas modern science deals with the "abstract" sign-concepts of a strictly verbal language, savage science semioticizes the world of the "concrete" into sign-objects that are organized into a hierarchy of classification systems. For instance, totemic animals are not childish fetishes, but differential signs coded into various structures and capable of rule-governed transformations, just like the phonemes of a language which are combined into various morphemes, lexemes, and syntagms until they generate discourse. Standing on the doctrine of the arbitrariness of the sign, Lévi-Strauss argues from the conventionality and the flexibility of savage thinking in myths, art, and social planning toward his thesis of the savage mind's sophistication: "From a formal point of view there is thus no fundamental difference between the zoologist or the botanist who allots a recently discovered plant the position *Elephantopus spicatus* Aubl., arranged for it by the system . . . and the Omaha priest who defines the social paradigms of a new member of the group by conferring the available name *Old-bison's-worn-hoof* on him. They know what they are doing in both cases" (216).

Lévi-Strauss's tactical deployment of semiotics against the evolutionary model of ethnography can be and has been reenacted by literary theorists who wish an alternative to the linear schema of influence and source studies, as well as by historians who want to practice a comparative history based on homologous relations and structures rather than chronological collections of facts. Particularly fruitful for developing a theory of intertextuality in these or other fields is Lévi-Strauss's notion of "*bricolage*" (*Savage Mind* 16–30). Strictly speaking, within the anthropological context, the *bricoleur* is the native mind itself, which thinks about problems and their solutions "mythically," or in terms of a "closed" set of "tools and materials" ordered into values by a "finite" set of rules. Although the *bricoleur* does not invent his own terms and operations but works with those already provided by the indigenous culture, the closure of *bricolage*, or its very systematicity, permits a potentially infinite number of messages to be generated from the same sign-objects. In this sense, Lévi-Strauss's savage *bricoleur* is not unlike T. S. Eliot's "catalytic" poet: like the mythmaker, the literary writer always begins with a "retrospective," a sort of dialogue with tradition, or the closed canon of classical texts that constitutes his cultural competence. As in Harold Bloom's theory of the anxiety of influence, the primitive mythmaker or carver of masks has to confront the texts of his "ancestors" before he, like the postromantic or modern poet, can proffer his own discourse. For both poet and mythmaker, therefore, originality is relative, consisting never of the absolutely new, but always of that paradigmatically virtual set of utterances "which will ultimately differ from the instrumental set [the intertexts of past and contemporary mythmakers, carvers, poets] only in the internal disposition of its parts" (*Savage Mind* 18). As a theory of intertextuality, then, *bricolage* would view the aesthetic dialectic between imitation and innovation in literary criticism as an illusory, superficial effect of the dynamics of deep structural transformations among homologous messages, or intertexts.

Lévi-Strauss's provocative comparisons of savage myths and Charles Dickens' *Great Expectations*, war clubs and cubist collages, totemism and science, invites a thoroughly interdisciplinary application of the theory of *bricolage*. Indeed, his masterwork, *Mythologiques* (1964–71, in four volumes) develops in this direction, since explanation of the system of South and North American Indian mythology involves explanation of the allied "languages" of social, economic, political, religious, sexual, and other domains of culture: "I claim the right to make use of any manifestation of the mental . . . activities of the communities under consideration which seems likely to allow me . . . to complete . . . the myth" (*The Raw and the Cooked* 4). In semiotic terms, *Mythologiques* constructs a multi-intertextual and intercultural space, made up of visual, verbal, kinesic, aural, animate and inanimate texts, all of which interrelate and determine each other's significations at several levels. In view of the extreme heterogeneity of the materials that he uses to build this vast semiotic system, Lévi-Strauss is a modern *bricoleur* par excellence. Certainly, the musical arrangement of the chapters and sections in the first volume, *The Raw and the Cooked*, is a deft bit of *bricolage*. More importantly, the mythical structure of Lévi-Strauss's own analysis of native myths serves as a declaration of the heuristic power of structuralism. Lévi-Strauss even goes so far as to claim that he has discovered the universal structure of the human mind—equally reflected in the Indians' myths, which are "homologous" to the symphonic scores of Wagner, which are "isomorphic" with the movements of the chapters in *The Raw and the Cooked*, which parallel the mind of the anthropologist himself: "It is in the last resort immaterial whether in this book the thought processes of the South American Indians take shape through the medium of my thought, or whether mine takes place through the medium of theirs" (*The Raw and the Cooked* 13).

Whatever we may think about the structural affinities among "concrete logic," "concrete music," and structuralism as a method of analysis, Lévi-Strauss's "ouverture" to a science of intertextuality is both attractive and perilous. To anticipate Derrida's critique, Lévi-Strauss appears intermittently blind and insightful with regard to the deconstructive implications of his marvelous intertextual, intercultural construction. The clash between the two heuristic metaphors that he applies in introducing his theories is a telltale index of a deeper conflict in his presuppositions. On the one hand, native myths are organized like "a nebula" that "gradually spreads" out from a center under the pressure of sequences of transformation groups, forming a "multi-dimensional body" (*The Raw and the Cooked* 3). On the other hand, the system of myths is like the process of crystallization which ensures—as we saw with Lotman's use of the same analogy—"a stable and well-defined structure." Since myth-as-nebula is an infinitely open semiotic system and myth-as-crystal is a complex but firmly closed system, we are faced with a fundamental contradiction in the nature of intertextuality. For, once we adopt the "crystal"-clear concepts of signs, codes, and structural relations among texts, when and how does the "nebula" of ever-expanding parallel and inverse transformations stop? It would seem, to import another Derridean phrase, that its very semiotic potential "decenters" the intertextual system, rendering both native mythology and Lévi-Strauss's *Mythologiques* radically indeterminate.

The way in which Derrida's critique of semiology and the social sciences has already insinuated itself into this discussion of Lévi-Strauss's structural anthropology is a fair demonstration of the ineluctable intertextuality of all discourse, or thought-in-language.

Throughout his work, Derrida focuses on the epistemological paradoxes in Western philosophy, which he analyzes and problematizes, showing how theories of representation, language, and reality "deconstruct" themselves by positing contradictory premises. In the essay entitled "Structure, Sign and Play in the Discourse of the Human Sciences," Derrida argues that the epistemological "*rupture*" made by structuralism in linguistics and ethnography is accompanied by a contradictory "redoubling" or "repetition" of precisely those metaphysical presuppositions about truth and meaning that structuralism sought to contest (278). His case in point is Lévi-Strauss's "Ouverture," the theoretical preface to *The Raw and the Cooked*. In order to break out of the restrictive historical model and open the field of anthropology to cross-cultural, synchronic comparisons, Lévi-Strauss refuses to locate a "key" or "origin" myth to which all the other myths discussed can be "traced" or from which they can be "derived." Rather, Lévi-Strauss asserts, we must approach mythology as a structure, or an intertextual space without an individual creator and without an absolute beginning or end: "There is no real end to methodological analysis, no hidden unity to be grasped once the breaking-down process has been complete. Themes can be split up *ad infinitum*" (*The Raw and the Cooked* 5).

Nevertheless, Derrida claims, Lévi-Strauss's treatment of structure invites the free "play" of intertextuality only to forbid it. The concept of structure permits permutation or transformation of the codes from various myths, but "grounds" or "centers" these relationships in a closed set of value-laden categories, such as the opposition between nature and culture or the corollary opposition between the raw and the cooked. By this subtle countermovement, structuralism reinstates the old "onto-theological" idea of an absolute origin or essence of Truth in the new form of the "transcendental signified" ("Structure, Sign, and Play" 280–81). In *Of Grammatology* (1967), Derrida extends this critique to Lévi-Strauss's statement on the purpose and methods of anthropology in *Tristes tropiques* (1955). Derrida debunks Lévi-Strauss's disparagement of civilized "writing" ("*écriture*") as a metaphysically invested bias against the "text" in which signifieds are graphically distanced from their signifiers, thus revealing the permanent gap between the signifier and the signified, between language and truth. This time, the transcendental signified is the "noble savage" and his prelapsarian, or rather romantic, communion with Nature which the modern Western observer, his head stuffed with intertextual baggage, can never recapture. As Derrida points out, however, natural man or man-without-"writing" is a fallacy, for the very fact that the most primitive savages, the Nambikawara, classify themselves by a double system of public and private names indicates their consciousness of textuality, or man-as-text: "If writing is no longer understood in the narrow sense of linear and phonetic notation, it should be possible to say that all societies capable of producing, that is to say of obliterating, their proper names, and of bringing classificatory difference into play, practice writing in general" (*Of Grammatology* 109).

In a characteristic maneuver, Derrida turns Lévi-Strauss's guiding theory of *bricolage* inside out. Ironically similar to the conservative mythmaker, Lévi-Strauss adopts the presuppositions and materials of the very tradition of empiricism that his structuralist project aims to supersede. Like all scientists who imagine that their theories represent progress over old ideas and methods, Lévi-Strauss is a *bricoleur* despite himself. Indeed, savage mythology and sophisticated science are equally intertextual, equally ideologically loaded, and equally indeterminate: "If one calls '*bricolage*' the necessity of borrowing one's concepts from the text of a heritage which is more or less coherent or ruined, it must be said that every discourse is '*bricoleur*' " (*Of Grammatology* 285).

Derrida's infamous pun on the "*différence*" between the signifier and the signified in the sign, and the epistemological "*différance*" or deferment of signification ensuing on this difference, poses a major problem for any semiotic theory of intertextuality. If the signifier is never simultaneous with the signified, then the formal analysis of the structures of a text—literary, visual, gestural, musical, ethnographic, and so on—can never be adequate to its virtual significations. The signified, or the final meaning of the text, will remain forever deferred by this "différence"/"différance" within the sign itself. What Derrida's deconstruction amounts to, then, is an iconoclastic theory of the necessary intertextuality of all discourse. Every text, every utterance, is an "interweaving" or a "textile" of signifiers whose signifieds are by definition intertextually determined by other discourses (*Positions* 26). It follows that each appreciative or critical interpretation is merely a tentative and partial "supplement" of a text, since the signifiers of a text bear only the "traces" of their multiple signifieds.[6] At the same time, each supplementation of a text has itself already been contaminated by previous discourses on that text and by other, presuppositionally related texts. In short, the play of "différence"/"différance" in the sign "ruptures" the very project of a semiotics of intertextuality, or a science of textual relations, because the text itself is an unstable process of illimitable intextual transformations. The very notion of intertextuality turns out to be a *mise-en-abîme*, an abyss of infinite semiosis at whose brink we stand, delighted or terrified.

The Intertextual Revolution

Structuralism uses intertextuality to posit certain formal connections among domains of culture hitherto studied separately under the historical or evolutionary models that dominated the humanities and the sciences. As its subversive and radical supplement, deconstruction uses intertextuality to open up the epistemological field so that any and all connections among human discourses may be made. Strikingly absent from both approaches to intertextuality is the presence of a subject—a speaker, author, reader, someone who thinks and feels and communicates through the text in question, someone who discovers the *inter-* in intertextuality. In this light, the work of Roland Barthes and Julia Kristeva may be seen as an attempt to reinscribe a trace of the subject, especially the sexual and political subject, into the space of intertextual relations.

Barthes' *Mythologies* (1957) is an application of Saussurean terminology, as filtered through Lévi-Strauss's theory of *bricolage*, to popular culture in contemporary France. Barthes treats ordinary objects and daily events, such as laundry soap and wrestling matches, as a coherent system of coded messages, or "myths," which redundantly convey a limited set of concepts to the populace. The criterion for modern "mythologies," however, is less their structure—that of a "second-order semiological system"—than their ideological contents. The innate "duplicity" of the signifier—signified relation enables the insertion of "bourgeois" values into every cultural sign. Since the average person seems unaware of the ideologically loaded signs that constitute "natural" things in life, it is up to the semiologist, or *"mythologue,"* to expose this intertextual conspiracy. Barthes' theory of mass culture as an intertextual system also suggests further inquiry into the connection between commercialism and intertextuality as a distinctively modern Western phenomenon. Yet, Barthes as semiotician is himself duplicitous, for under the banner of the science of signs he lambastes capitalism as an abuse of an ideally authentic mode of signification. Barthes finds himself, then, in the peculiar position of a Marxist semiologist: he has discovered the intertextual system that organizes French culture, but he has done so with ideological motivations that have, as he himself admits, undoubtedly skewed his selection of which texts to examine. In this sense, *Mythologies* are only Barthes' mythologies: "And what I was looking for in all this were significations. Are these MY significations? In other words, is there a mythology of the mythographer? Of course" (10).[7] We are left with the uncomfortable implication that any set of intertexts will always be only those intertexts noticed by the individual analyst.

S/Z (1970) makes an important contribution to the theory of intertextuality by redefining the text as both *multidisciplinary* and *multisubjective*. In the wake of Derrida's critique of semiology, Barthes now adopts a relativistic view of the sign, the subject, and the text. Surprisingly, it is the reader and not the text that wins the day in *S/Z*.[8] When Barthes proposes an "evaluative" typology for literature based on the opposition between the closed and the open text, his eye is less on the structure of the text than on what Julia Kristeva calls the "signifying practice" of the reader engaged with the text. Thus, the "classical" bourgeois text makes its reader into a passive "consumer" because it is "readable" ("*lisible*") only on the level of representation, where language is assumed to be transparently referential and ideologically innocent. In contrast, the "writable" ("*scriptible*") text liberates the reader to participate actively in the "work" ("*travail*") or "production" of literature itself. Each reader "rewrites" the text by discovering a new arrangement of signification: "The writable text is *ourselves writing*" (*S/Z* 6). Paradoxically, although Barthes espouses a deconstructive view of the sign, as evidenced by his defense of the "undecidability" of "connotations" in the "writable" text, he reinstates the individual subject at the very center, in the act of (re-)writing the text. After all, it is the subject—author, reader, analyst—who must make the intertextual connections that constitute the open text. Interpretation, then, depends on the subject's ability to gather up a variety of intertexts and bring them to bear on the given text: "*I read the text*" (*S/Z* 10). Of course, cautions Barthes, this "I" is himself or herself already a linguistically constituted, ideologically informed function of the wider intertextuality of his or her culture. The "I" is never "innocent," but always a selection of other (inter-)texts, so that the subject becomes as "plural" and "open" as the literary text.

The idea of the self as an intertextual site leads Barthes to read Balzac's story, "Sarrasine," in terms of a "*sémioclasm*" of the body. The dislocation of the signifier–signified relation, which causes what Derrida calls the "dissemination" of meaning in language, also dislocates the sexual identity of several of the characters in "Sarrasine." The beauty and femininity of the castrato singer, Zambinella, are discovered to be empty signifiers, without substantial referents to back them up. The amorous artist, Sarrasine, is tricked by the mirage of intertextual signifiers—Zambinella's clothing, hair, makeup, voice, gestures, friends—projects by society at large as well as by the narcissistic illusion that his own highly conventional-ized representations of Zambinella as an androgyne in painting and sculpture have produced. Ironically, Zambinella's very body becomes a plural text that unleashes a chain of intertextual signi-fiers forever separated from the true signified by the "différence"/ "différance" of his/her bisexuality. One could say that the unfor-tunate hero, Sarrasine, dies of intertextuality, both its surplus and its lack, since Zambinella both is and is not what all the outward signs indicate he/she is. The final lesson to be drawn here, however, concerns not only sexuality but politics. Barthes emphasizes the con-nection between the emptiness of the signs of gender and the emp-tiness of the signs of commerce in capitalist society. Like the body of the castrato Zambinella, money is a perverse sign without authen-tic origin or reference. Like Sarrasine, who is morally and mortally contaminated by "intersextuality," the bourgeois consumer is daily engaged in the prostitution of the marketplace (*S/Z* 39–40).

At the end of *S/Z*, Barthes comments that the logical conse-quence of his claims for the intertextual status of both text and reader is the textuality of the author himself. The cult of the authorial personality, so beloved and belabored by literary biog-raphers and critics, is superseded by the recognition that the so-called author is just another collection of (inter-)texts. In *Roland Barthes by Roland Barthes* (1975), Barthes offers us an autobio-graphical collage of photos, music sheets, cartoons, and "frag-ments" of writing which has as its subject not the person of the speaker, but the text-as-self, or rather intertexts-as-alternative-selves. Throughout this book, Barthes self-consciously plays with the signifier, teasing us with intertexts (Proust, Sartre), intratexts ("the trouble with avant-garde theories like mine . . . "), and auto-texts ("expanding on my favorite metaphors in *S/Z* . . . "), each of which differs from and so defers the ultimate signified—Barthes himself.[9] At one point, Barthes draws up a chart of some of the major sources for his theories ("Intertext," column 1), and the main intellectual systems he has espoused ("Genre," column 2), and the titles of his own books ("Works," column 3) (*Roland Barthes* 144–45). The "remarks" that follow fairly sum up Barthes' views on intertextuality. First, he distinguishes intertextuality from "a field of influence," preferring a pluralistic definition of interdiscur-sive relations that is rendered through metaphors: "a music of fig-ures," "a tissue," a "lacework," an "echo chamber," the mythical ship "Argo." Second, he retraces the paths of his own work— "(mythological) *interventions*," "(semiological) *fictions*," and "splinters, fragments, *sentences, phrases*"—not to assert any purposive development, but to observe the free systematicity of discourse, how "each phase is reactive: the author reacts either to the discourse which surrounds him (intertexts), or to his own discourse (intratexts and/or autotexts)" (*Roland Barthes* 145). Nevertheless, there is a seriousness and an anxiety amidst this celebration of the infinite text, the infinite self. The pleasures of writing and rewriting your own and others' texts can easily become a "lustreless" repetition of the same, bringing on a "hysterical," "clogged" feeling of being enclosed in one enormous Text: "This, then, is the Text, the theory of the Text. But again the Text risks paralysis . . . the Text tends to degenerate into prattle (*Babil*). Where to go next? That is where I am now" (*Roland Barthes* 71).

Unlike Barthes, who worries about the narcissistic gratifications of intertextuality, Julia Kristeva feels spurred on toward social revolution by the "productivity" of intertextual relations as they "work" the "materiality" of language and of historical reality (*Séméiotiké* 9–10).[10] Agreeing with Barthes on the necessity for a critique of semiology, Kristeva in *Séméiotiké: Recherches pour une sémanalyse* (1969) proposes a study of the "crisscrossing" ("*croisement*") of the subject, the signifier, and the process of culture as manifested in the text. The guiding principle of semanalysis and the special class of revolutionary texts that it describes is dialectical transformation. In contradistinction to signification, or the fixed relation between signifier and signified assumed by structural linguistics, "*signifiance*" is an activity of "confrontation" and "stratification" that reorganizes the semantic and grammatical categories of discourse, thereby challenging the dominant ideology of society as embodied in its language (*Séméiotiké* 11). "*Signifiance*," or the radical deployment of the signifier, produces the "*texte*," here defined as "une zone de marques et d'intervalles dont l'inscription non centrée met en pratique une polyvalence sans unité possible" ("a zone of marks and intervals whose decentered inscription [into ordinary discourse] puts into practice a polyvalence that cannot be "reduced to a unity") (*Séméiotiké* 13).[11] In other words, the "text" for Kristeva is a critical or "metalinguistic" act in which the subject scrutinizes previous and contemporary texts, affirming some and denying others in order to assert his or her own right to speak (*La Révolution* 341).[12] More specifically, intertextuality is a complex "procès de rejet multipliant la position du langage et du sujet" ("process of rejection that multiplies the position of language and of the subject"), a "*negativité*" that destroys old texts in order to create new texts (*La Révolution* 344).

As her mixed critical metaphors suggest, Kristeva's approach combines several modern theories on language and meaning, including those of Freud, Bakhtin, and Derrida, thereby making her own work exemplary of intertextuality as a "mosaic" of half-revealed, half-concealed citations from the discourse of others. While maintaining the positive importance of the dialogue between the speaker and the addressee, or the self and the other(s), Kristeva qualifies the status of the subject as a function of the deconstructive intertextuality of all discourse. Just as signification is rendered undecidable by *signifiance*, so the subject is projected into a vast intertextual space where he or she becomes fragmented or "pulverized" into an unending series of exchanges between his or her own and others' texts (*Séméiotiké* 89). In order to track down the traces of the subject in discourse, semanalysis borrows from psychoanalysis and from structural linguistics, the former accounting for the original productivity and the latter for the formal structure of the text. The "*géno-texte*" involves the paradigm of signifiers and the speaking subject, "I," who works to dislocate and revise the "tissue of language" ("*tissu de la langue*") as previously constituted by others' values and desires. The "*phéno-texte*" is the grammatical and semantic surface structure which stylistics mistakes for the final meaning of the text, but which is actually only the residue of the fuller "engendering" ("*engendrement*") of the text as a psychic and historical activity (*Séméiotiké* 219). It is important to note that intertextuality, in Kristeva's view, occurs at the "zero moment" of passage between the geno-text and the pheno-text, a moment during which the unconscious drives ("*pulsions*") of the subject erupt into language, struggling against the constraints on speech already established by the discourses—repressive and paternal intertexts—of others (*La Révolution* 340).

For practical purposes, Kristeva's most valuable contribution to the debate on intertextuality is the idea that an intertextual citation is never innocent or direct, but always transformed, distorted, displaced, condensed, or edited in some way in order to suit the speaking subject's value system. In her demonstration of the method of semanalysis on the poetry of Mallarmé and Lautréamont in *La Révolution du langage poétique*, Kristeva provides a detailed typology of intertextual relations based on the presuppositions, the grammar, and the semantics of the "reference" and the "transformative" texts (343–57). Given three major kinds of transformation—"oppositional," "permutative," and "indefinite"—we can formulate logical rules for the alterations that the producing text makes in its intertext. For instance, Lautréamont subverts the classical pattern of reasoning toward truth by permutating maxims from Pascal.

The intertext, "S'il se vante, je l'abaisse, s'il s'abaisse, je le vante" ("If he boasts, I put him down, if he demeans himself, I praise him"), represented by the formula $P(m_1t_1, m_2t_2)$, is permutated into "S'il s'abaisse, je le vante. S'il se vante, je le vante davantage" ("If he demeans himself, I praise him. If he boasts, I praise him even more"), or $P(m_2t_2, m_1t_1)$ (*La Révolution* 346).

Despite her meticulous analyses of the rhetorical and local operations involved in intertextual transformations, however, Kristeva fails to explain exactly which presuppositions are at stake (moral? religious? sociopolitical?) and to precisely what extent author *B* does change author *A*'s values by tampering with the structure of his or her language. For instance, Kristeva claims that, in volume 1 of *Poésies*, Lautréamont "appropriates" romantic discourse by critically transforming the discourse of several of its best known representatives. Kristeva then simply lists as intertextual citations the names of authors, characters, and a few titles which stand metonymically for romanticism in Lautréamont's work. It certainly seems debatable whether or not the texts of Hugo and Gautier, Byron and Poe can be treated as interchangeable variables for a complex system of cultural presuppositions spanning a century in at least three different national literatures (*La Révolution* 341). Moreover, as with Barthes, so with Kristeva, it is ultimately a question of the individual reader-analyst's cultural and literary competence in deciphering the intertext and its presuppositions: "Il s'agit donc de présuppositions généralisées jouant entre des ensembles discursifs dont l'un est donné, et dont l'autre (ou les autres) . . . est à reconstruire par le lecteur" ("It is therefore a question of generalized presuppositions that play among discursive wholes of which one is given, and the other (or the others) . . . must be reconstructed by the reader") (*La Révolution* 339). When Kristeva goes on to point out that we must verify which edition of Pascal's *Pensées* Lautréamont used for his parody, one cannot escape the uncanny feeling that we are back with Brower (1959), trying to reconstruct a historically accurate picture of the life and literary times of Alexander Pope by figuring out which editions of Dryden and Horace he read. The twin problems of intentionality and influence thus return, thinly disguised under the poststructuralist "productive" subject whose desires negate and transform the traditional canon of intertexts.

Intertextual Readers

According to Barthes and Kristeva, intertextuality is a revolutionary gesture directed by the modern text against the closure of the

signifier in bourgeois or representational discourse. In contrast, for
Michael Riffaterre and Gérard Genette, intertextuality is the normal *modus operandi* for all literature, classical and contemporary
alike. As a result, Riffaterre and Genette focus on what every
reader must know and do in order to understand fully the intertextual dimension of literature. But Riffaterre and Genette part
ways on the central issue of whether intertextuality should be
treated as an intuitive cultural practice or as a formal classification
system. While Riffaterre offers a series of ingenious close readings
to show how each literary text guides the reader towards its own
intertexts, Genette constructs a highly complex taxonomy of literary relations by way of a generic map for reading. In practice, the
choice between the detail of semantic analysis and the generalization of discourse theory seems moot, since every act of reading
explores lexical interpretations within certain generic conventions.

The reader's relationship to literature changes decisively as we
move from Kristeva's to Riffaterre's theory of intertextuality. For
Kristeva, the text organizes a frontal attack on the "logocentric
reader" by destabilizing the signifier and pluralizing interpretation
through an endless series of intertextual signifieds (*Séméiotiké* 255).
For Riffaterre, the text is rather a demanding but gentle paternal
guide that pushes the reader toward the correct interpretation by
marking the path generously with intertextual "traces": "L'intertexte laisse dans le texte une trace indélébile, une constante formelle
qui joue le rôle d'un impératif de lecture, et qui gouverne le dé-
chiffrement du message" ("The intertext leaves an indelible trace
in the text, a formal constant which plays the role of an imperative for reading, and which governs the decoding of the message")
("La Trace de l'intertexte" 5).[13] In *Semiotics of Poetry* and a series of
articles written since 1979, Riffaterre demonstrates that intertextuality is the major mode of "reader-perception" in poetry and the
source of many special literary effects such as humor, nonsense,
ambiguity, and obscurity (*Semiotics of Poetry*, 115–63). Of the theories of intertextuality examined so far, Riffaterre's is the most prag-
matically oriented, giving the reader–critic an almost step-by-step
method for handling a text and its intertext. But the main premise
that enables Riffaterre to work out this detailed guide to interpretation is both its greatest strength and weakness: to wit, that every
reader has the linguistic and cultural competence required to respond to the signals sent out by a text regarding its "proper" intertextual decoding.

The act of reading, Riffaterre argues, is a dynamic process that
entails at least two "levels or stages" of understanding the text. Re-

lying on his "linguistic competence," the reader of a poem begins
by assuming that its language has a familiar referential "*meaning*."
He or she soon discovers, however, all sorts of "ungrammaticalities"—deviations in syntax and/or in vocabulary—which do not
make sense in the framework of ordinary language. At this point,
the reader is forced to reread the poem and to employ his or
her "literary competence"—knowledge of the "descriptive systems"
available to the given culture and of "other texts"—in order to deduce the "*significance*" of the poem from the recurrent pattern of
its ungrammaticalities. The significance of the poem is never located in the first "*heuristic*" phase of reading, but only appears during the "*retroactive*" or "*hermeneutic*" phase, when mimesis is by-
passed in favor of semiosis. Most important, the "text's control"
over the reader at both stages of interpretation is "absolute," because the poem is a semantically and grammatically hierarchized
"structure" that needs to be understood in only one way—as a semiotic system of interlocked signs that are all "variants" of a "*matrix*" (*Semiotics of Poetry*, 4–6).

Intertextuality enters with the matrix, or the "hypothetical" structure that generates the entire poetic text. At the infralinguistic level
of the classeme or "sign production," the matrix of a given poem
interacts with the clichés and descriptive systems which are typical
of the "sociolect" and which are, therefore, assumed to be "already
actualized in set forms within the reader's mind." Departing from
the clichés "*fleur*" ("flower") and "*abîme*" ("abyss") in romantic discourse as a "*hypogram*," for example, a poem might generate its
"idiolect" out of a series of paradoxes, metaphors, and metonymies
based on this polar opposition (/light/ vs. /dark/, /good/ vs. /evil/,
and so on) (*Semiotics of Poetry*, 39–42). Although broadly cultural
and not marked by a quotation, this construction of an idiolectal
text from a descriptive system available in the sociolect is already a
case of intertextuality because the significance of the poem "cannot
be seen, let alone defined, without a comparison between the text
and its generator," here the pair of clichés.

At the level of "text production," intertextuality involves the concept of the "interpretant," which Riffaterre takes over from C. S.
Peirce, defining it as "a sign that translates the text's surface signs
and explains what else the text suggests" (*Semiotics of Poetry* 81).
The intertextual interpretant is the centerpiece of Riffaterre's theory of reading. Differentiating between "explicit" intertextuality,
or the easily tracked down quotation, and "implicit" intertextuality,
or the more elusive allusion, Riffaterre proposes a semiotic triangle
to account for the complex process of understanding triggered by

the presence of either type of intertextual marker in poetry or narrative (*Text Production*). Given the triple semiotic relation among the object, the sign, and the interpretant in Peirce, Riffaterre substitutes the intertext, the text, and a third text, or the secondary intertext, which "mediates" between the primary intertext and the text:

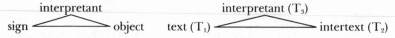

This schema has several major advantages. First, it acknowledges the fact that readers must usually bring more than one intertext to bear while deciphering the significance of a literary text. In one of Riffaterre's examples, a poem by Baudelaire is the intertextual interpretant that guides the intertextual relation between Lautréamont's *Les Chants de Maldoror* and Pascal's *Pensées*. The intertextual interpretant selects the features the former can use for his parody of the latter by providing a structural hypogram. However, Riffaterre claims, the difference in the messages of the interpretant as a poem in its own right and the intertext or the text is irrelevant to the successful functioning of the interpretant. This seems debatable since the reader must compare both intertext (T_2) and interpretant (T_3) in order to realize their mutual relevance to the topos parodied by the text (T_1). This objection notwithstanding, the semiotic triangle proposed by Riffaterre is superior to the simplicity of the traditional model of influence whereby text *A* affects text *B* in a linear relation that does not account for the multidirectionality of intertextual reading. At the same time, Riffaterre's triangle offers a practical alternative to Kristeva's abstract grammar of intertextual relations. Although less neat and scientific than Kristeva's mathematical formulae, Riffaterre's case-by-case treatment goes further in explaining the cultural presuppositions that inform transformations among text/interpretant/intertext.

Another advantage of Riffaterre's semiotic triangle is its reasonable reduction of the bewildering openness or infinitude of intertextual relations suggested by Derrida and deconstructionist theories of literature. Indeed, Riffaterre pointedly criticizes Barthes for failing to see the constraints that the structure of the text imposes on its own intertexts. Intertextuality is not a free association of the given poem or narrative with whatever previously read texts the individual can recall at the moment: "Ce concept d'un procès aléatoire expose Barthes à confondre avec l'intertexte des rapprochements accidentels dûs à des similitudes de lexique, de situation, à des ressemblances sur le plan de la référence apparente ou réelle au monde verbal" ("This concept of an aleatory process exposes Barthes to a confusion between the intertext and accidental connections due to similarities in lexicon, in situation, or to resemblances on the level of apparent or real reference to the non-verbal world") ("Sémiotique intertextuelle" 132). Rather, the text and its intertext(s) are variants of the same structural matrix. Thus, while he would agree with Barthes and Kristeva that the universe of discourse is essentially intertextual, Riffaterre parts company with them when he firmly grounds or "centers" all intertextual relations on the structural matrix of each text, an "origin" that guarantees significance as the reward at the end of the arduous reading process: "Undecidability marks a passing stage in the reader's progress toward interpretation" ("Interpretation and Undecidability" 238).

Yet, Riffaterre's faith in the systematicity of signs and texts leads him to adopt contradictory metaphors for the reader as both the subject and the object of intertextual discourse. At one moment, the reader plays the role of the powerful sleuth who hunts down the "ghost text" or intertext that haunts his reading of a poem, using his linguistic competence to locate the familiar stereotypes that the text has cleverly distorted (*Semiotics of Poetry* 91). At the next moment, the reader (always male) stubbornly resists the siren call of the text, refuses to play its idiolectal language game, and continually seeks "relief by getting away from the dubious words back to safe reality" (*Semiotics of Poetry* 165). The text here looms up before the reader like an angry tyrant, demanding that its intertexts be deciphered in just such a way and no other: "It [the text] is a hierarchy of representations imposed upon the reader, despite his personal preferences" (*Semiotics of Poetry* 12). While this picture of tug and pull between text and reader may fairly reflect the feelings of many, Riffaterre's conclusion that the reader need not ever identify the specific intertexts that motivate the text because of the formal structures that control his reading is not borne out by experience. Moreover, to concede that the reader's inability to find or recall the "hypogram of reference immediately does affect the content of his reactions" and then to insist that the reader's mere "perception of the grid of ungrammatical . . . phrases" is adequate for significance begs the question (*Semiotics of Poetry* 136). If the text is indeed "shaped like a doughnut," with the center being intertext and interpretant, then there will be more air than substance for that likely majority of readers who cannot identify the w/hole (*Semiotics of Poetry* 13).

Other conclusions that Riffaterre draws from the structurality of text/intertext and their control over the reader fly directly in the face of traditional influence and source studies. In recent articles, he takes great pains to distinguish his own very knowledgeable discussions of the contemporary context surrounding an intertext—for instance, Lautréamont's probable viewing of Proudhon's 1808 painting before writing a certain passage in *Maldoror* (1869)—from the plodding reconstruction of "filiations" practiced by "*la critique historiciste.*"[14] One of the strategic advantages of a semiotic approach to intertextuality, Riffaterre says, lies precisely in the logical necessity of positing an intertext whose structure the later text then expands or converts: "Nul besoin de prouver le contact entre l'auteur et ses prédécesseurs. Il suffit pour qu'il y ait intertexte que le lecteur fasse nécessairement le rapprochement entre deux ou plusieurs textes" ("There is no need to prove any contact between the author and his predecessors. It suffices that the intertext exist for the reader in order to make the necessary connection between two or more texts") ("Sémiotique intertextuelle" 131). Following this "principle of logical anteriority," which has "a mechanical, obligatory quality about it" (*Semiotics of Poetry* 15), Riffaterre also claims that the "monumentality" or systematicity of both text and intertext(s) renders their significance "relatively impervious to change and deterioration of the linguistic code" (21). Since the reader's linguistic and cultural competence is, as it were, already encoded in the text, and since the text itself is organized according to a matrix of intertexts, the importance of the historical dimension of literature gives way to that spatial arrangement of texts typical of structuralist and semiotic theories. Thus, placing himself in opposition to both historicism and deconstruction, Riffaterre offers the intertextual "trace" as the final guarantee of the significance of the text despite the shifting ideologies of readers and eras.

For those who feel bewildered by the various definitions of intertextuality on the contemporary literary scene, Genette's *Palimpsestes: La Littérature au second degré* (1982) promises clarification. Acknowledging that literature is fundamentally "transtextual," or a "second-degree" construct made out of pieces of other texts, Genette presents a taxonomy for five major types of transtextuality. In contrast to Barthes and Kristeva as well as Riffaterre, Genette considers intertextuality to be only one category of textual practice. Specifically, he restricts intertextuality to "une relation de coprésence entre deux ou plusieurs textes, c'est-à-dire . . . la présence effective d'un texte dans un autre" ("a relation of copresence between two or more texts, that is . . . the demonstrable presence of one text within another") (*Palimpsestes* 8).[15] Intertextuality can be further divided into three subcategories. While quotation ("*cita-*

tion") is the most explicit or clearly marked kind of intertextuality, allusion ("*allusion*") is the most implicit or unmarked. Plagiarism ("*plagiat*") falls in between these two poles as an unmarked but wholesale textual borrowing.

Of course, all three kinds of intertextuality raise the problem of the reader's literary competence and the author's intentions. Genette handles these chestnuts deftly: he sidesteps them by engaging in a polemic against "l'activité herméneutique du lecteur— ou de l'archilecteur" (*Palimpsestes* 16)—an allusion to Riffaterre's thesis of the ideal or "archreader" and his peculiar blend of semiotics and interpretation in *Semiotics of Poetry*. First, Genette complains that Riffaterre has so expanded the term "intertextuality" that it covers all of "literariness" or what Genette prefers to call "transtextuality." Second, Genette rejects the idea that all types of intertextuality must be implicit, hidden away in the deep matrix of the text and manifested only by ungrammaticalities on the surface of the text. Instead of the detailed semantic analyses carried on by Riffaterre, Genette argues that we should approach intertextuality and the other kinds of transtextuality through the larger units of discourse and genre analysis: "La 'trace' intertextuelle selon Riffaterre est donc davantage (comme l'allusion) . . . de l'ordre de la figure ponctuelle (du détail) que de l'oeuvre considérée dans sa structure d'ensemble . . . " ["The intertextual 'trace' according to Riffaterre is thus more (like the allusion) . . . on the level of the local figure (the detail) than on the level of the work considered as a structural whole"] (*Palimpsestes* 9). Consequently, the reader's relationship to the text should be viewed not as an overdetermined hunt for the ghost intertext, but as a reasoning process of elimination and identification based on generic and discursive rules: "J'envisage la relation entre le texte et son lecteur d'une manière plus socialisée, plus ouvertement contractuelle, comme relevant d'une pragmatique consciente et organisée" ("I see the relation between the text and its reader as more socialized, more openly contractual, as resulting from a conscious and organized practice") (*Palimpsestes* 16).[16] Genette's notion of the "contract" further implies that the reader need only know the categories and subcategories of the "architext," or the hierarchy of genres that organizes the field of literature and constitutes the fifth type of transtextuality, in order to achieve a full understanding of a text and its intertexts.

In view of the work done by Bakhtin, Barthes, and Kristeva on the ideological or cultural investment of literary structures that is brought to light by their very intertextuality, Genette's approach may seem overly formalistic and even superficial. In fact, however,

Genette does pay attention to the role of the reader and cultural constraints while clarifying some essential differences in the types of textual relations possible in literature. His second major category of transtextuality, or the "paratext" ("*paratexte*"), reminds us of the importance of the numerous classificatory indices that normally accompany a literary text. For example, the preface, epigraph, illustrations, and jacket cover of a novel constitute the pragmatic dimension of the contract between text and reader. The suppressed subtitles of Joyce's *Ulysses* which refer to Homer's *Odyssey* have decisively affected the critical response to that book.[17] Genette's third major category of transtextuality highlights another area that needs more study: "metatextuality" ("*métatextualité*"), or "la relation . . . de 'commentaire,' qui unit un texte à un autre texte dont il parle, sans nécessairement le citer" ("the relation of 'commentary,' which unites one text to another text about which the former speaks, without necessarily citing it") (*Palimpsestes* 10).[18] In this sense, the present essay is a complex instance of metatextuality since it quotes, paraphrases, and comments on twelve major theories of intertextuality. The interplay among titles of critical books is a common but very complex example of metatextuality which could lead to a study of the politics of interpretation.

The fourth category of transtextuality, or "hypertextuality" ("*hypertextualité*"), provides the focus for the rest of *Palimpsestes*.[19] The definition of hypertextuality, however, is laden with methodological pitfalls: "Toute relation unissant un texte B (que j'appellerai *hypertexte*) à un texte antérieur A (que j'appellerai, bien sûr, *hypotexte*) sur lequel il se greffe d'une manière qui n'est pas celle du commentaire" ["Any relation uniting text B (which I will call the *hypertext*) to an anterior text A (which I will call, of course, the *hypotext*) on which it is grafted in a way that is distinct from that of commentary"] (*Palimpsestes* 11–12). Unless one is willing to ignore the ideological dimension of discourse, the difference between structural hypertext and critical metatext will be hard to maintain. Is it adequate to observe, as Genette does, that *Ulysses* is a "simple" or "direct" "*transformation*" of the *Odyssey*, while the *Aeneid* is a "complex" or "indirect" transformation of the same hypotext? Surely, *Ulysses* is more than a "transposition" of the action of the *Odyssey* into modern Dublin; surely, the *Aeneid* does more with Homer's generic model for epic than simply fill it with new Roman contents. Likewise, the categorical distinction between hypertextuality, or formal and thematic relations between entire texts, and intertextuality, or local borrowings, does not hold in most cases. Take, for example, the literary parody—say, Tom Stoppard's *Rosencrantz and Guildenstern Are Dead* in relation to Shakespeare's *Hamlet*—in which text *B* quotes text *A* (intertextuality), criticizes text *A*'s theses (metatextuality), and borrows text *A*'s generic structure (hypertextuality). Can our interpretation of an intertextual allusion be separated from our understanding of the shared model for tragedy, or from the modern play's critique of the Renaissance play?

Ironically, Genette's project of clearing up the terminological jungle which has grown up around intertextuality produces a new thicket of theoretical coinages whose overlappings serve only to further obfuscate the reader's path toward literature.[20] Perhaps most damning of all is the fact that Genette's definition of hypertextuality, despite its structuralist cast, is almost identical to the traditional focus of influence and source studies—any relation between a posterior text *B* and an anterior text *A*. Genette's critical metaphor for hypertextuality, or the "grafting" of one text onto another, implies an organic model that belongs to historicism rather than to semiotics. His idea of the "derivation" of a new text from an old text hardly advances the old debate over the verification of sources and the reconstruction of the author's intention in using one text instead of another for his central inspiration. Genette is peripherally aware of these difficulties, as his scattered remarks about "pragmatics" suggest, but his commitment in *Palimpsestes* lies elsewhere—to the poetics of textuality and the universals of discourse.

It is instructive to compare Genette's model for hypertextual reading and Riffaterre's model for intertextual reading, for they represent the two major directions of literary semiotics: the formulation and classification of universals, and the interpretation of the various operations of signs within their cultural contexts. Both theorists work with a semiotic triangle which hypothetically reflects the relation between texts and the labor performed by the reader who discovers that relation:

Although Riffaterre and Genette agree that the reader must form a structural model according to which he or she can understand the text or hypertext in terms of the intertext or hypotext, the contents of that model are quite different. Riffaterre's reader guesses at the intertextual matrix in a poem by deploying semantic paradigms available in the ordinary language (descriptive systems and clichés) as well as knowledge of literary conventions and genres.

Genette's reader infers from all the literary performances he or she has encountered the generic model that governs the relation between hypotext and hypertext: apparently, neither the idiolect of the hypertext (Riffaterre's ungrammaticalities) nor the cultural information carried by hypotext or hypertext plays a decisive role in the reader's construction of this generic model. Another crucial difference between the two theories lies in the nature of the mediating text or corpus of texts at the top of the semiotic triangle. For Riffaterre, the intertextual interpretant is always quite specific and does not have to belong to the same genre as either the text or the primary intertext. For example, Baudelaire's poems bridge Pascal's maxims and Lautréamont's parody. For Genette, the generic model is a universal structure, "capable d'engendrer un nombre indéfini de performances mimétiques" ("capable of generating an indeterminate number of mimetic performances"), which requires that both hypotext and hypertext be of the same genre (*Palimpsestes* 13). As a result, Genette's triangle limits textual relations to one kind: that between hypotext and its genre, and that between hypertext and the same genre—or, the classical genus–species relationship. In contrast, Riffaterre's triangle allows for a threefold exchange: that between text and intertextual interpretant; that between intertextual interpretant and primary intertext; and that between primary intertext and text.

Oddly enough, Genette and Riffaterre arrive by divergent routes at the same conclusion that the intertext (hypotext) need not actually be discovered in order to achieve full understanding of the text (hypertext) in question. While Riffaterre argues from the semantic matrix, Genette argues from the generic matrix that recourse to history and biography is, theoretically, no longer necessary or desirable. Once semiotics has freed the text from time and place and personalities, however, the abyss of undecidability opens even wider. Indeed, at several points in *Palimpsestes*, Genette flirts with the fashionable deconstructionist view, remarking that any interpretative choice in this world of multitextual relations becomes a "simple affaire d'ingéniosité critique" ("simple affair of critical ingenuity"), or a subjective reading (*Palimpsestes* 16). Such asides sit uneasily with Genette's fundamental assumption of the validity of the structuralist project of locating literary universals. Much more characteristic is Genette's conclusion about the scientific value of his taxonomy: "Le rapport hypertextuel serait fixé, et donc neutralisé, et chacun pourrait . . . mesurer la distance et définir la transformation" ("Every hypertextual relation will be fixed, and thus neutralized, and everyone will be able . . . to measure the distance and define the transformation") (*Palimpsestes* 435). Certainly, Bakhtin would dispute Genette's cavalier assumption that the language and ideology of a text, especially one "dialogized" by other texts, can be "neutralized" merely by lifting out its generic structure. For her part, Kristeva would comment on the fallacy of fixing textual relations in light of the sociopolitico-historical processes that "work" the "materiality" of the text.

Most importantly, the conflict between formalism and pragmatics that marks Genette's work, as well as his quarrel with Riffaterre, typifies the great divide within literary semiotics at the present time. Alluding to Lévi-Strauss's concept of intertextuality in myth, or *bricolage*," Genette closes his book with a telling metaphor for hypertextuality—the *palimpseste*. Each literary or aesthetic text produces a palimpsest, superimposing several other texts which are never completely hidden, but always hinted at: "palimpseste, où l'on voit, sur le même parchemin, un texte se superposer à un autre qu'il ne dissimule pas tout à fait, mais qu'il laisse voir par transparence" ("[a] palimpsest, in which one sees, on the same parchment, the superimposition of one text onto another which the parchment does not completely hide, but permits us to glimpse through its transparency") (*Palimpsestes* 451). Like *bricolage* which both conserves and changes the mythology of a culture, the literary palimpsest hovers between originality and imitation. The idea that the other texts can be seen transparently through the centering text is highly dubious, though. Genette's interest in establishing a taxonomy causes him to stress imitation over innovation in a way that recalls Brower's somewhat simplistic use of quotations from Horace to show what Pope borrowed from the classics. More probably, the literary text carries out a polemical transformation (Kristeva) or at least a dialogue (Bakhtin) with the other texts that it notices, never fully assimilating or controlling their language or their ideology. Thus, like *bricolage* and the invisible "matrix" of the text, the "palimpsest" is another heuristic metaphor that reveals the paradox of structuralism and semiotics—theories of signification that invite an infinite play of relationships among texts, but only if the players stay within a binary or triadic system.

Intertextual Knowledge

In the introduction to volumes 5 and 6 of *A History of Modern Criticism*, René Wellek comes to the "resigned conclusion" that an "evolutionary history of criticism must fail" (*xxii*). Without relinquishing the right to "adjudicate the merits of different ideas" or establish a canon of criticism, and without falling into the trap of "complete relativism" to which historicism may lead, Wellek calls for a new "way of thinking of an internal history of criticism" (xx–xxi). In a strong sense, intertextuality as practiced by structuralists and semioticians offers an answer to the anxieties of influence and the need for a central tradition among what remains the majority of Anglo-American scholar-critics today. For, despite its formal apparatus of linguistic models and terminology, intertextuality is finally a conservative theory and practice. Like the methodology of source, influence, and biography which it replaces, the location of intertexts, intratexts, and autotexts takes place within a circumscribed field of literature that overlaps significantly with the canon or tradition proposed by early modern critics such as Matthew Arnold and T. S. Eliot. In effect, the "best that is known and thought in the world" is redefined as that set of text(s) on which the greatest number of intertexts converge. Thus, Genette ends up privileging Homer's *Odyssey* as the ur-hypotext to which the largest set of hypertexts from Virgil's *Aeneid* to Joyce's *Ulysses* can be related. Likewise, Kristeva's avant-garde authors ironically preserve the very bourgeois and Christian humanist establishment that they claim to reject by transforming and parodying, hence acknowledging the power of classics like Pascal's *Pensées* and the Bible in their writings. Perhaps the comparison between the "savage *bricoleur*" and the modern intertextualist is not so far off the ideological mark as we would like to think. If a leading theoretician such as Riffaterre can argue that its multiple interrelations with other texts, or "overdetermination," reveals the "exemplariness" and the "monumentality" of the literary text (*Semiotics of Poetry* 21), then no dire threat seems to be posed to the evaluative hierarchy of literature previously known under the labels of "tradition" or "classic."

Although he pointedly omits mention of Michel Foucault, Wellek challenges the recent theory of epistemic breaks as inadequate to explaining how literary critical history works: "There are no such complete revolutions in the history of criticism as Kuhn stipulates for the history of science" (*xxiii*). If several overlaps between influence and intertextuality can be found, it is nonetheless a fact of academic experience in America that intertextuality has changed both the practice of literature and the practice of literary criticism. In what sense, for instance, can the critic claim to "know" literature, literary history, or even one text if our thinking takes place within a constantly changing network of intertexts, past, present, and future? In *The Archaeology of Knowledge* (1974), Foucault addresses some of the epistemological issues that have emerged from the tension between the historical and the structural-semiotic models of textuality.[21] History and its disciplinary double, literary history, propose to give a permanent and therefore meaningful place to the texts produced by society. By insertion into a chronological order, itself motivated by the preference for certain ideological representations, certain historical texts or "documents" are transformed into "monuments," just as certain literary texts become "classics." However, Foucault argues, we have reified the central hypotheses of historicism since their construction in the nineteenth century, treating "period," "source," and "influence" as if they were facts and even universal truths instead of specific organizations of knowledge bound to certain socioeconomic and intellectual "conditions of possibility." Instead, Foucault proposes that we treat the concepts and terms of historicism as temporary "strategies" which attempt to master the "discontinuity" of actual time by organizing the otherwise random production and reception of literary texts according to the by-now familiar criteria.

Foucault recognizes, as does Derrida, that we cannot simply reject or forget the historical paradigm. Nonetheless, he urges critical theorists today to place its inherited concepts and methods under rigorous question, continuing to use them but, as it were, "under erasure." This critical practice, Foucault hopes, will permit us to "rethink" or rediscover the discontinuities of discursive events which have been previously "thought" in terms of "books" and, more recently, "texts." In effect, Foucault is calling for nothing less than a reorganization of knowledge. By observing the gap between the material unity of the book or the formal unit of the text, on the one hand, and their unpredictable "dispersion" across the dynamic space of "interdiscursivity," or the daily reading and (re-)writing of discourses, on the other, we approach the border of contemporary knowledge. On the margins of structuralism and semiotics—here taken as paradigms for modern knowledge about literature and language—the unitary text/book dissolves into its own intertextuality (witness the virtual disappearance of "the" text in Genette's taxonomy), just as the author and the reader take turns in a seemingly endless alterity utterly foreign to the subject–object relations of Cartesian subjectivity (as, for example, in Lacanian readings of the intertextual/intersexual itineraries of desire represented in literature).[22] From this angle, intertextuality presents itself not as a closed system of binary and triadic sign relations, but as an opening—not to say a "rupture"—toward a new epistemology whose terms we ourselves, still at least partially enclosed in the modern episteme, cannot quite "think," except to call its new space the "post-modern."[23]

The postmodern organization of knowledge both overlaps with and exceeds the recognition of the necessary interconnectedness of all discourse, or intertextuality. Intertextual knowledge "is limited, diagonal, partial" because "when he (man) attempts to define his essence as a speaking subject . . . all he ever finds" is "the already-begun of labour, life, and language" (Foucault, *The Order of Things* 330–31). Foucault's idea of the "always already" of our knowledge resonates with Bakhtin's emphasis on the fundamental interdiscursivity of the human world—"there exists an elastic environment of other, alien words about the same object"—and with Derrida's deconstruction of originary subjectivity and signification: "Il n'y a pas d'hors texte" ("There is no such thing as speaking or writing outside other texts"). The positioning of intertextuality on the border between modern and postmodern knowledge might help to account for the odd combination of ease and anxiety with which critical theorists today are rethinking literature and literary history in terms of space instead of time, conditions of possibility instead of permanent structures, and "networks" or "webs" instead of chronological lines or influence. From the point of view of a Foucauldian "archaeology," then, what seems to be disorganization and crisis in the knowledge and practice of literature and literary criticism may be rethought as a new "positivity" or a (re)construction through deconstruction of what we know and how we know it.

Notes

1. The best example of the debate over intentionality and the autonomy of the text remains W. K. Wimsatt and Monroe Beardsley, "The Intentional Fallacy," in *The Verbal Icon* 3–18.

2. The reader may wish to compare Bloom's definition of the final revisionary phase, or *aprophrades*, and Eliot's statement on the relationship of the poet to tradition:

> We shall often find that not only the best, but the most individual parts of his [a poet's] work may be those in which the dead poets, his ancestors, assert their immortality most vigorously. (48)

> I mean . . . the triumph of having so stationed the precursor in one's own work, that particular passages in *his* work seem not to be presages of one's own advent, but rather to be indebted to one's own achievement." (48)

3. For a solid introduction to basic concepts in semiotics, see Culler, *Structuralist Poetics* and *The Pursuit of Signs*, and Hawkes.

4. Lotman's definition of the artistic text as a secondary modelling system parallels Roland Barthes' discussion of cultural texts in *Elements of Semiology*; Barthes, in turn, credits Louis Hjelmslev.

5. For a thorough consideration of the place of intertextuality in Bakhtin's "philosophical anthropology," see Todorov, especially chapter 5.

6. The notions of the "supplement" and the "trace" are logical extensions of the gap in signification left by the *"différence"/"différance"* in the sign itself. See, for example, Derrida's development of the supplement and the trace in part 2 of *Of Grammatology* in regard to the debate over nature versus culture (101–316).

7. Since the standard English edition does not give the whole text of *Mythologies*, the translation here is my own.

8. The allusive title and reversible order of the seven sections of *S/Z* put into practice Barthes' theory of intertextuality as a "rewriting" (*"re-écriture"*) of previous texts gathered from various areas of cultural discourse by both the author and the reader. The self-conscious *auto*textuality of *S/Z* is also remarkable: notice how Barthes' theory generates the series of "annexes" and the deliberately misplaced epigraph to Bataille at the end of the book.

9. For a discussion of inter-, intra-, and autotextuality, see Dällenbach, and also Plottel and Charney.

10. The translations from *Séméiotiké* are mine. Pages are cited for the French text.

11. For an excellent overview of the various definitions of "text," see Todorov and Ducrot 356–61, 294–96.

12. Since the English version of *La Révolution du langage poétique* renders only part of the French text, translations here are my own. Pages are cited for the French text.

13. The translations of Riffaterre, "Sémiotique intertextuelle" and Riffaterre, "La Trace" are mine. Several other essays on intertextuality can be found in Riffaterre, *La Production du texte*, translated as *Text Production*.

14. For a semiotic approach to intertextuality that incorporates the historical dimension, see Jenny, and also Zumthor.

15. All translations from Genette's *Palimpsestes* are mine. Pages are cited for the French text.

16. Genette seems to have borrowed the concept of the social or cultural contract between reader and text from *Receptionsaesthetik*.

17. Genette does not acknowledge Riffaterre's extensive remarks about the intertextual function of titles in *Semiotics of Poetry* (see 99–109).

18. For a discussion of critical intertextuality or "metatextuality" in Butor, Barthes, and Blanchot, see Perrone-Moisés.

19. For other classifications of intertextuality, see Ben-Porat; Zumthor; Perri; and Sternberg.

20. Hutcheon offers some insightful remarks on the "contemporary

critical muddle regarding the *status* and, more significantly, the *locus* of textual appropriation," noting the displacement of subjectivity from author to reader, influence to intertext, in Barthes, Kristeva, and Riffaterre (230).

21. Although Foucault's discussion of historicism and structuralism throughout *The Archaeology of Knowledge* is pertinent to a consideration of the position of intertextuality within contemporary critical discourse, the concepts and terms referred to here can be found especially in ch. 2, sect. 1; ch. 3, sect. 4; and ch. 4, sect. 2.

22. Work remains to be done on the connections among and the epistemic conditions for "intertextuality" (Kristeva), "interdiscursivity" (Foucault), and "intersubjectivity" (Lacan). A prime example of the crisscrossing of the intersubjectivity of desire and the intertextuality of writing and reading is Lacan's analysis of Edgar Allan Poe's story in "Seminar on 'The Purloined Letter.'"

23. My use of the term "modern" does not exactly coincide with Foucault's definition of modernity in *The Order of Things*. There, he identifies the modern episteme with historicism and with structuralism, since both paradigms focus on "Man" as a "strange empirico-transcendental doublet" who is both the ground and the goal of knowledge as organized by anthropology, linguistics, and psychoanalysis—notably the three social sciences which have transformed the discourse of contemporary literary theory most powerfully (318). It seems to me, however, that Foucault, in emphasizing the role of "the unthought" and "the end of man" implicit in the literature and human sciences characteristic of the modern episteme, is suggesting the formation of another episteme altogether—the "post-modern." See chapters 9 and 10 in *The Order of Things* for Foucault's discussion of modernity and its fate: "In our day, the fact that philosophy is still . . . coming to an end, and the fact that in it perhaps, though even more *outside and against* it, in literature as well as in formal reflection, the question of language is being posed, prove no doubt that man is in the process of disappearing" (385; emphasis added).

Works Cited

Works are cited in text by date of publication in the original language. Page numbers refer to the standard English translation, unless otherwise noted.

Bakhtin, Mikhail. *Voprosy literatury i estetiki*. Moscow, 1975. Translated by Caryl Emerson and Michael Holquist under the title *The Dialogic Imagination: Four Essays*. Austin: University of Texas Press, 1981.

———. *Problemy poetiki Dostoevskogo*. 2d rev. ed. Moscow, 1963. Translated by R. W. Rotsel under the title *Problems of Dostoevsky's Poetics*. Ann Arbor, Mich.: Ardis, 1973.

———. *Tvorcestva Fransua Rable i narodnaja kul'tura srednevekov'ja i Renes-*

sansa. Moscow, 1965. Translated by Helene Iswolsky under the title *Rabelais and His World.* Cambridge, Mass.: M.I.T. Press, 1968.

Barthes, Roland. *Eléménts de sémiologie.* Paris: Seuil, 1964. Translated by Annette Lavers and Colin Smith under the title *Elements of Semiology.* New York: Hill & Wang, 1967.

———. *Mythologies.* Paris: Seuil, 1957. Translated by Annette Lavers under the title *Mythologies.* New York: Hill & Wang, 1972.

———. *S/Z.* Paris: Seuil, 1970. Translated by Richard Miller under the title *S/Z.* New York: Hill & Wang, 1974.

———. *Roland Barthes par Roland Barthes.* Paris: Seuil, 1975. Translated by Richard Howard under the title *Roland Barthes by Roland Barthes.* New York: Hill & Wang, 1977.

Ben-Porat, Ziva. "The Poetics of Literary Allusion." *PTL: A Journal for Descriptive Poetics and Theory of Literature* 1, no. 1 (1976): 105–28.

Black, Max. *Models and Metaphors: Studies in Language and Philosophy.* Ithaca: Cornell University Press, 1962.

Bloom, Harold. *The Anxiety of Influence: A Theory of Poetry.* New York: Oxford University Press, 1973.

Brower, Reuben A. *Alexander Pope: The Poetry of Allusion.* Oxford: Clarendon Press, 1959.

Culler, Jonathan. *Structuralist Poetics: Structuralism, Linguistics, and the Study of Literature.* Ithaca, N.Y.: Cornell University Press, 1975.

———. *The Pursuit of Signs: Semiotics, Literature, Deconstruction.* Ithaca, N.Y.: Cornell University Press, 1981.

Dällenbach, Lucien. "Intertexte et autotexte." *Poétique* 27 (1976): 282–96.

Derrida, Jacques. *De la grammatologie.* Paris: Minuit, 1967. Translated by Gayatri C. Spivak under the title *Of Grammatology.* Baltimore: Johns Hopkins University Press, 1976.

———. "Structure, Sign and Play in the Discourse of the Human Sciences." In *Writing and Difference,* translated by Alan Bass, 278–93. Chicago: University of Chicago Press, 1978.

———. *Positions.* Paris: Minuit, 1972. Translated by Alan Bass under the title *Positions.* Chicago: University of Chicago Press, 1981.

Eliot, T. S. "Tradition and the Individual Talent." In *The Sacred Wood: Essays on Poetry and Criticism,* 47–59. London: Methuen, 1920.

Foucault, Michel. *Les Mots et les choses.* Paris: Gallimard, 1966. Translated under the title *The Order of Things: An Archaeology of the Human Sciences.* New York: Random House, 1970.

———. *L'Archéolgie du savoir.* Paris: Gallimard, 1969. Translated by A. M. Sheridan Smith under the title *The Archaeology of Knowledge.* London: Tavistock, 1974.

Frye, Northrop. *Anatomy of Criticism.* Princeton: Princeton University Press, 1957.

Genette, Gérard. *Introduction à l'architexte.* Paris: Seuil, 1979.

———. *Palimpsestes: La littérature au second degré.* Paris: Seuil, 1982.

Greimas, A. J., and J. Courtes. *Sémiotique: Dictionnaire raisonné de la théorie du langage.* Paris: Hachette, 1979. Translated by Larry Crist, Daniel

Patte, et al. under the title *Semiotics and Language: An Analytical Dictionary*. Bloomington: Indiana University Press, 1982.

Hawkes, Terence. *Structuralism and Semiotics*. Berkeley and Los Angeles: University of California Press, 1977.

Hutcheon, Linda. "Literary Borrowing . . . and Stealing: Plagiarism, Sources, Influences, and Intertexts." *English Studies in Canada* 12, no. 2 (1986): 229–39.

Jakobson, Roman. "Closing Statement: Linguistics and Poetics." In *Style in Language*, edited by Thomas A. Sebeok, 350–377. Cambridge, Mass.: M.I.T. Press, 1960.

———. "Poetry of Grammar and Grammar of Poetry." *Lingua* 21 (1968): 597–609.

Jenny, Laurent. "La Stratégie de la forme." *Poétique* 27 (1976): 257–81.

Kristeva, Julia. *Séméiotiké: Recherches pour une sémanalyse*. Paris: Seuil, 1969.

———. *La Révolution du langage poétique: L'Avant-garde à la fin du XIXe Siècle: Lautréamont et Mallarmé*. Paris: Seuil, 1974. Translated by Margaret Waller under the title *Revolution in Poetic Language*. New York: Columbia University Press, 1984.

Lacan, Jacques. "Le Séminaire sur 'La Lettre voleé.'" In *Écrits*, 11–61. Paris: Seuil, 1966. Translated by Jeffrey Mehlman under the title "Seminar on 'The Purloined Letter.'" *Yale French Studies* 48 (1972): 39–72.

Lévi-Strauss, Claude. *La Pensée sauvage*. Paris: Plon, 1962. Translated under the title *The Savage Mind*. Chicago: University of Chicago Press, 1966.

———. *Le Cru et le cuit*. Paris: Plon, 1964. Translated by John and Doreen Weightman under the title *The Raw and the Cooked: Introduction to a Science of Mythology*. New York: Harper & Row, 1970.

———. *Tristes tropiques*. Paris: Plon, 1955. Translated by John and Doreen Weightman under the title *Tristes Tropiques*. New York: Atheneum, 1978.

Lotman, Juri. *Analiz poétícheskogo teksta: Struktura stikha*. London, 1972. Translated by D. Barton Johnson under the title *Analysis of the Poetic Text*. Ann Arbor, Mich.: Ardis, 1976.

———. *Struktura khudozhestvennogo teksta*. Providence, R.I.: Brown University Press, 1971. Translated by Gail Lenhoff and Ronald Vroon under the title *The Structure of the Artistic Text*. Ann Arbor: University of Michigan Press, 1977.

Perri, Carmela. "On Alluding." *Poetics* 7, no. 3 (1978): 289–307.

Perrone-Moisés, Leyla. "L'Intertextualité critique." *Poétique* 27 (1976): 372–84.

Plottel, Jeanine P., and Hanna Charney, eds. *Intertextuality: New Perspectives in Criticism*. New York: New York Literary Forum, 1978.

Riffaterre, Michael. *Semiotics of Poetry*. Bloomington: Indiana University Press, 1978.

———. "Sémiotique intertextuelle: L'Interprétant." In *Rhétoriques, sémiotiques*. Paris: Union Générale, 1979.

———. "La Syllepse intertextuelle." *Poétique* 40 (1979): 496–501.

———. "La Trace de l'intertexte." *La Pensée* 215 (1980): 4–18.

————. "Interpretation and Undecidability." *New Literary History* 12, no. 2 (1981): 227–42.

————. "Hermeneutic Models." *Poetics Today* 4, no. 1 (1983): 7–16.

————. *La Production du texte*. Paris: Seuil, 1979. Translated by Térèse Lyons under the title *Text Production*. New York: Columbia University Press, 1983.

Saussure, Ferdinand de. *Cours de linguistique générale*. Edited by Charles Bally, Albert Sechehaye, and Albert Riedlinger. Geneva, 1915. Translated by Wade Baskin under the title *Course in General Linguistics*. New York: McGraw-Hill, 1966.

Sternberg, Meir. "Proteus in Quotation-Land: Mimesis and the Forms of Reported Discourse." *Poetics Today* 3, no. 2 (1982): 107–56.

Stewart, Susan. *Nonsense: Aspects of Intertextuality in Folklore and Literature*. Baltimore: Johns Hopkins University Press, 1978.

Suleiman, Susan R., and Inge Crosman, eds. *The Reader in the Text: Essays on Audience and Interpretation*. Princeton: Princeton University Press, 1980.

Todorov, Tzvetan. *Mikhail Bakhtine: le principe dialogique*. Paris: Seuil, 1981. Translated by Wlad Godzich under the title *Mikhail Bakhtin: The Dialogical Principle*. Theory and History of Literature, vol. 13. Minneapolis: University of Minnesota Press, 1984.

Todorov, Tzvetan, and Oswald Ducrot. *Dictionnaire encyclopédique des sciences du langage*. Paris: Seuil, 1972. Translated by Catherine Porter under the title. *Encyclopedic Dictionary of the Sciences of Language*. Baltimore: Johns Hopkins University Press, 1979.

Wellek, René. *A History of Modern Criticism, 1750–1950*. Vol. 5. New Haven: Yale University Press, 1986.

Wellek, René, and Austin Warren. *Theory of Literature*. Rev. ed. New York: Harcourt, Brace, 1956.

Wimsatt, W. K., and Monroe Beardsley. "The Intentional Fallacy." In *The Verbal Icon: Studies in the Meaning of Poetry*, 3–18. Lexington: University Press of Kentucky, 1954.

Zumthor, Paul. "Le Carrefour des rhétoriqueurs: Intertextualité et rhétorique." *Poétique* 27 (1976): 317–37.

An Interview with Julia Kristeva

===

MARGARET WALLER

(translated by Richard Macksey)

The following interview took place in New York City in 1985. In these remarks, Kristeva traces the history of the concept of inter-textuality, discusses its importance in modern writing, and talks about America, her psychoanalytic practice, and her own writing. Her work on melancholy has since been published as *Le Soleil noir: Dépression et mélancolie* (Paris: Gallimard, 1987) and has been translated as *Black Sun: Depression and Melancholia* by Leon S. Roudiez (New York: Columbia University Press, 1989).—M. W.

Margaret Waller. How do you conceive of intertextuality? What are its formal and intrapsychic aspects? How do you distinguish it from Bakhtin's dialogism?

Julia Kristeva. One should perhaps emphasize the history of this concept, which has come to have rather wide currency, I think. Many investigators are using it to deal with important rhetorical and ideological phenomena in modern literature and in classical literature as well. I have a certain idea of the concept. At the beginning of my research, when I was writing a commentary on Bakhtin, I had the feeling that with his notions of dialogism and carnival we had reached an important point in moving beyond structuralism. French literary criticism at that time was especially fascinated by Russian formalism, but a formalism that limited itself to transposing notions proper to linguistics and applying them to the analysis of narrative.

Personally, I had found Bakhtin's work very exciting, particularly his studies of Rabelais and Dostoevsky. He was moving toward a dynamic understanding of the literary text that considered every utterance as the result of the intersection within it of a number of voices, as he called them. I discussed my reading with Roland Barthes, who was quite fascinated and invited me to his seminar—it was 1966, I think, and the seminar was held at 44 rue de Rennes—to make a presentation on Bakhtin. I think that my interpretation remains, on the one hand, faithful to his ideas, and demonstrates, on the other, my attempts to elaborate and enlarge upon them. Whence the concept of intertextuality, which does not figure as such in the work of Bakhtin, but which, it seemed to me, one could deduce from his work.

All of this is by way of showing you, with as much intellectual honesty as possible, the source of the concept of intertextuality, while at the same time underscoring the difference between this concept and that of, for example, dialogism. I see the following differences. In the first place, there is the recognition that a textual segment, sentence, utterance, or paragraph, is not simply the intersection of two voices in direct or indirect discourse; rather, the segment is the result of the intersection of a number of voices, of a number of textual interventions, which are combined in the semantic field, but also in the syntactic and phonic fields of the explicit utterance. So there is the idea of this plurality of phonic, syntactic and semantic participation. I think that what is new with regard to Bakhtin, is seeing this intervention of external plurality at different levels—not only at the level of meaning but at the level of syntax and phonetics, too. What interested me even more—and this seems to me unique—was the notion that the participation of different texts at different levels reveals a particular mental activity. And analysis should not limit itself simply to identifying texts that participate in the final texts, nor to identifying their sources, but should understand that what is being dealt with is a specific dynamics of the subject of the utterance, who consequently, precisely because of this intertextuality, is not an individual in the etymological sense of the term, not an identity.

In other words, the discovery of intertextuality at a formal level leads us to an intrapsychic or psychoanalytic finding, if you will, concerning the status of the "creator," the one who produces a text by placing himself or herself at the intersection of this plurality of texts on their very different levels—I repeat, semantic, syntactic, or phonic. This leads me to understand creative subjectivity as a kaleidoscope, a "polyphony" as Bakhtin calls it. I myself speak of a "subject in process," which makes possible my attempt to articulate as precise a logic as possible between identity or unity, the challenge to this identity and even its reduction to zero, the moment of crisis, of emptiness, and then the reconstitution of a new, plural identity. This new identity may be the plurality capable of manifesting itself as the plurality of characters the author uses, but, in more recent writing, in the twentieth-century novel, it may appear as fragments of character, or fragments of ideology, or fragments of representation.

Moreover, such an understanding of intertextuality—as indicating a dynamics involving destruction of the creative identity and reconstitution of a new plurality—assumes at the same time that the one who reads, the reader, participates in the same dynamics. If we are readers of intertextuality, we must be capable of the same putting-into-process of our identities, capable of identifying with the different types of texts, voices, semantic, syntactic, and phonic systems at play in a given text. We, too, must be capable of being reduced to zero, to the state of crisis that is perhaps the necessary precondition of aesthetic pleasure, to the point of speechlessness as Freud says, of the loss of meaning, before we can enter into a process of free association, reconstitution of diverse meanings, or kinds of connotations that are almost undefinable—a process that is a *re*-creation of the poetic text. I think, then, that this kind of writing, whose formal aspects I try to stress along with its intrapsychic aspects—and I think we must never discuss the one without the other—can only be accounted for by a reader who enjoys the complexity of the text and who places himself or herself on both levels at once.

This logic and dynamics, which may also be applied to classical texts, seem to me to be absolutely necessary for modern texts. This is true for poetic texts, which are characterized by great condensation, great polysemia: as examples I can cite the writings of Nerval or Mallarmé in particular. It is also true for the modern novel. The texts of Joyce are a very special example of this type. It is impossible to read *Finnegans Wake* without entering into the intrapsychic logic and dynamics of intertextuality. But it is true, too, for postmodernism, where the problem is to reconcile representation, the imposition of content, with the play of form—which is, I emphasize again, a play of psychic pluralization. And here, in postmodernism, the question of intertextuality is perhaps even more important in certain ways, because it assumes an interplay of contents and not of forms alone. If one reads Faulkner without going back to the Bible, to the Old Testament, to the Gospels, to American society of the period and to his own hallucinatory experience, I believe one cannot reconstitute the complexity of the text itself. This is valid for more recent literature as well. Once again, this question of content is not to be understood as being about a single content—"What does this mean in this sentence?"—but as a content that may be dispersed, traceable to different points of origin; the final meaning of this content will be neither the original source nor any one of the possible meanings taken on in the text, but will be, rather, a continuous movement back and forth in the space between the origin and all of the possible connotative meanings.

M. W. Given the applicability of the concept of intertextuality to modern texts that call into question the very concept of genre, would you agree with Bakhtin that the novel is the type par excellence of this polyphony?

J. K. Yes, I do agree, but provided we understand that ever since the rise of the novel in the West we have had an interminable novel, and the word becomes the generic term for a drastically expanded experience of writing. The term *roman* can now be applied to poetic writing incorporating a narrative element. It can also be applied to *récits* of a journalistic type that integrate the possibility of narrative, provided the category be expanded. It can be applied as well to the intermingling of autobiographical elements with essays and theoretical texts. These are all *romans*—as long as we understand "novel" as an intersection of genres and as a generalized form of intertextuality. If one identifies the novel with intertextuality, then every contemporary type of writing participates in it.

M. W. Even if it is poetry? Even if it incorporates . . .

J. K. Poetic elements, yes. Obviously if you are dealing with writing that is very fragmentary, very elliptical, as certain modern poetry is, then it is difficult to talk about novelistic elements. I will use the term *novel* when the narrative moment is really present, which is not the case with certain poetic texts that are quite chopped up. To these texts, then, we will not apply the word *roman*, but the question of intertextuality persists.

So, the concept of intertextuality encompasses both novel and poetry, even if the novelistic element can be taken today in a very broad sense. Intertextuality is perhaps the most global concept possible for signifying the modern experience of writing, including the classic genres, poetic and novelistic. And to the extent that these genres, in the classic sense of the term, are unrecognizable in the modern novel, perhaps we will be, as it were, freed from our obsessive appeal to genre if we accept the terms of intertextuality in characterizing the experience of writing.

M. W. Yes, but if I understand your global definition of intertextuality and of the novel's importance to it, then what is important is the *narrative* element, the *récit* element, even if it is fragmented, dispersed . . .

J. K. That defines the novel.

M. W. Yes, that's it.

J. K. Precisely. And I think it's an interesting distinction to maintain, at least in what concerns me, from the point of view of psychic activity. It is true that I see intertextuality as being just as applicable to modern poetic writing as to modern novelistic writing. But perhaps within this broadened concept of intertextuality, which concerns all contemporary writing, one can maintain a distinction between poetic and novelistic experience. For me, this distinction is interesting because it indicates different levels of psychic unity, and, in a certain way, some of the writer's possible defenses with regard to the crises that writing assumes. In the narrative experience the subject has access to more options for working things out with respect to moments of crisis, hallucination, loss, and risk of psychosis. The poetic experience is more openly regressive, if you will; it confronts more directly the moments of loss of meaning and perhaps, also, the maternal, the feminine, which obviously represents the solicitations of sexual pleasure and gratification and, at the same time, risk and loss of the self.

We can see this clearly in Nerval, to take a writer from whom we have some distance. When he writes a poem, which is very often a struggle against schizophrenic collapse or the threat of melancholia—"El Desdichado," for example, the Black Prince, "the black Sun of Melancholy"—the symbols mean a number of things one can inventory by using dictionaries of esoterica, but that's not the point. The essential point is precisely the polyvalence of the symbols, and the fact that we can add other connotations that perhaps even Nerval didn't recognize. If one also takes into account musicality, rhythmicity, alliteration, etc., this type of writing is obviously a temptation to go down as far as possible toward the semiotic, toward the confrontation of the subject with the object of loss, nostalgia, melancholia—in other words, that maternal form which may be conjured up as a dead mother, an absent mother. And it is an attempt to go down—note that the poet compares himself to Orpheus descending into Hell—an attempt that is totally vulnerable because it assumes the possibility of self-loss, and at the same time, accurate, because the poet pursues the vulnerability of the psychic experience to the very edge of non-meaning.

But what one can see is that when the poet feels he has won out in this regressive quest, he expresses his triumphant emergence with a narrative, or at least with the opening of a narrative. We see this in the first line of the last tercet of the sonnet:

> Et j'ai deux fois vainqueur traversé l'Achéron
> [And I have twice as a conqueror crossed the Acheron]

So Nerval uses an "I," with a verb in the perfect tense that moves us away from the poetic sense of fusion dominated by semiotic processes. He distances himself; he places himself in time. He begins again to tell a story in which, instead of mythical, esoteric, ambivalent, and indiscernible characters, there will appear two aspects of the feminine figure: the sighs of the saint and the cries of the witch—the mental and the carnal, if you will, the sublime and the sexual. It is as though from that point on one is dealing with protagonists in conflict, and beginning to tell a story. But it stops. It's a poem, and the narrative is not continued. Nonetheless, what I want to say is that the moment of triumph and mastery over the experience of conflict is the point at which narrative begins.

And this narrative overture Nerval will use more than once in his work. He will have real problems in writing stories like *Sylvie* and *Aurélia*. These incorporate not just the apparent or staged problems of the picaresque novel, which plays with a narrative that is broken up and rearranged in a radial pattern because this structure is conditioned and motivated by adventure itself, by the idea of adventure. Nor is Nerval's a case of a dismantling of the narrative mode, as in the *nouveau roman* with its attempt to overpower narrative logic. It is simply his inability to keep himself on a temporal line because the massive, archaic past will not go away. This remote past bursts out, breaking and destroying the narrative line. At that point we are seeing a polyphonic, intertextual narrative ruptured and broken by poetry. The phenomenon demonstrates that the subject of utterance is having difficulty keeping himself in the narrative mode. The poem does not turn out like a novel, properly speaking.

I chose this example to show to what extent narrative construction is the result of a "working-out" of the self, but also a defense and consolidation of the self in relation to its experience of crisis. I want to remark, too, upon the fact that in the contemporary world narrative writing, novelistic writing, doubtless takes on significance against a background of religious crisis, where we have no sacred discourses for reckoning with our experiences of crisis and rejoicing. Or else such discourses, when they do exist, are called into question as parts of a past difficult for modern society to accept without extremely problematic regressions. In this context, novelistic writing is an immense and very powerful means of guiding us most deeply into our crises and furthest away from them at the same time—a kind of repeated descent and reemergence such as Orpheus could not achieve, a sort of Orpheus experience, but that of a conquering Orpheus, a possible Orpheus, an Orpheus triumphant.

This is why the modern novel, which incorporates the poetic experience in an intertextual manner, is a tremendous opportunity for the sublimation of our crises and malaises. It is a kind of continuous lay analysis, and often perhaps weaker than psychoanalysis because it may lack the ideational means, the knowledge, the why and how of the psychoanalytic enterprise. But it may often be a more powerful tool than psychoanalysis because at times it presents us with situations that rarely appear in psychoanalytic treatment. Certain writers manage to lead us as deeply as possible into our malaises, where we seldom go except in dreams, and without always bringing back adequate accounts of those dreams.

M. W. I am struck by your definition of literature as a continuous lay analysis. You are currently working on melancholia and the imagination, and Nerval is one of the authors you will treat in this new book. Who will the other authors be? Why those and not others? And why nineteenth-century authors in particular?

J. K. It's a book that comes largely out of a fact observed in psychoanalysis: the high frequency of depression in the contemporary world. This is a very current phenomenon, even if it is unfashionable because we have no ideological or theoretical discourse valorizing depression. It eluded civilizations that enjoyed suffering or depression, and that indulgence was perhaps, sometimes, a way of aggravating the disorder, but also a way of helping people get through such periods. Our society is much more action-oriented, and those who are sad, or terribly boring, who move at a slow pace or do not speak, cannot be objects of fascination. We move them to one side and try to forget them.

There are civilizations, as I've said—the fifteenth century in particular, but also the nineteenth—that have tried to take depression into account after periods of religious crisis as at the end of the Middle Ages, or the end of the rapid rise of the rationalistic bourgeoisie with its belief in the goddess Reason and its crisis of religious values. The goddess Reason was an eighteenth-century idea which the nineteenth century called into question, and there was a subsequent return to the spiritual, the irrational, which signified not only a crisis in formal religion—"God is dead," Nietzsche said—but also a crisis in the belief in reason. So against this background the explosion of depression and melancholia attracted attention, and there was an attempt to find aesthetic forms and discourses to account for it. One can find such things, such rhetorical events, occurring again in modern and contemporary literature. One can take many of Faulkner's texts, for example, as tending in this direction. The American South, specifically the work of Flannery O'Connor, is shot through with depression, but knows it can find a way out. And then there are certain texts of Sartre, *Being and Nothingness* and *Nausea* in particular, that bear traces of attempts to redeem periods of depression. One can find these, too, in the nineteenth century—more direct than the modern examples, perhaps also more naive and, therefore, more striking.

I have tried not to write an encyclopedia of texts concerning and discussing depression. In the first place, I couldn't do it, and then, too, I wanted to reserve part of my book for clinical experience and what I hear coming from the couch. In particular, I have tried to report on certain configurations of female depression, which seems to be a question of current interest. So, amongst those texts or, rather, cultural artifacts, that have dealt with melancholia or presented themselves almost as courses of treatment, I have so far chosen three great works. I think now that I will stop there, but I'm not sure: I may add a fourth. There will be Holbein, the great painter, so sober and restrained, who, between Catholicism and Protestantism, tries to maintain a humanistic line, but precariously so, simultaneously serious and . . . at the limits of the possibility of representation, as though at the limits of artisticity. One wonders how it is possible to write and paint with so much restraint and sadness. I treat his work mainly through his painting, *The Dead Christ*. Then there will be Nerval, "the black Sun of Melancholy," his sonnet "El Desdichado," but also *Aurélia*. And Dostoevsky, insofar as he examines in a very explicit way the relationship of melancholia to religious crisis within the context of a political solution, which is, in fact, a current concern. One may wonder whether the choices of certain modern terrorists are not parallel to the terrorist choices of Dostoevsky's characters—Kirilov, Raskolnikov—whose actions range from suicide to the murder of a stranger and seem to be phenomena recurring in the modern political world. But Dostoevsky makes it possible for me to see them with more distance and, perhaps, with more objectivity. The reader, moreover, is bound to be struck by the similarities to the present day and can no doubt make the connection between terrorism and melancholy himself or herself.

M. W. And this same book will also be about your practice of psychoanalysis, especially female depression?

J. K. Actually, I will try to make depression comprehensible by presenting different types of patients, not all of them women. But I have also written a chapter where I concentrate more on various aspects of female depression.

M. W. I was wondering, because your "authors," so to speak, are men, and I was wondering about this gap . . .

J. K. I'm trying to find a woman author, too, but I'm having a lot of trouble because either I have to choose a very well-known woman author, and in that case the temptation of cliché or repetition is too great, or else . . .

M. W. But couldn't one say the same of Dostoevsky?

J. K. Not so much, perhaps, from the point of view of depression. What has been written about him has dealt more with his religion, his relationship to epilepsy, his polyphony. The presence of and apologia for suffering have been emphasized less; whereas, with women authors, this element, I think, was seen right away. The suffering of Virginia Woolf, or Sylvia Plath, or Charlotte Brontë, has often been discussed. I have wondered, by the way, whether it wouldn't be interesting to suggest, as an example of women writing melancholia or on melancholia, the work of a woman psychoanalyst. But I've not finished yet, so I'm not sure . . .

M. W. We'll wait and see. Can you see something beyond psychoanalysis, or are you so comfortable with it that the question of political commitment, or anything else, doesn't even come up? Is there anything missing, theoretical perhaps, or practical, that bothers you, in the sense that it indicates to you that there is still another stage to get to, not now, but later on?

J. K. You mean, do I feel comfortable or do I . . . You seem to have the impression that I feel comfortable for the present with doing psychoanalysis. If one feels comfortable, one doesn't do psychoanalysis. [Laughter.] Psychoanalysis is a response to an enduring uneasiness which is not necessarily a simple existential uneasiness, but rather an intellectual discomfort. And I believe that psychoanalysis is the discourse of the intellectual life, if the intellectual life is also characterized by this uneasiness and a constant questioning of meanings, heritages, doctrines, and appearances. Now psychoanalysis as I understand it—I know this does not correspond to the various and often very controversial portrayals of psychoanalysis we may receive in America as well as in France—has the advantage of being a fusion, if you will, an intertextuality of practice and theory. It is the great obsession of our culture.

At the end of the nineteenth century, we constructed quite advanced and very abstract theoretical systems that found themselves at a certain point in a state of culpability—that is, cut off from practical experience. At that moment, the available solutions were two. Either one could follow this development to its logical conclusion by pushing the isolation even further and shutting oneself off in a universe of metalanguage meeting metalanguage—analytical philosophy, among other things, or at least one possible version of it—or one could, dialectically, try to make theory and practice meet. The consequences of this second strategy are Marxism, various forms of sociology, of political commitment, etc., that are not innocent and that can often lead to catastrophic results, as much because they may involve an abdication of the intellect as because they represent a social and political dogmatism that betrays any moral aspiration.

I believe psychoanalysis has the advantage, with Freud's innovations, of linking theoretical work with action, of being a bridge between contemplation and efficacy, between theoretical construct and treatment. And you never have one without the other. You cannot be a good theoretician, a good analyst, without being a good practitioner. If you are one or the other, either something is wrong in your practice or something is wrong with your theory. One often hears, "but there may be people with a lot of insight who don't produce theories." I can't say that theory must necessarily be written down, but in their insight these people already have concepts of how they function, and of how the psyche functions—so a certain modalization is present to guide them in their practice. This point seems to me very crucial for the analytic adventure.

The second point is that psychoanalysis is a discourse that is not closed, contrary to certain images presented by certain kinds of analytic practice which portray it as the mere repetition of Freud. We are in a continuous confrontation with the living discourses of society—the new malaises and symptoms, but also new ways of relating to image, public life, sexuality, biology, and procreation. With regard to all of these, psychoanalytical discourse is called upon to break new ground, to be a sort of continuous creation, if it wants to keep up with people and to make it possible for them to find their own ways of responding to these existential questions. Expanded in this way, analysis does not at all appear to me to be a closed system that we will some day have to discard. It incorporates and displaces discourses. The practices of the teaching of literature and literary criticism can only be nourished and enlightened, finding both resources and greater lucidity, through contact with psychoanalysis.

M. W. You have often spoken of the United States in your writings. I am thinking in particular of the article in *Polylogue* . . .

J. K. "From Ithaca to New York."

M. W. Yes, in that, and also in "My Memory's Hyperbole," which you wrote for *The Female Autograph* [Domna C. Stanton, ed. (New York: New York Literary Forum, 1984), 261–76]. You were talking there primarily about France, and about the sixties and seventies . . .

J. K. And it ends that way?

M. W. It ends—

J. K. —with America.

M. W. With America and the United States. Right. So, why America? Of course it has to do with your personal life, with the fact that you are here every three years. But would there be other reasons?

J. K. Yes, there are many reasons, and it's true that we must perhaps begin with personal reasons—especially in the case of a psychoanalyst—we all know that! I must say that I am very fortunate to have been invited by Columbia University to come every three years and teach in the Department of French. It's a very good university, and the students always welcome me with a great deal of kindness and curiosity. They ask questions that stimulate me a great deal because they have a way of listening to theoretical discourse "psychologically," existentially. Their questions are always based on an experience that may or may not be connected with the concepts, but it is always stimulating for the one to whom the questions are addressed. So there has been a sort of adoption of me at Columbia which is very flattering.

But I think we must go a little beyond that, since there are a number of reasons that have always made me feel very favorably disposed toward American life and the American experience. First of all, I say this in the context of a certain centralization of political, administrative, and ideological life in France that is our legacy from royalty, from Bonaparte. American federalism—the polyvalence of centers of decision making in the publishing and academic worlds, but also, I believe, in the government (and I admit I've had little opportunity for observing the latter, but it strikes me that it works in this way)—American federalism seems to be a more favorable and adequate response to the problems people face today than the centralization of Europe, in general, and France, in particular.

Second, there is a big problem facing European communities today, that of racism or polyracism. We are turning into a polyracial or polynational society. From across the Mediterranean, masses of Arabs, Africans, etc., are spreading through France. The political structure of France, on the one hand, and the French mentality, on the other, are not capable of taking in this phenomenon because they—our cultures—are extremely strong and coherent and find themselves absolutely incapable of absorbing these "invasions." We find ourselves in a sort of face-off, with conflicts that threaten to result in catastrophe in the coming years. I am not necessarily speaking of right-wing political groups, who play up such things and take advantage of the malaises. Those groups, in my opinion, ultimately are used by parties on the right *as well as* parties on the left in a rather subtle and dangerous political game. But that's all part of the current scene.

I simply think that, even if it is a long-term prospect, there must be a resolve to recast our ways of thinking, which is very difficult, given our cultural heritage. From this point of view American society, which is a society of immigrants, already a conglomerate and a mosaic, can provide an example of how, *practically*, to resolve these questions. That said, I do not think the American model can be exported to Europe or that we can have the same attitude as Americans, since conditions are not the same. You do not have the cultural heritage France has, which is a kind of identity that feels itself invaded and reacts to that invasion. So, we will have to find our own solutions, but the example of American tolerance, of American pragmatism, of dealing with the other on various levels of daily existence while allowing him his autonomy on the levels of his deep cultural and religious choices—these kinds of solutions are interesting for Europeans to envision and contemplate. Thus, the American model continues to interest me very much.

However, perhaps I have failed to stress something which exists in the articles you mentioned and which is extremely important in terms of the intertextuality of the world. Europe, to my mind, remains a locus of civilization, of the art of living, and of that capacity to assume the law without forgetting pleasure. Americans, perhaps, are in the process of discovering and trying to assimilate this lesson from Europe, after having had an offended attitude with regard to what they considered to be European cultural arrogance. I have often heard American friends speak of feeling rejected by the prestige that Europeans believe they have, which leads them to be a little condescending toward representatives of American civilization. Well, I think things have changed somewhat in that regard, and I think the American world—perhaps because Europe, too, is more receptive—feels more receptive toward Europe. We may, at some point, achieve a mutuality of reciprocal respect.

M. W. What struck me in your memoir was your speaking of the rather special autobiographical form that combines the *I* and the *we*, the first-persons singular and plural. It was so problematic and paradigmatic, your personal story and also the story—

J. K. Of the Tel Quel group.

M. W. Of the Tel Quel group. I was wondering whether you thought you would perhaps some day write about . . .

J. K. Yes, the whole story.

M. W. And if so, if you would write something novelistic, or would it be more of a documentary account. What form would it take, and in what style and language?

J. K. I don't know! I am, indeed, asked that question because of the text called "Memoir," and because one half of "L'Hérétique de l'amour" is a text on maternity that contains a rather poetic and subjective section. Because of that, good friends of mine have suggested that I take up a more fictional kind of writing. I don't know. For the moment, I think that psychoanalytic interpretation, which is very close to the economy of fiction, completely absorbs that kind of desire. I don't really need to produce an object, detached from myself, based on my life story, because I feel that in psychoanalytic interpretation there is a discourse that, while more or less detached from direct reference to biography, does go, nevertheless, by way of my own life story to meet the life story of the other person. There is a back-and-forth movement there that spares me the need for novelistic writing.

At times, I think the important thing would be to write, if not a novel, then at least an account of those years of personal theoretical work that marks French culture of the sixties and seventies and continues to mark it in a certain way which will make it part of literary history—there should be an assessment of that period. But I think that the period has not yet come to a close and that we don't have enough distance from it yet. Maybe some day it should be done, but not now. In any case, when the question comes up of whether I can see myself as a writer of fiction, I can see myself as one later on . . . if life goes on! That would be an activity for one who had emerged somewhat from the action. I see it a bit like the characters of Ronsard—in the evening by the fireside, after the story proper. For the moment I feel too much involved in the story in question to take stock of it. One could answer that novelistic writing does not assume any distance, and that to write a novel means by definition to remain immersed in the action. But for now, again, psychoanalytic interpretation takes the place of that; I must add, moreover, that theoretical writing, along with psychoanalysis and literary criticism, absorbs certain subjective elements, and for the moment this gives me enough balance without my needing to move into fiction. There is also the fact that to the extent that French is still, after all, a foreign language for me, I feel a certain reticence about writing anything literary in French. Although I am competent in French, I think it is perhaps not well enough connected, organically, with my unconscious for me to produce valid creative work.

M. W. Whereas you were saying yesterday, of Beckett, that after his mother's death he wrote in French. So it was possible for him to write in two languages.

J. K. Yes . . . but a rather special kind of writing, and one that may correspond to some deep rupture or distress in Beckett's personality, something that makes it necessary for writing—which, in any case, is translation—in his case to be explicitly translation on a direct level, between two languages, and not merely between an affective life and a personal language. Beckett's is a rather special psychic life, and I . . . my distress is not of that order.

M. W. One last question: you said that your work in psychoanalysis and literary criticism absorbs, so to speak . . .

J. K. A certain need for fiction.

M. W. Yes. And that your choosing to be a literary critic has something to do with your personal history. Your choice of texts, I would say, is also a very personal choice.

J. K. Yes, of course.

M. W. So why certain texts and not others? You work on all different kinds of texts. What ties them together?

J. K. Maybe I am an intertextual personality. I have a lot of facets, like a diamond. I really think that if there is a "pattern," it is the borderline between sense and nonsense, between the semiotic and the symbolic. Obviously it takes different forms in different centuries for various people. But what interests me is the dividing line. I have had the feeling that the human condition, insofar as it involves the use of speech, is very fragile, and that writing explores that fragility. I try to find examples of literary texts where this fragility appears to have maximum visibility.

M. W. And in your psychoanalytic practice, too . . .

J. K. Well, there it rather depends on the people who present themselves, but I find this stage appearing there, too, in a very flagrant way, and times of crisis, whether hysterical or depressive, touch on this same question of borders. So I am fairly sensitive to this fragility; I believe I'm trying to help people cope with it.

The Gray Area

A Selected Bibliography
of Intertextual, Postmodern, and Contemporary
American Studies

===

JENNIFER JENKINS

Studies on intertextuality in contemporary narrative are legion. A large body of critical work on issues of intertextuality in Latin American, European, and Quebecois literature exists, focused in part on the work of Jorge Luis Borges, Gabriel García-Márquez, Alain Robbe-Grillet, Marcel Proust, and Claude Simon. While some of this work is cited here, I have tried to limit references to those which directly contribute to the theory of the intertext and those which deal specifically with contemporary, or postmodern, American culture and narrative. The nature of this project frustrates such attempts, however, and several critical works on other literatures and periods are cited for their theoretical approaches and instructive treatment of texts (Jane Gallop, Bruce Morrissette, John Carlos Rowe). Needless to say, intertextual studies extend beyond literary factionalism. Theories of the intertext occur in areas as seemingly diverse as hermeneutics, narrative theory, cultural anthropology, psychoanalysis, and political theory (Hal Foster, Fredric Jameson, Jacques Lacan). A smattering of titles in these disciplines is also included, as a starting point rather than as a definitive list of references. Finally, most of the citations resist a single rubric; the few subdivisions are designated to loosely divide the material by form and content.

Intertextuality

Alter, Robert. *Partial Magic: The Novel as Self-Conscious Genre*. Berkeley and Los Angeles: University of California Press, 1975.
Althusser, Louis. *Aesthetics and Politics*. London: New Left Books, 1977.
Altman, Charles F. "Intertextual Rewriting: Textuality as Language Formation." In *The Sign in Music and Literature*, edited by Wendy Steiner. Austin: University of Texas Press, 1981.

Angenot, Marc. "L'Intertextualité: enquête sur l'émergence et la diffusion d'un champ notionnel." *Revue des sciences humaines* 189 (1983): 121–35.

———. "Lecture intertextuelle d'un texte de Freud." *Poétique* 56 (1983): 387–96.

———. "Intertextualité, interdiscursivité, discours social." *Texte* 2 (1983): 101–12.

Arrive, Michel. "Pour une théorie des textes poly-isotopiques." *Langages* 31 (1973): 53–63.

Atkinson, R. "The Citation as Intertext: Towards a Theory of the Selective Process." *Library Resources and Technical Services* 28, no. 2 (1984): 109–19.

Auerbach, Eric. *Mimesis: The Representation of Reality in Western Literature.* Translated by W. R. Trask. Princeton: Princeton University Press, 1953.

Bakhtin, Mikhail. *Problems of Dostoevsky's Poetics.* Translated by R. W. Rotsel. Ann Arbor, Mich.: Ardis, 1973.

———. "Discourse Typology in Prose." In *Readings in Russian Poetics*, edited by L. Matejka and K. Pomorska. Ann Arbor: University of Michigan Press, 1978.

———. *The Dialogic Imagination: Four Essays.* Edited by Michael Holquist. Translated by Caryl Emerson and Michael Holquist. Austin: University of Texas Press, 1981.

———. *Rabelais and His World.* Translated by Helene Iswolsky. Cambridge, Mass.: M.I.T. Press, 1968; Bloomington: Indiana University Press, 1984.

Barthes, Roland. "De l'oeuvre au texte." *Revue d'esthétique* 24, no. 3 (1971): 225–32.

———. "Réponses." *Tel Quel* 47 (1971): 89–107.

———. "Intertexte." In *Encyclopaedie Universalis* vol. 15 (1973).

———. *S/Z.* Paris: Seuil, 1970. Translated by Richard Miller, under the title *S/Z.* New York: Hill & Wang, 1974.

———. *Image, Music, Text.* Translated by Stephen Heath. New York: Hill & Wang, 1977.

———. *Roland Barthes by Roland Barthes.* Translated by Richard Howard. New York: Hill & Wang, 1977.

Bassnet-McGuire, Susan. *Translation Studies.* New Accents. London: Methuen, 1980.

Baudrillard, Jean. *For a Critique of the Political Economy of the Sign.* Translated by C. Levin. St. Louis: Telos Press, 1981.

Beaugrande, Robert de. *Text, Discourse, and Process: Toward a Multidisciplinary Science of Texts.* Norwood, N.J.: Ablex Publishing, 1980.

Béhar, Henri. "La Réécriture comme poétique—ou le même et l'autre." *Romanic Review* 72, no. 1 (1981): 51–65.

Bellemin-Noël, Jean. *Le Texte et l'avant-texte.* Paris: Larousse, 1972.

Ben-Porat, Ziva. "The Poetics of Literary Allusion." *PTL: A Journal for Descriptive Poetics and Theory of Literature* 1, no. 1 (1976): 105–28.

———. "The Poetics of Allusion—A Text Linking Device—in Different Media of Communication (Literature versus Advertising and Journalism)." In *A Semiotic Landscape: Proceedings of the International Association for Semiotic Studies, Milan 1974*, edited by Seymour Chatman, Umberto Eco, and J. M. Klinckenberg. The Hague: Mouton, 1979.

Bilous, Daniel. "Intertexte/pastiche: l'intermimotexte." *Texte* 2 (1983): 135–60.

Bjornson, Richard. "Translation and Literary Theory." *Translation Review* 6 (1980): 13–16.

Bloom, Harold. *The Anxiety of Influence: A Theory of Poetry*. New York: Oxford University Press, 1973.

———. *A Map of Misreading*. New York: Oxford University Press, 1975.

———. *Poetry and Repression: Revisionism from Blake to Stevens*. New Haven: Yale University Press, 1976.

Booth, Wayne. *Critical Understanding: The Powers of Pluralism*. Chicago: University of Chicago Press, 1979.

Bouazis, Charles, ed. *Essais de la théorie du texte*. Paris: Galilée, 1973.

Brandt, Per Aage. "La Pensée du texte (de la littéralité de la littérarité)." In *Essais de la theorie du texte*, edited by Charles Bouazis. Paris: Galilée, 1973.

Britton, Celia. "The Dialogic Text and the 'texte pluriel.'" *Occasional Papers* (University of Essex Language Centre) 14 (1974): 52–68.

Brenkman, John. "Narcissus in the Text." *Georgia Review* 30, no. 2 (1976): 293–329.

Bruckner, M. E. "Concluding Remarks . . ." *Littérature* 41 (1981): 104–08.

Bruss, Elizabeth W. *Beautiful Theories: The Spectacle of Discourse in Contemporary Criticism*. Baltimore: Johns Hopkins University Press, 1982.

Brutting, Richard. *"Ecriture" und "text": Die franzosische Litteraturtheorie "nach dem Structuralismus."* Bonn: Bouvier Verlag, 1976.

Butler, Christopher. *Interpretation, Deconstruction, and Ideology*. London: Oxford University Press, 1981.

Carlos, Alberto J. "Nacha Regules y Santa: Problemas de intertextualidad." *Symposium: A Quarterly Journal in Modern Foreign Literatures* (Syracuse, N.Y.) 36, no. 4 (1982–83): 301–7.

Carroll, David. *The Subject in Question: The Language of Theory and the Strategies of Fiction*. Chicago: University of Chicago Press, 1982.

Certeau, Michel de. *Heterologies*. Translated by Brian Massumi. Theory and History of Literature, vol. 17. Minneapolis: University of Minnesota Press, 1986.

Chambers, Ross. *Story and Situation: Narrative Seduction and the Power of Fiction*. Theory and History of Literature, vol. 12. Minneapolis: University of Minnesota Press, 1984.

Chatman, Seymour, Umberto Eco, and J.-M. Klinckenberg, eds. *A Semiotic Landscape: Proceedings of the International Association for Semiotic Studies, Milan 1974*. The Hague: Mouton, 1979.

Chevalier, Anne. "Du détournement des sources." *Revue des sciences humaines* 196 (1984): 65–79.

Christensen, B. "Problèmes méthodologiques d'une lecture intertextuelle: Prise de la prose." *Revue Romane* (Copenhagen) 17, no. 2 (1982): 55–63.

Christensen, Inger. *The Meaning of Metafiction: A Critical Study of Selected Novels by Sterne, Nabokov, Barth, and Beckett.* Bergen and Oslo: Universitetsforlaget, 1981.

Clifford, James, and George E. Marcus, eds. *Writing Culture: The Poetics and Politics of Ethnography.* Berkeley and Los Angeles: University of California Press, 1986.

Cohn, Dorritt. *Transparent Minds: Narrative Modes for Presenting Consciousness in Fiction.* Princeton: Princeton University Press, 1978.

Compagnon, Antoine. *La Seconde Main ou la travail de la citation.* Paris: Seuil, 1979.

Coward, Rosalind, and John Ellis. *Language and Materialism: Developments in Semiology and the Theory of the Subject.* New York: Routlege & Kegan Paul, 1977.

Crowley, Roseline. "Toward the Poetics of Juxtaposition: 'L'Après-Midi d'un Faune.'" *Yale French Studies* 54 (1977): 33–44.

Culler, Jonathan. *Structuralist Poetics: Structuralism, Linguistics, and the Study of Literature.* Ithaca, N.Y.: Cornell University Press, 1975.

———. "Presupposition and Intertextuality." *Modern Language Notes* 91, no. 6 (1976): 1380–96.

———. *The Pursuit of Signs: Semiotics, Literature, Deconstruction.* Ithaca, N.Y.: Cornell University Press, 1981.

———. *On Deconstruction: Theory and Criticism after Structuralism.* Ithaca, N.Y.: Cornell University Press, 1982.

Cury, Maria Zilda Ferreira. "Intertextualidade: Una Pratica Contradictoria." *Cadernos de Linguistica e Teoria da Literatura* 8 (1982): 117–28.

Dällenbach, Lucien. "Intertexte et autotexte." *Poétique* 27 (1976): 282–96.

———. *Le récit speculaire: Essai sur la mise en abîme.* Collection Poétique. Paris: Seuil, 1977.

Danow, David K. "M. M. Bakhtin's Concept of the Word." *American Journal of Semiotics* 3, no. 1 (1984): 79–98.

Davies, Howard. "*Les Mots* as *Essai sur le don:* Contribution to an Origin Myth." *Yale French Studies* 68 (1985): 57–72.

Davis, Robert Con, and Ronald Schleifer, eds. *Rhetoric and Form: Deconstruction at Yale.* Norman: University of Oklahoma Press, 1985.

Delas, Daniel. "Propositions pour une théorie de la production textuelle et intertextuelle en poésie: 'Airs' de Philippe Jaccottet." *Romanic Review* 66, no. 2 (1975): 123–39.

Deleuze, Gilles, and Félix Guattari. *Anti-Oedipus: Capitalism and Schizophrenia.* Translated by Robert Hurley, Mark Seem, and Helen R. Lane. New York: Viking, 1977.

de Man, Paul. *Allegories of Reading: Figural Language in Rousseau, Nietzsche, Rilke, and Proust.* New Haven: Yale University Press, 1979.

———. "Hypogram and Inscription: Michael Riffaterre's Poetics of Reading." *Diacritics* 11, no. 4 (1981): 17–35.

———. "Dialogue and Dialogism." *Poetics Today* 4, no. 1 (1983): 99–107.

———. *The Resistance to Theory.* Foreword by Wlad Godzich. Minneapolis: University of Minnesota Press, 1986.

Dembowski, Peter, "Intertextualité et critique des textes." *Littérature* 41 (1981): 17–29.

Derrida, Jacques. "Structure, Sign, and Play in the Discourse of the Human Sciences." In *The Structuralist Controversy*, edited by Richard Macksey and Eugenio Donato. Baltimore: Johns Hopkins University Press, 1972.

———. *Of Grammatology.* Translated by Gayatri C. Spivak. Baltimore: Johns Hopkins University Press, 1976.

———. "Signature Event Context." In *Glyph* 1: Johns Hopkins Textual Studies, Baltimore: Johns Hopkins University Press, 1977. 172–97.

———. *Writing and Difference.* Translated by Alan Bass. Chicago: University of Chicago Press, 1978.

———. *Dissemination.* Translated by Barbara Johnson. Chicago: University of Chicago Press, 1981.

Descombes, Vincent. *Objects of All Sorts: A Philosophical Grammar.* Translated by Lorna Scott-Fox and Jeremy Harding. Baltimore: Johns Hopkins University Press, 1983.

Eco, Umberto. *The Role of the Reader: Explorations in the Semiotics of the Text.* Bloomington: Indiana University Press, 1979.

Eisenzweig, Uri. "Un concept plein d'interêts." *Texte* 2 (1983): 161–70.

Eli Blanchard, Marc. *Description: Sign, Self, Desire, Critical Theory in the Wake of Semiotics.* The Hague: Mouton, 1980.

———. "Up against the Text." *Diacritics* 11, no. 3 (1981): 13–26.

Esrock, Ellen. "Literature and Philosophy as Narrative Writing." In *Ideas of Order in Literature and Film*, edited by Peter Ruppert, Eugene Crook, and Walter Forehand. Tallahassee: University Presses of Florida, 1979.

Ette, Ottmar. "Intertextuality: A Literary and Social Approach." *Roman Z Lit* 9, nos. 3–4 (1985): 497–522.

Faria, Almeida, Fernando Namora, Teresa Salema, and Vergilio Ferreira. "O Autor, a Intertextualidade e o leitor." *Coloquio* 75 (1983): 54–57.

Fitch, Brian T. *The Narcissistic Text: A Reading of Camus' Fiction.* Toronto: University of Toronto Press, 1982.

Foster, Hal. *Recodings: Art, Spectacle, Cultural Politics.* Port Townsend, Wash.: Bay Press, 1985.

Foucault, Michel. *Language, Counter-Memory, Practice.* Translated by D. F. Bouchard and S. Simon. Ithaca, N.Y.: Cornell University Press, 1977.

Foust, R. E. "Poetics, Play, and Literary Fantasy." *New Orleans Review* 9, no. 3 (1982): 40–44.

Francoeur, Louis. "The Dialogical Semiosis of Culture." *American Journal of Semiotics* 3, no. 1 (1985): 121–30.

Frow, John. "Who Shot Frank Hardy? Intertextuality and Textual Politics." *Southern Review: Literary and Interdisciplinary Essays* (South Australia) 15, no. 1 (1982): 22–39.

———. *Marxism and Literary History.* Cambridge: Harvard University Press, 1986.

Frye, Northrop. *The Anatomy of Criticism.* Princeton: Princeton University Press, 1957.

Gaillard, Françoise. "Code(s) littéraire(s) et idéologie." *Littérature* 12 (1973): 21–35.

Gallop, Jane. *Intersections: A Reading of Sade with Bataille, Blanchot, and Klossowski.* Lincoln: University of Nebraska Press, 1981.

———. *The Daughter's Seduction: Feminism and Psychoanalysis.* Ithaca, N.Y.: Cornell University Press, 1982.

Garavini, Fausta. "Le Misanthrope travesti; hypertexte occitan." *Littérature* 50 (1983): 91–103.

Gelley, Alexander. *Narrative Crossings.* Baltimore: Johns Hopkins University Press, 1987.

Genette, Gérard. *Introduction à l'architexte.* Collection Poétique. Paris: Seuil, 1979.

———. *Narrative Discourse: An Essay on Method.* Translated by Jane E. Lewin. Ithaca, N.Y.: Cornell University Press, 1980.

———. *Palimpsestes: La littérature au second degré.* Collection Poétique. Paris: Seuil, 1982.

Gomez-Moriana, Antonio. "Intertextualité, interdiscursivité, et parodie: pour une sémanalyse du roman picaresque." *Journal canadien de recherche sémiotique* 8, nos. 1–2 (1980–81): 15–32.

Graff, Gerald. *Literature against Itself: Literary Ideas in Modern Society.* Chicago: University of Chicago Press, 1979.

Gray, Floyd, and Marcel Tetel, eds. *Etudes sur le XVIe siècle pour Alfred Glausser: Textes et intertextes.* Paris: Nizet, 1979.

Grivel, Charles. "Les Universaux de texte." *Littérature* 30 (1978): 25–30.

———. "Thèses préparatoires sur les intertextes." In *Dialogizität*, edited by R. Lachmann. Munich: W. Fink Verlag, 1983.

Groupe d'Entrevernes. *Signes et paraboles: sémiotique et texte évangelique.* Paris: Seuil, 1977.

Hamon, Philippe. "Texte littéraire et métalangage." *Poétique* 31 (1977): 261–84.

———. "Texte et Ideologie." *Poétique* 49 (1982): 105–25.

Harari, Josué, ed. *Textual Strategies.* Ithaca, N.Y.: Cornell University Press, 1979.

Harvey, Irene E. *Derrida and the Economy of Différance.* Bloomington: Indiana University Press, 1986.

Hassan, Ihab Habib. *Paracriticisms: Seven Speculations of the Times.* Urbana: University of Illinois Press, 1975.

Hawkes, Terence. *Structuralism and Semiotics.* Berkeley and Los Angeles: University of California Press, 1977.

Hayles, Katherine. *The Cosmic Web: Scientific Field Models and Literary Strategies in the Twentieth Century.* Ithaca, N.Y.: Cornell University Press, 1986.

Hempfer, Klaus, and Gerhard Regn, eds. *Interpretation: Das Paradigma der Europäishen Rennaisance-Literatur. Festschrift für Alfred Noyer-Weider zum 60 Geburtstag.* Wiesbaden: Franz Steiner Verlag, 1982.

Heyndels, Ralph. "Intertexte, institution, pédagogie." *Neohelicon* 10, no. 1 (1983): 301–9.

Holland, Michael. "De l'intertextualité: métacritique." *Texte* 2 (1983): 177–92.

Hoy, David Couzens. *The Critical Circle: Literature, History, and Philosophical Hermeneutics*. Berkeley and Los Angeles: University of California Press, 1978.

Hutcheon, Linda. *Narcissistic Narrative: The Metafictional Parodox*. New York: Methuen, 1984.

———. "Literary Borrowing . . . and Stealing: Plagiarism, Sources, Influences, and Intertexts." *English Studies in Canada* 12, no. 2 (1986): 229–39.

Iat, Geneviève. "Intertextualité, 'transposition,' critique des sources." *Nova Renascenca* 4, no. 13 (1984): 5–20.

Ivanov, V. V. "The Significance of M. M. Bakhtin's Ideas on Sign, Utterance, and Dialogue for Modern Semiotics." In *Semiotics and Structuralism: Readings from the Soviet Union*, edited by H. Baran. White Plains, N.Y.: International Arts and Sciences Press, 1976.

Jameson, Fredric. "Magical Narratives: Romance as Genre." *New Literary History* 7, no. 1 (1975): 135–64.

———. *The Political Unconscious: Narrative as a Socially Symbolic Act*. Ithaca, N.Y.: Cornell University Press, 1981.

Jefferson, Ann. "Intertextuality and the Poetics of Fiction." *Comparative Criticism: A Yearbook* (Cambridge, England) 2 (1980): 235–50.

Jensen, Sevend Bøggild. "Kulturanalyse og Intertekstualitet." *Litterature og Samfund* 35 (1982): 17–29.

Jenny, Laurent. "La Stratégie de la forme. *Poétique* 27 (1976): 257–81.

———. "Sémiotique du collage intertextuel ou la litterature a coups de ciseaux." *Révue d'ésthetique* 3–4 (1978): 165–82.

Jitrik, Noe. "Lo vivido, lo teorico, la coincidencia." *Cuadernos Americanos* 2, no. 253 (1984): 89–99.

Johnson, Anthony. "Allusion in Poetry." *PTL: A Journal for Descriptive Poetics and Theory of Literature* 1, no. 3 (1976): 576–87.

Kawin, Bruce F. *The Mind of the Novel: Reflexive Fiction and the Ineffable*. Princeton: Princeton University Press, 1982.

Kellman, Steven G. *The Self-Begetting Novel*. New York: Columbia University Press, 1980.

Kibédi-Varga, Aron. "Pour une histoire intertextuelle de la littérature." *Degrés* 12, nos. 39–40 (1984): g.1–g.10.

———. *Théorie de la littérature*. Paris: Picard, 1981.

Kiremidjian, G. K. "The Aesthetics of Parody." *Journal of Aesthetics and Art Criticism* 28 (1969): 231–42.

Klinkowitz, Jerome. *The Self-Apparent Word: Fiction as Language/Language as Fiction*. Carbondale: Southern Illinois University Press, 1984.

Kristeva, Julia. "Problèmes de la structuration du texte." In *Théorie d'ensemble*, edited by Tel Quel. Paris: Seuil, 1968.

———. *Séméiotiké: Recherches pour une sémanalyse*. Paris: Seuil, 1969.

———. *Le Texte du roman: Approche sémiologique d'une structure discursive transformationelle*. Approaches to Semiotics, edited by Thomas A. Sebeok. The Hague: Mouton, 1970.

———. *Desire in Language: A Semiotic Approach to Literature and Art*. Edited by Leon S. Roudiez. Translated by Thomas Gora, Alice Jardine, and Leon S. Roudiez. New York: Columbia University Press, 1980.

———. *Revolution in Poetic Language.* Translated by Margaret Waller. New York: Columbia University Press, 1984.

Krysinski, Wladimir. *Carrefour des signes: essais sur le roman modern.* The Hague: Mouton, 1981.

———. "The Intertext of the Novel and Comparative Space." *Canadian Review of Comparative Literature* 11, no. 4 (1984): 469–77.

———. "The Dialectical and Intertextual Function of Irony in the Modern Novel." *Canadian Review of Comparative Literature* 12, no. 1 (1985): 1–11.

Lacan, Jacques. *Ecrits: A Selection.* Translated by Alan Sheridan. New York: Norton, 1977.

LaCapra, Dominick. *Rethinking Intellectual History: Texts, Contexts, and Language.* Ithaca, N.Y.: Cornell University Press, 1983.

———. *History and Criticism.* Ithaca, N.Y.: Cornell University Press, 1985.

Lachmann, R. ed. *Dialogizität.* Munich: W. Fink Verlag, 1983.

Laurette, Pierre. "A l'ombre du pastiche: la réécriture—automatisme et contingence." *Texte* 2 (1983): 113–34.

Leitch, Vincent B. *Deconstructive Criticism: An Advanced Introduction.* New York: Columbia University Press, 1983.

Lemke, J. L. "Ideology, Intertextuality, and the Notion of Register." In *Systemic Perspectives on Discourse. Vol. 1. Selected Theoretical Papers from the 9th International Systemic Workshop,* edited by James O. Benson, 275–94. *Vol. 2. Selected Applied Papers from the 9th International Systemic Workshop,* edited by William S. Greaves. Advances in Discourse Processes 15. Norwood, N.J.: Ablex Publishing, 1985.

Leps, M.-C. "For an Intertextual Method of Analyzing Discourse." *Europa* 3, no. 1 (1979–80): 89–102.

Levi, A.H.T. "Histoire littéraire, intertextualité et civilization." In *Etudes francaises en Europe non francophone,* edited by Jozef Heinstein. Warsaw: Panstwowe Wydawnictwo Naukowe, 1981.

Liao, Ping Hui. "Intersection and Juxtaposition of Wor(l)ds (Intertextuality)." *Tamkang Review: A Quarterly of Comparative Studies between Chinese and Foreign Literatures* 14, nos. 1–4 (1985): 395–411.

Link, Jurgen. "Interdiscourse, Literature, and Collective Symbols: Theses towards a Theory of Discourse and Literature." *Enclitic* 8, nos. 1–2 (1984): 157–65.

Logan, Marie-Rose. "L'Intertextualité au carrefour de la philologie et de la poétique." *Littérature* 41 (1981): 47–49.

Lukacher, Ned. *Primal Scenes: Literature, Philosophy, Psychoanalysis.* Ithaca, N.Y.: Cornell University Press, 1986.

McHale, Brian. "Free Indirect Discourse: A Survey of Recent Accounts." *PTL: A Journal for Descriptive Poetics and Theory of Literature* 3, no. 2 (1978): 249–87.

Malcuzynski, M.-Pierette. "Critique de la (dé)raison polyphonique." *Etudes Francaises* 20, no. 1 (1984): 45–56.

———. "Polyphonic Theory and Contemporary Literary Practices." *Studies in Twentieth-Century Literature* 9, no. 1 (1984): 75–87.

Marks, Elaine. "Lesbian Intertextuality." In *Traditionalism, Nationalism, and*

Feminism: Women Writers of Quebec, edited by Paula Gibert. Contributions in Women's Studies, no. 53. Westport, Conn.: Greenwood Press, 1985.

Mastrangelo Bové, Carol. "The Text as Dialogue in Bakhtin and Kristeva." *Revue de l'Université d'Ottowa/University of Ottowa Quarterly* 53, no. 1 (1983): 117–24.

Mavrodin, Irina. "Voyage à travers l'espace-temps poïétique." *Cahiers roumains d'études littéraires* 4 (1980): 77–82.

Megill, Allen. *Prophets of Extremity: Nietzsche, Heidegger, Foucault, Derrida.* Berkeley and Los Angeles: University of California Press, 1985.

Melville, Stephen. *Philosophy beside Itself: On Deconstruction and Modernism.* Theory and History of Literature, vol. 27. Minneapolis: University of Minnesota Press: 1986.

Meyer, Herman. *Das Zitat in der Erzahlkunst.* (English title, *The Poetics of Translation in the European Novel.*) Stuttgart: Carl Ernst Poeschel, 1961.

Miller, J. Hillis. *Aspects of Narrative.* New York: Columbia University Press, 1971.

———. *The Linguistic Moment: From Wordsworth to Stevens.* Princeton: Princeton University Press, 1985.

Miller, Nancy. "D'une solitude à l'autre: vers un intertexte feminin." *French Review: Journal of the American Association of Teachers of French.* (Chapel Hill, N.C.) 54, no. 6 (1981): 797–803.

Morawski, Stefan. "The Basic Function of Quotation." In *Sign, Language, Culture,* edited by A. J. Greimas and R. Jakobson, et al., 690–705. The Hague: Mouton, 1970.

Morrissette, Bruce. *Intertextual Assemblage in Robbe-Grillet from Topology to the Golden Triangle.* Fredericton, New Brunswick: York Press, 1979.

Net, Mariana. "Towards a Pragmatics of Poetic Intertextuality." *Revue Roumaine de Linguistique* 28[20], no. 2 (1983): 159–62.

Neuman, Shirley. "Figuring the Reader, Figuring the Self in Field Notes: 'Double or Noting'." *Open Letter* 8–9 (1984): 176–94.

Norris, Christopher. *Deconstruction: Theory and Practice.* London: Methuen, 1982.

———. *The Deconstructive Turn: Essays in the Rhetoric of Philosophy.* London: Methuen, 1983.

———. *Contest of Faculties: Philosophy and Theory after Deconstruction.* London: Methuen, 1985.

Ollier, Claude. "Les inscriptions conflictuelles." *Pratiques* 10 (1976): 81–90.

Olsson, A. "Intertextuality—the meeting point between texts." *Bonniers Literara Magasin* 53, no. 3 (1984): 155–66.

Pacheco, Carlos. "La intertextualidade y el compilador: Nuevas claves para una lectura de la polifonia en Yo el Supremo." *Revista de Crítica Literaria Latinoamericana* (Lima, Peru) 10, no. 19 (1984): 47–72.

Pavel, Thomas. "The Borders of Fiction." *Poetics Today* 4, no. 1 (1983): 83–88.

Perezfir, G. "Model of Intertextuality in Literature." *Romanic Review* 69, nos. 1–2 (1978): 1–14.

Perri, Carmela. "On Alluding." *Poetics* 7, no. 3 (1978): 289–307.

Perrone-Moisés, Leyla. "L'Intertextualité critique." *Poétique* 27 (1976): 372–84.

Popovic, Anton. "Sémiotique intertextuelle: l'interpretant." *Revue d'esthe-tique* 1–2 (1979): 128–50.

———. "La trace de l'intertexte." *La Pensée* 215 (1980): 4–18.

———. "Communication Aspect in Slovak Literary Scholarship." In *Language, Literature, and Meaning II: Current Trends in Literary Research*, edited by John Odmark. Amsterdam: Benjamins, 1980.

Quere, H. "Discours, texte(s), textualité." In *A Semiotic Landscape: Proceedings of the International Association for Semiotic Studies, Milan 1974*, edited by Seymour Chatman, Umberto Eco, and J.-M. Klinckenberg. The Hague: Mouton, 1979.

Reichler, C. "On the Notion of Intertextuality: the Example of the Libertine Novel." *Diogenes* 113–114 (1981): 205–15.

Reis, Carlos. "Intertextualité et lecture critique." Translated by Yves Gourgaud. *Canadian Review of Comparative Literature* 12, no. 1 (1985): 46–55.

Ricardou, Jean. *Pour une théorie du Nouveau Roman.* Paris: 1971.

———. "Le Texte survit a l'excité" (Réponse à Michael Holland). *Texte* 2 (1983): 193–216.

Riese, Utz. "Zwischen Realismus und Postmodernismus." *Weimarer Beitrage: Zeitschrift für Literaturwissenschaft, Ästhetik und Kulturtheorie* 31, no. 3 (1985): 517–23.

Riffaterre, Michael. "The Self-Sufficient Text." *Diacritics* 3, no. 3 (1973): 39–45.

———. "The Poetic Function of Intertextual Humor." *Romanic Review* 65, no. 4 (1974): 278–93.

———. "Paragrammes et signifiance." *Semiotext[e]* 2, no. 1 (1975): 15–30.

———. "Intertextual Scrambling." *Romanic Review* 68, no. 3 (1977): 197–206.

———. *Semiotics of Poetry.* Advances in Semiotics, edited by Thomas A. Sebeok. Bloomington: Indiana University Press, 1978.

———. "La Syllepse intertextuelle." *Poétique* 40 (1979): 496–501.

———. "Sémiotique intertextuelle: l'interpretant." *Revue d'ésthetique* 1–2 (1979): 128–50.

———. "Intertextualité surréaliste." *Mélusine* (Lausanne) 1 (1980): 27–37.

———. "Syllepsis." *Critical Inquiry* 6, no. 4 (1980): 625–38.

———. "La Trace de l'intertexte." *La Pensée* 215 (1980): 4–18.

———. "Interpretation and Undecidability." *New Literary History* 12, no. 2 (1981): 227–42.

———. "Ponge intertextuel." *Etudes françaises* (Montreal) 17, nos. 1–2 (1981): 73–85.

———. "L'intertexte inconnu." *Littérature* 41 (1981): 4–7.

———. "Descriptive Imagery." *Yale French Studies* 61 (1981): 107–25.

———. "Hermeneutic Models." *Poetics Today* 4, no. 1 (1983): 7–16.

———. "Semantic Analysis of Intertext." (Réponse à Uri Eisenzweig) *Texte* 2 (1983): 171–75.

———. *Text Production.* Translated by Térèse Lyons. New York: Columbia University Press, 1983.

———. "Intertextual Representation: On Mimesis as Interpretive Discourse." *Critical Inquiry* 11, no. 1 (1984): 141–62.

Rigolot, Carol. "L'Amerique de Saint-John Perse: Referentielle ou intertextuelle?" In *Espaces de Saint-John Perse*, vol. 3. Aix-en-Provence: Centre Saint-John Perse, Université de Provence, 1981.

Rimmon-Kennan, Shlomith. "Paradoxical Status of Repetition." *Poetics Today* 1, no. 4 (1980): 151–59.

Robbe-Grillet, Alain. "Order and Disorder in Film and Fiction." *Critical Inquiry* 4, no. 1 (1977): 1–20.

Rojas, Carlos. "Goya como protagonista: El arte como medida y limites de la novela." In *Selected Proceedings: 32d Mountain Interstate Foreign Language Conference*, edited by Gregorio C. Martin, 275–284. Winston-Salem, N.C.: Wake Forest University Press, 1984.

Rorty, Richard. *Philosophy and the Mirror of Nature.* Princeton: Princeton University Press, 1979.

———. *Consequences of Pragmatism.* Minneapolis: University of Minnesota Press, 1982.

Rose, Margaret. *Parody and Metafiction.* London: Croom Helm, 1979.

Roventa, D. "Intratextual/Intertextual . . ." *Degrés* 28 (1981): g.1–g.6.

Rowe, John Carlos. *Through the Custom House: Nineteenth-Century American Fiction and Modern Theory.* Baltimore: Johns Hopkins University Press, 1982.

Ruprecht, Hans-Georg. "Du formant intertextuel. Remarques sur un objet ethnosémiotique." *Actes sémiotiques: Documents de recherche du Groupe de Recherches sémio-linguistiques* (Ecole des Hautes Etudes en Sciences Sociales/Centre National de Recherche Scientifique) 3, no. 21 (1981): 1–27.

———. "Intertextualité" *Texte* 2 (1983): 13–22.

Rusinko, Elaine. "Intertextuality: The Soviet Approach to Subtext" *Dispositio: Revista Hispanica de Semiotica Literaria* (Ann Arbor, Mich.) 4, nos. 11–12 (1979): 213–35.

Ruthrof, Horst. *The Reader's Construction of Narrative.* London: Routledge & Kegan Paul, 1981.

Said, Edward. "What Is Beyond Formalism?" *Modern Language Notes* 86 (1971): 933–45.

———. *Beginnings: Intention and Method.* Baltimore: Johns Hopkins University Press, 1975.

———. *The World, the Text, and the Critic.* Cambridge: Harvard University Press, 1983.

Schick, Ursula. "Narrated Semiotics or an Intertextual Tangle?" (Translation of "Erzahlte Semiotik oder intertextuelles Verwirrspiel? Umberto Ecos Il nome della rosa.") *Poetica* (Amsterdam) 16, nos. 1–2 (1984): 138–61.

Schmeling, Manfred. "Textuelle Fremdbestimmung und literarischer Vergleich." *Neohelicon* 12, no. 1 (1985): 231–39.

Scholes, Robert. *Fabulation and Metafiction.* Urbana: University of Illinois Press, 1979.

Segre, Cesare. *Semiotics and Literary Criticism.* Translated by John Meddemen. The Hague: Mouton, 1973.

Servodidio, Mirella. "Oneiric Intertextualities." In *From Fiction to Metafiction: Essays in Honor of Carmen Martin-Gaite*. Lincoln: University of Nebraska Press, 1983.

Seung, T. K. *Structuralism and Hermeneutics*. New York: Columbia University Press, 1982.

Siegle, Robert. *The Politics of Reflexivity: Narrative and the Constitutive Poetics of Culture*. Baltimore: Johns Hopkins University Press, 1986.

Singer, Alan. *The Metaphorics of Fiction: Discontinuity and Discourse in the Modern Novel*. Tallahassee: University Presses of Florida, 1983.

Smith, Barbara Herrnstein. *On the Margins of Discourse*. Chicago: University of Chicago Press, 1978.

Sollers, Philippe. "Niveaux sémantiques d'un texte moderne." In *Théorie d'ensemble*, edited by Tel Quel. Paris: Seuil, 1968.

———. *Writing and the Experience of Limits*. Edited by David Hayman. Translated by Philip Barnard with David Hayman. New York: Columbia University Press, 1983.

Spanos, William V., Paul A. Bove, and Daniel O'Hara. *The Question of Textuality: Strategies of Reading in Contemporary American Criticism*. Bloomington: Indiana University Press, 1982.

Starobinski, Jean, ed. "Le Texte dans le texte. Extraits inédits des Cahiers d'anagrammes de Ferdinand de Saussure." *Tel Quel* 37 (1969): 3–33.

Steele, Peter. "Scriptor Ludens: The Notion and Some Instances." *Canadian Review of Comparative Literature* 12, no. 2 (1985): 235–63.

Steiner, George. "Text and Context." In *On Difficulty*. New York: Oxford University Press, 1980.

Sternberg, Meir. "Proteus in Quotation-Land: Mimesis and the Forms of Reported Discourse." *Poetics Today* 3, no. 2 (1982): 107–56.

Stewart, Susan. *Nonsense: Aspects of Intertextuality in Folklore and Literature*. Baltimore: Johns Hopkins University Press, 1978.

Szegedy-Maszak, Mihaly. "One of the Basic Concepts of Research in Historical Poetics in Hungary: Repetition." In *Language, Literature, and Meaning II: Current Trends in Literary Research*, edited by John Odmark. Amsterdam: Benjamins, 1980.

Suleiman, Susan R., and Inge Crosman, eds. *The Reader in the Text: Essays on Audience and Interpretation*. Princeton: Princeton University Press, 1980.

Tel Quel. *Théorie d'ensemble*. Paris: Seuil, 1968.

Todorov, Tzvetan. *Mikhail Bakhtin: The Dialogical Principle*. Translated by Wlad Godzich. Theory and History of Literature, vol. 13. Minneapolis: University of Minnesota Press, 1984.

Tompkins, Jane P., ed. *Reader-Response Criticism: From Formalism to Post-Structuralism*. Baltimore: Johns Hopkins University Press, 1980.

Tyler, S. A. "Ethnography, Intertextuality, and the End of Description." *American Journal of Semiotics* 3, no. 4 (1985): 83–98.

Ulmer, Gregory L. *Applied Grammatology: Post(e)-Pedagogy from Jacques Derrida to Joseph Beuys*. Baltimore: Johns Hopkins University Press, 1985.

Valdes, Mario J. and Owen Miller, eds. *The Identity of the Literary Text*. Toronto: University of Toronto Press, 1985.

Veron, Eliseo. "Pour une sémiologie des operations translinguistiques." *Versus* 4 (1973): 81–100.

Vilar de Kerkhoff, Ada. "Echo et Narcisse: Réflections et réfractions du rapport titre-texte sur l'espace de la traduction." *Texte* 4 (1985): 127–35.

Voldeng, Evelyne. "L'Intertextualité dans les écrits feminins d'inspiration feministe." *Voix et Images: Littérature Quebecoise* (Montreal) 7, no. 3 (1982): 523–30.

Vultur, Smaranda. "Text si intertext: Possibilitati de abordare si delimitari." *Studii si Cercetari Linguistice* 29, no. 3 (1978): 347–57.

———. "Situer l'intertextualité." *Cahiers roumains d'études littéraires* 3 (1981): 32–36.

———. "A propos des configuration intertextuelles." *Cahiers roumaines d'études littéraires* 4 (1984): 72–78.

Warning, Rainer. "Imitation und Intertextualität: Zur Geschichte lyrischer Dekonstruktion der Armortheologie." In *Interpretation: Das Paradigma der Europaishen Rennaisance-Literatur. Festschrift für Alfred Noyer-Weider zum 60 Geburtstag,* edited by Klaus Hempfer and Gerhard Regn. Wiesbaden: Franz Steiner Verlag, 1982.

Waugh, Patricia. *Metafiction: The Theory and Practice of Self-Conscious Fiction.* London: Methuen, 1984.

Wilden, Anthony. *System and Structure: Essays in Communication and Exchange.* London: Methuen, 1980.

———. "Montage: Analytic and Dialectic." *American Journal of Semiotics* 3, no. 1 (1984): 25–48.

Wolf, Bryan J. "A Grammar of the Sublime, or Intertextuality Triumphant in Church, Turner, and Cole." *New Literary History* 16, no. 2 (1985): 321–41.

Yaari, Monique. "Osmose ou parodie: Une Lecture intertextuelle des Paludes." *French Forum* (Lexington, Ky.) 10, no. 3 (1985): 325–37.

Young, Robert, ed. *Untying the Text: A Post-Structuralist Reader.* London: Routledge & Kegan Paul, 1981.

Zijderveld, Anton. *On Clichés: The Supercedure of Meaning by Function in Modernity.* London: Routledge & Kegan Paul, 1979.

Zima, Peter. "De la structure textuelle à la structure sociale: Les contributions formalistes et structuralistes à la sociologie de la littérature." *Revue d'ésthetique* 2–3 (1976): 186–222.

———. "L'Histoire dans le texte." *Revue de l'Université de Bruxelles* 3–4 (1979): 298–303.

———. *Textsoziologie.* Stuttgart: Metzler, 1980.

———. *Semiotics and Dialectics: Ideology and the Text.* Amsterdam: Benjamins, 1981.

———. "Littérature et société: Pour une sociologie de l'écriture." In *Théorie de la littérature,* edited by Aron Kibédi-Varga. Paris: Picard, 1981.

Zumthor, Paul. "Le Carrefour des rhétoriqueurs: Intertextualité et rhétorique." *Poétique* 27 (1976): 317–37.

———. "Intertextualité et mouvance." *Littérature* 41 (1981): 8–16.

———. "L'Intertexte performanciel." *Texte* 2 (1983): 49–59.

JENNIFER JENKINS

Contemporary American Narrative

Allen, Mary. *The Necessary Bleakness: Women in Major American Fiction of the Sixties.* Urbana: University of Illinois Press, 1976.

Altieri, Charles. "From Symbolist Thought to Immanence: The Ground of Postmodern American Poetics." *Boundary* 2 1 (1973): 605–41.

Baumback, Jonathan. *The Landscape of Nightmare: Studies in the Contemporary American Novel.* New York: New York University Press, 1965.

Bellamy, Joe David. *The New Fiction: Interviews with Innovative American Writers.* Urbana: University of Illinois Press, 1974.

Bradbury, Malcolm. *The Modern American Novel.* Oxford: Oxford University Press, 1983.

Bryant, Jerry H. *The Open Decision: The Contemporary American Novel and Its Intellectual Background.* New York: Free Press, 1970.

Caramello, Charles. *Silverless Mirrors: Book, Self, and Postmodern American Fiction.* Tallahassee: University Presses of Florida, 1983.

Class, Dietmar. *Entgrenztes Spiel: Leserhandlungen in der postmodern amerikanischen Erzählkunst.* Stuttgart: Steiner, 1984.

Davis, Robert Con. "The Case for a Post-Structuralist Mimesis: John Barth and Imitation." *American Journal of Semiotics* 3, no. 3 (1985): 49–72.

D'haen, Theo. "Postmodernism in American Fiction and Art." In *Approaching Postmodernism,* edited by Douwe W. Fokkema and Hans Bertens, 211–31. Amsterdam: Benjamins, 1986.

Ditsky, John M. "The Man on the Quaker Oats Box: Characteristics of Recent Experimental Fiction." *Georgia Review* 26 (1972): 297–313.

Federman, Raymond. "Fiction in America Today or the Unreality of Reality." *Indian Journal of American Studies* 14, no. 1 (1984): 5–16.

Godden, Richard, and Rhodes, Pamela. "The Wild Palms: Faulkner's Hollywood Novel." *American Studies* 28, no. 4 (1983): 449–66.

Gresset, Michel, and Noel Polk, eds. *Intertextuality in Faulkner.* Jackson: University Press of Mississippi, 1985.

Harris, Charles B. *Contemporary American Novelists of the Absurd.* Princeton: Princeton University Press, 1961.

Hassan, Ihab Habib. *Radical Innocence: Studies in the Contemporary American Novel.* Princeton: Princeton University Press, 1971.

———. *Contemporary American Literature 1945–1972: An Introduction.* New York: Ungar, 1973.

Hendin, Josephine. *Vulnerable People: A View of American Fiction since 1945.* New York: Oxford University Press, 1978.

Hellman, John. *Fables of Fact: The New Journalism as New Fiction.* Urbana: University of Illinois Press, 1981.

Hicks, Jack. *In the Singer's Temple: An Essay on Contemporary American Fiction. Prose Fictions of Barthelme, Gaines, Brautigan, Piercy, Kesey, and Kosinski.* Chapel Hill: University of North Carolina Press, 1981.

Hicks, Walter J. *The Metafictional City.* Chapel Hill: University of North Carolina Press, 1981.

Hollowell, John. *Facts and Fictions: The New Journalism.* Chapel Hill: University of North Carolina Press, 1977.

Karl, Frederick R. *American Fictions, 1940–1980: A Comprehensive History and a Critical Evaluation.* New York: Harper & Row, 1983.

Kazin, Alfred. *The Bright Book of Life: American Novelists and Storytellers from Hemingway to Mailer.* Boston: Little, Brown, 1973.

Klein, Marcus, ed. *The American Novel since World War II.* Greenwich, Conn.: Fawcett, 1969.

Klinkowitz, Jerome. *Literary Disruptions: The Making of a Post-Contemporary American Fiction.* 2d ed. Urbana: University of Illinois Press, 1980.

———. *Literary Subversions: New American Fiction and the Practice of Criticism.* Crosscurrents/Modern Critiques, 3d ser. Carbondale: Southern Illinois University Press, 1985.

LeClair, Tom, and Larry McCaffery. *Anything Can Happen: Interviews With Contemporary American Novelists.* Urbana: University of Illinois Press, 1983.

McCaffery, Larry. *The Metafictional Muse: The Works of Coover, Gass, and Barthelme.* Pittsburgh: University of Pittsburgh Press, 1983.

———. "And Still They Smooch: Erotic Visions and Revisions in Postmodern American Fiction." *Revue francaises des études americaines* 9, no. 20 (1984): 275–87.

McConnell, Frank D. *Four Postwar American Novelists: Bellow, Mailer, Barth, and Pynchon.* Chicago: University of Chicago Press, 1977.

Mailloux, Steven. *Interpretive Conventions: The Reader in the Study of American Fiction.* Ithaca, N.Y.: Cornell University Press, 1982.

Malmgren, Carl Daryll. *Fictional Space in the Modernist and Postmodernist American Novel.* Lewisburg, Pa.: Bucknell University Press, 1985.

O'Donnell, Patrick. *Passionate Doubts: Designs of Interpretation in Contemporary American Fiction.* Iowa City: University of Iowa Press, 1986.

Olderman, Raymond. *Beyond the Waste Land: A Study of the American Novel in the Nineteen Sixties.* New Haven: Yale University Press, 1972.

Oleksy, Elzbieta. "*Tempora mutantur et fabulae mutantur in illis*: Some Reflections on Post-Modern American Fiction." *Studia Anglica Posnaniensia: An International Review of English Studies* 14 (1982): 315–22.

Packman, David. "The Kosinsky Controversy." *Cross Currents: A Year-book of Central European Culture* 3 (1984): 265–67.

Parker, Herschel. *Flawed Texts and Verbal Icons: Literary Authority in American Fiction.* Evanston, Ill.: Northwestern University Press, 1984.

Putz, Manfred. *The Story of Identity: American Fiction of the Sixties.* Stuttgart: Metzler, 1979.

Rupp, Richard H. *Celebration in Postwar American Fiction.* Coral Gables, Fla.: University of Miami Press, 1970.

Sammarcelli, Françoise. "La Chambre aux échos: Notes sur l'intertextualité restreint dans LETTERS de John Barth." *Delta English Studies* 21 (1985): 105–25.

Spinker, Michael. *American Literature and Social Change: William Dean Howells to Arthur Miller.* Bloomington: Indiana University Press, 1984.

Stark, John O. *The Literature of Exhaustion: Borges, Nabokov, and Barth.* Durham, N.C.: Duke University Press, 1974.

Stevick, Philip. *Alternative Pleasures: Postrealist Fiction and the Tradition.* Urbana: University of Illinois Press, 1981.

Tani, Stefano. *The Doomed Detective: The Contribution of the Detective Novel to Postmodern American and Italian Fiction.* Carbondale: Southern Illinois University Press, 1984.

Tanner, Tony. *City of Words: American Fiction 1950–1970.* New York: Harper & Row, 1971.

Wallace, Ronald. *The Last Laugh: Form and Affirmation in the Contemporary American Novel.* Columbia: University of Missouri Press, 1979.

Weinberg, Helen. *The New Novel in America: The Kafkan Mode in Contemporary Fiction.* Ithaca, N.Y.: Cornell University Press, 1970.

Zavarzadeh, Mas'ud. *The Mythopoeic Reality: The Postwar American Nonfiction Novel.* Urbana: University of Illinois Press, 1976.

Zurbrugg, N. "Burroughs, Barthes, and the Limits of Intertextuality." *Review of Contemporary Fiction* 4, no. 1 (1984): 86–107.

Studies of Postmodern and Contemporary Literature and Culture

Arac, Jonathan, ed. *Postmodernism and Politics.* Theory and History of Literature, vol. 28. Minneapolis: University of Minnesota Press, 1986.

Barth, John. *The Friday Book: Essays and Other Nonfiction.* New York: Putnam, 1984.

Benamou, Michel, and Charles Caramello. *Performance in Postmodern Culture.* Madison: Coda Press, 1977.

Bulter, Christopher. *After the Writer: An Essay on the Contemporary Avant-garde.* Oxford: Clarendon Press, 1980.

Burnham, Jack. *Great Western Salt Works: Essays on the Meaning of Post-Formalist Art.* New York: George Braziller, 1974.

Eagleton, Terry. "Capitalism, Modernism, and Postmodernism." *New Left Review* 152 (1985): 60–73.

Eco, Umberto. "Innovation and Repetition—Between Modern and Postmodern Aesthetics" *Daedalus* 114, no. 4 (1985): 161–84.

Federman, Raymond, ed. *Surfiction: Fiction Now and Tomorrow.* 2d ed. Chicago: Swallow Press, 1981.

Foster, Hal, ed. *The Anti-Aesthetic: Essays on Postmodern Culture.* Port Townsend, Wash: Bay Press, 1983.

Fokkema, Douwe W. *Literary History, Modernism, and Postmodernism.* Harvard University Erasmus Lectures, Spring 1983. Amsterdam: Benjamins, 1984.

Fokkema, Douwe W., and Hans Bertens, eds. *Approaching Postmodernism.* Amsterdam: John Benjamins, 1986.

Gardner, John. *On Moral Fiction.* New York: Basic Books, 1978.

Garvin, Harry R., and James Heath, eds. *Romanticism, Modernism, and Postmodernism.* Lewisburg, Pa.: Bucknell University Press, 1980.

Gass, William. *Fiction and the Figures of Life.* New York: Knopf, 1970.

Gilman, Richard. "The Idea of the Avant-Garde." *Partisan Review* 34 (1972): 382–96.

Grossvogel, David I. *Limits of the Novel: Evolution of a Form from Chaucer to Robbe-Grillet.* Ithaca, N.Y.: Cornell University Press, 1968.

Guerard, Albert J. "Notes on the Rhetoric of Anti-Realist Fiction." *Tri-Quarterly* 30 (1974): 3–50.

Hafrey, Leigh. "The Gilded Cage: Postmodernism and Beyond." *Tri-Quarterly* 56 (1983): 126–36.

Hassan, Ihab Habib. *The Dismemberment of Orpheus: Toward a Post-Modern Literature.* New York: Oxford University Press, 1971.

Humm, Peter. "Reading the Lines: Television and New Fiction." In *Re-Reading English,* edited by Peter Widdowson. London: Methuen, 1982.

Hutcheon, Linda. "A Poetics of Postmodernism." *Diacritics* 13 (1983): 33–47.

———. *A Theory of Parody: The Teachings of Twentieth-Century Art Forms.* London: Methuen, 1985.

Jameson, Fredric. "Postmodernism, or the Cultural Logic of Late Capitalism." *New Left Review* 146 (1984): 53–92.

Johnsen, William A. "Toward a Redefinition of Modernism." *Boundary 2* 2 (1974): 539–56.

Kroker, Arthur, and David Cook. *The Postmodern Scene.* New York: St. Martin's, 1986.

Lodge, David. *The Modes of Modern Writing: Metaphor, Metonymy and the Typology of Modern Literature.* London: Edward Arnold, 1977.

Lyotard, Jean-François. *The Postmodern Condition: A Report on Knowledge.* Translated by Geoff Bennington and Brian H. Massumi. Theory and History of Literature, vol. 10. Minneapolis: University of Minnesota Press, 1984.

MacCannell, Dean, and Juliet Flower MacCannell. *The Time of the Sign: A Semiotic Interpretation of Modern Culture.* Bloomington: Indiana University Press, 1982.

McCord, Phyllis. "The Ideology of Form: The Nonfiction Novel." *Genre* 19 (1986): 59–79.

Morrissette, Bruce. "Post-Modern Generative Fiction: Novel and Film." *Critical Inquiry* 2, no. 2 (1975): 223–62.

Newman, Charles. *The Post-Modern Aura: The Act of Fiction in an Age of Inflation.* Evanston, Ill.: Northwestern University Press, 1985.

Palmer, Richard E. "Postmodernity and Hermeneutics." *Boundary 2* 5 (1977): 363–94.

Poggioloi, Renato. *The Theory of the Avant-Garde.* Translated by Gerald Fitzgerald. New York: Harper & Row, 1971.

Poirier, Richard. *The Performing Self: Compositions and Decompositions in the Language of Contemporary Life.* New York: Oxford University Press, 1971.

Robbe-Grillet, Alain. *For a New Novel.* Translated by Richard Howard. New York: Grove Press, 1964.

Rochberg, George. "The Avant-Garde and the Aesthetics of Survival." *New Literary History* 3 (1971): 71–92.

Said, Edward. "Contemporary Fiction and Criticism." *TriQuarterly* 33 (1975): 231–56.

Schmidt, S. J. "The Fiction Is That Reality Exists: A Constructivist Model of Reality, Fiction, and Literature." *Poetics Today* 5, no. 2 (1984): 253–74.

Sears, Sallie, and Georgianna W. Lord, eds. *The Discontinuous Universe: Selected Writings in Contemporary Consciousness.* New York: Basic Books, 1972.

Spanos, William V. "The Detective and the Boundary: Some Notes on the Postmodern Literary Imagination." *Boundary* 2 1 (1972): 147–68.

Thiher, Allen. *Words in Reflection: Modern Language Theory and Postmodern Fiction.* Chicago: University of Chicago Press, 1984.

Toulmin, Stephen. "The Construal of Reality: Criticism in Modern and Postmodern Science." *Critical Inquiry* 9 (1982): 93–111.

Trachtenberg, Stanley, ed. *The Postmodern Moment.* Movements in the Arts, no. 1. New York: Greenwood Press, 1985.

Vernon, John. *The Garden and the Map: Schizophrenia in Twentieth-Century Literature and Culture.* Urbana: University of Illinois Press, 1973.

Wasson, Richard. "From Priest to Prometheus: Culture and Criticism in the Post-Modern Period." *Journal of Modern Literature* 3 (1974): 1190–1208.

Wheelis, Allen. *The End of the Modern Age.* New York: Basic Books, 1971.

Wilde, Alan. "Irony in the Postmodern Age: Toward a Map of Suspensiveness." *Boundary* 2 9, no. 1 (1980): 5–47.

———. *Horizons of Assent: Modernism, Postmodernism, and the Ironic Imagination.* Baltimore: Johns Hopkins University Press, 1981.

Ziolkowski, Theodore. "Towards a Post-Modern Aesthetic." *Mosaic* 2 (1969): 112–19.

Special Numbers of Journals

INTERTEXTUALITY:

"L'Autoreprésentation: Le Texte et ses miroirs." *Texte* 1 (1982).

"Codes littéraire et codes sociaux." *Littérature* 12 (1973).

"Collages." *Revue d'ésthetiques* 3–4 (1978).

"La Farçissure: Intertextualités au XVIe siècle." *Littérature* 55 (1984).

"Forum on Mikhail Bakhtin." *Critical Inquiry* 10, no. 2 (1983).

"L'Intertextualité: Intertexte, Autotexte, Intratexte." *Texte* 2 (1983).

"Intertextualité: Third International Colloquium on Poetics." Organized by Michael Riffaterre. New York: Columbia University Press, 1979.

"Intertextualités." *Poétique* 27 (1976).

"Intertextualités Médiévales." *Littérature* 41 (1981).

"Intertextuality." *American Journal of Semiotics* 3, no. 4 (1985).

"Intertextuality: New Perspectives on Criticism." *New York Literary Forum* 2 (1978).

"The Language of Difference: Writing in Quebec(ois)." *Yale French Studies* 65 (1983).

"Linguistique et littérature, Colloque de Cluny 16–17 avril, 1968." *La Nouvelle Critique.* Special number (1968).

"Mikhail Bakhtine, son cercle, son influence." Colloquium of Queen's University Bakhtin Circle. Kingston, Ontario, October 7–9, 1983.
"Problèmes d'intertextualité." *Sémiotique et Bible* 15 (1979).
"Romans et Intertextes/Novels and Intertexts I." *Canadian Review of Comparative Literature* 11, no. 4 (1984).
"Texte Contre-Texte." *Littérature* 48 (1982).

CONTEMPORARY AMERICAN NARRATIVE:
"A Supplement on Contemporary American Fiction." *Boundary 2* 5, no. 1 (1976): 21–137.
"Current Trends in American Fiction." Edited by Raymond Federman and Carl R. Lovitt. *Substance* 27 (1980).
"Novel vs. Fiction: The Contemporary Reformation." Edited by Jackson I. Cope and Geoffrey Green. *Genre* 14, no. 1 (1981).
"White on White: Contemporary American Fiction/Current Theory." Edited by Robert Con Davis. *Arizona Quarterly* 39, no. 4 (1983).

POSTMODERN LITERATURE AND CULTURE
"Modernism and Postmodernism." *New Literary History* 3, no. 1 (1971).
"Special Issue on Modernism and Postmodernism." *Studies in Twentieth-Century Literature* 5, no. 1 (1980).
"Engagements: Postmodernism, Marxism, Politics: A *Boundary 2* Symposium." Edited by Jonathan Arac. *Boundary 2* 11, nos. 1–2 (1982–83).
"Poetics of the Avant-garde." *Poetics Today* 3, no. 3 (1982).
"Postmodernism, History, and Cultural Politics." *Enclitic* 8, nos. 1–2 (1984).
"Postmodern Genres." Edited by Marjorie Perloff. *Genre* 20, no. 3 (1987).

Bibliographies

Bruce, Don. "Bibliographie annotée: écrits sur l'intertextualité." *Texte* 2 (1983): 217–58.
McCaffrey, Lawrence F., ed. *Postmodern Fiction: A Bio-Bibliographical Guide.* Movements in the Arts, no. 2. New York: Greenwood Press, 1986.
Perri, Carmela. "Allusion Studies: An International Annotated Bibliography, 1921–1977." *Style* 13, no. 2 (1979): 179–225.

Contributors

PATRICK O'DONNELL is Professor and Director of Graduate Studies in the Department of English at the University of Arizona, where he teaches American literature and literary theory. He is the author of *John Hawkes, Passionate Doubts: Designs of Interpretation in Contemporary American Fiction,* and many essays on modern and contemporary American fiction. He is the editor of *New Essays on* The Crying of Lot 49, forthcoming from Cambridge University Press, and is at present working on two books: *Echo Chambers: The Representation of "Voice" in the Modern Novel* and *American Historics: Essays on the Writing of American Literary History.*

ROBERT CON DAVIS teaches at the University of Oklahoma. He has published widely on literary theory and American literature, and has edited *The Fictional Father: Lacanian Readings of the Text* and coedited *Rhetoric and Form: Deconstruction at Yale.* Currently, he is coeditor of the *Oklahoma Project for Discourse & Theory.* He has recently completed *Paternal Romance: Zeus, Yaweh, and the Politics of Narration.*

CHARLES CARAMELLO is Associate Professor of English and Comparative Literature at the University of Maryland. He is the author of *Silverless Mirrors: Book, Self and Postmodern American Fiction* and of numerous articles on modern and postmodern literature. His book on Henry James and Gertrude Stein is forthcoming from the University of North Carolina Press.

HENRY LOUIS GATES, JR., the W. E. B. DuBois Professor of Literature at Cornell University, is the author of *Figures in Black: Words, Signs, and the 'Racial' Self, The Signifying Monkey,* and many essays on black American literature and literary theory. He is the editor of several books, including the thirty-volume Oxford–Schomburg Library of Black Women's Writings.

KATHLEEN HULLEY is Associate Professor of English at the University of North Dakota, where she directs the Group for Interdisciplinary Theory and Praxis (GITAP) and teaches American literature, critical theory, and women's studies. She has edited a collection of essays on Grace Paley, as well as the collection *Objectivity, an Interdisciplinary Issue, Pleasure and its Discontents,* and *Colonization in Race, Class, and Gender.* She has written articles on postmodernism and feminist theory and is currently writing a book on the city in literature.

LINDA HUTCHEON is Professor of English and Comparative Literature at the University of Toronto. Her books include: *Narcissistic Narrative: The Metafictional Paradox, Formalism and the Freudian Aesthetic, A Theory of Parody,* and, forthcoming, *A Poetics of Postmodernism: History, Theory, Fiction, The Canadian Postmodern: Essays on Contemporary English–Canadian Fiction,* and *Postmodern Representation: Complicity and Critique.*

JENNIFER JENKINS is a doctoral candidate in English at the University of Arizona.

JULIA KRISTEVA, a major figure in the history of semiotics, is a practicing psychoanalyst and Professor of Linguistics at the University of Paris VII-Vincennes. Her works include *Séméiotiké: Recherches pour une sémanalyse*, *La Révolution du langage poétique* (translated as *Revolution in Poetic Language*), *Pouvoirs de l'horreur* (translated as *Powers of Horror: An Essay on Abjection*), *Histoire d'amour* (translated as *Tales of Love*), and *Soleil noir: Dépression et mélancolie* (translation forthcoming as *Black Sun: Depression and Melancholia*).

JOHN T. MATTHEWS is Associate Professor of English at Boston University, where he teaches American literature. He is the author of *The Play of Faulkner's Language* and many articles on modern American literature. He is a coeditor of *The Faulkner Journal*, and is currently completing a book on frame narration in American literature.

THAïS MORGAN is Assistant Professor of English at Arizona State University, where she teaches history of criticism, contemporary literary theory, and interdisciplinary studies. Her articles on theory and Victorian literature have appeared in *Semiotica*, *American Journal of Semiotics*, *Victorian Poetry*, and in *The Muse of Apollo*, forthcoming from Oxford University Press. She is coeditor of *Reorientations: Theory, Pedagogy, and Social Change*, and is working on a book about the politics of tradition from 1860 to 1920. Her translation of Gérard Genette's *Mimologiques* is forthcoming from the University of Nebraska Press.

JOHN CARLOS ROWE is Professor of English and Comparative Literature at the University of California–Irvine. He has written extensively on American literature, critical theory, and cultural poetics. His books include *Henry Adams and Henry James*, *Through the Custom-House: Nineteenth-Century American Fiction and Modern Critical Theory*, and *The Theoretical Dimensions of Henry James*. He is also coeditor of a special issue of *Cultural Critique* on representations of the Vietnam War.

RONALD SCHLEIFER teaches at the University of Oklahoma and is editor of *Genre*. He is also coeditor, with Robert Con Davis, of the *Oklahoma Project for Discourse & Theory*. He has published widely on modern literature and criticism, and is the author of *A. J. Greimas and the Nature of Meaning* and coeditor of *Contemporary Literary Criticism*. Presently, he is completing *Criticism and Modernism*.

GABRIELE SCHWAB is the author of *Samuel Becketts Endspiel mit der Subjektivtät* and *Entgrenzungen und Engrenzungsmythen* (currently being translated for Harvard University Press as *Subjects Without Selves*). She teaches English and Comparative Literature at the University of California–Irvine, and has published several essays and articles in English on literature, literary theory, and cultural criticism.

ALAN SINGER is Associate Professor of English at Temple University. He is the author of *A Metaphorics of Fiction: Discontinuity and Discourse in the*

Modern Novel and *The Charnel Imp*, a novel. His contribution to this volume is part of a work-in-progress, *Narrative Knowing: The Subject of Action in Ideology and the Novel.*

MARGARET WALLER, translator of Julia Kristeva's *Revolution in Poetic Language* and numerous other articles, is Assistant Professor of French at Pomona College. She is currently at work on a book about figures of gender and power in the French romantic novel.

HEIDE ZIEGLER is Professor and Director of the Institut für Literaturwissenschaft Amerikanistik at the University of Stuttgart. She has published books in German on William Faulkner's short stories and on irony in modern literature. Her publications in English include *The Radical Imagination and the Liberal Tradition: Interviews with Novelists* (with Christopher Bigsby), *John Barth*, and an edited collection: *Facing Texts: Encounters Between Contemporary Writers and Critics.* She is currently working on a book about the comic imagination.